Mc

TRIMBLE

TRIMBLE

9/48047

HENRY MCDONALD

BLOOMSBURY

The publishers wish to thank Faber & Faber for permission to reproduce an extract
from 'Autumn Journal XXIV', by Louis MacNeice, *The Collected Poems of
Louis MacNeice*, Faber & Faber, London, 1966, and Gill and Macmillan
for permission to reproduce an extract from *14 May Days* by Don Anderson,
Gill and MacMillan, Dublin, 1994.

First published in Great Britain 2000
This paperback edition published 2001

Bloomsbury Publishing Plc, 38 Soho Square, London W1D 3HB

A CIP catalogue record for this book
is available from the British Library

ISBN 0 7475 5315 7

10 9 8 7 6 5 4 3 2 1

Typeset by Hewer Text Ltd, Edinburgh
Printed by Clays Ltd, St Ives plc

CONTENTS

Acknowledgements   vii

Prologue: No Celebrations in Ulster's Hebron   1

1. A State of Siege, a Sense of Service   8

2. Vanguard Days   33

3. From out of the Wilderness   68

4. The Road to Westminster   106

5. A Man for All Factions   142

6. Towards a Long Good Friday   179

7. A Longer Hot Summer   218

8. Nobel, No Guns, No Government   258

9. A Last Leap of Faith   307

Epilogue: 'We've Jumped, You Follow'   327

Notes   347

Bibliography   355

Index   356

A Note on the Author   360

ACKNOWLEDGEMENTS

This book is in large part based on interviews with more than a hundred sources, some of whom preferred to be off-the-record. To those who wished to remain anonymous I am extremely grateful and understand fully their reasons for remaining in the shadows. Among the many named others to whom I owe a debt of gratitude are: Professor Anthony Alcock, Jack Allen, Roger Alton (my editor at the *Observer*), Don Anderson, Tim Attwood, Dr Arthur Aughey, Ernest Baird, Glen Barr, my dear friend Professor Paul Bew, Kelvin Boyes, David Brewster, David Burnside, Lord Cranborne, Leslie Cree, Ciaran Crossey (one of the dynamic duo from the Linenhall Library's superb political collection), Fred Crowe, Tony Crowe, 'Big Jim' Curran (my 'chauffeur' through those dark winter journeys across Northern Ireland), Jim Cusack, Jeff Dudgeon, Ruth Dudley Edwards, Sir Reg Empey, Lord Fitt, Brian Garrett, Gordon Gillespie, Professor Tom Hadden, my agent Bill Hamilton, Eoghan Harris, Ray Haydn, Chris Hudson, John Hunter, Will Hutton, the Reverend Brian Kenaway, Gary Kent, David Kerr, Stephen King, the Reverend David Knox, Lord Laird, Professor Simon Lee, John Lloyd, Dr Gordon Lucey, Alban Maginnis, Ken Maginnis, Seamus Mallon, Walter McAuley, Bob McCartney, Sam McClure, Tina McCombe, Chris McGimpsey, Michael McGimpsey, Alan McKillen, David McNarry, Frank Millar Junior, Austin Morgan, Alan Morton, Yvonne Murphy (part two of the Linenhall's dynamic duo), Sean O'Callaghan, Malachi O'Doherty, Finbarr O'Farrell, Ian Paisley Junior, Henry Reid, Ken Reid, Lee Reynolds, Jim Rodgers, A.T.Q. Stewart, John D. Taylor, Willie Thompson, David Trimble, Andy Tyrie, Paul Webster (my deputy editor at the *Observer*), Harry West, Barry White Junior and Jim Wilson.

Finally, an apology to the two women in my life – Claire and Lauren. I must have seemed like a stranger to you both during those long months of research and writing. A big thank-you, a tender hug and lots of kisses for putting up with me at this testing time.

Prologue:

No Celebrations in Ulster's Hebron

10 December 1998. The grey bleakness of an Ulster town in the depths of winter is flecked with slashes of Orange. There is orange on the telegraph poles, orange on the trees, orange on the hedgerows. Ribbons and bows of orange are tied to railings and bushes all over the quaint nineteenth-century churchyard. Only the tattered red, white and blue of the union flag flying flaccidly above the stone bridge interrupts the blur of orange all around.

Out on the rural edge of Portadown, in the heart of David Trimble's Westminster constituency, the scene is almost bucolic. There is a row of little cottages with potted plants outside on the window sill; in another field a group of well-fatted cows have just bedded down on the grass, signalling the onset of rain; while the church itself could feature in any painting of the English countryside. Yet the calm around Drumcree belies the fact that this is Ulster's Hebron, a religious and cultural citadel as important to hard-line Protestants as the West Bank town is to Jewish settlers.

The eerie peace here resembles a battlefield granted temporary respite. To the right of the church a World War I-style trench has been dug into the field, and from the air it looks like an untreated wound scarring the earth beneath. On the nationalist side of the line there are British Army arc lights which are switched on at night to illuminate the protestors who gather here. The previous day local loyalists claimed to have found a listening device under the bridge.

Almost a thousand miles away in Oslo David Trimble is being presented with the Nobel prize for peace, but in the very centre of the area he represents there are no celebrations. Drumcree and the violent sieges associated with it every July for the last five years are a focal point for the virulent sectarian conflict that still blights Northern Ireland, peace prize or no peace prize. Many in this constituency and outside it believe it was the Drumcree conflict in 1995 that got David Trimble elected leader of the Ulster Unionist Party. He sided with the Orangemen who defied a ban on them marching over the bridge towards the Garvaghy Road, a Catholic enclave in Protestant-dominated Portadown. Today the very people he supported back then, when the annual Orange Order parade first became an international focus for confrontation, regard his Nobel prize at best as a joke and at worst as the ultimate betrayal.

It is the 128th day of the Drumcree siege and no one here is celebrating Trimble's global adulation. He may have internationalized the unionist cause, but some of his former followers think it was for too high a price. In a caravan inside the church grounds Harold Gracey, the District Master of the Portadown Orange Order, is counting money. He lays the coins out in neat cylindrical piles, all of which are destined for a box marked 'Drumcree Fighting Fund'. There is a portable television by the window but it is switched off. At 12.25 p.m. David Trimble and John Hume, the leader of the SDLP, the Social Democratic and Labour Party, are about to take the stage in Oslo. Gracey is asked if he wants to watch the ceremony, but shakes his head in disgust. 'Why would I want to watch *that*?' he says, almost spitting the last word out. When I suggest that Trimble might donate some of the £200,000 Nobel prize money to the fighting fund, Gracey just turns his head away.

Gracey was once a key supporter of Trimble's in Portadown. Three days after he was first elected to Parliament in May 1990, Gracey marched with him through the town in an Orange parade that became a *de facto* Trimble victory rally. Now Gracey would not and could not be seen in his company, given that many of the Orangeman's friends regard their MP and Northern Ireland's First Minister-designate as a traitor to the loyalist cause.

Others at Drumcree go further than Gracey. As Trimble delivers his speech, which is just audible from a car radio outside the church, Ivor Young, a former member of the Ulster Defence Association, arrives on the road and starts to walk down towards the police line. He wears a white baseball cap with 'Northern Ireland' emblazoned in red on the front. Young is unimpressed by his MP's performance: 'Everybody thought Trimble was a godsend. Here was a man backing up the loyalist orders who was well educated and articulate. It was the Orange Order that put him into Westminster, but now he has turned his back on the Protestant people.'

In Oslo the Ulster Unionist leader is committing more heresies, at least to the small group of hard-liners gathered at Drumcree. In his Nobel lecture Trimble becomes the first senior Unionist leader to admit the mistakes of the past, to acknowledge that the old Stormont regime that ended with the eruption of the Troubles in 1969 *did* discriminate against Catholics. 'Ulster Unionists fearful of being isolated on the island built a solid house, but it was a cold house for Catholics,' Trimble tells his audience. The gap between the MP and constituents like Young and Gracey is fast becoming a chasm.

Young and I walk to the graveyard where in July 1996 Trimble wagged his finger at a line of RUC riot police who had trained their guns, loaded with plastic bullets at protesting Orangemen. What would happen, I ask, if Trimble came here now?

'There's no chance of him turning up – he would not be accepted. If he comes to Portadown town centre he has to be accompanied by bodyguards. He would be run out of here.' Then Young has a confession to make: 'The first time I ever voted for an Ulster Unionist in my life was when David Trimble stood as a candidate here. I really thought that this was a man who could promote the Protestant cause. I regret even talking to him now.' Then he adds menacingly: 'There'll be trouble sooner or later. This thing is building up.'

And what of the Nobel prize? Is he not proud that his own MP was the international statesman whose face graced the cover of *Newsweek* magazine this week?

'Well, the way I thought about it, it was a joke. I think most people here think the same – it's become one big joke. There won't be too many television sets turned on this morning in Portadown,' Young predicts. He returns to the Protestant loyalist side of the line just as the rector of Drumcree church drives by.

So how did Trimble come in a few years to alienate Young, Gracey and the others who saw his election as a godsend? In his address in Oslo he quotes Amos Oz, the Israeli author and advocate of peaceful compromise with the Palestinians. He makes a reference to Oz's definition of a political fanatic as 'someone who is more interested in you than in himself', that is, someone who wants to force you to be religiously, racially or geographically perfect. The men huddled in Harold Gracey's caravan and on the road outside Drumcree church fit that description. They yearn for a Protestant Parliament for a Protestant people; they believe in the possibility of the restoration of a loyalist Arcadia with them on top and the Catholics at the bottom; they truly imagine they can rewind history. A few even believe that the Ulster people are in fact the lost tribe of Israel, locked in an eternal struggle against the Papist hordes around them. For these extremists, Drumcree is their Megiddo. The ongoing violence at Drumcree has spawned several new anti-ceasefire loyalist terrorist factions such as the Red Hand Defenders, led by a group of fanatical self-appointed Protestant pastors who think they are fighting a holy war. The RDH, who killed their first victim, a Catholic police constable called Frankie O'Reilly, in a blast bomb attack at Drumcree, have also threatened 'traitors' on the unionist side. The arch 'traitor' for this army of God is David Trimble.

The First Minister-designate refers to them in Oslo. 'We have a few fanatics who dream of forcing the Ulster British people into a utopian Irish state, more ideologically Irish than its own inhabitants want. We also have fanatics who dream of permanently suppressing northern nationalists in a state more supposedly British than its inhabitants actually want.'

It is appropriate that David Trimble should line up alongside Amos Oz because, if there are any credible parallels between conflicts around the world, then the Northern Ireland Troubles come closest to the Israeli–Palestinian tragedy. Irish republicans often try to draw another international parallel, with South Africa under apartheid; here, Catholics represent the blacks and the unionists the Afrikaners. This ludicrous reductionism has led to the ad nauseam repetition by Sinn Fein leaders such as Martin McGuinness of the mantra 'Unionism needs a De Klerk' – that is, someone who can tell the unionists that the game is up for their imagined privileges inside Ulster's laager. That analogy is laughable, since the position of Catholics in Ulster does not begin to compare, in the present or even the past, with the plight of black people under the apartheid regime. However, Israel and Northern Ireland do have some more obvious parallels. They are essentially struggles based on conflicting national rights – the right of the nationalists to live in a unitary state clashing with the right of the unionist majority wish to remain linked with Britain. And as in

Israel, the Troubles are further complicated by a dangerous, centuries-old mix of mutually hostile religions. There are even geopolitical similarities, given the 'narrow ground' which Israeli and Palestinian, nationalist and unionist, are fighting over in the Middle East and Ireland.

So if the men on the hill at Drumcree are Ulster's equivalent of the Jewish fundamentalists occupying the centre of Hebron, then David Trimble is perhaps Northern Ireland's Yitzak Rabin. Rabin was the warrior turned peacemaker, the chief of staff of the Israeli Defence Forces whose lighting victory in the 1967 Six-Day War led to the capture of places like Hebron. However, he was eventually prepared to relinquish these Palestinian towns for the sake of a peace settlement. In a strange way Rabin became the victim of his earlier success. The triumph of the Six-Day War sparked an outbreak of messianic fervour in Israel and led to the proliferation of Jewish settlements on the West Bank. Almost twenty years later, some of those Jews who in the early 1970s colonized the occupied territories thanks in part to Rabin's military triumph regarded him as a traitor for wanting to return that land.

In a less dramatic way Trimble too has travelled the road from staunch uncompromising loyalism to reach an accord with Irish nationalism and, in his own words, 'end the internal cold war on this island'. He too is suffering from his earlier successes. In 1974 he played an important back-room role in bringing down the last power-sharing administration in Northern Ireland – the only victory for Ulster Protestants in decades of setback. Winning in 1974, it could be argued, exaggerated the unionists' sense of their own strength vis à vis the nationalists as well as their real influence over subsequent British government policies. 'Victory' in eighteen days in May 1974 was Ulster's Six-Day War – a temporary triumph with corrupting consequences. Trimble was one of the back-room generals who coordinated the loyalist uprising more than a quarter of a century ago. Ever since, unionists and loyalists have paid a heavy price for that win – paradoxically, their position inside the UK has been progressively weakened since May 1974. Winning back then destroyed any short- to medium-term prospect of an internal political settlement inside Northern Ireland. Trimble's presence on the podium today in Oslo is in part a recognition of how one of the generals of 1974 tried to make amends for the corrosive triumphalism that followed the toppling of the power-sharing regime.

Rabin paid the ultimate price for his own journey – assassination at the hands of a Jewish fundamentalist named Yigal Amir. Trimble too faces grave danger. It is not an exaggeration to suggest that some of the wilder fanatics in places like Portadown would follow Amir's example. Certainly by the time Trimble was awarded the Nobel prize, the paroxysm of verbal abuse directed at him from Orange ultras had started to reach Israeli proportions. Before his death Rabin was constantly harassed outside his home and accused of selling out; posters appeared, some depicting him in an Arab kaffiyeh headdress and others, more sinister, showing his face in a rifle sight. On the motorway leading into Portadown flyovers, pillars and road signs have been pasted with posters bearing the slogan 'Trimble – MI5 Agent'. There are weekly protests outside the Trimbles' house in nearby Lisburn. His wife receives constant abusive telephone calls from hard-liners determined to make the family's life a misery. One of his former friends in the constituency has gone so far as to urge Trimble to do the honourable thing and shoot himself as atonement for his alleged treachery. Rabin's life was emblematic of the struggle within Zionism between the rational and the irrational, the secular and the messianic. The latter stages of Trimble's political career have equally been a tussle between the emotional and pragmatic wings of unionism. Trimble, like Rabin, is prepared to give up some ground to his enemies so that the overall siege of his state can be lifted.

After watching the televised ceremony in Oslo I drive to the Drumcree shop in the centre of Portadown, which has become a shrine to the local siege. It stocks Drumcree chocolate bars, Drumcree keyrings, Drumcree lighters and Drumcree monkey hats with three tiny figures dressed like the Blues Brothers in dark suits with Orange sashes; there is even an Airfix-style model of the siege, with plastic soldiers pointing their rifles at a photograph of the Orangemen on the hill. Among the many tapes on sale is one by James Galway, the renowned international flautist who learned to play his instrument in a loyalist flute band in North Belfast during the 1960s. When I tell the woman behind the counter that Galway was in Oslo today and played a tune in honour of Trimble and Hume, she presses the stop button on the cassette player and replaces the tape with *Songs of the UVF*. On the walls are pictures of those who support the men on the hill – among the politicians is Ian Paisley. The youthful Free Presbyterian gospel singer Paul Berry is also on view: he entertains protestors at Drumcree with his own version of the *Dad's*

Army theme tune which begins, 'Who do you think you are kidding, Mr Trimble . . .' I ask the lady in the shop if David Trimble's portrait will ever grace her walls. 'Only if he changes his attitude, and I doubt he will,' she replies.

The largest town in David Trimble's constituency is at war with itself. When you go down the Garvaghy Road there is a permanent police presence protecting Catholic homes in Craigwell Terrace. Parallel to Garvaghy is the Tunnel, a narrow, depressing road with derelict flats on one side and a sausage factory on the other. It was the scene of a disputed Orange march in 1985 when the British government prevented a traditional parade passing Catholic homes. For decades the nationalists of the Tunnel had lived under siege during the marching season while the RUC penned them into their homes as the loyalist bands and Orangemen swaggered triumphantly past. On the right are the Protestant houses and Corcrane Orange Hall. There are loyalist halls all over the world, from Ghana to Canada, Australia to South Africa, but this one is the most frequently attacked of them all, and today it is covered in paint-bomb splashes and republican graffiti. There is a palpable sense of hatred and menace on either side of this road which no amount of good will in Oslo, Washington, London or anywhere else can dilute in the near future.

Even back in the relative sanity of post-ceasefire Belfast no one has been putting out the flags for the two Nobel laureates. This reflects the cautious mood across the community: a feeling that the peace is not finally sealed, and that a new conflagration at Drumcree or other sectarian flashpoints could still destroy the political agreement that David Trimble and others had pieced together earlier in the year.

On my way home I travel along the Upper Ormeau Road in South Belfast and wonder if his supporters' fears for his safety are an exaggeration. At the very worst Trimble could be hamstrung by his right wing; their opposition will make it impossible for him to take the next step towards a historic compromise with republican-ism. But, just as I dismiss the idea that others on the wilder shores of loyalism might take their bitterness and sense of let-down to a terrifying conclusion, I notice that on the wall of the Good Shepherd Catholic church someone has scrawled in fresh paint: 'D.T. is dead.'

A State of Siege, a Sense of Service

On the eve of a critical annual conference for the Ulster Unionist Party on 24 October 1998, when his leadership was on the line, David Trimble took time out to receive a family heirloom. At a private ceremony in the White Horse Hotel outside Derry city, he was presented with a World War I canvas kitbag. According to the man who found it it had belonged to Trimble's maternal grandfather, W.H. Jack, a native of Derry and former unionist mayor of the city. For decades it was assumed to have been left behind during the mass Protestant exodus from the west bank of the city following the outbreak of the present Troubles in August 1969. In the slime and slaughter of the Somme his grandfather had sought some comfort in the bag, in which he both slept and ate. Tony Crowe, a unionist historian who had bought the kitbag at an auction in Derry a year before, had even discovered in it a number of original military-issue salt biscuits still in their wrappers. One or two had been opened and partially eaten: Captain Jack must surely have nibbled on them in the trenches to stem his gnawing hunger. Trimble was visibly moved when he was given the memento, a tangible connection with his political and cultural antecedents. For David Trimble grew up in a psychological atmosphere dominated by an ever-present state of siege and a sense of unbroken service to the British crown. His grandfather's story symbolizes these twin concepts running through Trimble's own history. Captain Jack links him with Derry, a city where Ulster Protestants still feel embattled, and the bag reminds him of the family's long-standing tradition of service in the British armed forces.

With the exception of the victory of King William III (William of

Orange) at the Boyne in 1690, there are two key events which, more than any other, have shaped the Ulster Protestant consciousness and bind Trimble to his roots – the siege of Derry of 1689 and World War I. The latter event illuminates the historic contradiction in Ulster unionism's attitude towards Britain. The thousands who signed up in 1914 demonstrated their Britishness by serving the nation in time of war. But the all-Protestant militia from which these volunteers came, the Ulster Volunteer Force, had originally been set up two years earlier to oppose by force of arms the Westminster Parliament's proposals for Home Rule in Ireland. A loyalty to the crown was tempered by an occasional, sometimes violent, disloyalty to its government.

The Protestant majority in Ulster were overwhelmingly opposed to self-rule from Dublin and threatened a civil war in Ireland in opposition to the Liberal government's plans. Their hostility to the policy was best summed up in the phrase 'Home Rule is Rome Rule'. In response, nationalists in the South set up their own underground army, the National Volunteers, to fight the UVF. The UVF was set up by Sir Edward Carson, a Dublin-born barrister and passionate unionist who had defended the Marquess of Queensbury during his infamous libel trial against Oscar Wilde. Ironically, civil war was only averted by the onset of World War I, in which Irishmen from both sides of the Home Rule divide were slaughtered.

Grandfather Jack had joined Carson's UVF during the Home Rule crisis and only transferred to the 10th Enniskillen Regiment when the Ulster Volunteers were incorporated into the British Army and renamed the 36th Ulster Division. Shortly after taking the King's shilling Jack gained a commission as a captain and in 1915 he trained at Finner Camp in Bundoran, now the main Irish Army base in north-west Ireland. He first saw action at the Somme in July 1916 when the 36th Ulster Division suffered appalling casualties – two thousand men were killed on the first day of the battle. Incredibly, Captain Jack survived and returned to Derry at the end of the war.

Trimble, however, can trace his ancestors, particularly the Cahoons on his maternal grandmother's side, right back to the 1640s. It was at this time that Protestant immigrants from western Scotland (known as planters) first came to north-west Ireland, to areas such as Donegal and the new and rapidly expanding settlement on the river Foyle which was to become Derry. In terms of scale and character the colonization of Ulster matched the contemporary English migration to North America. But in Ulster the majority of those who crossed the Irish Sea to seize new land came from Scotland. Their arrival provoked not only a land war with the displaced native Irish but also a religious conflict, given that the planters were primarily of Presbyterian stock and the Irish were Catholic. The antecedents of today's ethno-religious conflict can be found in the seventeenth-century plantation of Ulster.

The Cahoons initially settled in Doagh Island (now in the Irish Republic) but moved to Derry city around 1680. Nine years later the city became a key battleground in the Williamite wars that followed the Glorious Revolution of 1688, when Mary Stuart, with the aid of her Dutch husband, Prince William of Orange, and his allies overthrew James II. William and Mary's assumption of the English throne marked the end of absolutism and the survival of constitutional monarchy, and the extension of the war into Ireland was aimed at preventing the restoration of a Catholic monarchy in England.

Derry was already a place of refuge for Protestant planters when the conflict spilled over into Ireland. Following an earlier Catholic rebellion in 1641 against the Ulster plantation, many Protestants had flocked from regions like East Donegal into the relative safety of the newly built Maiden City of the north (so called because it was the planters' first urban settlement there, predating Belfast). Fortress Derry had successfully repelled two earlier sieges by Catholic armies, described by the eminent Ulster historian A.T.Q. Stewart as simply 'dress rehearsals'[1] for the real thing in 1689.

On one level the 1689 siege of Derry was a turning point in the history not only of the British Isles but of the entire European continent. William's reasons for invading England and eventually Ireland were not altogether altruistic. He feared that an English king aligned to Louis XIV would become a useful ally to the French in their aim of subjugating the Dutch Republic. Sixteen years before the 1688 Revolution, an alliance of France and England had defeated the Dutch. William wanted to avoid a repetition of that event and with it the complete domination of Europe by Louis. The Vatican, too, opposed the French king's bid for continental hegemony: Alexander VIII celebrated William's victory over James II's mostly Catholic army in Ireland by conducting a special mass. It is a fact lost on most Orangemen today that the Pope was one of William's strongest supporters in the struggle.

At a more parochial level, Derry was a crucial battleground in William's war against James because the fate of the Protestant settlement depended on the city holding out. James's armies had over-run Protestant settlements across the north of Ireland and it appeared that the entire island might fall under his control.

Symbolically, the siege of Derry was the genesis of a number of important myths that still have resonance today. The Ulster loyalist battle-cry of 'No surrender', for instance, first echoed around Derry's walls during the three-month siege when, despite fever and starvation, its inhabitants refused to bend to James's armies. The loyalist suspicion of any compromise as a potential betrayal was first personified in the figure of the Robert Lundy, the governor of the city, who sought to negotiate a surrender during the darkest days of the siege. His plans were thwarted, and his effigy has been burned on Derry's walls every December since. As A.T.Q. Stewart has wryly noted, if Lundy hadn't existed the loyalists of north-east Ulster would have invented him. A 'Lundy', therefore, has long since entered the Ulster Protestant lexicon as a term for someone who sells out the cause; it is a label that has recently and very frequently been applied to David Trimble.

The fact that Trimble's ancestors fought at the siege has always been a source of immense pride to him. 'My grandmother who hailed from the Maiden City was intensely proud of the fact that her ancestors had successfully endured the siege,' he wrote. 'She ensured that her grandchildren had proper appreciation of the heroism displayed by the defenders of Derry.'[2]

The central Protestant heroes of the siege were the local apprentices, who shut the city's gates just in time to prevent James II's army from entering Derry. The mythos of the Apprentice Boys was born, and out of it emerged a loyalist marching institution. Trimble himself is an Apprentice Boy. Even if he wanted to, he would find it impossible to escape the legacy and ignore the ancestral voices that still haunt so many in Northern Ireland.

Following the siege, the Cahoons became a prominent Protestant family in Derry. In the late nineteenth century Trimble's great-grandfather went into the building business. The Cahoons lived at that time in a large three-storey merchant's house in Eden Terrace, on the edge of what today is the republican Bogside; in the nineteenth century, however, it was home to the Protestant merchant classes. In the 1990s Eden Terrace's religious and political affiliations have changed: it is now populated mainly by Catholic professionals and students who attend the nearby Magee College. The Cahoons played a major part in the reconstruction and expansion of the city in the first half of the twentieth century. For instance, they won the contract to build Altnagelvin, Derry's main hospital on the east bank of the river Foyle, after World War II. Yet by the late 1940s the firm had gone bankrupt through a series of bad contracts and unwise investments.

Before the money went, however, the Cahoons had enough confidence to move back and forward into Donegal on the north-western Irish seaboard even after Ireland was partitioned in 1922 and Donegal was incorporated into the new semi-independent Irish Free State. Despite having been part of the ancient province of Ulster, Donegal was now excluded from the unionist-dominated state of Northern Ireland. Six of the nine ancient Ulster counties contained significant Protestant majorities. The inhabitants of the others, Donegal, Cavan and Monaghan, felt under threat from the mainly Catholic Irish Free State and thousands of them – though not the Cahoons – fled into Northern Ireland. Trimble's mother, baptised Annie Margaret Elisabeth Jack but commonly known as Ivy, was actually born in Buncrana, a seaside Donegal town with a once-thriving Protestant community. In a historic twist, during the recent Troubles the town became one of the main havens for members of the Provisional IRA's Derry Brigade on the run from the security forces across the border in Northern Ireland.

Trimble's father William, too, had his roots in a region of pre-partition Ireland that is now in the Irish Republic. He was the son of a Presbyterian farmer in Co. Cavan who also had to flee into fortress Northern Ireland. So the Trimble sense of siege is coloured not just by the experiences of the Jacks and Cahoons under the walls of Derry. As he grew up the young David often heard tales of his other ancestors besieged in the mainly Catholic Irish midlands. There is another family legend, less easy to confirm than the Derry one, that the Trimbles (the name is derived from the Northumberland Turnbulls, emphasizing the Trimbles' origins as planters from the English–Scottish borders) were burned out of their homestead during the troubles of the 1920s when Ireland was partitioned. William Trimble's father George had been in the Royal Irish Constabulary and would certainly have been a prime target for republicans. In the 1920s the RIC were mercilessly hunted down by Michael Collins's IRA during the Irish War of Independence because they were seen as the local 'eyes and ears' of the British Army. When the unionist-dominated Northern Ireland state was founded in 1921 George Trimble saw the writing on the wall and moved to Belfast, transferring his loyalty to the newly formed and mainly Protestant Royal Ulster Constabulary.

Trimble's father William grew up in Belfast, in an area that, just like Derry's Eden Terrace, was once a Protestant middle-class redoubt and has since been penetrated by socially aspiring Catholics. Like many rural police officers who came to the big city in post-partition Ulster, Trimble's grandfather gained rapid promotion and eventually became head constable at Donegall Pass RUC station – yet another example of the pattern of service running through the Trimble family tree. Until very recently David Trimble has protested that there was no family tradition of involvement in the main Protestant religious/cultural institution, the Orange Order. But latterly he has discovered that his grandfather George had in fact been District Master of Ballynafeigh Orange Lodge in the Upper Ormeau for several years. (Seventy years later, George Trimble's old Ballynafeigh lodge became the focus of world media attention given its involvement in a disputed Orange parade passing through the now mainly Catholic nationalist Lower Ormeau Road.)

The Trimbles were far from wealthy and in the pre-Welfare State era George could not afford the fees for William's studies at Queen's University, Belfast after his son had passed the matriculation exam at the age of sixteen. Instead, William entered the Northern Ireland Civil Service and found himself working as a clerk in the Minister of Labour during World War II. He met Ivy in the Derry office of the Labour Ministry, where she too was a clerk, and they married in 1941.

David Trimble was born on 15 October 1944, the middle child of three. He came into the world in a period when the position of unionists inside the UK was starting to look more secure than at any time since the state was founded in 1921. Although Britain was still fighting a war, the Allies were already on European soil and victory over Hitler was clearly in sight. (Among the thousands of British troops battling their way towards Nazi Germany was one James Molyneaux, a young NCO from Northern Ireland who took part in the liberation of Belsen and thirty years later would become leader of the Ulster Unionist Party.) The unionist government of Northern Ireland had provided sea and air bases and, more importantly, thousands of its own citizens (all volunteers) for the British war effort. In contrast, Eamon de Valera's Irish Free State remained neutral. Moreover, IRA collusion with Nazi agents fuelled a number of unionist myths about Irish treachery and deceit. There were stories, for instance of Belfast IRA members in the blackout lighting the way with torches for Luftwaffe bombers. (Exaggerated myths like this conveniently ignored the fact that de Valera's government had ruthlessly suppressed republican violence during the war as a sop to Churchill.) There was a general feeling within the unionist population that once again they had demonstrated their loyalty to the crown in time of need, and that this would surely be rewarded in the face of Irish Free State subterfuge.

At the time of his birth David Trimble's family were living in Bangor on the Co. Down coast, which for any lower middle-class Presbyterian family seemed a world apart from the geopolitical uncertainties that their ancestors had faced in Derry, Cavan and Longford. More than most towns in Northern Ireland, Bangor aptly fits Margaret Thatcher's infamous description of the Province being as 'British as Finchley'. In the 1940s and 1950s this seaside resort ten miles east of Belfast was a relatively prosperous, mainly Protestant town. Until the advent of the package holiday to the Spanish Costas, Bangor was a popular tourist trap for the Protestant working class in nearby Belfast and even further afield in western Scotland. The seafront was dominated by the kiss-me-quick architecture of amusement arcades, dodgem rides, mini-pools and large, imposing boarding houses. But behind this veneer of vulgarity lay a tier of solid, late nineteenth-century houses that were home to the town's burgeoning middle classes.

The Trimbles lived first in a terraced house in the centre of the town at King Street, then in 1948 moved to a larger home on Victoria Road where young David, a shy, quiet boy, had some of his happiest childhood memories. 'Just a few yards down from the house where I lived was an alley through to Seacliff Road beside the sea. I could get from there in two to three minutes . . . you could climb right on to the rocks and of course the rocks became my playgrounds. It was a very peaceful place to play.' Another of his early recollections is the end of the post-war austerity associated with Clement Attlee's government: 'I can remember when sweets came off ration and getting sweets for the first time. Before that we never knew what sweets were.'[3]

Sweets or no sweets, the period in which Trimble spent his childhood is seen by unionists as a 'golden age'. The constitutional position of Northern Ireland inside the United Kingdom seemed secure following Ulster's contribution to the war effort. Eire's transformation into the Irish Republic in 1948 failed to change the status quo north of the border. By the mid-1950s the Province was enjoying an increase in living standards, although this prosperity was not experienced by many in the Catholic/nationalist community. Moreover, they were still trapped in a state of which they wanted no part. The IRA continued, though quite unsuccessfully, to attempt the violent overthrow of the Northern Ireland state.

Nor was lacking a share in the new-found prosperity necessarily limited to Catholic families. Although Trimble's father was secure in a civil service job for life, the pay was only average and the family lived frugally. The Trimbles, as David points out, accepted their lot and did not grumble about being unable to afford the new products of the mass consumer age: 'I was conscious that as a family we weren't quite as well off as other friends' families. In the late 1950s some of them had televisions, but we didn't for a long time. I can't say there was any sense of deprivation – there were just things we couldn't afford.'[4]

David was sent first to Central primary school and then to the larger Ballyholme primary, where he began to show signs of his father's academic abilities. His sister Rosemary and brother Iain both failed the eleven-plus entrance exam for grammar school, but David won a scholarship. His father decided to send him to Bangor grammar, a non-denominational school only a few hundred yards from the house. Some of the other more elite grammar schools were linked to the Church of Ireland and a boy such as David might feel ill at ease there on account of both his humble background and his Presbyterian religion. Trimble's memories of the school are not entirely positive – in fact it was here that he encountered the first of many obstacles that were put in the way of his early ambitions.

I had a chequered career at school as I think I must have been something of a late developer. The first thing we did when entering the school was to sit a test. It was a teacher called Ernie

Brown, who said the usual things, 'Oh, you think you're good because you've passed your eleven plus,' and so on, 'but you're not.' He said he would take us down a notch. He lifted up one of the scripts from the test to show how ghastly we were, and of course it was mine. So I found myself in the B stream, and through the early years I was at the bottom of the B stream.[5]

But from the age of fourteen the young Trimble's results started to improve. He adored history but had to fight hard for a place in the advanced senior history class (the equivalent of today's A-level) which the headmaster, Randall Clarke, took himself.

There were only seven of us in that class, and I disliked Randall intensely as a person because he was fussy and was reluctant to let me in. For the first months of that course he kept telling me how lucky I was to be in it. I didn't like particularly his view on Irish history, but it has to be said the experience of being there was good. In second year, for instance, we were doing seventeenth-century history and the book that he used was by a chap called David Gough, and that was a university text. So in that sense he stretched us, and he did eventually concede in the two years that I was there that I was very good.[6]

His best subject, however, was ancient history, at which he gained the equivalent of an 'A' grade. He admits to a 'slight arrogance' for being disappointed at the time that his mark was less than 100 per cent.

Did he ever get a proper insight into the 'other side' of Irish history, given that he was brought up in such a stable Protestant/unionist environment?

The only Irish history I ever did at school was . . . seventeenth-century Irish, British and European [which would have included the siege of Derry and the Battle of the Boyne]. So it gave me some knowledge of the other side, because most people who went to state schools came out with no sense of Irish history at all. I learned Irish history, but it was in a British and more importantly a European context.[7]

Historical heroes often offer clues to later political development. Trimble's choice of the English Civil War was complex. 'I tended to be with the people, the Commonwealth. But at the same time I thought that while the Royalists were wrong they were also romantic, whereas the Roundheads were right but offensive.'[8]

While at Bangor grammar Trimble got embroiled in a darker episode. A fellow pupil alleged that in early 1961 Trimble had been part of a gang of boys who bullied him.

> It took the form of a series of humiliations and constant harass-
> ment. . . . It was like mind games. I was a shy wee person and
> they seemed to know the right buttons to press to embarrass me
> in front of other people. They would make fun of my hair and my
> uniform and they would wait for me to come in late in the
> mornings. They would tease me about every possible thing they
> could find. I didn't want to go to school at all by the end of it.[9]

The pupil acknowledges that Trimble was not vicious compared to other boys in the gang. He despised Trimble, however, because he was a school prefect who 'took every opportunity to humiliate me'. When his anger reached boiling point be decided he was going to get his revenge. He went to a Bangor gunsmith and bought an old .303 rifle with the stock removed and the barrel cut to two inches. 'I made my own round of ammunition. I'd gotten hold of a couple of bullets and I drilled a hole in the percussion camp of the round and filled it with gunpowder from penny bangers, and I put a ball bearing in on top of it and took it to school with me. I was going to frighten or shoot Trimble because I was so traumatized by it all.'[10] However, He never got his opportunity as he was caught with the gun by a teacher who handed him over to the local RUC.

Trimble's own frustrations were not confined to the academic field. Like millions of other boys growing up at the beginning of the jet age he wanted to be a pilot and dreamed of flying modern fighters for the Royal Air Force. He was hearing the call of service that had taken his grandfather Captain Jack into the armed forces. But poor eyesight from an early age prevented him fulfilling this youthful ambition (his brother Iain did join the RAF, where he became a mapper and aerial photographer). A number of militar-istic youth organizations competed for the loyalty of Bangor boys who were keen on putting on uniforms and playing war games. When he was thirteen Trimble became a member of both the Sea

Scouts and the Air Training Corps, eventually opting to stay with the latter for several years. 'I was more interested in the possibility of flying and shooting than scouting activities. The funny thing was that the Scout troop was a largely middle-class affair whereas the ATC only contained two grammar school boys. Oddly, the Scouts were rougher, rugby-playing boys, and I wasn't really a physical person so I stayed with the ATC.'[11]

The ATC was where he met another Bangor boy, Leslie Cree, who was to exert a major influence on the early part of his life. Cree, already an NCO, became the leader of a pack of cadets, including Trimble, all of whom have remained close friends. 'I remember this wee quiet lad, gangly and wearing glasses, with red hair, coming to join up one night, Cree said. 'He was quite reserved, even a bit shy. . . . I was fifteen and already considered myself a veteran, so I took Davy under my wing.'[12] Cree recalls that Trimble's uniforms were pristine and his shoes always gleaming – he took the ATC very seriously.

The boys trained on alternate weekends at RAF Aldergrove on the northern outskirts of Belfast; at Ballykelly, which was a joint British-American air base during the war and is still in use today; or on board HMS *Eagle*, one of the ships in Lough Foyle assigned to the RAF's Coastal Command in the 1960s. Despite being short-sighted, according to Cree and other ATC comrades Trimble became a proficient marksman on the firing range. On the annual camps at RAF bases in Scotland Trimble won awards for shooting at falling plates, and quickly learned how to fire a .303 rifle, a .22 rifle and a Bren machine gun. Firing rifles and machine guns, map-reading, glider training, aircraft recognition and generally preparing for war were helping this shy, bookish boy from Victoria Road emerge from his shell. 'He came out of the ATC a different person from when he first joined,' asserts Cree. 'Although he was a little reserved, he was also resolute. Davy showed he could lead – he could take orders, but also give them.'[13]

The summer camps were not just an opportunity to test map-reading skills or get lost in the Highlands; the teenage Bangor squadron would often slip off at night to a local pub and convince the landlord or landlady that they were old enough to be served. According to Cree, Trimble was one of the first out of the door of the barracks and into the pub, where they would spend the evening playing cards, chatting mess-room gossip or even arguing about politics. Meanwhile, back at home Trimble and Cree got into a number of scrapes: 'I remember David driving his first car. . . . I had an old Rover 75 and David found this Rover 60. . . . On his first outing he hit this pole and that was the end of his driving for many years. We weren't injured, but it put him off for a long time.'[14]

The Bangor ATC squadron had an eclectic taste in music ranging from classical to rock'n'roll. Cree said that in those years Trimble was an Elvis fanatic. 'I tried to convert him to Buddy Holly but without much success. It was only Elvis and the classical composers.' However, he showed no interest in soccer at a time when Ulster-born players like George Best were international superstars; instead, Trimble went along with Cree to motorcycle grand prix.[15]

Cree was leader of the group and it was natural for Trimble to follow him into another militaristic institution of which both are still members – the Orange Order. Cree belonged to the Bangor Abbey Orange Lodge and persuaded the reticent Trimble to come and join. Yet despite the fact that they were both Orangemen, Cree's and Trimble's best friends in the ATC included a number of Catholic boys from Bangor and nearby Newtonards; Alan McKillen was one of them. He recalls: 'David was religion-blind. He just wasn't interested in what you were. He was never aloof from someone because of his or her religion, or treated anyone differently because of who he or she was. We were all like that as squaddies in the ATC. No one in the ATC at that time was bigoted or sectarian – absolutely no one.'[16]

As unlikely as it may seem today, given the violent confrontations over Orange parades in recent summers, McKillen and the other Catholics in the squadron would watch Cree and Trimble marching through Bangor on the Twelfth of July. This, however, was the period just before the eruption of the Troubles, and Bangor at least was generally sectarian-free for Catholic boys like McKillen, who were insulated from the discrimination and repression that their peers faced in other parts of Northern Ireland.

Although Trimble's short-sightedness precluded him from training as a fighter pilot, along with Cree and McKillen he was allowed to take glider lessons. They trained at RAF Aldergrove and Syndenham, the home of Queen's University's air squadron, and eventually gained their glider pilot licences in the late 1960s. Yet for all his friend's love of flying, Alan McKillen never imagined that

Trimble was ever cut out for a career in the armed services. 'He was one of the boys all right, but he was still a bit different from the rest of us. Even at fifteen or sixteen you could tell he was quite intellectual, that he was on his way to a university degree, perhaps even to Oxford or Cambridge. He was well read and could argue about many subjects, including world politics, so we didn't bother arguing with him about politics.'[17]

Indeed, having put thoughts of the RAF behind him, Trimble's burning ambition was to study history at Queen's University, Belfast. However, two roadblocks stood in his way: misinformation and a lack of money. Trimble had dropped Latin after his junior exams, but in his penultimate year at Bangor grammar he was told that he could not take a history degree at Queen's without it. He took up Latin again, but soon realized he was not going to pass it in time. Meanwhile the family was also facing financial difficulties and David started to come under pressure from his father to go straight into full-time employment, preferably following his footsteps into the civil service. Trimble applied for a junior post in the Ministry of Finance, but discovered just before he left school that Latin was no longer compulsory for history undergraduates. By then, however, it was too late to reapply to Queen's as he had been accepted by the Ministry, and a sense of service to his father and the rest of the family made him feel obliged to take up the post.

So while the academic life had eluded him for the time being, and he was not destined for glory with the RAF, at least Trimble's years in the cadets forced the introverted, bespectacled boy to go out into the world. More importantly, perhaps, it brought him into contact with Catholic boys of the same age, something of which many Protestant children had little or no experience while growing up in the last two decades of Stormont rule. In retrospect his involvement with the ATC can be read as the weedy intellectual kid wanting to play with the big boys. This pattern of wanting to be one of the lads – even the tough, hard-drinking, hard-fighting ones – was to be replicated later in his political career.

In the mid-1960s the first rumbles of the political earthquake which would shake the unionist regime to its foundations were heard from beneath the apparently peaceful surface of Northern Ireland. Through the use of its armed police force and the B Specials, the unpaid but uniformed part-time branch of the Ulster Special Constabulary, the unionist government had effectively defeated an earlier IRA offensive, the border campaign of 1956–62 which was aimed at undermining the Northern Irish and British governments and ending partition. Its defeat, after twelve volunteers and six RUC officers had been killed, and thirty-two members of the Northern Ireland security services injured, led to serious disarray within Irish republicanism. After a major rethink the IRA began to pursue a new, peaceful, socialist path which outraged republican traditionalists.

In 1966 the Stormont government called up the B Specials again as it whipped up hysteria about a new republican threat. Among their number were some of Trimble's old comrades. 'A lot of the chaps with me in the ATC had gone into the Special Constabulary – Leslie, Winston, and George Patton who was a crack shot,' he recalled. 'They were mobilized around 1966 in case something major happened, although I still felt the mid-sixties were a period of optimism and new prosperity.'[18] In Protestant eyes, the Specials were seen as an important reserve force which could be sent into action at times of crisis to protect their state; Catholics, on the other hand, loathed the 'B men', whom they regarded as a brutal sectarian militia.

This volatile situation was further hyped by the rantings of the Reverend Ian Paisley, an ambitious Free Presbyterian firebrand from Ballymena. Paisley was leading a new crusade of Protestant hard-liners against the twin beasts of religious/ecumenical rapprochement with Rome and the new political entente between Terence O'Neill's administration in Belfast (he had taken over from Lord Brookeborough in 1963) and Sean Lemass's modernizing government in Dublin. When O'Neill invited Lemass to Belfast for talks in 1965 he was denounced by Paisley, who threw snowballs at both prime ministers.

The tensions had first boiled over in riots in central Belfast in 1964, at the time of a general election called by Sir Alec Douglas-Home. Paisley's supporters threatened to march on the Catholic Falls Road in order to take down Irish tricolours (still a banned symbol in Northern Ireland under the Flags and Emblems Act) in the window of the Republican Clubs' headquarters. Fifty years after the 1916 rising it seemed to many unionists that violent republicanism was being resurrected from the ashes of the defeat of the border campaign.

Trimble, who in the summer of 1964 had just started working at the Land Registry office in Fermanagh, was not enthusiastic about Terence O'Neill, who was belatedly trying to reach out to nationalists within Northern Ireland. The Prime Minister was, for example, visiting Catholic schools and entering into detente with the Dublin government. Trimble admits he would have been more impressed by Brian Faulkner, O'Neill's Home Affairs Minister, who had played an active role in suppressing the IRA border campaign. Faulkner was a political figure full of contradictions. Friends and opponents alike praised him for his energy in attracting new industry as the modernizing Minister of Commerce in 1963. Yet his career was marked by a hard-line reputation won in 1950 for leading an Orange parade through the Longstone Road, a Catholic area near Kilkeel in Co. Down. It could said that the Longstone Road march was a prequel to the defiance that Trimble was to demonstrate at another contentious march forty-five years later in Drumcree, Portadown.

The deployment of armed forces by Stormont reached a peak in 1966, reflecting a widely held one-dimensional view of Irish republicanism as the ever-present mortal threat to their state. Unionists of all hues had failed to analyse the evolving nature of the IRA and Sinn Fein following the republican movement's defeat in 1962 at the end of the border campaign. Under the leadership of Cathal Goulding, the IRA embarked on a major soul-searching exercise and opened up a new dialogue with left-wing intellectuals, writers, journalists and academics. These were the first incremental steps away from United Ireland-or-nothing nationalism towards a peaceful socialist path. The surest evidence of the new republican departure under Goulding was the disillusionment of more traditional republicans such as Joe Cahill, who drifted out of the IRA towards the end of the 1960s and whose careers were only resuscitated in the sectarian storm that blew across Northern Ireland in the early 1970s.

Although some of his friends in the ATC were called up by the B Specials two years later, David Trimble showed little interest in local politics when he matriculated at Queen's in 1964. His main concern was to take advantage of a civil service scheme which would finally allow him to go to university. Suitable employees could take part-time law degrees at Queen's University, leaving their offices for a few hours every day to study and attend lectures. Trimble and another young man who had come up from Dungannon to work in the Land Registry, Herbie Wallace, were both accepted for the law course. Wallace believes that at that stage Trimble did not have any plans either to enter academia or to practise as a solicitor; rather, like him, he would use his law degree to scale the heights of the civil service. Wallace also saw no signs of interest in entering Northern Ireland politics. 'Even in the Land Registry he was a fairly bookish person who read very widely, knew lots about any topic you raised and wasn't shy about expressing his opinions. But he seemed more interested in national British politics. I think then his views would have been conservative in terms of mainstream politics – he wasn't particularly active or interested in the local scene.'[19]

The Students' Union on University Road was the birthplace of political careers ranging from that of John Taylor, who became Home Affairs Minister under the last unionist government, to Bernadette Devlin, the nationalist civil rights activist and future Mid-Ulster MP. But, recalls Wallace, 'We never really got involved in student life as we were simply in and out. We were slightly older than other students and had more commitments. We came up to Queen's, attended our lectures and went back to work at the Land Registry.'[20]

Trimble and Wallace had been told by one of the senior lecturers, William Twinning, that they were both capable of first class honours if they took leave of absence from their jobs in their final year and concentrated on their studies. Trimble discovered that because he had been out of school for three years he was entitled to a mature student grant, and asked for a ten-month sabbatical from the civil service. Wallace, married with a mortgage, opted to remain a part-timer on full pay. But the two friends continued to work together on the course, and Wallace appreciated Trimble's help: 'I found it an advantage to study with him as we were able to discuss things and work them out. It was particularly useful for me when he decided to go full-time because he had more time to spend in the library. He was decent enough to share information he picked up . . . we weren't competitive, we looked after each other.'[21]

In his fourth, full-time year at Queen's Trimble worked hard and remained more or less oblivious to the political debate raging just a few hundred yards away in the Students' Union, which had by then become a cradle for the leadership of the Northern Ireland civil rights movement. Contrary to unionist propaganda, the Northern

Ireland civil rights movement was a reformist rather than a revolutionary movement. It argued for equality for Catholics within the Northern Ireland state, demanding an end to anti-Catholic discrimination in areas such as housing, employment and local government. O'Neill was the first unionist leader to recognize the necessity of treating Catholic citizens equally within the state, but in the stormy atmosphere of the mid- to late 1960s Protestants were led to believe that the civil rights movement was a republican Trojan horse designed to push Ulster by stealth into a United Ireland. Thirty years later David Trimble would pick up from where O'Neill had left off, but in the meantime David Burnside, who was press officer for the Ulster Unionist Party's student branch at Queen's in the late 1960s, said he never recalled Trimble turning up for a single public meeting, protest or rally in the four years he spent on the campus.[22]

While his peers protested, Trimble was preoccupied with a blossoming relationship with a colleague at the Land Registry, Heather McCombe. His first serious love affair, it surprised those around him, particularly at work. Herbie Wallace found it hard to believe that Trimble and Ms McCombe were an item. But even at the early stages of the romance, Wallace could see problems ahead:

> They had a liaison at one of our Christmas parties while we were still part-time students working in the Registry, but I was really surprised that they started seeing each other regularly. Heather was a very outgoing and bubbly girl, whereas David wasn't a social animal at all. She had an attractive face but was very plump. They really were a match of opposites – she wasn't very intellectual, while David was cerebral. It was a strange union.[23]

In July 1968 David Trimble made it on to page one for the first time in his life. The local newspaper, the *North Down Spectator*, recorded that: 'William David Trimble, 39 Clifton Road, Bangor, gained the degree Bachelor of Law with First Class Honours, the only Queen's student to do so for the three years. David achieved this while studying part-time at Queen's and working in the civil service.'[24] The article must have been given him immense satisfaction, particularly as many of his detractors at Bangor grammar school would have seen it. He felt a real sense of achievement after the earlier frustrations. The summer of 1968, when the rest of the student world from Paris to Prague, Belfast to Belgrade, was in revolt, was a personally satisfying one for Trimble. Within the space of a couple of months he had married Heather McCombe and, as a result of his first class degree had been offered the post of Assistant Lecturer at Queen's law faculty, starting in the new autumn term.

The wedding, in August 1968, was a top hat and tails affair. The couple were married at Donaghadee Church of Ireland, outside Bangor, and the reception was held in the Dunallen Hotel, where Heather's teenage brother worked as a part-time barman. William McCombe, who has since had a partial sex change and now insists on everyone addressing her as Tina, took an instant dislike to his new brother-in-law and his family.

> I thought he was very boring. He was the sort of chap who would have sat on a Sunday afternoon in my mother's house and watched seven hours of cricket on television – county cricket, mind, not even Test cricket – sit with his feet up and his glass of wine and not speak a word. He never spoke to me; he never held a conversation. It was always just, 'Hello', 'Yes' or 'Goodbye', and that was it.[25]

Given Trimble's social awkwardness and shyness, inevitably there was no stag night. William/Tina McCombe remembers the wedding day because he refused to wear a top hat over his long hippie-style hair, even though he was an usher. This seemed to upset Trimble's mother.

> She put on these airs and graces and reminded us all that she lived in Clifton Road in her posh voice. I didn't like his sister Rosemary, either – she thought she really was somebody, just because she worked in Glasgow's department store in New-tonards. The knees-up in the Dunallen Hotel consisted of a meal and then everybody disappeared. There was no partying in the bar afterwards.[26]

But despite his differences with his new brother-in-law Tina McCombe remembers that the young couple did seem at the time to be very much in love – although, like others who kept their counsel, he never imagined that their marriage would last.

In conjunction with lecturing, Trimble had to take the exams for the Northern Ireland Bar which brought him to the law courts in central Belfast twice a week. While there he often wondered whether he should turn away from academia into legal practice. It would have been an opportune time to become a barrister or solicitor, for legal aid had been introduced to Northern Ireland the previous year. (Had he done so, it would have coincided with a big legal explosion, because when the Troubles erupted in 1969 the number of terrorist- and criminal-related cases increased dramatically.) However another sense of service, a duty that he felt he owed to Queen's law faculty given their offer of a job, persuaded him to stay on. He still ponders, though, on what might have been: 'When I first went down to the law courts in September 1968 the Bar was still comprised of about sixty persons, and of everybody who was in practice at that time, up to about 1970, nearly all of them did very well. I often wonder what might have happened – would I have been a much richer man today?'[27]

While Trimble busied himself with academic life, the world just outside his door was changing dramatically. In the month he took up his new post the Trotskyite group People's Democracy, which had an active branch at Queen's, organized a civil rights demonstration outside Belfast City Hall. The Unionist government sent the RUC in to break up the march, which ended in violent scuffles between police and students. Meanwhile, at a similar civil rights demonstration in Derry, a peaceful protest which had been attacked by the RUC ended with young nationalists throwing petrol bombs and looting shops in the city centre. In the same month the Nationalist Party at Stormont withdrew from its role as the government's official opposition; it was demanding radical reforms of the electoral system including 'one man, one vote', together with an end to religious discrimination against Catholics and to the Stormont regime's repressive legislation. One wing of the Unionist Party led by O'Neill attempted damage limitation, offering a series of internal reforms and the sacking of the more hawkish cabinet members such as Craig, who was held personally responsible for the police's over-reaction in Derry. Realizing the PR disaster that had befallen his government, at the end of 1968 O'Neill gave his famous 'Ulster at the crossroads' address in which he set out a five-point reform programme. It included the introduction of 'one man, one vote'; a review of the draconian

Special Powers Act; and the establishment of a commission to investigate allegations of vote fraud and discrimination against Catholics in Derry.

Trimble, like many other unionists at that time, appeared to have been living in a state of denial over the well-documented cases of discrimination and bigotry against the nationalist minority. In fact in 1968 he was taking those allegations against the Unionist regime very personally:

> On the Cahoon side, Jack did a couple of terms as Unionist mayor of Londonderry in the late fifties. This heavily influenced my attitude to the civil rights movement, which seemed to focus on Londonderry in terms of allegations of discrimination in housing, jobs and so on. Now I knew what Jack was like as a person and believed him to be someone of irreproachable character. Yet here were these people saying beastly things about him, and I thought, 'That can't be right – there's something wrong here.' I thought, 'Uncle Jack can't be doing that.' There was a disjunction between the allegations and what I knew of the personality.[28]

It was to take David Trimble thirty years to acknowledge publicly that Catholics were discriminated against under the old Stormont government. His radically different attitude in 1968 may in part be explained by the siege mentality that still colours much of unionist thinking within Northern Ireland. In the 1960s there were plenty of unionists who could personally recall Northern Ireland's violent birth in the 1920s and the risks that the infant state faced, in particular the ever-present fear of invasion by the Republic. Even during the years of stability and prosperity this sense of embattlement had never truly dissipated. None of this is to excuse the poisonous bigotry behind the deliberate discrimination and electoral malpractices, but it does help put the state of denial into a historical and, in Trimble's case, personal perspective.

At least discrimination was something of which no one could accuse Trimble personally in his teaching. The majority of his students, some of who held strong left-wing and republican views, regarded him as scrupulously fair. Many also recall that in a new age of informality in dress and speech, with some lecturers rivalling their students in chic shabbiness, Trimble stood out: despite his youthfulness he looked deeply conservative. In the vogue hippie parlance of the era, he would have been known as a real square! John Hunter, who came down to Belfast to study law from the Glens of Antrim, a mainly Catholic enclave on Northern Ireland's north-east coast, remembers this aspect of Trimble:

He always wore a Burton's suit and a shirt and tie at lectures and tutorials. Trimble would address you as 'Mr Hunter' – he never used your first name. He seemed to fit into the rather staid atmosphere around Queen's before the Troubles. In contrast there were other young lecturers who wore jeans, grew their hair long and went out drinking with us. There was even one academic – who must remain anonymous – who used to invite me to dinner with his girlfriend. We would have a meal, a drink, talk revolutionary politics and then he would roll some joints. I could never imagine in a million years David Trimble doing something like that.[29]

Hunter, who has since become one of Northern Ireland's leading libel experts and has acted as legal adviser for several Ulster newspapers, suspects that Trimble's cold-fish attitude to his students masked a deeper shyness, an affliction which he has never fully conquered. 'He was intelligent, but a little remote. I got the impression back then that he was slightly uncomfortable standing up in front of a class and lecturing thirty or so people. But he was conscientious, fair and you never got the impression he cared about your background. His lectures weren't stunning but he was workman-like. He got you through the course.'[30]

In an odd sense David Trimble's social conservatism, whether in lifestyle, dress or politics, mirrored that of another bespectacled young man also with a promising political career ahead of him; John Major. The former British Prime Minister has been cruelly caricatured on television's *Spitting Image* as Mr Grey, the nerdish accountant sipping the glass of sherry in the kitchen, oblivious to the sexual, narcotic and political hedonism next door during the greatest party in human history – the late 1960s. Major's *Spitting Image* caricature could have easily fitted the Trimble persona of 1968–9. The sixties seemed to pass both men by.

The young radicals marching past Trimble's office down the University Road in late 1968 and early 1969 dreamed of transforming the civil rights movement, with its moderate reformist demands, into a vehicle for socialist revolution. Fired up with the same radicalism as students in Paris, West Berlin, Prague and other major cities throughout the world, they believed that civil rights could be harnessed to overthrow both unionist Northern Ireland and the 'bourgeois clerical-dominated' state in the south. Yet their dream of worker-student revolution in Ireland was fast evolving into a real-life nightmare of sectarian communal violence. The North was in fact moving from civil rights to the edge of civil war.

Following a series of resignations from his cabinet in early 1969, O'Neill was forced to step down on 28 April, indicating a shift to the right inside the Ulster Unionist Party. The new leader, Major James Chichester Clark, was determined to quell the civil rights disturbances with a security crackdown. The UUP's violent resistance to change culminated in the B Specials going on the rampage in nationalist districts of Belfast and Derry: both the Specials and loyalist counter-demonstrators attacked civil rights demonstrations. In August that year loyalist mobs joined with armed B Specials to attack Catholic homes on the interfaces between the Falls and Shankill Roads in Belfast. The conflagration in the city threatened to spread across the Province as the Stormont regime's grip on the situation started to slip. On 15 August Labour Prime Minister Harold Wilson was forced to send British troops to Belfast, who were at first seen by the beleaguered Catholics there as saviours from a loyalist pogrom. A month later the Army constructed the first so-called peace line, a Berlin Wall-style barricade separating Catholic and Protestant areas in the city. In October Wilson sent the Home Secretary, James Callaghan, on a four-day fact-finding trip, the result of which was a series of reforms such as the disarming of the RUC and the disbanding of the B Specials. The latter move provoked fury within the loyalist community and rioting broke out on the Shankill Road. Three people died, including Constable Victor Arbuckle, the first policeman to be killed in the Northern Ireland Troubles – ironically, at the hands of the renascent loyalist UVF. By the end of the year the Unionist regime's power in Northern Ireland had been severely weakened.

O'Neill's reforms had come too late, given the vicious sectarianism that had been unleashed on the streets. The attacks by extreme loyalists helped create a new anti-reformist traditional physical-force movement – the Provisional IRA – comprised of republican traditionalists who disagreed with the Official IRA's leader, Cathal, Goulding, who had shifted the movement on to a Marxist political path and away from physical force, and young Catholics who had watched their streets burn at the hands of Protestant mobs. August 1969 was, however, only a prelude, and greater disasters were to befall Northern Ireland in the next decade. Even a young university lecturer like David Trimble found himself being sucked into the maelstrom. Between 1968 and 1972 Trimble lived in North Belfast in a shared flat in Kansas Avenue, a large tree-lined street of three-storey houses which runs between the Cavehill and Antrim Roads, close to where Protestant and Catholic enclaves intersect. In the late 1960s Kansas Avenue was still a reasonably prosperous religiously mixed area populated by teachers, doctors, civil servants and students, though in the 1970s it would become one of the most dangerous parts of Northern Ireland.

Trimble's bus ride to Queen's every morning in 1970–1 would take him past burning vehicles through army checkpoints and across broken glass and debris from the overnight rioting. The bus provided 'a terror tour of the hot spots of the early Troubles'. He was often struck by the contrast between the surreal calm around Queen's and the violent chaos all round him in North Belfast:

> I remember walking down the Antrim Road to Queen's on a bright spring day in 1972 when a policeman stopped me outside the local RUC station. He told me not to go down there as the police had come under fire – it was close to the Newington [a nationalist area]. I don't know why I said it, but I told the police officer I thought the shots were from an automatic rifle. He looked at me suspiciously, as if wondering why I would know a thing like that. I thought I was going to be arrested. By then shootings and riots were almost a daily thing in the area, so I decided to move back to Bangor.[31]

The Troubles were even encroaching on to the campus. One of Trimble's undergraduates had been arrested in August 1971 when Brian Faulkner, who had succeeded Chichester Clark as Premier in March, persuaded Edward Heath's government to introduce internment without trial. Internment was a total public relations disaster for Heath and an even bigger security debacle for Faulkner. RUC intelligence on republican suspects was hopelessly outdated. Most of those arrested in the initial swoops were either loyal to the Goulding-led Official IRA or simply non-involved nationalists who subsequently became radicalized as a result of their experiences at the hands of the British Army: those who executed the policy of internment were among the greatest recruiting sergeants for the belligerent Provisionals.

Initially the British troops were welcomed by Belfast's beleaguered Catholics. The soliders were seen as their saviours from a mass loyalist pogrom. Catholics felt that the forces of the Stormont state – the RUC and B Specials – were merely the armed wing of unionism and would do nothing to prevent extremist Protestant mobs attacking their areas. Local IRA men in West Belfast seethed at the sight of Catholic women serving tea to British troops on the Falls Road in 1969. The British Army had, for the moment at least, displaced the IRA as the defenders of the Catholic community.

But the honeymoon was soon over, and before long there were daily clashes between troops and civilians. Trimble gleaned first-hand knowledge of what was happening in republican areas from his brother-in-law, who had joined the Parachute Regiment in 1968 and was on a tour of duty when internment was introduced. From his quizzing of William McCombe, it was obvious to Trimble that many squaddies were using brutal methods during arrests and interrogations. Some soldiers saw internment as their chance to get back at the rioters, snipers and bombers by using excessive force. In turn this simply drove more young nationalists into the Provos' arms. Trimble's concerns about internment, however, were by no means ethical or moral, he simply felt that Faulkner had bungled it. Police and troops acting on poor intelligence were detaining the wrong people, while the Provisional IRA's ranks continued to swell.

Trimble's student internee had been one of his brightest pupils, and a few months after internment he received a letter from the young man. It was postmarked 'Long Kesh', the new World War II-style prison camp outside Belfast where hundreds of political inmates including future Sinn Fein leaders such as Gerry Adams were being detained. The student, who had by then joined the Marxist Official IRA wing housed in Cage 2 of Long Kesh, appealed for help from Trimble to enable him to continue his studies while he was interned. Much to the surprise of the internee, Trimble, an Orangeman and by then an uncompromising unionist, wrote back and obliged him. 'He went out to Long Kesh and met the prison governor on my behalf. The governor agreed that I could study, and Trimble would be allowed to come once a week and give a tutorial one-to-one with me in the visiting area. The arrangement lasted from late 1971 to May 1972.'[32]

Conditions in Long Kesh were primitive, with inmates held in Nissen huts that baked in summer and froze in winter. There was only a rudimentary drainage system and the food was poor. Given the spartan environment, a study area for Trimble's student was seen as a luxury by his comrades.

> Trimble went to the governor and raised the issue with him. He said I needed somewhere private to study as you were sharing a hut or cage with lots of other prisoners and there was no peace. Eventually they agreed to let me use the medical hut in the central reservation of the camp. I would go there every morning at nine o'clock and sit at a desk between two filing cabinets in a corner away from the sick beds.[33]

The former Official IRA prisoner never forgot Trimble's endeavours in helping him keep up his course work in such extraordinary circumstances. 'I think he thought he was simply doing his job. When I was freed in May 1972 I was accepted back into Queen's. On returning to Queen's it has to be said Trimble never showed any animosity towards me, nor did he even comment about where I had been for the last eighteen months. I can only guess that he saw it as his professional duty to help me go on with the course.'[34]

Whatever polite truce may have prevailed inside the confines of Queen's University between the recently released internee and his lecturer, on the outside the two had become deadly political enemies. By 1972 the sense of siege was reaching manic levels within the unionist community. It was compounded by a general feeling that something needed to be done, that Ulster was in crisis, and the call to serve was becoming irresistible. Trimble, like thousands of other young unionists, many of whom had never been involved in politics before, was about to answer that call.

2

Vanguard Days

By the summer of 1972 Northern Ireland had descended into a vortex of savage sectarian warfare. Ninety-six people were killed in the month of July alone – an average of three deaths every day. On 31 July the centre of Belfast had been devastated by a series of no-warning car bombs as the Provisional IRA bombed its way to the negotiating table with the British government. At night the city was blacked-out and deserted as assassins hunted their quarry. One of the emerging new Protestant street militias, the Ulster Defence Association, built barriers at the interface of Catholic and Protestant communities and announced the creation of no-go areas. Considerable tracts of Northern Ireland were becoming ethnically divided, with thousands forcibly expelled from their homes. Indeed, it could said that the first example of ethnic cleansing in post-war Europe occurred not in the Balkans but in Belfast. Meanwhile, the Provisional IRA's ranks had been further swelled earlier in the year by the events of 30 January, when the Parachute Regiment shot dead thirteen people during a banned civil rights march; a fourteenth victim died in hospital a short time later. The resultant widespread disgust in Ireland culminated in the burning-down of the British Embassy in Dublin. Many IRA volunteers who later became prominent in the armed struggle, such as the Derry-born writer Shane Paul O'Doherty, said they joined the Provos to get revenge for what happened on Bloody Sunday. By the start of July the Provos had held secret talks with Northern Ireland Minister William Whitelaw and British officials in London. For the loyalists of Ulster it seemed that Doomsday was indeed approaching, that a United Ireland was on the horizon. Many of them concluded that the move towards Dublin rule could only be resisted on the streets and, if need be, by force. Following the abolition of Stormont on 28 March loyalist workers had staged a two-day Province-wide industrial stoppage, but it had totally failed to alter Ted Heath's plans.

Out of the chaos in which unionism found itself emerged a man whose political career had seemed to be over in 1968 when he was sacked from Terence O'Neill's cabinet. As Minister for Home Affairs, Bill Craig had been ultimately responsible for the RUC's brutality during the 1968 civil rights march, and now he was back with a vengeance. On 9 February Craig had formed the Vanguard Movement, a pan-unionist alliance of disgruntled members of the Unionist Party, former B Specials, Orangemen and various factions of the loyalist paramilitary underworld. Craig, an intelligent and able right-winger, advocated that the only way to defend the union from the British government's appeasement of the IRA was through industrial action and mass meetings. In Craig's nimble, Machiavellian mind these protests would scare the British government into not yielding any further concessions to republicanism. The MP for East Antrim had left the Unionist Party in disgust at what he saw as O'Neill's and later Faulkner's craven sell-out. Many unionists who mistrusted the religious fundamentalism and blustering rhetoric of Ian Paisley believed that they had found a new secular messiah in the figure of Craig.

He organized a series of mass rallies around Northern Ireland which climaxed in a monster meeting in Belfast's Ormeau Park on 18 March, less than a week before Heath took the decision to impose direct rule from Westminster. More than sixty thousand Protestants turned up to hear rabble-rousing speeches from the platform that included a promise from Craig that Vanguard could 'liquidate the enemy', meaning the IRA and all shades of republicanism. Many of those at the rally wore paramilitary-style uniforms. The atmosphere was menacing, with hundreds of Vanguard 'marshals' in their armbands and crash helmets standing alongside groups of young Protestant thugs known as the Tartan gangs, who hovered at the edge. David Trimble was not at Ormeau Park, although many of his generation who were later to become some of his closest aides did attend. Trimble was still behaving like a passive observer, watching from the sidelines as these political seizures gripped the Province.

Craig had attracted a wide range of individuals, including fledgling paramilitary killers, Protestant trade unionists, former policemen and, most surprisingly of all, young, mainly right-wing intellectuals. One of the things that struck Trimble about Craig when he first met him was that he was well read. For instance, Trimble is fond of reminding people that it was Bill Craig who introduced him to the work of Karl Popper. The philosopher's *Poverty of Historicism* attacked the fundamental basis of Marxism at a time when Communism was still in vogue on campuses across the world, including Trimble's own university. It is still one of his favourite texts.

Among other academics who joined Vanguard in the early 1970s was a European-studies specialist at the University of Ulster, Professor Anthony Alcock. It was not just because Craig was more robust in defending the union that Alcock followed him. Unlike Paisley, who stood against Britain's entry into the European Economic Community (now the European Union) in 1974, Craig wanted Vanguard to be in favour of the EEC. This impressed a pro-European like Alcock.

> I signed up shortly after Britain's referendum on joining the EEC. Most of the university in Coleraine was staffed by English people who showed absolutely no interest in political issues to do with Northern Ireland. The main reason I followed Craig was that [he] thought Europe was a good idea. I actually ran Vanguard's 'Keep Britain in Europe' campaign in Co. Londonderry. The other reason for choosing Vanguard was that I was never interested in traditional Orange or rural values, which dominated Ulster Unionism in Londonderry.[1]

There were many other unionist Young Turks who were equally fed up with the ineptitude of the old Unionist Party leadership. They looked to Craig as their man of action, as someone who could galvanize a demoralized unionist population into fighting back. These men were impatient with the old party, which was run on the lines of a medieval court, with the blue-blooded leadership making all the decisions while the foot soldiers did the donkey work. Reg Empey, for instance, who had simultaneously joined the Young Unionists at Queen's and the party's Bloomfield branch on his East Belfast home territory, recalled:

My first experience of a Unionist Party branch meeting was a bad one. I tried to raise a number of social issues. This was in the late 1960s when I discovered to my horror the conditions some people were living in. We had gone down to visit a number of houses in Ethel Street off the Albertbridge Road and discovered places that were more like dungeons than homes. They had outside toilets, jaw-box [deep old-fashioned china] sinks, water running down the walls. I tried to raise the state of these houses at the first branch meeting and the party stalwarts were horrified. We were told that this was politics and we were only to involve ourselves in the day-to-day running of the party, that issues like this were matters for the cabinet at Stormont. Naturally we Young Unionists at Queen's wanted action, we wished to change things. When Vanguard came along in 1972 we saw our chance and left the party.[2]

David Burnside was another young man attracted to Vanguard's militant activism, contrasting it to the catatonic Unionist Party leadership which had sleep-walked into the crisis. Burnside had been press officer for the Young Unionists at Queen's and, like his fellow student Reg Empey, was totally disillusioned with the party hierarchy. 'In 1972 I was still chairman of the Young Unionists at Queen's and at that time the party was still an integral element of the Conservative and Unionist Party of Great Britain. But Heath betrayed us and that was it. I found it hard to be part of a party connected to the Conservatives any more.'[3]

Trimble, on the other hand, appeared to stumble into Vanguard by pure chance. Several members of his Orange lodge such as Albert Smith and George Green, a former B Special, were prominent Vanguard figures in Bangor. Green, who headed the Ulster Special Constabulary Association, was a key influence on Trimble now that Leslie Cree was no longer living in Northern Ireland. (Cree had gone to work in the gas industry in Co. Waterford in the Republic just before the Troubles erupted.) Green was a father figure to many younger loyalists and Orangemen in the North Down constituency, where he had been involved in unionist politics for decades. Green and Smith persuaded Trimble to address Vanguard members in North Down on the new voting system to be introduced by the British government as part of its post-Stormont reform programme – proportional representation. Trimble had happened to mention to Green during a lodge meeting that he had read up on the new system, and Green thought that this young Orangeman was intelligent and trustworthy enough to explain the vagaries of PR to people more used to first-past-the-post permanent majority rule.

Both Burnside and Trimble were getting noticed and rose quickly up the Vanguard ranks, although, while Burnside was quickly brought into Craig's inner sanctum, he believes that it was Trimble who was chosen to be the leader's anointed one. Trimble was appointed chairman of the North Down association and brought into the organization's ruling council. Burnside, given his experience of handling the media at a politically turbulent university like Queen's, was appointed Vanguard's press officer. Burnside concurs with the widely held view that it was principally George Green who encouraged Trimble to join up and eventually stand for election. So how did this shy academic who had never bothered with unionist politics at Queen's in the late sixties and early seventies strike Burnside?

> He was extremely bright and articulate. We worked a lot together from the autumn of 1972 to the end of 1974. We were regarded as Vanguard's main back-room boys. And Craig encouraged us to write policy documents, generate ideas about the way forward. Craig's movement wasn't just about rallies and protests – it was really the only unionist organization at the time which thought things through, tried to find a real alternative to direct rule. David was part of all that from an early stage.[4]

However, others close to Craig were more hostile towards Trimble, whom they regarded as a young upstart exercising a disproportionate and ultimately malign influence on their leader. They were suspicious of this grey man from academia who within a few months had shot up the Vanguard ranks. One of these detractors, a prominent figure in unionist politics in the 1970s, declared:

> In those days Trimble was very hard to pin down. He was always a total mystery man because he lectured at Queen's and yet here he was mixing with strange company that included paramilitaries. None of us were ever really familiar with his family or personal background, or indeed any other details about him. He

was always a sort of figure that made people wonder exactly
what his motives were.[5]

These remarks are important because, with the benefit of hindsight,
many of Trimble's former friends-turned-enemies have tried to hint
that he was working to a long-term agenda in 1972–3. Another
former Vanguard member who is now an Ulster Unionist councillor has even gone so far as to allege that Trimble was recruited by
MI5 at Queen's and ordered to infiltrate Vanguard. But these
outlandish claims seem to be influenced more by paranoia and
personal bitterness than to be founded on hard facts. It was, after
all, Craig who promoted bright young men such as Trimble,
Burnside and Empey. Moreover, Trimble did not actively petition
to join Vanguard – all the evidence points to the fact that Bill Craig
discovered him. Trimble had no sinister motive for joining Vanguard, he was not seeking out a secret army. The allegations of MI5
plants and infiltrations say much more about the widespread
feelings of betrayal among Vanguard hard-liners that Trimble
was to generate more than two decades later.

Vanguard was, of course, not just a coalition of students and
unionist intellectuals. The movement engaged in street politics and
inevitably this drew in paramilitaries. The clandestine loyalist paramilitary world in the early 1970s was a disparate alliance, based on
the unstable lines of Presbyterian anarchy. The competing and
sometimes overlapping bodies ranged from the oldest illegal organization, the Ulster Volunteer Force, to its satellite group Red Hand
Commando, the Ulster Defence Association, the Orange Volunteers
and so on. In many cases there was considerable cross-over between
the various armed groups and Vanguard. Andy Tyrie, for instance, a
plump West Belfast community activist with a thick black moustache and dark-tinted glasses, was both the nominal head of the UDA
in Northern Ireland and a member of Craig's Vanguard.

It was at this time that Trimble first came into contact with the
loyalist paramilitaries. Tyrie recalled meeting Trimble and taking
an instant liking to him. He makes some telling comments which
demonstrate how seriously Trimble was committed to the loyalist
cause in the early 1970s:

Down through the years I've met many politicians who blustered,
who said Ulster will fight but never did any of the fighting

themselves. I have to say from the first day I met David Trimble with Craig I knew that he would be prepared to put a uniform on to fight for the defence of his country. I always found David Trimble at any time I met him to be far-sighted. He didn't look at the immediate picture – he was always keen to see how we could politically outmanoeuvre Sinn Fein and the IRA. He said to me once that he felt political violence wasn't necessarily the answer, but at the same time I don't think he would have shirked responsibility if he had been put in a position to take up arms. I felt he would have done it, because he didn't lack courage.[6]

The alphabet soup of loyalist extremism, with its UVFs, UDAs, RHCs, OVs and so on, was still not full enough for Bill Craig. He wanted his own private army. At the same time as he created the Vanguard political movement, he oversaw the establishment of the Vanguard Service Corps. Ostensibly the VSC was Craig's praetorian guard, which marshalled the mass rallies and provided security for leading unionist politicians on the platforms. According to a number of sources who were active in loyalist paramilitarism in the early 1970s, David Trimble was for a short time a member of the VSC.

The man who swore Trimble into the organization said he had no hesitation in joining what was technically a legal group but in reality was another Protestant paramilitary force. Sam McClure would later hold talks with nationalist leaders like Paddy Devlin and John Hume, but in the early 1970s he was a militant loyalist deeply involved with both the VSC and the more overtly terrorist Red Hand Commando. According to McClure, the VSC was a phantom army of several thousand men with an officer class and even uniforms although it never actually took up arms, rather lay dormant in the event of a doomsday. Neither was it an illegal organization. 'There were two chiefs of staff who put the five thousand together. It was divided into areas east and west of the [river] Bann. I looked after the VSC in the east and an Orangeman from Lisburn commanded the western area, which stretched right down to Enniskillen.'[7]

McClure, a pub owner from East Belfast, was one of Vanguard's chief recruiting sergeants for both the political and military wings. He would head-hunt potential VSC recruits and initiate them at Vanguard's newly acquired headquarters in Hawthornden Road, a quiet, tree-lined street in a middle-class suburb about a mile from Stormont. 'You swore allegiance to the country and to saving Ulster. David came of his own volition. Trimble would be the first to admit that he was as militant as you can get. Everybody who joined knew that the VSC was a potential army in waiting.'[8]

Like Tyrie, McClure got on well with Trimble from the outset and regarded him as an important asset in terms of his speech-writing abilities and the legal-constitutional advice that he could offer. In contrast McClure disliked Trimble's new colleague Reg Empey, describing him as a 'wimp'. McClure refuses to divulge his own exact position in the VSC – he will only admit that he was a 'senior member'.[9] He has confirmed that from late 1972 his organization held a series of meetings with the more active loyalist terrorists in the UDA and UVF; but he is at pains to stress that Trimble was only an ordinary VSC member and was certainly not senior enough to have been involved in the early talks between Vanguard's military wing and the other proactive terror groups. However, McClure did share Tyrie's assessment of Trimble as someone prepared to take up arms in the event of outright confrontation – though Tyrie emphasizes that Trimble was not a 'hands-on' man in relation to loyalist terrorism. His involvement was more on the political side.

Trimble's own recollections of the VSC are vague. His view was that most people 'never knew what the VSC did'. Moreover, he is convinced that Craig set up the quasi-paramilitary VSC as a tactic to keep the other, more deadly loyalist paramilitary groups under the Vanguard umbrella: 'It was constructed in order to give him [Craig] membership of the board of the loyalist coalition that included groups like the UDA.' He accepts that many in Vanguard, including himself, might have been prepared to take up arms in the event of outright civil war.

The atmosphere in 1972–3 meant that many people were thinking things were going rapidly downhill – we were heading for an awful crash, we were going to be in a war situation. It's easy enough to talk about this in hindsight, but who can tell how I would have been involved in that? There were plenty of people who were happy to do their bit. You could see easily enough how people in that time got caught up in all kinds of activity.[10]

Jim Wilson was a former Unionist Party member in Ballyclare who, like Burnside and Empey, had grown tired of the innate conservatism of the old unionist establishment. Wilson dismissed the Unionist Party as being as politically militant as the Mothers' Union. 'They didn't know how to fight dirty, they didn't get out into the streets. They had meetings in each others' houses, and most of the conversation was about how they had better tea in somebody else's house.' Wilson is candid about Vanguard and its military wing: 'It was on the fringes of illegality. I make no apologies for saying that I was on the fringes of paramilitary activity. I didn't go down the road that other people did, but I shared the aspirations of those who took to the streets. I was more interested in the political side, like David, but I think we both admired those taking to the streets.'[11]

One of the most energetic and able young loyalists rising through Vanguard was Glen Barr, who also happened to be the head of the UDA in Derry. Barr, an articulate working-class trade unionist, said that at times it was difficult to tell the difference between the UDA and Vanguard in certain areas. He met Trimble at the beginning of 1973 along with Tommy Herron, the UDA's East Belfast commander who was later murdered in an internal loyalist dispute. Trimble met with them to advise on political and constitutional matters in the run-up to the United Loyalist Council's general strike in February 1973.

> Davy was always anxious to mix with the boys, the paramilitary men, because that was the fashionable thing to do in those days. You had to be a friend of Tommy Herron and guys like that if you were going to be something big in the community. Davy was very much part and parcel of the fringe group that was always there. He would never have been privy to the UDA's discussions and stuff like that, but certainly he was very much there when there were meetings between Vanguard and the UDA representatives.[12]

In other words, Trimble was never party to the who, what and why of UDA assassinations, and was never involved in the planning of strategies of loyalist paramilitarism.

It may have seemed exceptionally odd for a mild-mannered lecturer who had recently moved into prosperous middle-class

Bangor to be dabbling with the paramilitary underworld. His reasons for joining the VSC may in part have been connected to his sense of service from the time he spent in the ATC playing war games. Perhaps they may have been rooted even deeper in the past, to those older traditions personified by Captain Jack and the Cahoons in the siege of Derry. Some close associates suspect that they may also have had something to do with the concept of the weedy guy out on the fringes of the gang wanting to belong.

His political relationship with the loyalist paramilitaries was to deepen further in the mid-1970s when he became one of their advisers on politico-constitutional matters. But there was a price to pay for Vanguard's association with the armed loyalist groups. In early 1973 Craig had formed the United Loyalist Council, made up of Vanguard, all the loyalist paramilitary forces and hundreds of Protestant trade unionists. On 7 February it declared a general strike in protest at direct rule from Westminster. The ULC hoped to intimidate Edward Heath into restoring Stormont, but the day of action degenerated into a self-defeating orgy of violence as five people were shot dead and seven wounded in several shooting incidents across Belfast. One of the victims was a fireman killed by a sniper in Sandy Row, a Protestant enclave close to the city centre; he was targeted simply because he was trying to put out blazes started by loyalist mobs. In addition there were eight bombings and thirty-two arson attacks, the latter mainly directed at Catholic-owned businesses and homes. Ordinary law-abiding unionists were further sickened when the day ended with loyalist gunmen firing on the British Army. The irony of pro-state terrorists shooting at troops towards whom they were proclaiming their loyalty was not lost on them.

As Don Anderson, one of the ablest of the local journalists who covered the strike, put it, the February 1973 stoppage set 'Protestant against Protestant'.[13] There was mass intimidation against even Protestant workers who did not wish to join the protest. Craig, Trimble and others had to learn a hard lesson from the debacle – unless they had the mass of the unionist people on their side, political strikes were doomed. But it was a lesson they learned well.

While Craig, Trimble and their colleagues flirted with the loyalist paramilitaries it should never be overlooked that the latter carried out blatant and brutal sectarian carnage. In 1972–3 the

UDA, UVF, RHC et al. had killed almost two hundred people between them. The latter year saw the advent of the so-called torture killings in which Catholics were picked up at random, beaten savagely and then hacked to death. Invariably these victims were politically uninvolved nationalists who just happened to have been in the wrong place at the wrong time. The loyalists were fond of claiming that they were 'terrorizing the terrorists', but in reality their collective callousnesss probably drove even more Catholics to support the Provisional IRA.

By mid-1973 the old Ulster Unionist Party was in utter disarray. In the May local elections party candidates were split into two opposing camps – Official Unionist and simply Unionist. The division came about over Brian Faulkner's response to a government White Paper, drawn up by Heath's Secretary of State for Northern Ireland William Whitelaw, which outlined plans for a seventy-eight-member constituent assembly. Faulkner reluctantly backed Whitelaw's proposals since he could see no alternative, but a substantial minority within the UUP opposed the deal. Their principal objection was Whitelaw's insistence that power would only be devolved back to the Province if the unionists agreed to share power in a coalition government with the nationalist SDLP.

Faulkner's problems increased a month later, when the elections to the Assembly were held on 28 June. The pro-Faulkner bloc won just twenty seats, while an alliance of anti-White Paper loyalists including Vanguard and the Reverend Ian Paisley's theocratic Democratic Unionist Party gained thirty. The majority of Protestant voters had rejected Whitelaw's plans, but despite this the Secretary of State pressed ahead. Any new political initiative would surely founder due to this inbuilt instability.

The Assembly election provided David Trimble with his first taste of the political hustings. This sharp-featured, fresh-faced twenty-nine-year-old must have cut an incongruous figure beside the stolid pension-aged ex-police officers and businessmen pounding the pavements of North Down.

The main thrust of Trimble's campaign strategy was to attack Brian Faulkner, a man he had once admired as a unionist modernizer. The North Down Vanguard ticket's election leaflets included one with a cartoon lampooning Faulkner as London's lapdog. It depicted Whitelaw holding out a bone to a dog bearing Faulkner's face with the bubble caption: 'Please, please sir. I swear I won't wreck your Assembly.' The message on Trimble's first election manifesto was brief but extremely uncompromising. It had promised that the three Vanguard candidates, Trimble, George Green and Ken Leckey, would 'not allow murderers and quislings to destroy Ulster and hand it over to republicans'. The term 'quisling' clearly meant Faulkner; words like that were to come back and haunt David Trimble more than two decades later.

Despite their vigorous campaign, in which they covered all the main towns of the constituency including Trimble's home patch in Bangor, none of the three Vanguard men was elected. In fact North Down bucked the overall trend against Faulkner, with all three Official Unionist candidates managing to get elected. George Green had encouraged Trimble to stand and, even though he only polled 163 first-preference votes, he believes he got something out of the bruising experience of defeat. After all, Trimble had been the late call-up to the Vanguard ticket so he could be philosophical about his paltry vote. 'One of the stalwarts said to me, "You won't get very many votes, but you've done yourself a world of good in this campaign." He turned out to be absolutely right – I didn't get many votes, but people involved in politics were noticing me.'[14] At the Bangor Vanguard's AGM the following October Trimble was elected chairman of the constituency association – which, it turned out, was in part thanks to Craig's prompting.

Following the election Trimble spent much of the summer organizing the Vanguard political party, speaking at meetings and travelling to local branches across Northern Ireland. This energetic disciple of Craig struck up a number of friendships with local Vanguard leaders that were to prove invaluable in years to come. They included people like Fred Crowe, a Vanguard councillor on Craigavon district council whose area took in Orange heartlands like Portadown. Crowe, a car dealer, often used Trimble for non-political legal advice, particularly when he was offered buy-outs from larger car firms. Crowe said he instantly recognized Trimble as someone who could best articulate the unionist case.

In the very early stages I thought of him as someone who could have a tremendous future in politics. We spent a lot of time together because in 1973 David didn't drive [since the accident with his ATC mate Leslie Cree in his teens]. So I chauffeured him about in the rural parts of Ulster. We sat for hours in the car going to this meeting and that. All he wanted to do was talk politics, although he always did so in a calm, reasoned manner. He was never a demagogue. He wasn't one of those people who keep shouting 'No Surrender!' all the time until there's nothing left to surrender.[15]

Crowe shared the Craigavon council chamber with a number of republican councillors, one of whom, he knew, was also a senior Official IRA member. The Officials had declared a unilateral ceasefire the previous year in a bid to help end the sectarian carnage. Their ceasefire also marked another ideological step by the Officials away from violent nationalism towards a peaceful, socialist path. The Provisionals, however, rejected the Officials' continued pleas for them to follow suit, and accused the OIRA of 'running away from the struggle'. However, the OIRA ceasefire won them some new and unlikely admirers in the unionist community. Crowe struck up a friendship with Malachy McGurran, the chairman of the Republican Clubs (the OIRA's political wing in Northern Ireland) on the local council. During one of their marathon car journeys around mid-Ulster, Crowe told Trimble about this relationship. 'David was amazed. It impressed him that here were people who were involved with the IRA and their whole opinion had seemed to change. He told me he even felt that this was a good omen – if they could be changed, maybe others could be changed too in the future.'[16]

Vanguard had become a nursery for the new unionist and loyalist talent that had been held back in the atrophying years of Unionist Party monopoly rule. The organization also created a number of lasting political friendships which were to help Trimble later in his career. Reg Empey remembers being impressed by Trimble's skills in debate, at which he outshone most of his contemporaries. Empey became one of Trimble's close friends in the early Vanguard years, and like Fred Crowe in mid-Ulster, acted as his chauffeur in Belfast. 'Our relationship was very amicable because I respected him and always thought he had great potential. I don't think that in that period we ever had an argument.'[17]

But while the future seemed bright on the political front, on a personal level things were falling apart. Heather had joined the newly formed Ulster Defence Regiment shortly after its establishment in 1970, and by the early 1970s, she and Trimble had drifted apart. Herbie Wallace's and her brother's warnings that the pair were incompatible had rung true. Within a year Trimble would seek a divorce.

Throughout 1973 and early 1974, Trimble lived a double life, attending meetings and rallies at which Bill Craig predicted a Protestant uprising and then returning to the cloistered atmosphere at Queen's, where he could leave the pressures of Vanguard activism behind. His involvement with loyalist street politics had raised a few eyebrows among the university establishment, but little could be done to stop his activities outside the campus. Professor Tom Hadden, a colleague in the law faculty, was one of the few who defended his right to be politically involved. Hadden, a left-winger with little sympathy for Trimble's political stance, nevertheless applied consistent logic: if other lecturers such as his friend Kevin Boyle were engaged in leftist politics, then Trimble had a right to be active in loyalism.

> If anyone asked my opinion about it I would automatically make the comparison with Kevin Boyle's position. . . . Kevin . . . had been defended by Professor Newark [the head of department] on the basis that it wasn't really anybody's business what you did in your personal capacity. . . . Newark . . . had advised him to make sure he did his faculty duties and not to let his outside duties interfere with his work. If he did that he would be fully supported. So I had to apply the same logic to David Trimble.[18]

However, others in the faculty were never to forgive Trimble for his Vanguard days and were to use it against him a few years later.

Despite the warnings that the Protestant electorate had sent out to Whitelaw in June, that autumn the Secretary of State went ahead with his power-sharing plan. In November he managed to hatch a deal between Brian Faulkner's unionists and the SDLP under Gerry Fitt. The agreement was secured the following month at a conference at the Sunningdale civil service college in Berkshire. Its two main elements were a power-sharing executive comprising nationalists and unionists, and a Council of Ireland.

The package underscored Northern Ireland's position within the UK for as long as a majority wished to remain British, but the new Stormont Parliament would not run on the lines of simple majority rule. In effect power-sharing meant that the unionist majority would agree to a partnership government with Gerry Fitt's SDLP. Even though unionists held most seats in the Assembly, the number of cabinet posts would be equally divided between them and the SDLP.

The 'fishbone in the gullet', as Don Anderson colourfully describes it, for unionists was the creation of a Council of Ireland. Although the Council of fourteen ministers could only act by unanimous decision, thus giving the unionists an effective veto over the cross-border body, the perception on the ground was that this was a Trojan horse which would deliver defeat and destroy the union. As Anderson wryly points out, perception is everything in Northern Ireland even if cold logic told unionists the opposite. The situation was not helped, either, by some SDLP politicians such as Hugh Logue who trumpeted the view that the Council was a stepping-stone towards a United Ireland. In fact it was Logue who first drew the analogy between the Council and the Trojan horse.

Within the Faulkner camp there was a sense of despair, exacerbated by the belief that London, having abolished Stormont, was ready to hand over Ulster to the Republic through a series of complex constitutional con tricks. Some senior unionist figures, convinced that the union was already finished, had already given up the UK ghost. In January 1974 the prominent Belfast barrister Desmond Boal, a former Unionist MP and one-time ally of Ian Paisley, argued that Ulster loyalists should cut a deal with Dublin to initiate a new federated Ireland. Boal urged unionists to negotiate now from a position of relative strength to get the best possible arrangement with the South. Vanguard unionists were appalled by what they saw as Boal's morbid defeatism, and it was Trimble who led the intellectual offensive against his advocacy of federalism. This attack on Boal in a Sunday newspaper was actually the first occasion on which Trimble called for independence for Ulster; it was not in later pro-UDI documents, which his opponents are still keen to produce in order to embarrass him. Nor would it be the last time that Trimble locked horns with any eminent unionist QC who predicted the end of the union.

In his article, entitled 'Independence may be the only alternative to a United Ireland', Trimble agreed that in the light of direct rule and the Sunningdale Agreement Boal's prognosis that 'the union with Great Britain has been gravely, perhaps mortally, wounded' was probably correct. However, Trimble attacked Boal's assertion that an independent Ulster was, neither economically nor politically, a viable option.

> Mr Boal's conclusion that independence would be disastrous rests on two assumptions. First – that all subsidies from Britain would cease and, second, that 'ruthless supression of one third of the population would be necessary'. Mr Boal's assumption that Britain would be so eager to be rid of our problems that she would pay someone to relieve her of this embarrassment logically applies to a form of independence.[19]

However, Trimble demonstrated naïveté in his assault on Boal's second assumption, that only violent suppression could force nationalists to accept an independent Ulster.

> Of course there are circumstances where the Northern minority [i.e. Catholics] as a whole would oppose independence and there are some ultra republicans who would oppose independence in any circumstances. But if independence was accompanied with guarantees against untrammelled Protestant hegemony (and it is not the policy of the Loyalist parties to create such a hegemony) then there is the very real prospect of a form of independence not leading to chaos.[20]

The likelihood was, in fact, that large numbers of nationalists, particularly in western parts of the Province where they were and still are in a majority, would have violently opposed a loyalist UDI in 1974. The only viable form of independence would have been the violent repartitioning of Northern Ireland, with the loyalists controlling everything east of the river Bann. This, of course, would have meant the forced repatriation of thousands of Catholics to the west and the creation of recalcitrant nationalist enclaves in Belfast. Although Trimble's argument was both radical and naïve, the article did contain a few hints of his own vision of a secular unionism. Firstly, the rejection of 'untrammelled Protestant hegemony' showed that, even in the dark days of the early 1970s when others were yearning and fighting for the return of a Protestant Parliament for a Protestant People, Trimble seemed more interested in a pluralist, non-sectarian Ulster. The article also contained another idea which was to resurface in a new political initiative twenty-five years later – a Council of the British Isles.

At the beginning of 1974 a new Protestant workers' organization had been formed, the Ulster Workers' Council. It was pledged to have no alignment to any one unionist party, although it supported the anti-White Paper loyalist parties in opposing Sunningdale. The UWC had planned a general strike for 8 February, but postponed it due to internal disagreements. Twenty days later its political allies had other things to worry about – Edward Health had called a snap general election for the 28th as part of his struggle with the miners over 'Who governs Britain?'. Here was a chance for the anti-Sunningdale coalition to show the world what the Protestants of Ulster really thought of the power-sharing deal.

Brian Faulkner had resigned from the UUP's leadership the previous month, following the rejection of Sunningdale by his party's ruling council. He was replaced by Harry West, a Fermanagh farmer who had been Faulkner's Agriculture Minister in 1971. For the general election West aligned the UUP with the DUP (Democrative Unionist Party) and Vanguard to form the United Ulster Unionist Council (UUUC) which delivered a stunning blow to Faulkner's pro-Agreement unionist faction. The coalition took over 50 per cent of the votes – the clearest indication yet that the majority of unionists rejected Faulkner's power-sharing executive with Gerry Fitt.

Trimble did not seek a nomination for any of the Westminster seats, preferring to run the Vanguard machine which helped elect Craig as MP for East Belfast and the Reverend Robert Bradford in the south of the city. Trimble's diligence was now getting him noticed beyond the confines of Vanguard. John Laird had become the youngest-ever Stormont member in 1970 at the age of twenty-six. Now the head of one of Northern Ireland's most successful PR agencies he first met Trimble at a UUUC conference in the Northern Counties Hotel in Portrush on the North Antrim coast two months after their electoral triumph. Laird recalled Trimble as a man in monastic isolation, like some dedicated member of an ultra-left sect who is committed to the cause to the point of asceticism.

That was my first sighting of Trimble, although I had heard about him in the undergrowth. When I first saw him I thought he was Harold McCusker [another Unionist MP] because he looked a bit like Harold – those black-rimmed glasses and the severe haircut. At the conference Trimble was the ultimate back-room boy. He was up all night writing drafted documents. He wasn't a guy who rushed to the bar for a few drinks with anybody else, or even to go out for a walk. He would spend hours in his hotel room writing the documents for Craig and Co.[21]

The Portrush UUUC conference baulked at a general strike as the best tactic of bringing down the Northern Ireland executive. Harry West, for instance, was known to be at most lukewarm about another industrial stoppage. Instead, the UUUC decided to organize a Boycott Irish Goods campaign in the North. To the loyalist militants this looked like a cop-out. The Ulster Workers' Council was not even informed about the UUUC's conference, so decided to go it alone and force the politicians' hands. Tyrie and Barr, who held posts inside both the UDA and the UWC, demanded a meeting on 13 May with Ernie Baird (Craig's second-in-command), Paisley and John Taylor, another man who was to play a key role in Trimble's later career. Tyrie and Barr informed them that they had planned a strike for the following day, thus presenting the politicians with a *fait accompli*.

Although the UUUC representatives needed to be persuaded of the merits of the strike, Trimble was keen. In his view the politicians needed to be prodded along, and the time was now ripe to challenge Faulkner's authority. While others wobbled, Trimble was an early and enthusiastic supporter of what was to become the most successful revolution against the British government since World War II. Trimble's attitude stands in sharp contrast to that of other Vanguard luminaries such as the Reverend Robert Bradford, who on the first morning of the strike urged workers to return to their jobs because he felt it was the politicians' job to destroy the executive. Another anti-power-sharing unionist, Willie Thompson, a UUUC assembly man from Co. Tyrone, also spoke out against the strike. Twenty-five years later Thompson would be the militant and Trimble the moderate.

The new Labour government and most of the media foolishly dismissed the strike and predicted its collapse. However Harold Wilson and his new Secretary of State for Northern Ireland, Merlyn Rees, should have realized the danger the Province was now in. Already on the first day the largest power station in the

Province, Ballylumford near the port of Larne, was down to half capacity. As night fell there were power cuts over large areas. The UWC, with the combined strength of the UDA and UVF muscle, was able to control petrol distribution. It issued passes to workers in essential services such as hospitals as well as to staff at large industrial complexes such as the missile manufacturers Short's whose machinery needed to be serviced around the clock. In loyalist areas the paramilitaries were even able to control the supply of milk to schoolchildren. Trimble was able to use his influence to help his old friend Leslie Cree, now working for Calor gas distributors in Belfast, obtain the necessary passes to deliver vital supplies to hospitals and other essential services.

Inevitably the UDA, UVF and other smaller terror groups used intimidation. Workers were turned away from barricades by masked men armed with clubs and sticks. Some UDA pickets were given cameras to photograph people who tried to get through, although in many cases the cameras had no film in them. Other men in army jackets went around workplaces 'persuading' employees to down tools and go home. At the Harland and Wolff shipyard in East Belfast eight thousand workers turned up for a mass meeting, expecting to hear speeches from UWC leaders. Instead they were informed that if their cars were still in the company car park by two o'clock they would be burned.

Intimidation, however, was not the prime reason for the UWC's success. The fourteen-day strike was genuinely popular with the Protestant working class. The Irish Congress of Trades Unions and the British TUC attempted to organize back-to-work marches, but they were pitiful failures with only a few hundred, mainly left-wing activists, turning up. Even the conservative-minded middle-class unionists who were uncertain about general strikes had little sympathy for Faulkner's power-sharing executive.

Critically, the British Army and the RUC did not attempt to quell the strike. The UDA and UVF were under orders not to get into armed confrontations with the security forces, a lesson well learned from the 1973 debacle. If the RUC attempted to remove a UDA barricade, the men in the paramilitary-style uniforms did not resist but moved it to another location. Instead of violent clashes the UDA and UVF opted to play cat and mouse with the police. (While the loyalist paramilitaries attempted to scale down their violence during the strike in Northern Ireland, the Republic remained a target. On 17 February the UVF left two massive car bombs in Dublin and Monaghan. The no-warning explosions killed twenty-eight people, all civilians, including two baby girls. The Dublin bombing was largely the work of the Belfast UVF, while the Monaghan bomb was placed by the UVF's so-called Mid Ulster Brigade. It is worth pointing out that some of the loyalist leaders who attended meetings at Hawthornden Road, which had become the strike HQ, and drew up strike strategy with UUUC politicians had first-hand knowledge of the planning and execution of this strategy. The other theory – that British intelligence was somehow involved in the bomb attacks, on the grounds that loyalists were incapable of exploding devices of this magnitude themselves – is ludicrous. The UVF had bombed Dublin two years before, and during the early 1970s were responsible for a number of similar atrocities against Catholic targets in Northern Ireland.

Although the paramilitaries played a vital role in putting men on the streets and warning reluctant strikers of the risk of reprisals, a number of central players in the stoppage agree that David Trimble's organizational skills were also invaluable. Hawthornden Road must have seemed an unlikely venue from which to plot a coup d'état. One wonders what the polite people of this leafy suburb thought of the beefy men with dubious credentials who turned up in their area to discuss the overthrow of a government alongside the 'respectable' politicians who built future careers on promises neither to talk to nor negotiate with terrorists. Trimble's most vivid memory of Hawthornden Road during the strike was the bizarre sight of the Reverend Robert Bradford setting his dogs on British soldiers. 'There was a large garden around the house and the Army used to place undercover soldiers in the grass, quite blatantly for all to see. Robert Bradford used to arrive every morning with his two pet terriers which he let off the leash. They used to bark and yelp at the soldiers.'[22]

Trimble had two tasks throughout the strike: co-editing *The Bulletin* (the daily news-sheet of the strike committee) and giving political and legal advice to the UWC. He worked on *The Bulletin* with Harry Smith, a UDA man and close associate of Glen Barr. It became a vital part of the UWC's propaganda war. With most television sets turned off through lack of power the only cross-community broadcasting organization was BBC Radio Ulster, which was supplied with a daily digest of the UWC's actions through Trimble and Smith. According to many broadcast journalists working at the BBC's Ormeau Avenue headquarters, *The Bulletin*'s reports were normally quite accurate and useful given that they provided daily up-to-date information on which roads were blocked by loyalist pickets. In fact they were so precise that the Northern Ireland Office accused the BBC of playing into the strikers' hands by discouraging workers from taking their cars on to the roads because there were so many reports of blocked routes. As Anderson puts it: 'When the UWC said that deliveries of animal feed would halt, they halted. When it announced that Belfast was to be left without domestic gas, it happened. When it threatened to remove all remaining workers from power stations if the army was used, it did so.'[23] In other words, the BBC had to pay heed to *The Bulletin* because it was a fairly accurate digest of UWC activity on the streets – so much so that the SDLP accused the Corporation of pro-strike bias. The irony of this charge was that prior to the stoppage most loyalists thought the BBC was pro-republican!

Trimble's most critical contribution came just a few hours before a pivotal broadcast by Harold Wilson on Saturday, 25 May. Trimble helped draft the statement from the strike coordinating committee, which by then had expected Wilson to introduce martial law as a means of breaking the UWC. Trimble's prints are all over the statement, particularly in its fine legal-constitutional points:

> The Ulster Workers' Strike is not an act of rebellion against a lawful authority but a protest within the law against the denial of the rights of the democratic wishes of the majority of the Ulster people. The loyalty of the majority in Ulster is unchallengeable and their allegiance to Her Majesty the Queen cannot be called into question. The British Government has refused to heed the voice of the majority democratically expressed in the last election. They have imposed on the people a form of government which would not be imposed on any other part of the United Kingdom. This imposition is even contrary to Section 2 of their legislation, the Constitution Act 1973, which requires any Executive to have widespread support in the community.

On the same day as the statement Trimble made another invaluable offering to the UWC's strategic plans. Rumours had spread overnight that Wilson intended to arrest the strike leadership, including Glen Barr. It was Trimble who suggested that Barr, Tyrie, the trade unionists and other industrial/paramilitary leaders should slip out of Hawthornden Road and set up an alternative HQ at a secret location on the Ballybeen housing estate at the edge of East Belfast. In their place would sit the UUUC leadership, which included Assembly members and a number of MPs. Trimble's idea was that when the British Army kicked in the door they would find themselves in the embarrassing situation of having to intern elected representatives, including members of the Westminster Parliament. The Machiavellian plan demonstrated that Trimble had a grasp of political manipulation. As the UWC left Hawthornden Road he handed each man a copy of Hueston's *Essays on Constitutional Law*, which, he pointed out, contained a good article on martial law. The loyalists might find it useful over the next few days if Wilson went ahead with his military crackdown.

However, the trap Trimble set for Harold Wilson never materialized, as the British cabinet was already hopelessly divided over the use of troops to break the strike. Military advisers had been warning Merlyn Rees that the British Army would not be able to hold down a Protestant uprising if it was used to smash the stoppage. If a few hundred activists in the IRA could hold down sixteen thousand British troops, how could the military suppress a mass outbreak of violence from unionists?

Harold Wilson opted for economic and political blackmail instead. Everyone in Northern Ireland waited for his address to the nation. Some were disappointed because a power cut in Derry ensured that television screens went off air – surely an omen for the government. Opponents and supporters of the executive alike agree that Wilson's speech was a disaster from which Brian Faulkner's government could not recover. These were the words that inadvertently delivered the fatal blow:

The people on this side of the water, British parents, have seen their sons vilified and spat upon and murdered. British taxpayers have seen the taxes they have poured out almost without regard to cost – £300 million this year with the cost of the army operations on top of that – going into Northern Ireland. They see property being destroyed by evil violence and are asked to pick up the bill for rebuilding it. Yet people who benefit from this now viciously defy Westminster, purporting to act as though they were an elected government – people who spend their lives sponging on Westminster and British democracy and then systematically assault democratic methods. Who do these people think they are?

Listening to the speech in Hawthornden Road, Trimble was jubilant. Wilson had lumped the UWC with the IRA, thus further alienating the entire Protestant population. The Prime Minister had not made it clear enough to the British public that it was the IRA and not loyalists who were killing British troops, certainly not the UWC. Moreover, the 'spongers' label was a propaganda godsend to the strike committee. Within hours politicians, trade unionists and ordinary loyalists were pinning pieces of sponge to their lapels in protest at Wilson's remarks. Almost every Protestant in a community which had always shown loyalty to Britain at times of national crisis had been accused of sponging on the state. The insult therefore cut deep into the unionist pysche. Glen Barr agreed with Trimble that Wilson had gifted the UWC a major PR coup. Support for the strike grew across Protestant parts of Ulster, and by Tuesday 28 May Brian Faulkner's executive was on the verge of outright collapse. That morning Faulkner's twelve back-benchers voted to open negotiations with the UWC despite resolute SDLP opposition. Several hours later Northern Ireland's last Prime Minister went to Merlyn Rees to ask him to open up dialogue with the strikers. Rees refused and Faulkner promptly resigned. The power-sharing executive was truly finished.

Protestants celebrated on the streets of Belfast while the SDLP withdrew from Stormont, a dejected and sullen party angered at the British government's inability to prevent the coup d'état. The world's media gathered outside Hawthornden Road for reaction from the UWC. A French radio reporter approached Sam McClure for a comment. 'I said something to him like this strike was a people's revolution – this is something similar to the one you had, only it's not as bloody as the one you had,' McClure recalled.[24]

David Trimble had played a back-room but strategically important role in the most successful rebellion within the UK since World War II. His role in the strike was to mark him out as a hardliner for years to come. John Hume, who had been Energy Minister throughout the strike and watched his authority eroded by the loyalists on the street, was deeply affected by the 1974 stoppage. Hume believed the central lesson was that until the British government confronted unionism or, as he tastelessly put it, 'lanced the boil', there would no progress inside Northern Ireland. It is not surprising that constitutional nationalists like Hume were to harbour a deep suspicion of Trimble long after the events of May 1974. Even the non-nationalist labourite wing of the SDLP continued to nurse a grudge against him decades later. In the eyes of its leader Gerry Fitt, no friend of John Hume or the Hibernian nationalist wing of the SDLP, the Queen's law lecturer was one of the guilty men who had destroyed a real chance of political stability and compromise in the 1970s.

Throughout the strike Trimble had adhered to Professor Newark's advice not to let politics get in the way of academic professionalism. He still attended his lectures and tutorials at Queen's, crossing pickets lines, sometimes with the aid of a UWC travel pass, en route to South Belfast. But although he continued to teach competently and treated his students fairly, many of them were deeply resentful of Trimble's involvement in the strike. May was examinations month at Queen's and, thanks to the power cuts, many students were studying at night by the light of oil lamps. Some students were even prevented from travelling to Queen's or were late for their exams having been held up at loyalist barricades on main routes into the city.

One of Trimble's students from 1973–6 was Alban Maginnis, an SDLP supporter from North Belfast who had to run the gauntlet of loyalist pickets every morning as he travelled from his home in the Antrim Road area. Eventually things got so bad that in May 1974 Maginnis moved in with a friend in a Queen's hall of residence in order to take his second-year exams. His memories of Trimble at that time were mixed.

> I had cordial relations with him as a teacher, but there was no great warmth. He was a good law lecturer who taught well and didn't allow politics to enter his teaching. I have to say I did feel a certain resentment towards him because of his pivotal role in that strike. He was one of the main organizers, one of the brains behind it, and I still think the fall of the power-sharing executive was one of the greatest tragedies to befall Northern Ireland or indeed Ireland. I think that, had it survived, then we would have

been well on the way to reconciliation. He was scrupulously fair in his dealings with students, but I couldn't help feeling he had brought something down which I thought at the time was very, very good.[25]

Maginnis, who later became the first nationalist Lord Mayor of Belfast, said there was a mood of deep despondency within the university following the fall of the power-sharing government. 'Politics started to die at Queen's. I think people there were becoming more and more alienated from politics. There had been a great period of political debate in the late sixties there, and now it was dead. Our politics had degenerated into sectarian civil war, so I think students were turned off and disillusioned. This was made worse by the destruction of the executive.'[26]

While Trimble faded back into academic life, politics in Northern Ireland was suspended in deep freeze. Rees announced the establishment of a Constitutional Convention of the major parties to hammer out an alternative to the Sunningdale Agreement. Loyalist paramilitaries including Sam McClure held secret meetings with the SDLP at a house in Belfast's Malone Road area, while the IRA met with Protestant churchmen in Feakle, Co. Clare. The result of the latter discussion was an IRA Christmas ceasefire starting on 22 December, which the Provos extended into early 1975. Although the death toll for 1974 was 294, there were signs that, despite the collapse of the power-sharing executive, there could be fresh political movement in the new year.

At the end of March Harold Wilson, whose government had been re-elected the previous October, visited Stormont and announced elections to the Constitutional Convention. It was an attempt to revive the old Assembly, but without any precondition such as power-sharing or a Council of Ireland. Trimble and Raymond Jordan were selected by Craig to stand as Vanguard's candidates in South Belfast. He was finally heading for his first seat in a Parliament.

Trimble opened his campaign on 11 April with an assurance that, despite the previous year's victory in the strike, Vanguard was not seeking to humiliate the nationalists: 'We are not approaching this Convention in a mood of triumph or with the intention to exclude or degrade any section of our people. We would invite the minority to come in from the cold of their self-imposed exile and to abandon their sterile anti-partitionism that prompted, encouraged and prolonged it.'[27]

Again, while Trimble seemed to be appealing to nationalists to stop being nationalists, there are further signs that he was not aligned to the anti-Catholic Protestant supremacism advocated by other elements of the UUUC. However, the complex nature of Trimble the politician was demonstrated six days later in his second policy statement of the campaign, in which he bitterly attacked the SDLP: 'The SDLP manifesto speaks of trust. How can there possibly be trust with a party who clearly tried to use the power-sharing executive and the Council of Ireland to manipulate Ulster into an All-Ireland state? Men who we know wish to subvert the state cannot possibly be admitted to government.'[28] The problem for Trimble was that a few months later this is exactly what he would be arguing for – the SDLP in coalition with the UUUC.

A lighter note was sounded in the campaign when local newspapers reported that Trimble was actually teaching two of the SDLP's youngest candidates in the election – Alban Maginnis and Aidan Larkin, by then both postgraduates studying for the Bar. Unaware of Maginnis's resentment towards him over the UWC strike, Trimble commented: 'We get on very well in the class and both are very good pupils, but there is no mention or allusion to politics at all. If that happened in the class it would probably make the relationship rather awkward.'[29] In the event neither Maginnis nor Larkin was elected.

Trimble almost didn't make it to the Stormont Convention himself. When the ballot papers were counted on 1 May he polled 2429 first-preference votes – 4402 behind the quota in the constituency. The Northern Ireland system of proportional representation involves the single transferable vote for multi-member constituencies. Seats are won through reaching a quota, which is calculated in this way. Say there are three seats in a constituency and one hundred valid votes are cast. The number of votes is divided by the number of seats plus one (100 divided by 4 = 25). Then an extra 1 is added to the 25 to make 26, which is the quota. The candidate or candidates who reach the quota on the first count get elected. If no candidate achieves the quota, or there are still seats unfilled, the lowest-polling candidate is eliminated and his/her second preferences are added until another candidate reaches 26, and so on until all three seats are filled.

Although he was ahead of fellow Vanguard candidate Ray Jordan, Trimble had an agonizing wait until the ninth count to be elected. He finally reached the quota with 7240 votes, thanks to the elimination of Jordan. When Craig heard that Trimble had got in, close aides reported that he was particularly delighted. The Convention elections had been a triumph for Vanguard. Craig's party won fourteen seats, two more than Ian Paisley's DUP.

Over the summer the parties held a series of talks to find a new way forward. Trimble drafted a number of key documents to be submitted by Bill Craig in the course of discussions with the SDLP. Relations in particular between Vanguard and the SDLP were sometimes fraught and sometimes cordial. Trimble accused the SDLP of trying to discredit the Ulster Defence Regiment, while Paddy Devlin warned Vanguard that his party would not be intimidated into any new arrangement. Yet Trimble also praised Gerry Fitt's party for accusing the IRA of attempting to provoke a 1969-style 'tribal collision' over the summer in a bid to derail the Convention talks.

Trimble's stature within Vanguard was growing, especially given his frequent contributions to the debates in the newly resurrected Stormont Parliament. On 27 June, for instance, he made a well-constructed speech on the issue of whether or not the Convention should be televised. Surprisingly for someone who had master-minded the UWC's propaganda campaign the previous year, Trimble was lukewarm about allowing cameras into the chamber, as the press reported:

> In the nineteenth century newspapers had carried verbatim reports of important debates in parliament. Now there seemed to be a concentration on headlines and the presentation of attractive packages. If broadcasting went ahead it might lead to members trying to introduce points which were not exactly relevant to the debate, or trying to score points. There was also the question of the quality of debate and whether it was of a high standard. They would not want to reduce the confidence of elected representatives any more than it had already been.[30]

He therefore abstained in the motion that the proceedings be televised, which was defeated by a large vote. So the Northern

Ireland public never got to see some of the antics of the politicians they had elected acted out on television!

A fortnight before the Convention reconvened after the summer recess Bill Craig stunned the unionist political establishment by submitting a document which suggested a 'Voluntary Coalition' with the SDLP. He stressed that this was not power-sharing but rather a voluntary arrangement which would bring the minority into a new Northern Ireland government at times of national emergency. Given the intensified sectarian violence of 1975, this seemed an appropriate time for a national-emergency government. However other UUUC leading lights such as Ian Paisley and Craig's deputy Ernie Baird were outraged, and many of them laid the blame for this concept firmly at the door of David Trimble. They felt that Craig was rolling back the gains made during the UWC strike. One of Craig's former allies, for instance, believes Trimble was the manipulator who sold the idea of the Voluntary Coalition to the Vanguard leader.

> He and Craig became very close over the Voluntary Coalition concept. I am not sure whether David sold it to Bill or Bill sold it to David. I rather suspect it was the former. My objection to the Voluntary Coalition was that there was no such a thing. Once you bring people into government you can't put them out. The Voluntary part of the concept was a figment of Trimble's and later Bill Craig's imagination.[31]

When the UUUC's leadership met on 8 September the only vote cast in favour of the Voluntary Coalition was Bill Craig's. On 13 October Paisley called for his expulsion and won the backing of several Vanguard members, including Ernie Baird and Reg Empey. The same day the Orange Order came out in favour of the Paisleyite line inside the UUUC. The Grand Master of the Orange Order in Belfast, Thomas Passmore, accused Craig of departing from the UUUC's election stance about not sharing power with nationalists. It would not be the first time that the Orange Order would turn against the ideas of David Trimble. But some within the UUUC were uneasy about the demands that Craig should be kicked out. John Laird said it represented a personal dilemma. 'It would be with a heavy heart that we would expel anyone. We don't want divisions inside the loyalist ranks to get any deeper.'[32]

Twenty-four hours later Craig and Trimble, along with Glen Barr and George Green who had also supported the Voluntary Coalition, were suspended from the UUUC. Although the majority of Vanguard stood loyally by Craig, nine dissidents led by Baird now allied themselves to Paisley.

At the end of October Craig suffered a double humiliation: he was expelled from the UUUC's parliamentary party at Westminster, and then his Vanguard supporters were ejected from the loyalist coalition. Craig was once again on his own.

Trimble hit back on 3 November, accusing Ian Paisley of backtracking on the Voluntary Coalition idea. He claimed that Paisley had originally supported the idea in discussions on 26 August, just before the end of the summer recess. Paisley was accused of backing down following pressure from his own Free Presbyterian Church, a vehemently anti-Catholic anti-power-sharing religious sect. Naturally Paisley strongly denies this.

Regardless of the recriminations, any chance of political progress or compromise was effectively dead. Moreover, unionism was now more divided than ever. At this time there were three distinct unionist camps: the rump supporters of Brian Faulkner, who now called themselves the Unionist Party of Northern Ireland; the pro-Craig Vanguard unionists, along with the UDA; and finally the hard-line UUUC led by Paisley, Baird and Harry West.

Trimble has always regarded the rejection of the Voluntary Coalition as a missed opportunity for unionism. From a position of relative strength, unionism, or at least a section of it, had been offering nationalists a chance to participate in a government that, unlike that proposed in the Sunningdale Agreement, did not include an All Ireland dimension. Unionism had had a chance to be magnanimous in victory but had foolishly squandered it. He would fight on inside Vanguard and at the Convention, but he knew that any chance of his way forward was slight. Vanguard as a coherent movement stumbled on, but the split over the Voluntary Coalition had mortally wounded the organization, effectively ending the possibility of Trimble's mentor, Bill Craig, becoming the leader of unionism.

In the midst of the Voluntary Coalition row Trimble was busy putting together another political document, this time for the loyalist paramilitary leadership. The UDA, UVF and Red Hand Commando had founded a parallel political alliance known as the

Ulster Loyalist Coordinating Committee, which in early 1975 consulted with a number of unionist academics, businessmen and economists on the viability of an Independent Ulster. Two of the prime movers in the subsequent paper, entitled 'Your Future – Can Ulster Survive Unfettered?' were David Trimble and the economist John Simpson. Trimble had helped write what was in effect the first-ever serious political document produced by the loyalist paramilitaries.

The document set out the economic case for independence, which included a coalition government with Catholic representatives. Within the ground-breaking document was a sub-section headed 'External Affairs', which probably reflected Trimble's views on relations with the Irish Republic and acted as a pointer to his position on the issue twenty years later: 'We assume an independent state responsible for its own external defence. We also assume the Republic of Ireland will be a friendly and not a hostile neighbour,' the authors wrote. And then they added: 'We would suggest that Ulster be an independent republic within the Commonwealth and we can envisage cross-border co-operation on matters of mutual interest. Indeed it might be possible to expand this into some community of the British Isles for all the people of these islands, English, Scots, Welsh, Ulstermen and Irishmen are in fact independent.'

Trimble was not just still flirting with loyalist terrorists, he was giving them political and constitutional advice. While the UDA, UVF and other satellite groups were engaged in sectarian slaughter, their political representatives were showing a great deal more flexibility towards nationalists than were the 'respectable' politicians of the UUUC. And although Trimble's embrace of Ulster nationalism, even to the point of Protestant republicanism, was a radical departure from established unionist politics, his advocacy of the Community of the British Isles and cross-border bodies actually predates Tony Blair's vision of a federated, decentralized Britain twenty-two years later.

At the beginning of 1976 Trimble was elected Vanguard's deputy leader, and almost immediately went on the offensive against his former comrades in the UUUC. The acrimony from the 1974 strike was poisonous. Trimble accused the UUUC of hypocrisy after the unionist coalition revived talks with the SDLP. With Baird now in the opposing camp, Trimble was the leading voice in Vanguard after Craig. He decided on a new tack, campaigning for a referendum on the Voluntary Coalition. Trimble and Craig, along with Glen Barr and George Green, tabled a motion calling on the Secretary of State to hold such a referendum. But it was up to the Convention's business committee to ratify which motions could go forward to Merlyn Rees, and, given that Vanguard had no presence on the UUUC-dominated committee, the motion was never going to be accepted.

The exchanges between rival unionists became more bitter, and the rhetoric of David Trimble started to sound dangerously radical to more conservative unionists. On 4 March Trimble clashed with John Taylor in a Convention debate. He accused Taylor of running away from a referendum on Voluntary Coalition because in a magazine interview he had accepted that a majority would come out in favour of it. Taylor retorted that Trimble was misrepresenting what he had said. The atmosphere deteriorated further when Ian Paisley rose to speak. Paisley referred to a story doing the rounds at Queen's about a member of Vanguard who was a lecturer in law at the university. Whether it was true or not, Paisley told the Convention, it concerned the accidental discharge of a personal firearm by this person in the home of a young lady. He was clearly referring to Trimble, and the Vanguard deputy leader was enraged. There were cries from the Vanguard benches for Paisley to withdraw his comments, but the DUP leader refused to give in. He ended his highly personalized attack on Trimble by pointing out that he had been prepared to smear former Vanguard colleagues as 'being something inside this chamber and another thing outside it'. It seemed that Paisley was using this as his justification for raising in a Convention debate the rumours about Trimble firing a gun in his former girlfriend's flat. When Paisley still refused to give way, Trimble, Craig, Barr and Green stormed out of the chamber.[33] Trimble has never clarified exactly what went on during the alleged incident in the flat. It is true that he held a firearm for personal protection, but to infer that he used it to threaten a former girlfriend could be interpreted as a typical piece of Paisley hyperbole.

Before the walk-out Trimble had also issued a warning about the possibility of a new loyalist rebellion: 'Where there was a political issue which could not be settled by political means then at some stage the time came when force was ultimately the only way to resolve the dispute.'[34] He then added that he hoped the Province had not come to that point. This echoed a grim prognosis that Trimble had given the previous month, when he predicted that unless the unionists cut a deal with the SDLP Northern Ireland would slide into civil war. Trimble was now playing the role of Ulster's new Cassandra. His logic suggested that it was either a Voluntary Coalition or bust.

Trimble and his colleagues, however, were now outcasts within the broader unionist family. They did not serve the cause of future unionist unity with their threat on 10 May that they were prepared to split the unionist vote by putting up Vanguard candidates against UUUC MPs in the next general election. One of their most hated targets was Enoch Powell, the former Conservative Health Minister who had been dimissed from the Tory cabinet in 1968 for his overtly racist 'rivers of blood' speech. As well as being a ranting racist Powell was a strong supporter of the unionist cause at Westminster. Much to the dismay of many devolutionists inside the Ulster Unionist Party, Powell was given the nomination for a seat in South Down. The imperialist epigone was returned to Westminster under the UUP banner in the October 1974 election, despite the mocking of Ian Paisley who quite brilliantly labelled this mercurial political misfit as the 'Wolverhampton Wanderer' – a play on Powell's old constituency and the football team from the same town. Trimble too could not conceal his loathing of Powell, regarding him as exerting a malignant influence over unionist politics. He still blames Powell for playing a central part in the opposition to the Voluntary Coalition.

> It was Powell in the autumn of 1975 who led the attack on the Voluntary Coalition. He was the one who deluded the unionist leadership, particularly people at the top, into thinking the best way forward was full integration inside the UK. That was a shame, because from a unionist point of view the Voluntary Coalition was a much better arrangement than Sunningdale. There would have been no Irish cross-border dimension. It was a marvellous opportunity, and it was blown thanks in no small part to people like Enoch Powell.[35]

Trimble and Craig, however, may have been whistling in the wind regarding the SDLP accepting the Voluntary Coalition. Gerry Fitt has since confirmed that he never had any great enthusiasm for the concept. 'I knew the unionists would in the end not accept it, so I didn't hold out much hope.' Even today Fitt is reserved in his judgement of Trimble, which probably reflects his bitterness over the destruction of the 1974 executive and his personal regret about Brian Faulkner's demise: 'I don't think I should say what opinion I have of him. All I'll say is I don't think Trimble could ever compare with Faulkner.'[36]

The rump of Vanguard continued to exist after the Convention petered out in mid-1976. By then, however, Vanguard was no longer the mass movement which had once threatened to supplant the UUP as the leading force of unionism. Meanwhile the UUUC indulged in its own Arcadian fantasies. It set up a sub-group known as the United Unionist Action Council under the leadership of Paisley and Baird, whose aim was to repeat the success of the 1974 strike and this time restore Protestant majority rule. Trimble and Craig were opposed to the strike, as was Glen Barr. Harry West's Ulster Unionist Party also refused to take part. Despite the lack of unionist unity, the UUAC declared a general strike on 3 May 1977. This time, however, the stoppage turned out to be a dismal failure. Crucially, the committee failed to win the support of the Ballylumpford power workers, so industry and commerce did not grind to a halt as they had three years earlier. Paisley and Baird's twin demands for local control over security and a return to majority rule were not met. And although the UDA had backed the strike, a number of key figures in the organization were reluctant to take part. Glen Barr said there was little enthusiasm for the new strike in many so-called UDA brigade areas.

Andy Tyrie asked me up to Belfast to advise them after the first week of the 1977 strike, and I said the only advice I will give you is how to get this thing called off. I can't advise you how to win it this time, because you can't. I told them it was going to fail because you cannot pull the same tactic off twice. A good shop steward never repeats his winning strategy again – he does something new. The government would be ready for you this time, and of course they were. Trimble thought very much on the same lines as me about the 1977 strike – it was a disaster. In the long run it was fatal for unionism because it exposed a weakness in our armour. We showed we couldn't cripple the country industrially again, and subsequent British governments took note of that.[37]

By mid-1977 the British government had given up on politicial initiatives, preferring a 'security first' policy under the new Secretary of State, Roy Mason. The former Yorkshire miner with a reputation for being tough on law and order introduced the SAS into trouble spots such as South Armagh. His crackdown on terrorism was also directed at loyalists, with major swoops against UVF and UDA personnel in areas such as East Antrim. Harsh interrogation techniques were employed by the RUC to break terrorist suspects. The net result, though, was a dramatic reduction of violence in Mason's term of office, which saw the annual death toll decline from 295 in 1976 to 77 in 1978.

In this constitutional vacuum Trimble saw little future in a political career and retreated into academia. He had correctly analysed the attitude of the SDLP, which, having been traumatized by the collapse of the executive and the rejection of the Voluntary Coalition, was poised to abandon the search for an internal solution to Northern Ireland's problems. Even before the exit of Gerry Fitt and Paddy Devlin and the replacement of their policies by a more traditional nationalist/republican stance under John Hume, Trimble prophesied that the party was 'turning its back on Northern Ireland politics and was joining with the backwoods-men of Fianna Fail in sterile anti-partition-ism'.[38] It was a bleak but accurate assessment of the SDLP's new departure.

His old guru Bill Craig meanwhile found himself an increasingly isolated and irrelevant figure within the unionist community. By early 1978 Vanguard had virtually ceased to exist as a functioning political party; reverting to its former role as a pressure group, it was eventually absorbed completely into the Ulster Unionist Party. A year later, in the May general election which saw Margaret Thatcher come to power, Craig lost his East Belfast seat to Ian Paisley's Democratic Unionist Party deputy Peter Robinson by a mere sixty-four votes. Craig's departure came at a time of fragmentation within the unionist body politic. Unionism was now divided into four separate parties – Ian Paisley's DUP, the Official Unionists under Harry West, Vanguard, and Brian Faulkner's Unionist Party of Northern Ireland. The factionalism has since grown increasingly worse. Today unionism is represented in the Northern Ireland Assembly by seven competing parties.

Craig never recovered from the defeat and faded into political obscurity. A quarter of a century after leading Ulster loyalism to its famous victory in the May 1974 strike, Craig lives in virtual isolation in Donaghadee on the North Down coast. He is prone to severe bouts of depression and rarely sees any of his old comrades and friends. One of the few ex-Vanguard colleagues who keep in touch with him is Sam McClure, the man who swore Trimble into the organization's military wing back in the early years of the Troubles.

McClure still backs Trimble, claiming that 'if you scratch David's surface you will still find a Vanguard man deep down'. His comments reflect the central importance of the Vanguard days on Trimble's development. If Gerry Adams's political and intellectual training college was the cages of Long Kesh in the 1970s, then Trimble's was in Hawthornden Road and on the streets of loyalist Belfast with Vanguard during that same period of massive social upheaval. McClure recently called Craig to ask him if he would be willing to talk publicly about his former protégé. Craig declined, stating wearily over the phone that 'I don't really want to talk about how Ulster is being sold out'.[39]

From out of the Wilderness

At first they thought someone was hammering on the huge door of number 21 University Square. David Trimble was drinking coffee in the lecturers' rest area while Herbie Wallace had just put on the kettle for a cup of tea. For a few seconds they never even thought it was shots at all. Then someone did start banging on the door, shouting that there had been a shooting outside. Trimble ran out and found his colleague Edgar Graham dying in the street just yards from the university library. The oasis of peace in the pleasant environs of University Square had finally been violated on 7 December 1983.

The IRA had targeted Graham, the rising star of Ulster Unionism, as he was on his way to lecture students. Wallace remembers Trimble's reaction: 'David was first out and I followed. The most vivid recollection I have is of Edgar's face, which was incredibly red. Then I was hit by this sense of disbelief. David appeared calm – he didn't seem to go to pieces. But who knows what he was feeling inside? They were particularly close, but he never showed any emotion.' Wallace had been one of the last people to see Graham alive that fateful morning. As he was walking up Botanic Avenue from the railway station Graham was driving down it, and the two waved at each other. Wallace assumed it was just another normal day – that Graham was going for his daily newspapers before joining his colleagues for coffee.[1]

As Trimble approached Graham's body Dermot Nesbit, another unionist lecturer at Queen's, shouted to him that their friend had been shot. Trimble was angry that he was not able to identify the gunmen in the mêlée as terrified students and security staff fled across University Square. The confusion brought to mind another shooting incident a few months earlier when the IRA had attempted to assassinate the Lord Chief Justice, Robert Lowry. Four shots were fired from a sub-machine gun, and one of them injured a Queen's professor outside the staff common room which Lowry was about to visit. Trimble had seen the gunman but was annoyed with himself for not acting quickly enough – if he had run to the back of the common room towards the fire escape he could have recognized the entire IRA gang.

At the time of his assassination Edgar Graham had been the darling of the Ulster Unionist Party. Although not yet thirty he was already a leading light, having risen rapidly from chairman of the Young Unionists in 1981 to become the UUP's honorary secretary a year later. In a strange way his meteoric rise in the UUP mirrored Trimble's in Vanguard. Just before his death he had written two pamphlets for the party's Devolution Group, of which Trimble was a member. And the Ulster Unionist Upper Bann MP, Harold McCusker, thought so highly of Graham that he had asked the young law lecturer to make legal submissions on behalf of widows of IRA terrorism to the European Commission on Human Rights.

The Provos would undoubtedly have been aware of Graham's potential as a dangerous opponent given his high public profile in the revamped Northern Ireland Assembly, to which he had been elected in 1982. However, this potential was underlined inadvertently by a writer on Irish affairs. According to Sean O'Callaghan, an IRA killer turned Irish police agent, this writer, a guest speaker at a Sinn Fein-organized seminar, pointed out that Graham was one of the most capable unionists to emerge in more than a decade. Although his remark was probably an innocent analysis of Graham's prospects of UUP leadership, it helped convince the IRA that this future foe should be removed. There may have also been a more immediate reason for targeting Graham. Sylvia Paisley (no relation to the DUP leader), a unionist student who later married RUC Chief Constable Sir Jack Hermon, told Trimble that republicans at Queen's had been outraged by some of Graham's remarks during a recent debate in the Students' Union, when he had spoken on the use of the supergrass system to convict IRA and loyalist suspects. 'Sylvia told me they were besides themselves with rage in the debate because of Edgar's performance. She believed – and I find it credible, too – that led immediately to Edgar's murder, because we know it was students who murdered him.'[2]

Ironically, Graham had informed Trimble just a week before his murder that he felt at risk from loyalist paramilitaries after criticizing them for their threats to Maze prison staff. Trimble said Graham was so convinced that he would be assassinated by loyalists that he had made arrangements for his own funeral. In the end he just happened to be wrong about where the bullets would come from.

The terror unit selected to carry out the assassination included a now-leading Belfast member of Sinn Fein. More than twenty years later one wonders if the IRA men who singled out Edgar Graham on that cold, grey morning in December 1983 have ever considered, in hindsight, that they might have got the wrong man? That the real target should have been the other unionist law lecturer taking his coffee break across the street in number 21 University Square?

This was not the first time that one of Trimble's political colleagues had been assassinated by the IRA. Almost two years earlier, on 14 November 1981, a five-man IRA team had shot dead the Reverend Robert Bradford at his Finaghy constituency office. Trimble, who had known Bradford in their Vanguard days, only learned about the murder that evening. The Belfast lawyer and Northern Ireland Labour Party activist Brian Garrett broke the news:

Robert Bradford had been murdered around lunchtime and David hadn't heard about it. I met him in the bar of the Grand Opera House during a break in the concert. I happened to mention to him that it was terrible that Bradford had been killed. At first he thought it was another politician, Roy Bradford, one of Brian Faulkner's allies, but then I said it was the Reverend Robert and he had been murdered in Finaghy. He seemed stirred beyond the ordinary. It froze him. Was it grief? Was it fear? It was almost as if he was petrified. I remember saying to him, 'I'm really sorry I had to tell you that, David.' I felt as if I had hit a very raw nerve in David somewhere.[3]

The IRA said they had killed Bradford because he was 'one of the key people responsible for winding up the loyalist paramilitary machine'. Unionists, however, saw the murder as an attempt to provoke a loyalist backlash. Other close aides of the South Belfast MP believe it was in part an attempt to silence one of their most outspoken critics, combined with revenge for the death of ten IRA men on hunger strike in the Maze. Republicans blamed Thatcher's obstinacy for the deaths, since her refusal to accede to any of the prisoners' five demands for political status had prolonged the crisis. The motivation behind Bradford's murder appeared more visceral than strategically political; Graham's assassination, however, had more long-term significance, given that the Provisionals thought they had removed a future unionist leader from the scene.

Even outsiders looking in on the Byzantine world of Ulster Unionism were convinced that Edgar Graham was an anointed one. David Trimble, on the other hand, seemed at this time an even more isolated figure than Bill Craig. Herbie Wallace noted the contrast in the lecturers' political fortunes in the early eighties:

> Before Edgar was murdered his star was very much in the ascendant, whereas Trimble at that stage had very little political influence. Edgar was a real operator who appealed to the leadership. He had a much more measured, diplomatic approach, whilst David had always said what he thought. Although David and Edgar saw eye to eye on political matters, their approaches to handling the party were radically different.[4]

If Graham had been the blue-eyed boy at the start of the new decade, Trimble was still seen by many in the Ulster Unionist hierarchy as one of the black sheep. He had followed Craig into the UUP in February 1978, but from the outset had aroused suspicion among senior party members. In fact Trimble was lucky to have got into the party at all. Although he only wanted to become a member of his local branch in Bangor, his application was vetted at the highest level – right up to the party's executive committee. Michael McGimpsey, now a senior aide to Trimble, remembers the problems he faced: 'In those days, if you had ever stood against the party in an election and you subsequently wanted to join it, your application had to be vetted in the headquarters at Glengall Street. The rule used to be that you needed a two-thirds majority to be accepted.'[5] In fact the rules were bent for Trimble. A hundred and three voted for him while a hundred were opposed – too tiny a majority for a party card. But Trimble had admirers in high places, one of whom was the then UUP leader Harry West.

Trimble's organizational and PR skills had impressed West during the UWC strike, and he thought the young man might be a valuable asset now that he was knocking on Glengall Street's door: 'I was very, very happy to have him on board. I welcomed him because he was an educated chap who could be of real assistance to the party. I had seen the way he worked with Bill Craig and he seemed to be what we needed at the time – well spoken, well read.'[6] While others took a malign view of this Vanguard Johnny-come-lately in their midst, Harry West would continue to encourage Trimble throughout his career in the UUP.

Those who did not share West's enthusiasm included the rump of Vanguard who had broken with Bill Craig and Trimble over the Voluntary Coalition. Jim Wilson had joined the UUP with the Ernie Baird faction and had deliberately run down the Vanguard machine in his native Ballyclare. Wilson admits that there was initial hostility to Trimble both from those who had left Vanguard with Baird and from the UUP loyalists who had stayed true to Glengall Street in the early 1970s. There was even a degree of personal jealousy. ' "Upstart" was the word most used by some senior people regarding Davy. They saw him as a real threat – probably because he had more ability than they did.'[7]

John Taylor said questions were posed about why former Vanguard people were signing up for the UUP. Were they trying to infiltrate Ulster Unionism in the same way that British Trotsky-ists were clandestinely entering the Labour Party? Taylor, however, stresses that he thought it was right to absorb the brightest and best of Vanguard in order to harness their abilities. He even put his earlier differences with Trimble over the Voluntary Coalition aside and asked him to become his agent for the European Elections in 1979.

The election, on 7 June, was a triumph for Taylor. He took the third and last Euro-seat on the sixth count with a total of 153,466 votes, behind Ian Paisley and John Hume. But it proved disastrous for Harry West. The UUP had put up two candidates – Taylor would take votes from east of the river Bann while the leader stood in the west. The party had hoped to make it a clean sweep of all three seats for unionism, but West was eliminated in the fifth count. Shortly afterwards he decided to resign from the leadership.

Taylor puts much of his own success down to Trimble's organizational skills:

> David certainly drew up a good programme of canvassing for me. That worked to my advantage, because even recently I heard Martin Smyth [a Protestant minister and former Vanguard member who became the UUP's MP for South Belfast after the assassination of Robert Bradford] say that if Harry West had only canvassed more in that election he would have done better. Harry took it very laid back, but David and I went to town on it. We canvassed nearly every unionist street in Belfast. Remember, this was a massive campaign because this was the first Euro-campaign ever fought in Northern Ireland and the Province is an entire constituency.

Trimble was a Euro-enthusiast at the time, Taylor recalled, and he found his election agent extremely useful: 'He knew Europe inside out. He knew about the politics of individual European countries, and the strengths and locations of the various communities inside member states.'[8]

Despite his contribution to Taylor's victory, rapid rise for Trimble through the UUP ranks was effectively blocked by the elevation of James Molyneaux, the party's South Antrim MP, to leader in 1979. A former British Army NCO, Molyneaux was deeply respected in the party and well connected in the various loyalist marching institutions, including the Orange Order. Molyneaux's critics accused him of quietly shifting the UUP away from devolution towards a policy of fully integrating Northern Ireland within the UK, with only a limited increase in powers to local government. A retiring, tight-lipped, modest bachelor with impeccable manners, 'Wee Jim', as he is still affectionately known in the party, was seen as a safe pair of hands. He was someone who could exercise real influence with the Tories behind closed doors at Westminster while the likes of Paisley blustered and thundered outside.

The pro-devolutionists in the party, though, were concerned that Molyneaux had fallen under the spell of Enoch Powell, the arch-integrationist. Molyneaux's pro-integration tendencies may in fact have been encouraged in May 1979 when the Tories won the general election. Margaret Thatcher, the new Prime Minister, had declared herself to be an ardent unionist who would brook no let-up in the fight against the IRA. It seemed that the Molyneaux wing of Ulster Unionism was convinced that the union was safe in Maggie's hands. Others, however, were not so sure that Moly-neaux's slow, patient approach could yield results. As one internal critic put it: 'It was all very well for Wee Jim to boast that he was having tea with the Queen Mother or Maggie and that they assured him that the union was safe. Nobody in the British government, Labour or Tory, could be trusted – they should have all been treated with suspicion.'[9]

The political prospects for a committed devolutionist like Trimble seemed bleak, so he tried to advance his career at Queen's instead. Even his political opponents in the law department thought his chances of moving up the ladder there looked more promising. Trimble was known to his colleagues as a 'black-letter lawyer' – someone who checks the statute book or common law and teaches from the texts. The other wing of the department consisted of the 'sociological lawyers', those who looked at the way the law operated and its effect on society. Very roughly, this dichotomy split along right–left lines in the late 1970s and early 1980s. However, both wings came together in the early 1970s to produce a pamphlet which is still used by the Northern Ireland Housing Executive, the body in charge of public-sector accommodation. It was an unlikely academic marriage: Trimble the black-letter lawyer working with the left-wing sociological lawyer Tom Hadden to produce 'Northern Ireland Housing Law', which was to become standard issue for housing officers during the period of massive public-sector recon-struction. Hadden recalls that in 1978–9 he and Trimble took turns every fortnight to travel to Derry to teach law to housing officers. He was struck by Trimble's diligence and competence: 'I don't think he was a star turn for the students – they didn't rush to his lectures. But he always got the job done.'[10]

Hadden thought Trimble might be useful in another field, political journalism. In 1978 he had taken over as editor-in-chief of *Fortnight*, Northern Ireland's principal current-affairs maga-zine. Hadden had been involved with the publication since its inception eight years earlier but had had to leave when he took up a teaching post in British Columbia. When he returned from Canada he found things in a state of chaos: 'It was being run on the lines of a Bennite cooperative and the place was a mess.'[11] He was also concerned that there was no significant unionist voice writing regular features. Hadden was particularly interested in publishing political gossip and in-house analysis from inside the unionist camp, and he realized he had the perfect candidate just next door to him in 21 University Square.

Trimble revelled in the role of 'Calvin MacNee', a nom-de-plume that *Fortnight* had used since 1970. He was paid between £20 and £30 per column and contributed regularly until the early 1980s. It is hard to discern exactly which of the Calvin Macnee pieces Trimble penned, given that other political commentators shared the pseudonym. Some, such as in the March 1978 edition, are obviously his work. This article was written shortly after the Provisional IRA firebomb attack at the La Mon Hotel in East Belfast, which killed twelve people, and Trimble was clearly deeply affected by the atrocity: 'I find it very difficult to address myself to writing a political column with the bloody events at La Mon still in my mind. Political judgements seem so superficial in a context where human lives can be extinguished in such a casual and cavalier fashion.' Yet he went on to berate fellow unionists' reactions as 'mindless inanities' and singled out two leading figures of Ulster Unionism in West Belfast, the Orange Order's chief in the city, Thomas Passmore, and Jean Coulter. In the same article Trimble attacked the *Sunday Times*'s Ireland correspondent, Chris Ryder, for speculating that the bomb attack was a Provo demonstration of intent to Fianna Fail, then the Republic's ruling party, which was having its annual conference. This seemed slightly unfair on Ryder, given that he was an outspoken critic of terrorist violence. At the end Trimble added: 'It seems unhelpful in that it suggests that our condition of violence is simply a product of a carefully orchestrated strategy of rationally grounded decision making.'

Through Trimble's MacNee articles *Fortnight* readers were given the odd glimpse into the closed grey world of Ulster Unionism. In the November 1979 edition Trimble analysed the European election results and correctly concluded that it had dealt a massive blow to the party's devolutionist wing. In that article there was the broadest of hints that Jim 'Iceman' Molyneaux might have pushed Harry West aside:

The election did for poor Harry too. I'm told that no sooner were the results in than he got a call from Jim Molyneaux telling him in no uncertain terms to quit. . . . The change in leadership will also make it more difficult for the pro-devolution group in the party. The direct-rule-is-the-best-we-can-get group is now firmly in control, and with the party leader happily ensconced at Westminster with the largest majority in the UK, it's hard to think how he can be unseated.

He then sounded a prophetic note: 'Unless of course Maggie Thatcher takes it into her head to pull the rug out again. Of which more anon.' Trimble was clear about Thatcher – unionists should never trust their Tories.

In the following edition, which spanned December 1979 and January 1980, Trimble aka MacNee took a pot shot at Molyneaux. The UUP leader was angry that the Tories' first political initiative on Northern Ireland, a series of talks with party leaders headed by Secretary of State Sir Humphrey Atkins, did not meet his demands. MacNee poked fun at Molyneaux, noting that 'the problem for Jim is that his miscalculations were and are all wrong. . . . Jim Molyneaux thought that before he helped bring down the Labour government, he had a promise by the Tories to introduce a new tier of local government. He saw that promise in the Tory manifesto and fondly believed that it and it alone would be Atkins' initiative.' It was not, of course, and MacNee seemed to delight in the sight of the integrationists being made to look foolish by Thatcher's man. MacNee predicted that the Prime Minister would never forgive Molyneaux for effectively snubbing the Atkins conference – again a piece of shrewd insight given Thatcher's later U-turns on Ireland. The same article contained dark hints of a looming split between the integration and devolution wings of the UUP – hardly a sign of a man happy with the direction in which his party was going.

Trimble's disdain for Paisley is a continual theme in his Calvin articles. He was contemptuous of Paisley's 'Carson Trail' in 1981 when the DUP leader embarked on a Northern Ireland-wide crusade against the growing rapprochement between Thatcher and Irish Premier Charles Haughey, warning of an impending threat to the union from this new alignment. Paisley was trying to emulate Sir Edward Carson, who in 1912 had undertaken a tour of the Province in opposition to Home Rule, and followed the same route as that of the original unionist leader. In these 1980s' rallies

Paisley issued dire warnings to loyalists that the constitutional position of Northern Ireland was now under the same threat as at the time of the Home Rule crisis. His aim was to drum up mass loyalist street protests to frighten Thatcher into not making concessions to Haughey over Northern Ireland's status within the UK.

In the midst of his campaign, a reaction in part to Robert Bradford's murder, Paisley set up a Third Force of DUP-sponsored vigilantes. The Force appeared at a number of his rallies and even organized the odd roadblock. In one notorious incident several Third Force members were photographed on a hillside waving firearms certificates in the air – a clear threat that the phantom vigilante group could be transformed into a private army.

Trimble via MacNee was completely dismissive of Paisley's Third Force. In a Christmas/New Year edition of *Fortnight* in 1981–2, Trimble wrote in a piece entitled 'Reverend Rampages': 'It is not too difficult to imagine situations where there are clashes between Third Force patrols and the army or police. The consequences could be incalculable. We could find ourselves slowly sliding into the same mess as the Lebanon. But that would only happen if the Third Force imitated the Lebanese Christians and sought to openly supplant the lawful forces.' Paisleyites might retort that this is exactly what Trimble and co. were prepared to do whilst in Vanguard, particularly during the UWC strike! However, in the same piece Trimble did accurately predict that the Third Force would slowly peter out along with the Carson rallies.

The Calvin MacNee period illustrates that in his early UUP days Trimble was not the average party hack forever churning out the Glengall Street line. The tone of many of the articles is wry and facetious. His constant targets were Molyneaux, naturally Paisley, and John Hume who had become the leader of the SDLP in 1980. At times his pieces read like the devolutionist's revenge on a unionist leadership that invested too much faith in Thatcher. He also raged at the new SDLP nationalism that had walked away from an internal solution to Northern Ireland's problems. The mere fact that Trimble was prepared to write at all for what was commonly regarded as a left-of-centre political magazine demonstrates that he was still an unusual figure in unionism – one prepared to meet the opposition head on, unlike other unionists who ran away from debate and wrapped themselves up in comfortable clichés. He was eventually sacked from the MacNee column in the early 1980s when the Dublin-born journalist Andy Pollak took charge of the magazine. Hadden was still on the editorial board and, although he thought Pollak mistaken in letting Trimble go, he did not interfere with the new editor's decision.

Trimble may have been breaking new ground outside Queen's by advocating the unionist/devolutionist line in a soft-left publication such as *Fortnight*, but the establishment did not see a major role for him in the university hierarchy. By the early 1980s he was deputy dean of the law faculty, but soon found that this was about as far as he could go – the ghosts of Vanguard haunted him at every turn. Herbie Wallace asserted that his past was definitely a hindrance:

> I think if David had been a member of a respectable party like the Alliance Party there would not have been the same mutterings about his political involvement. I can't prove it, but I think his politics didn't go down well in the university because he was seen as being on the extremes, whereas the university wanted to portray itself as a moderate and constructive influence on the community.[12]

Even those who were politically opposed to Trimble believe his academic advancement was handicapped for these reasons. Tom Hadden accepts that the opposition based their campaign against Trimble mainly on his earlier role in Vanguard.

The post of dean of the law faculty fell vacant at the start of 1986 and Trimble decided to apply for it. As deputy dean he must have thought his chances were reasonable, but within days colleagues noted the emergence of a *de facto* 'Stop Trimble' movement. Given that the post was an elected one, Herbie Wallace suggested he should be Trimble's campaign manager. Wallace accuses a number of key figures in the department of making sure Trimble failed to get the job, but he also feels that his candidate's prospects were damaged by Young Unionists at Queen's who tried to exploit the opposition by alleging that the university was engendering an anti-unionist ethos. Trimble was 'very hurt' by the determination of some members of the faculty to stop him, according to Wallace. Brian Garrett believes Trimble was 'politically incorrect' for Queen's at a period when the university was trying to shed its pro-union image – it was under pressure to ditch such symbols of unionism as the playing of the National Anthem and the attendance of the RUC band at graduation ceremonies. Queen's was also the frequent target of nationalist grievances over the under-employment of Catholics in certain faculties and in the senior tiers of the university's administration. Trimble was possibly the right man but at the wrong time.

He suffered a second humiliation a year later when he applied for the post of director of the Institute of Legal Studies. The Institute, of which Trimble had been acting head in its infancy, offered graduates in other disciplines the opportunity to take courses leading to a legal career. His only rival was Mary McAleese, a Catholic former law student with strong nationalist opinions who had once complained of naked sectarianism at Queen's. McAleese had been an adviser to the Catholic Church at the time of the Irish government's New Ireland Forum, a multi-stranded attempt to draw up a report on the island's constitutional future in the face of the growing electoral strength of Sinn Fein. In 1984 she provoked unionist fury when, in an interview with the *Irish Times*, she said she could understand the 'anger, hurt and provocation that pushes people into the [IRA]'. On another occasion she described Northern Ireland as an 'archetypal police state'.[13] When McAleese was selected instead of Trimble several Ulster Unionist MPs tabled a question in Parliament about her qualifications for the post; McAleese hit back, accusing them of being upset that a Catholic nationalist woman had got the job. Trimble's initial reaction was that he should take the case to the Fair Employment Agency, the semi-state body which investigated allegations of discrimination on the grounds of religion or politics – he was convinced that he had been denied the post because of his politics, a view encouraged by Young Unionist right-wing radicals who had befriended him at Queen's. Yet in the end he did not, deciding it would have been improper to embroil himself in a sordid legal battle with his own university. Even Trimble's allies in the department felt he would have been wrong to do so. Wallace felt sorry for his old friend, but also acknowledged that McAleese had been 'an excellent appointment'.[14]

But Trimble could still be grateful to Queen's for one important personal achievement, as it was where he found the love of his life. Daphne Orr was one of his students while he was going through a painful divorce from Heather. Friends said the end of Trimble's first marriage had been a bitter affair at the outset: 'David told me that he told Heather he knew about her affair and that he had had a very robust conversation with her. He said he wouldn't be back until she was out of the house. I suspect that at that stage he had already realized that the marriage was a mistake, that they were incompatible, and I think he now had his excuse to get out of it.'[15] Brian Garrett recalls Trimble down at the law courts in 1976 waiting for his divorce to come through. 'I remember being surprised to see him on his own. He told me this was his divorce day and yet there he was alone. Normally when people get divorced they bring someone along with them for support. But he just stood there alone – it was very odd.'[16]

Daphne and Heather at least had one thing in common: they both knew Herbie Wallace. He had worked with Heather in the Land Registry office, and now he was also teaching Daphne at Queen's.

The couple met at an end-of-term summer party after, as Trimble is often at pains to point out, his student had graduated. They were married in August 1978 at the local Methodist church in Daphne's home town, Warrenpoint, a seaside resort near the Irish border made notorious a year later when the IRA killed eighteen British soldiers nearby. Trimble's best man was his brother Ian; Daphne's bridesmaids were her twin sisters Caroline and Judith. Wallace was particularly delighted to see his old friend given a second chance: 'Daphne was always going to be and continues to be a super-supportive wife for David. They had much more in common.'[17] Other close friends of the couple agree that from the beginning Daphne became a rock in David's life. 'Davy wouldn't be where he is today without Daphne. That's sounds like a cliché, but it happens to be true. She sacrificed her own career for David and later their children. She is the calming influence in Davy's life.'[18] (It is a measure, perhaps, of the political obscurity into which David Trimble retreated in 1978 that when Daphne's local paper, the *Mourne Observer*, reported the wedding, it only mentioned that the groom was a 'barrister and law lecturer'. There was no mention of his position in either Vanguard or the Ulster Unionist Party.)

Although Trimble stood out as a rather stiff, reserved and conservative character at Queen's, his tastes beyond politics and academia were surprisingly catholic. Close friends noted that when he found an interest in something it quickly turned into an obsession. His passion for opera, for instance, developed shortly after he married Daphne, and one Queen's colleague said he reached the point where 'he could bore for Ireland in opera'.[19] Nor was he the typical meat-and-two-veg Ulsterman. On holiday in Italy shortly after his second marriage he discovered pasta. Following the Italian trip, dinner party guests at the Trimbles' noticed that David didn't just go out and buy supermarket pasta like everyone else but insisted on making his own. He would then 'entertain' the table with a lecture on how he made it with his own pasta machine. Unlike most Ulstermen, particularly in the unenlightened late seventies and early eighties, Trimble was quite fond of cooking for the family, which he still does as a means to unwind.

In contrast to the strict teetotalism of some leading figures in unionism (Paisley refers to alcohol as the 'Devil's buttermilk'), Trimble's other passion is wine. In fact he regarded himself as an expert to the point where it began to irritate his closest colleagues. At a law department Christmas lunch in the early eighties Herbie Wallace decided to play a trick on the would-be wine buff.

We were in a restaurant near Queen's, and David was waxing lyrical about this red wine he had chosen. I didn't drink red at the time because I thought it gave me a worse headache than white. When he got up to go to the gents I flicked some of the ash from the cigar I was smoking into his wine. After David came back he took another sip and said, 'Oh yes, you don't know what you're missing.' I told him later what I had done and he laughed. Perhaps it was a little malicious, but I wanted to point out that he wasn't always the expert he believed himself to be.[20]

Beyond law Trimble read widely, particularly history, his favourite subject as a schoolboy. In 1979 he was asked to join an interview panel as a non-specialist to see Paul Bew, a young Cambridge postgraduate who had applied for a post in Queen's history department. The most serious question posed actually came from Trimble. He had read Bew's book *The State in Northern Ireland*, and impressed the author by displaying genuine interest rather than indignation at its contents (Bew had discovered new evidence confirming Winston Churchill's long-term view that a United Ireland was inevitable). Bew, who has since become Professor of Politics at the university, remembers that Trimble appeared very well informed about Irish history, particularly recent developments in Irish historical studies. In the late 1970s Bew and Henry Patterson (his co-author on *The State in Northern Ireland*) were part of a new wave of young historians who had gravitated towards the Workers' Party – the political heirs of the Official IRA. Revisionism in Irish history was in vogue, as left-wing intellectuals in Belfast and Dublin demolished the traditional nationalist narrative of Irish history (the view that Irish history has been an unbroken struggle by the Irish people to force the invading British out of their country – a view that excludes the Ulster Protestants and their sense of Britishness). The growing relationship with Bew was to have a profound impact on Trimble's political development in the mid- to late 1990s. Bew recalls that Trimble possessed an 'intellectual curiosity' unlike that of any other unionist politician he had met before. He took a keen interest in the development of the Workers' Party, which sometimes bordered on admiration; this was the logical evolution of his conversations with his Vanguard colleague Fred Crowe about the changing nature of Official Republicanism and the possibility of other republicans going down the same road. Bew became friendly with this unorthodox unionist lecturer in law. Some of his reflections on Trimble's home offer an insight into the man's personality. Bew was, for instance, struck by his inability to throw away newspapers and academic articles. He recalled that the genteel chaos of the family's home in a middle-class suburb of Lisburn was that of the scatterbrain academic rather than the potential political high flier.[21]

Meanwhile in the UUP Trimble kept the devolution flag flying at a time when the party was lurching towards integrationism. At the party's annual conference in October 1978 Trimble and Craig had tabled an amendment defending the principle of devolution, but under pressure from the leadership it was withdrawn. The former Vanguard 'upstarts' continued to press for a devolved government at the next two party conferences, but each time the UUP hierarchy ensured that a vote was not taken on the issue. At a fractious AGM on 18 October 1980 Trimble found himself in the opposing camp against John Taylor, who spoke against voting on the devolution issue. The Molyneaux wing of the party were determined not to allow any debate on the matter, claiming that devolution was dead in every part of the UK including Northern Ireland. Trimble lambasted the party leadership for putting faith in integration, telling delegates: 'Integration was based on misconceptions. Integration would end with Northern Ireland's union resting with two sovereign governments in London and Dublin.'[22]

The anti-integrationist group, comprising Trimble, Edgar Graham and Davy McNarry, were frustrated at the inaction of the Molyneaux leadership. The devolution cabal met once a month throughout 1980 at the Europa Hotel, where they discussed tactics and policy. McNarry recalls that Trimble was one of the more conservative-minded members of the group who did not want to do anything to undermine Molyneaux publicly. However, McNarry and Trimble both agreed that the UUP should adopt a positive approach to a new political initiative from Thatcher's Secretary of State, Sir Humphrey Atkins. Molyneaux chose to boycott the talks instead, which the devolution group regarded as a disastrous mistake. McNarry said Trimble was exasperated at the UUP's attitude to the Atkins talks.

> David saw very clearly that we were a party going nowhere. The new leadership wanted us to be as British as Finchley, and that sounded lovely to everybody. Our views about the need for a new Stormont were not taken on board. The result was we spurned a real chance to cut a new deal with the SDLP at the Atkins talks before the rise of Sinn Fein. As a result we have ended up with Sinn Fein being allowed to grow into what is has now become.

McNarry believes that integrationism was also a convenient mask to hide behind for those Ulster Unionists who could not stomach the idea of sharing power with Catholics. 'At the Atkins talks David wanted the party to talk about co-opting unionism and nationalism into a partnership government. History will have to judge who blew that chance – after all, look what they have ended up with,' he added. Trimble shares this analysis that Atkins, like the Voluntary Coalition, was a wasted opportunity and helped pave the way for the rise of Sinn Fein in the 1980s. As a result of their opposition to the Molyneaux line Trimble and McNarry were, in the latter's words, 'sent to Coventry for a while'.[23] But in 1980 Trimble, Craig and McNarry produced a policy document for the Ulster Unionist Council.

In the wake of the Tories' Westminster victory Jim Molyneaux and his integrationist allies dismissed Trimble's dire warnings about Dublin involvement as scaremongering. Thatcher was surely a convinced unionist whose steely opposition to the demands of republican prisoners in the Maze prison's H-Block for political status – demands which included the right to refuse prison work, the right to refuse to wear prison uniform, and the right to free association amongst fellow republican prisoners; in other words, the right to be treated differently from ordinary criminals – confirmed their view that the lady was not for turning on Northern Ireland. Their confidence in Thatcher seemed to be underpinned when she appeared to turn down the recommendations of the Irish government-sponsored New Ireland Forum report in 1984. The Prime Minister's dismissal, at an Anglo-Irish summit at Chequers on 19 November 1984, of the pan-nationalist report's three recommendations – a unitary Irish state, a federal Ireland or joint authority between Dublin and London – prompted the headline writers to sum up Thatcher's attitude in the infamous phrase 'Out, out, out.' Garret Fitzgerald, the Irish Premier, was initially outraged at Thatcher's behaviour during the summit, accusing her of being 'gratuitously offensive'. Molyneaux was delighted at Dublin's dismay. His faith in Thatcher had not been blind, he concluded. While unionists feted her apparent rejection of the Forum report, Trimble was the spectre at the feast, pointing out that the Prime Minister did not actually spurn everything the Irish wanted. He said the UUP was too busy celebrating victory to notice that a deal was still going to be done between Thatcher and Fitzgerald behind their backs. Trimble remembers shortly after the summit attending a UUP conference in Newcastle, Co. Down at which the delegates were euphoric about Thatcher's alleged snub to Fitzgerald. He went among the delegates warning them that all was not well, but many of the party's stalwarts laughed off his concerns.

It took someone with a legal mind like Trimble's to pore over the communiqué issued after Chequers to spot the dangers lurking beneath the veneer of Thatcher's rejection:

At that press conference someone asked her a question about the proposals for a unitary state, a federal Ireland and then a third idea. She couldn't remember what the third one was, and you could see an official whispering in her ear. Then she said, 'And that is out, too.' She never said, 'Out, out, out.' What stuck in my mind was she didn't know what the proposals were in full. Therefore the summit meeting with Garret Fitzgerald was not actually a discussion of the Forum proposals. This was about something else. I then looked at the communiqué and I saw the hints about something quite different going on between the government, including cultural matters, issues of identity and all the rest of it. I remember saying that London and Dublin were going to do a deal.[24]

A year later Trimble would be proven right and Molyneaux shown to have been entirely wrong about Thatcher's true intentions.

A by-product of the Chequers communiqué was the establishment by Trimble of the Ulster Society, a polito-cultural pressure group to promote the pro-British identity in Northern Ireland. He realized that the summit's references to respecting nationalist culture and identity would translate into money for the promotion of the Irish language, Gaelic games, music, dance and so on. Culture would become, in Trimble's words, a 'new battlefield' and unionists would have to prepare for a counter-offensive. Although the most vivid expression of unionist/British identity was Orangeism, Trimble guessed correctly that any London/Dublin initiative on Irish culture would be designed to bypass the Orange Order. Unionists therefore needed a non-sectarian, non-political front to mop up any funding available.

The Ulster Society was an important staging post in Trimble's political career for two reasons. Firstly, it was a means of injecting fresh confidence into unionism at a time of renascent republican political activity. Irish republicanism had been galvanized by the 1981 hunger strike at the Maze prison in which ten IRA and Irish National Liberation Army (INLA) prisoners had died. The hunger strike had not only provided a springboard for Sinn Fein's political fortunes, it had also renewed nationalist interest in the Irish language and Irish culture. Republicans who were confident about their own identity taunted unionists by accusing them of being a non-people, of having no real culture of their own. The Ulster Society provided a vehicle for unionists to prove otherwise. Secondly, Trimble's innovation formed a focus for a new cadre of disaffected young unionists who wanted more than the UUP could ever give them. Some of his critics have accused the Ulster Society of becoming 'Trimble's Militant Tendency', on the same lines as the Labour Party's Militant wing in the 1980s which Neil Kinnock accused of being a party within a party. In the Ulster Unionists' case, the Trimble Militants were accused of operating a secret caucus inside the party. As one early Ulster Society activist put it: 'Trimble gave us a new sense of identity beyond singing "God Save the Queen" at the end of every party conference and marching on the Twelfth of July. The Ulster Society became a cultural front in the war against republicanism.'[25]

Interestingly, Trimble saw the Society reaching out beyond the narrow confines of Ulster Protestants. Another early recruit, John Laird, said that one of the Society's first objectives was to disseminate into Catholic schools their material on Edward Carson, the impact of World War I and the creation of the Northern Ireland state. Trimble was determined to show Catholic schoolchildren that there was another side to Irish history than the traditional nationalist narrative; in particular, he was keen to draw attention to the huge numbers of Irish Catholics killed fighting for Britain in both world wars. Trimble's attempt to introduce unionist history into Catholic schools is perhaps an early indication of his later project to desectarianize unionism, to make the union more relevant to Catholics in general. The Ulster Society grew throughout Northern Ireland and beyond. It eventually set up branches, based on individual and corporate membership, not only in the Province but also in England, Scotland and Wales as well as in countries such as Canada, the USA, South Africa and Australia where the Ulster Protestant diaspora was scattered.

Many of the young intellectuals and students attracted to the Ulster Society would play key roles in Trimble's ascent through the UUP in the late eighties and early nineties. One of the most enthusiastic of the radicals was Gordon Lucy, who had first met Trimble when he was a schoolboy on a visit to the 1975 Convention at Stormont. As a young history graduate he attended both the Society's preliminary meeting in March 1985 at the Park Avenue Hotel in East Belfast and its first AGM there the following June, at which Trimble was elected chairman. For Lucy the Ulster Society was 'exhilarating, exciting, a breath of fresh air in unionist politics'. He acknowledges that its creation not only provided Trimble with a support group of younger energetic professionals and students, but also plugged him into the UUP's local party branch network across Northern Ireland: 'The thing that did help his political development would have been his willingness to address branch meetings and go along to lectures and talks in the back of beyond. So he got to know lots of people. The Ulster Society played a very useful role in raising his profile in the party.'[26]

The Ulster Society also attracted into its ranks a number of students like John Hunter and Drew Nelson who were to emerge as loyal Trimble allies in the UUP. Given that the Society attracted the flotsam and jetsam of unionism, including those out on the fringes of Ulster Unionism such as Belfast Independent Unionist councillor Nelson McCausland, many in the UUP leadership viewed it with deep suspicion. Some even regarded the Society as a focus for right-wing extremism. This, however, seems to be an unfair charge given that the Society attracted liberal unionists as well as hard-liners. The dangers for Trimble lay in the future, given that many whom he gathered around him at the inception were to turn out more extreme and uncompromising in their politics than he had ever been even in the Vanguard days.

Trimble's most important contributions to the Ulster Society were two historical pamphlets, one on the Easter Rising and the other on the foundation of the Northern Ireland state. The Easter Rising was the most important historical turning point of Irish history in the twentieth century. Until Easter 1916 Irish national-ism had pursued a peaceful path towards Home Rule within the British Empire. The attempted coup by more extreme nationalists, led by the poet Padraig Pearse and the Labour leader James Connolly, was seen as a stab in the back by the British at a time when the nation was at war with Germany. The rebellion had initially lacked popular support throughout the country, but British over-reaction, culminating in the execution of the leaders, who were quickly transformed into martyrs, galvanized the repub-lican movement and led to a ferocious war between the newly formed Irish Republican Army and the British forces.

In the early 1980s it was still unheard of for a unionist to write about Irish republicanism; some could barely speak the name of the beast. The thirty-five pages of *The Easter Rebellion of 1916* are as much an apologia for unionism as a résumé of the central event which shaped Irish history in the twentieth century. Trimble drew a lot of inspiration from the new wave of revisionist historians who had challenged much of the mythos of the Rising. In the final section, entitled 'Artificial Entity', Trimble argues that nationalism could have gained Home Rule for Ireland just before the outbreak of World War I had it accepted the reality of partition. Another interesting point is that Trimble bases his argument on an earlier critique of the Rising by a Jesuit priest, one Father Shaw. He notes that Shaw's reassessment, first published in the journal *Jesuit Studies* in 1966, was turned down for wider circulation at this time – the Rising's fiftieth anniversary. Shaw made three major criticisms of the uprising: that it made partition inevitable; that it led to the Irish Civil War; and that the state it subsequently created ignored the nationalist dead of World War I. One could never imagine Ian Paisley founding his argument for Northern Ireland's existence on the arguments of a Jesuit priest; it seems that Trimble, however, felt intellectually comfortable doing so.

Trimble noted that Easter 1916 stored up trouble for the future – it left a sense of unfinished business in Irish nationalist minds. When he wrote about the fiftieth anniversary commemorations poisoning the political atmosphere in Northern Ireland he might have been thinking of his own friends in the ATC who were called up in 1966. The 'rising tide of republican propaganda' was in his mind partly to blame for the re-formation of the Ulster Volunteer Force in the same year and the re-energizing of Ian Paisley's style of unionist street politics throughout the late sixties.

The key weakness in Trimble's pamphlet, reflecting a man hell-bent on hard-line security solutions in the 1980s, was his analysis of the execution of the 1916 rebels. Trimble defended the action of Britain's most senior army officer in Ireland, Sir John Maxwell, who gave the order for Padraig Pearse, James Connolly, Thomas Clarke and the other leaders to be sentenced to death. Maxwell's heavy-handed approach created a potent myth of republican martyrdom, the consequences of which Ireland is still suffering. Trimble, though, tried to see it from Maxwell's viewpoint:

Maxwell has been criticised; but it is doubtful if his actions can be fairly impugned. There were only two courses open to him. Either he was moderate and restrained and released his prisoners to conciliate nationalist opinion, or he applied the law strictly and so permanently removed all the seditious elements from society. With 500 dead as a result of the rebels' actions and proof of treasonable contact with the enemy – in what was the greatest war the world had seen – there was really no choice.[27]

This hang-'em-high analysis might have sounded well to the unionist grassroots, but the fact remains that the cruelty of the executions and the subsequent stupidity of the British in imposing an unpopular conscription policy effectively galvanized Sinn Fein at the expense of John Redmond's moderate Nationalist Party. Sixty-five years later it seemed the British and the unionists had learned nothing from the lessons of 1916 when they resisted prisoners' demands for political status in H-Block, which led to the deaths of ten republican inmates on hunger strike at the Maze prison. And just as Redmond was the loser after 1916, so too (nearly) was John Hume's SDLP in the early 1980s when the modern moderate nationalist leader was almost eclipsed by a renascent Sinn Fein.

Trimble's other major work for the Ulster Society, *The Foundation of Northern Ireland*, gives clues to the other side of his political philosophy – his pragmatism. His undisputed hero in the period leading up to partition was Sir James Craig, a unionist businessman and prominent Orangeman who was to become Northern Ireland's first Prime Minister. In fact Trimble sought to resurrect Craig as the true champion of unionism to the detriment of Sir Edward Carson – an act of heresy for any unionist. Carson, a Unionist in the integrationist mode, was bitterly opposed to the partition of Ireland and wanted the entire island – not just the north-east – to remain within the Empire. While Carson was the great demagogue of unionism before partition, Craig became the arch-pragmatist, realizing that unionism would have to cut its losses in the south and take what it could get in Ulster – the six counties comprising what was to become Northern Ireland.

Trimble wrote his pamphlet in a period when talking to republicans was still an absolute taboo for any unionist. However, he pointed out that Craig had set the example in 1920 by engaging with the enemy rather than running away from them. He praised Craig for entering into discussions firstly with Michael Collins, the IRA chief of staff during the Irish War of Independence, and then with Eamon de Valera, who later became Irish Premier. Craig displayed flexibility on emotive issues such as the release of IRA prisoners. One of the key elements of the first Craig–Collins pact, in early 1922, was the Northern Ireland Prime Minister's agreement to reprieve a number of IRA prisoners under sentence of death in a Derry prison. The releases were part of a peace plan between the Unionist administration in Belfast and the Provisional government in Dublin. Trimble, like Craig, was to come under fire from his own side at the end of the century for appearing soft on the release of IRA prisoners. Although Craig employed repressive measures against the northern Catholic minority, such as the deployment of the hated B Specials in nationalist areas, he also once again showed flexibility. Another aspect of the Craig–Collins pact was the Unionist leader's assurances to Dublin that Belfast Catholics who had been expelled from their workplaces by Protestant mobs would get their jobs back once there was an economic upturn in the Province. Craig demonstrated a grasp of new realities which Carson never did. Nor was Trimble's historical hero ideologically or emotionally tied to the notion of 'not an inch' to nationalism. Instead, Craig calculated that the surrender of a few inches here and there in border negotiations might just secure the overall objective of Northern Ireland staying remaining in the UK.[28]

'At home, there were some who were ready to criticise Craig, but what was not in dispute, was his enormous physical and political courage,' Trimble wrote. He went on to point out that Craig had proved to Lloyd George's government that he had not been intransigent, given that he had been willing to talk to the IRA leader Collins and the Sinn Fein chief de Valera. Seventy-seven years later Trimble had to face the same criticisms for talking to the republican enemy at the time of the Good Friday Agreement. When asked recently which of the two major unionist historical figures he preferred to associate himself with, Trimble answered unsurprisingly: 'I would say Craig actually because he did the dirty work. He did the deal with Collins – he went to Dublin to negotiate while Carson lapsed into manic depression.'[29]

One of the principal aims of Trimble's Ulster Society was to instil fresh confidence in an uncertain and apprehensive unionist community. The year of its inception turned out to be the most traumatic for unionism since the abolition of Stormont thirteen years earlier. For nearly eighteen months prior to the establishment of the Ulster Society in June 1985 Trimble had been an unwelcome Cassandra inside the UUP, issuing constant warnings about the grave threat to unionists from Thatcher's growing relationship with Dublin. Now he and his old mentor Bill Craig had hard evidence to prove that a sell-out was in the offing.

In the spring of 1985 Bill Craig was contacted by a number of sources inside the Conservative Party who warned him about a new London–Dublin political agreement. Craig was so disturbed that he emerged from semi-retirement to convey the dangers to the unionist leadership. He first contacted a number of trusted allies, in particular Trimble and Fred Crowe. Trimble agreed with Craig's analysis that the threat from a looming Anglo–Irish initiative was real. He helped Craig draft a letter, in the latter's name, which was sent to Ian Paisley and Jim Molyneaux.

The original draft, which I have obtained, is dated 21 June 1985 – five months before the British and Irish governments signed the Anglo–Irish Agreement at Hillsborough. It began with a hand-written 'Dear Jim', and went on to inform the UUP leader that:

> The present formal arrangements between London and Dublin will shortly be given more substance and greatly expanded to the extent that in practice though not in form a constitutional change will be effected. The fear of the so-called 'Protestant backlash' is the only limiting factor. I would like to think that this gives the loyalists an opportunity to deter [ie the proposed Anglo–Irish Agreement], as opposed to the present situation where it affects only the timing of decisions.

Craig then went on to predict a form of joint authority between the two governments: 'The present London–Dublin agreement giving Dublin a right to formal machinery for consultation is probably based on an exchange of notes between the governments. The current talks in Dublin eyes will lead to a treaty relationship with very elaborate machinery based on that of the Nordic Council or something similar to be implemented gradually.' In other words Craig, Trimble and their allies accurately presaged the establishment of the Anglo–Irish Secretariat at Maryfield outside Belfast. Although the exact source of Craig's original information has never been revealed, it appears that they were well versed on the shape of the Anglo–Irish Agreement before it was signed.

To counter the Agreement, Craig proposed the creation of an 'Ulster pact' to unite the disparate unionist factions. Incredibly, the unionist leadership chose to ignore Craig's concerns. Molyneaux was still indulging in a fantasy – that Thatcher was ideologically committed to unionism, and that this still exerted considerable influence at Westminster.

This fantasy was exposed on 15 November when Margaret Thatcher and Garret Fitzgerald met at Hillsborough Castle outside Belfast to sign the Anglo–Irish Agreement. The accord was the most far-reaching political development between the two governments since 1920, and for the first time since partition gave the Republic some say in Northern Ireland's internal affairs. The kernel of the declaration was the establishment of a joint conference of British and Irish ministers backed up by a secretariat at Maryfield on the fringe of loyalist East Belfast. This secretariat, staffed by Irish civil servants, would be able to monitor political, security and fair employment issues in Northern Ireland on behalf of the nationalist minority. There was now a direct channel into government for Catholic grievances to get tangible results on discrimination, heavy-handed policing and cultural matters.

One of the unspoken aims of the Hillsborough Accord was to shore up John Hume's SDLP in the face of a growing Sinn Fein electoral threat. The Anglo-Irish Agreement, which was immediately rejected by Sinn Fein, gave the SDLP direct input into British and Irish government policy-making. Yet while constitutional nationalists feted the declaration, unionists were outraged.

There was a deep sense of anger and betrayal, particularly among Ulster Unionists, over what the British government had done. A day after the communiqué was issued the DUP and UUP announced that their fifteen MPs would resign their Westminster seats and fight by-elections since the British government refused to test the Agreement in a referendum. On 20 November there were ugly scenes outside Belfast City Hall when loyalist councillors including George Seawright, a notorious sectarian bigot who once called for Catholics to be incinerated, attacked the new Secretary of State, Tom King. Three days later up to a quarter of a million people turned up for a mass protest against the Agreement outside Belfast City Hall, where effigies of Margaret Thatcher were burned beside the platform. The sense of sell-out was summed up by Harold McCusker's speech in the House of Commons. Almost in tears, just a week after the Agreement he spoke of his shame at having been treated so contemptuously by his own government.

Trimble, a lonely flag-bearer for devolution in the UUP, got no comfort from telling the leadership, 'I told you so.' He even felt sorry for Molyneaux: 'He was misled. Molyneaux placed too much faith in some Tories. In the run-up to the Anglo–Irish Agreement there were cabinet ministers who ran up to him and said, "Don't worry, Jim. Everything's OK." I don't know if there was deliberate misinformation . . . but Jim was taken in by these people.'[30] Other former Vanguard comrades were not so kind. Fred Crowe was furious that Molyneaux had not heeded Bill Craig's warning the previous June that an Agreement might be signed in the autumn. The resentment of Molyneaux's handling of the situation was to smoulder for a decade, then reignited in the mid-1990s and paved the way for Trimble's rise to the top.

The Vanguard outsider was now winning new friends inside the UUP given that his gloomy assessments of the British government's real plans were being proved correct. In the autumn of 1985 Trimble was guest speaker at several party branch meetings across the Province. He was getting noticed, and a new audience of suspicious, fearful unionists was listening. He told the UUP's Aughnacloy branch in Co. Tyrone that Thatcher's letters to Paisley and Molyneaux stressing that UK sovereignty would not be diminished were meaningless. With the eagle eye of a constitutional lawyer, Trimble had spotted that the Thatcher letters did not rule out arrangements which would mean Ulster being treated differently from other parts of Britain. 'The first assurance without the second is worthless,' he wrote. 'There is more to being part of the United Kingdom than being subject to the sovereignty of the United Kingdom government.'[31]

A month after the Agreement was signed, Trimble was invited by the UUP's Knock branch in East Belfast to give a legal analysis of the Hillsborough Accord. He again accused the British government of misleading unionists by claiming that the joint ministerial conferences would not have executive powers. The conference, he said, was not just consultative given that it would take greater control of security matters and address nationalist concerns over the RUC and UDR. 'The police have lost their independence from Government control and the Chief Constable has lost what tattered remnants of integrity he may once have possessed.'[32]

It was clear that the British government was prepared to face down unionist opposition on the streets to the Anglo–Irish Agreement. On 14 January 1986 Tom King warned that the by-elections caused by the Unionist MPs' resignations would not change

Wesminster's cross-party support for the Agreement. The by-elections produced mixed results for the unionists. Their overall vote increased, but the party's MP for Newry and Armagh, Jim Nicholson, lost his seat to the SDLP's deputy leader and justice spokesman, Seamus Mallon, by 2583 votes.

When the protest poll failed to budge Thatcher, the unionists attempted to repeat the success of 1974 by calling a one-day general strike. The unionist 'Day of Action' halted most of industry and disrupted public services, leading to massive power cuts across the Province. However, the day ended in disaster for the strike committee because loyalist terrorists fired on RUC patrols in North Belfast. This alienated a large section of unionist middle-class opinion which loathed the Agreement but was horrified to find loyalists firing on 'their' police force. Further loyalist arson attacks on the homes of RUC officers throughout the first full year of the Agreement proved even more counter-productive, as they put further distance between militant working-class Protestants and the middle-class support base of Ulster Unionism.

The unionists failed to persuade the British government to ditch the Accord. Their power inside the House of Commons was sharply reduced, and their use of the strike weapon was a tactical blunder given Thatcher's trenchant resistance to the miners in 1984–5. On 13 March Tom King sent an extra battalion of British soldiers to the Province to counter growing loyalist street violence. The UUP and DUP leadership were confused about how best to make Thatcher change her mind: argument or force. The deployment of more troops indicated that Thatcher was prepared to confront them if they chose the latter option. In fact, by late spring/early summer the security forces had turned their guns on protesting loyalists in Portadown who had objected to the rerouting of several Orange parades away from the Catholic Tunnel area of the town.

As the first anniversary of the Anglo–Irish Agreement approached, unionists looked no nearer to toppling it. In many cases their protests, such as the boycott of British ministers in the Northern Ireland Office, were petering out. Trimble watched with dismay as the UUP and DUP leaderships mishandled and bungled the protest campaign. The quiet university lecturer believed more radical measures were needed to defeat the Agreement, and once again he fell into the orbit of the loyalist paramilitaries he had worked with during the UWC strike.

The body capable of bringing together the militants of unionism was already in existence when the Agreement was signed. The Ulster Clubs had been set up a month before Hillsborough with the stated aim of opposing the rerouting of loyalist parades. After Hillsborough the movement pledged to destroy the Anglo–Irish Agreement. By January 1986 it claimed to have eight thousand members in forty-eight branches. One of its earliest members was David Trimble, who through his work with the Ulster Society was brought on to the organization's Grand Committee.

The Ulster Clubs' ruling body contained several paramilitary leaders including John McMichael, the new supreme commander of the UDA. The mass movement at times resembled a Vanguard old boys' society, and among its ranks were several colleagues of Trimble's from the 1974 strike. One of them was Sam McClure, the man who had sworn him into the Vanguard Service Corps in the early seventies. McClure said that the thinking behind the Clubs was that, while they could not resurrect Vanguard, the new organization would be Vanguard under another name. And, like Vanguard, the new force had its own military wing, the Ulster Corps. Although Trimble never joined the Ulster Corps he must have known about its existence, McClure asserted, given that he eventually became chairman of the Ulster Clubs movement.

The Corps comprised people who were in the VSC – it included people like the late John McMichael and Alan Wright, the Clubs' first chairman. It was organized throughout Northern Ireland but mid-Ulster was particularly important. Just like the VSC, it was an army in waiting which encompassed different paramilitary groups and those not aligned to any. The Ulster Corps still exists in skeleton form today.

McClure defined Trimble during this period as a 'really red-hot militant'[33] who regarded anyone breaking the boycott of NIO ministers as a traitor to the cause.

Trimble's role in the Ulster Clubs, and his association with loyalist figures such as John McMichael, may partly explain the source of unproven allegations of the existence of a high-powered committee of businessmen, unionist politicians, RUC officers and Protestant paramilitaries which directed a loyalist terror campaign throughout mid-Ulster. These claims first surfaced in a Channel 4 television documentary entitled *The Committee*, broadcast in the autumn of 1991. While it is true that Trimble sat at the same table in the Ulster Clubs with McMichael, McClure, Tyrie and others, in no way did he have any knowledge of the UDA's assassination campaign, and neither would he have approved of such actions. Even his enemies inside loyalism deny that he had any knowledge of loyalist terrorist activity. The active loyalist groups, the killers of the UDA and UVF, deeply mistrusted all so-called respectable unionist politicians. They were disillusioned because the main-stream unionist parties had made them do the donkey work during the UWC strike but then took all the glory for themselves. The same unionist parties who in some cases had goaded them into war but then condemned the loyalists also sickened them when they did their dirty work for the politicians. The second-in-command of the UVF in Northern Ireland dismissed Trimble's involvement with the alleged committee:

Nobody would have trusted a unionist politician with informa-tion about who we were going to shoot next. The idea that the politicians and policemen were directing us was absurd. If we had been colluding on a structured scale with the RUC then why did so many more of us get arrested and end up in jail? If we had top-level information on republican targets from the police there would have been countless more republicans buried up at Mill-town cemetery. As for taking orders from the likes of Trimble – that's laughable. If we had taken orders from the politicians we would have been beaten in a few weeks.[34]

None the less Trimble was prepared, as he was in 1974, to envisage a situation in which constitutional unionist politicians would have to step outside the law. Ten days before the first anniversary of the Hillsborough Agreement, he spoke in militant terms about fighting it. The constitutional expert from Queen's warned that the day was coming soon when unionists would have to use extra-parliamentary activity to defeat the London–Dublin deal. Although he was dis-dainful of the fiasco that was Ulster Resistance – the Protestant militia founded by Ian Paisley but disowned by him in the same year – he had no objection in principle to mobilizing a citizens' army:

Do you sit back and do nothing or move outside constitutional forms of protest? I don't think you can deal with the situation without the risk of an extra-parliamentary campaign. I would personally draw the line at terrorism and serious violence. But if we are talking about a campaign that involves demonstrations and so on, then a certain element of violence may be inescapable.[35]

Although Trimble said he hoped violent confrontation could be avoided, he feared that Ulster was on the precipice of major conflict: 'I do think we are standing on the verge of a scuttle by HMG [Her Majesty's Government], even of civil war. If are not actually on the verge we are very close to it.'[36] This was militant talk at a time of resurgent loyalist paramilitary violence and widespread ethnic tension across Northern Ireland. He was not, of course, involved in the direction of loyalist terrorism; nevertheless such language was stoking up fears of a British withdrawal in a time of increasing sectarian violence.

Trimble's militancy extended beyond the Ulster Clubs and into the UUP itself. He was a bitter critic of unionist MPs who decided to break their boycott of Westminster. Even John Taylor, the man who promoted him in the 1979 Euro elections, felt Trimble's wrath. Ulster Clubs activists had picketed Taylor's Strangford constituency office after he had made a statement that it would be prudent for unionist MPs to return to the House of Commons. Trimble appeared to support the picketing, pointing out that 'The Northern Ireland Office would throw its hat in the air if the MPs were to go back. I think the party in the country would be very opposed to a return.'[37]

Trimble also clashed with Ken Maginnis, an ebullient, silver-haired former UDR major with a walrus moustache who had represented Fermanagh/South Tyrone since 1983. Maginnis, the darling of the UUP's liberal wing, deeply mistrusted private armies and mass movements like the Ulster Clubs. He accused the Clubs of deepening the splits inside unionism and damaging its credibility, given their open association with paramilitaries. However, Trimble defended the Clubs: 'Contrary to what Ken Maginnis said, the Clubs are not "promoting divisions and causing distractions". They are actually promoting greater unity.'[38]

While he had been popular inside the Ulster Clubs, at the end of

1987 Trimble's prospects inside the UUP looked severely limited. He had crossed swords with two of the party's leading lights and then went on to snipe at Molyneaux's old mentor, Enoch Powell: 'I think the Unionist Party is really quite foolish to allow Enoch Powell to sit in the Commons – it obscures the situation. It also raises hopes among certain people that they might get back into the system.'[39] The 'certain people' he was hinting at undoubtedly included Molyneaux. Many in the party hierarchy took note of the 'Vanguard upstart's' remarks and concluded that here was a dangerous man who still could not be trusted. They would try their utmost to curb his career inside the UUP.

Although not involved in loyalist terrorism Trimble continued to give occasional snippets of constitutional advice to the UDA leadership, in particular during the anti-Agreement struggles. Andy Tyrie has confirmed that at this time he and John McMichael would seek out Trimble for political guidance. McMichael and Trimble belonged to the same Apprentice Boys' Club in Lisburn and would have met on the Ulster Clubs' Grand Committee too. However, they also saw each other outside these institutions. Tyrie recalled that in late 1986 he and McMichael often went to Trimble's home. 'David lived in Lisburn. Many times we went to his house and saw him there and we would discuss things – political matters only.'[40]

At the time the two UDA front men were engaged in a series of talks with politicians, constitutional experts, historians and other intellectuals with a view to drawing up a new political initiative. The result of their deliberations was the *Common Sense* document, the launch of which on 29 January 1987 made headline news in Northern Ireland and the Republic. Paradoxically for a movement engaged in sectarian assassination, the UDA had seemingly shown more sensitivity to nationalist fears than had the established unionist parties. It envisaged a Northern Ireland Assembly, an all-party government (like the Vanguard Voluntary Coalition), a Bill of Rights and a written constitution. The proposals received a fairly favourable response across Britain and Ireland; even the leader of the latter's four million Catholics, Cardinal Tomas O'Fiach, praised the document. John Hume commented that, despite the fact that it had come from a 'surprising source', his party regarded *Common Sense* as 'constructive'.

Although Trimble was only one among many intellectuals whom

the UDA consulted, his contributions form some of the central tenets of the *Common Sense* document. And while his input was not as direct as it had been in the *Ulster Unfettered* pamphlet his prints are clearly all over it, especially those sections dealing with the Bill of Rights and a constitution. Tyrie said that he and McMichael were in regular contact with Trimble in the build-up: 'We consulted him on the *Common Sense* document because he was a constitutional expert. We could never have put the document together without asking people what they thought, and that included Trimble.'[41]

The Glengall Street establishment's mistrust of Trimble was bolstered by what they saw as his retreat into political extremism throughout the anti-Agreement protests. They were alarmed in particular at his resurrection of the idea of independence for Northern Ireland. In August 1989 he had advocated dominion status for Ulster outside of the UK but within the Commonwealth. To the UUP establishment his ideas seemed dangerously close to the original *Ulster Unfettered* document that he had helped write for the loyalist paramilitary leadership back in 1975.

After the Anglo–Irish Agreement unionism was locked in an internal intellectual struggle over the future. One wing, led by Robert McCartney, argued for equal citizenship in the UK; in practice this meant the formation of local branches of the main British parties – Labour, Conservative and Liberal Democrat – in Northern Ireland. McCartney's Campaign for Equal Citizenship claimed that, if the major parties organized in the Province, the nature of politics there would be transformed from sectarian dogfights to class-based issues. The CEC attracted a weird alliance composed of unionist conservatives disenchanted with the Orange tribalism associated with the UUP; former Marxist writers like the then *Financial Times* journalist John Lloyd; pro-union trade union-ists who were involved in the UWC strike; and left-wing intellec-tuals such as the University of Ulster politics lecturer Dr Arthur Aughey.

Although at the time of the 1974 strike Trimble had worked with many of the far-left activists from the British/Irish Communist Organization (a Stalinist ginger group which believed Ireland was divided into two nations – one Irish, the other British), he now found himself on the other side of the debate. He now described integration as 'an emotional spasm', which was unrealistic given that the British government did not really want to integrate Ulster fully into the UK. Referring to his historical hero, Sir James Craig, Trimble pointed out that the first unionist government had asked Lloyd George for dominion status prior to partition. His call for 'self-determination'[42] was remarkably similar to the UDA's 1970s' concept of an independent Ulster. The unionist critics of independence, whether in its full-blown or dominion status phase, such as those in the CEC were quick to point out that this would inevitably lead to a Protestant Ruritania in which Catholic nationalists would have to be violently suppressed.

In February 1988 the Ulster Clubs published a fifteen-page pro-independence document written by Trimble called *What Choice for Ulster?*. In it he outlined the various options facing unionists: equal citizenship/integration, devolution, a united Ireland and dominion status. His objections to devolution are interesting given that they are founded on the British and Irish governments' insistence that a devolved administration in Belfast will only come about if unionists accept power-sharing and an Irish dimension – a version of which has come to pass ten years later. Trimble-the-hawk was also sceptical about devolution because any future Assembly, under some form of Anglo–Irish patronage, would have no control over security. The demolition of devolution as an option included a triumphalist jibe at Brian Faulkner:

> The 1973 Assembly had even less power than Stormont. Crucially, it had no control over internal security matters. It is ironic that the Prime Minister, who resigned in 1972 rather than acquiesce in the removal of these powers, tamely agreed in 1973 to accept office as a 'Chief Executive' in an administration with no power over security . . . when his administration met its first test in 1974 it was shown to have no significance!

His dismissal of devolved government in 1988 on the grounds that it would be a toothless, subservient administration would come back to haunt him, for in the late 1990s Trimble's opponents would deploy exactly the same arguments he had once used against Brian Faulkner and devolution.

His concept of independence was on the same lines as that of Canada, Australia and New Zealand – autonomous sovereign states which retained a special relationship with Britain through membership of the Commonwealth. Addressing nationalist concerns, he drew historical analogies with Sir James Craig who had negotiated with Michael Collins during the early months of the Northern Ireland state. In 1921–2 Craig had attempted to offer nationalists in the north some concessions. Trimble now urged modern loyalists to do the same in a new, independent Northern Ireland: 'We must not aim for UDI and must strive to avoid a violent parting, rather we must seek the necessary changes by agreement. We should say to Irish nationalists in our midst, "A united Ireland is impossible, but a united Ulster is possible and we invite you to be part of it." ' As a concession to nationalists, Trimble also dug up his old idea (first articulated in *Ulster Unfettered*) of a Council of the British Isles. It would encompass the now devolved governments in Belfast, Cardiff and Edinburgh in a new body along with the Dublin and London administrations. Such a Council would bring the Irish Republic into a new pan-British context and was therefore attractive to unionists.

Trimble's own militancy never extended further than chaining himself to the gates of the tax office in Lisburn. But he was prepared to be open about the price loyalists would have to pay if they wanted dominion status – in other words independence. One of the advantages of dominion status, he argued, was that loyalists could regain control of security policy. London was not interested in unleashing the security forces against the IRA. Loyalists, on the other hand, had nowhere to go and would have to defeat republicans militarily in order to secure independence. He accepted that this might lead to a 'Beirut-style' situation with massive cross-community violence: 'We would hope to avoid the horrors of Lebanon and the dangers of repartition, but that depends on circumstances beyond our control.'[43] In his reference to repartition, Trimble was perhaps more candid about unionism's real intention if it ever lost its in-built majority status within Northern Ireland. Many unionist politicians have hinted that, instead of succumbing to the wishes of a future nationalist majority inside a six-county context, they would rather repartition the Province on an east–west basis.

In its hour of need, if Britain withdrew and repartition was looming, Trimble indicated he would support the creation of an Ulster citizens' army: 'There must be no stunts. Ulster Resistance was a disaster and the Third Force ended up being the Third Farce.

The last thing we need are stunts or bombast. People have heard it all before too many times – we don't want empty words or gestures. We do have the potential for an organisation like the original UVF, but we have to do it seriously.'[44]

It was and is a bizarre contradiction that on the one hand Trimble was helping the UDA construct a compromise with nationalists based on the lines of the old Voluntary Coalition while on the other he was prepared to contemplate the logical consequences of an independent Ulster – repartition and the violent suppression of a republican minority in Northern Ireland. Even as he was moving closer to the UUP mainstream at the end of the 1980s Trimble was also calling for (in certain extreme circumstances) the establishment of a new private loyalist army. He had been making some progress through the party after the Agreement was signed, having been elected chairman of the Official Unionist Association in Lagan Valley, Jim Molyneaux's parliamentary constituency. In the same year, 1988, he was also elected on to the party's ruling executive.

Yet there were many figures in the upper echelons of the UUP who were still uncertain about Trimble's credentials. According to a number of high-placed sources in Glengall Street in the late 1980s, Molyneaux distrusted Trimble; and Enoch Powell, who still exercised considerable influence over a section of the party, loathed the 'Vanguard upstart'. 'He was not regarded as a natural Official Unionist,' asserted one of these sourced. 'Powell mistrusted Trimble and warned people about him.'[44]

Their uncertainty was deepened by Trimble's maverick behaviour. Although he railed against Unionist MPs who broke the ministerial boycott, Trimble became the lone wolf of the British–Irish academic conference circuit. He was a regular attender at the annual British–Irish Association meetings that brought together top politicians, diplomats, security chiefs, journalists and academics from London, Dublin and Belfast. These conferences, held at various colleges in Oxford, Cambridge, London and the Midlands, were the occasion for keynote speeches by Irish and British ministers. Trimble defended his attendance on the grounds that BIA gatherings were academic affairs at which unionists should not be afraid to put the intellectual case for the union. The majority of unionist politicians refused to engage in any debate with their Irish opponents, but Trimble was different.

On his first BIA meeting, at Keele University, Staffordshire in 1986, he befriended a number of Catholic writers and journalists from the Republic, one of whom was to have an important bearing on his future thinking. Ruth Dudley Edwards was a historian who had just written a devastating account of the life of Padraig Pearse, the leader of the 1916 Rising. At the time she was still in thrall to John Hume, but was anxious to hear the other side of the Northern Ireland story too. She bumped into Trimble in a corridor and was struck by the fact that this taciturn unionist academic did not seem to know anyone at the conference. Edwards admits that she was 'still struggling with stereotypes about Ulster Protestants, assuming them all to be dour, teetotal bigots. He changed my perceptions.'[45] She invited Trimble to a post-conference party in her room at Keele at which the other guests included Paul Bew. Edwards recalls that Trimble was one of the last to leave, at about three in the morning, following heated political discussions lubricated by several bottles of wine. They became firm friends, corresponding when Trimble was in Northern Ireland and meeting for dinner when he travelled to London. His closest aides say Edwards has become of one of his confidants and advisers at times of crisis.

In 1988 he put himself forward for nomination as the UUP candidate for the Euro election to be held that June. From the outset Trimble had several powerful allies, including the outgoing member, John Taylor. It seemed that Taylor had forgiven Trimble over the Ulster Clubs' picketing of his constituency office. Taylor believed Trimble 'would have presented a first-class image for Ulster in Strasbourg'.[46] Rather than limiting himself to playing the traditional role of the Northern Ireland Euro representative – ensuring that subsidies continued to flow for local agriculture – Trimble, in Taylor's eyes, could have given the international community a vision of unionism radically different from the bellicose bellowing of Ian Paisley inside the Strasbourg Parliament. Taylor argued throughout the party that Trimble would act as a perfect counterpoint to John Hume, who had brilliantly used the EU stage to promote the Irish nationalist cause worldwide. However, Taylor could not come out openly for Trimble given that he was the retiring MEP and, more importantly, that there was a deep well of sympathy within the UUP for the front runner, Jim Nicholson. He had lost his Newry and Armagh seat to the SDLP in the 1986 by-elections, and there was a widespread feeling that the party owed him one.

The selection convention was held in Belfast's Europa Hotel on 7 May. As expected, the eight hundred-strong Ulster Unionist council voted heavily in favour of Nicholson. While Trimble believed the sympathy vote meant Nicholson was always going to win, Taylor suspected his former Euro election agent had thrown it away on the day through a mixture of modesty and naïveté:

> I told him off immediately after the meeting in the nicest of ways. I said to him he was too honest because he told the truth when asked a crucial question from the floor: 'What is your knowledge of a second language?' David replied that he had a general understanding of French, which was a total understatement. Jim Nicholson answered by saying he was almost fluent in French and if selected would take lessons to improve upon this. I won't comment on Jim's grasp of French, but David was too modest. David had made a great speech on European political issues and social policies, but he never mentioned once the issue which commands the largest slice of the EU budget – the Common Agricultural Policy. He never mentioned agriculture from the beginning to the end of his speech.[47]

Given that a large segment of the delegates included farmers from mid-Ulster and the border regions, Trimble's chances of nomination were completely doomed.

Although beaten, Trimble was unbowed. At the end of the selection meeting Jim Wilson, an old Vanguard colleague who was by then the UUP's general secretary, walked up to him to commiserate. Wilson, now commonly regarded as Molyneaux's chief enforcer inside Glengall Street, shook Trimble by the hand. 'He asked me, "David, why are you always on the margins of the party?" I took that as being indicative of a general sea change in attitudes towards me among some, though not all, at the top.'[48]

This sea change was reflected at the UUP's annual conference the following autumn when Trimble finally scored a victory inside the party. The constitutional affairs debate saw the party's devolutionists triumph at last. Trimble had moved the main motion, which stated 'implacable opposition' to the Anglo–Irish Agreement. He then accepted an amendment from Michael McGimpsey that Northern Ireland needed devolution with meaningful powers. While Trimble urged delegates not to allow the issue to become 'another arid debate on integration and devolution' it was clear that the devolutionist wing was turning the tables. Some three hundred delegates backed the motion, with only a handful voting against. The upshot of the vote was that, even though Molyneaux was still party leader, his integrationist option had finally been shot to pieces. It was Trimble the devolutionist who was now swimming with the tide inside Ulster Unionism.

Yet as the new decade dawned Trimble was still a relatively minor figure in the UUP. He was on the party's executive as well as having been appointed the UUP's legal affairs spokesman, but seemed to have little prospect of further progress in his political career. Although he was almost out of the local wilderness after the Vanguard years, it was to take a tragic twist of fate to catapult him into the national political limelight.

4

The Road to Westminster

Harold McCusker died of throat cancer on 9 February 1990, just two days after his fiftieth birthday. The Upper Bann MP's death was a bitter blow to the Ulster Unionist Party, given that he was one of their more formidable spokesmen in a sea of uninspiring grey men. In black and white photographs he bore an uncanny similarity to David Trimble with his flat, neatly parted hair and thick-lensed glasses. And, like Trimble, McCusker was an unorthodox unionist politician. In 1979 McCusker stayed true to his own labourite principles when he, alone amongst unionists, supported Jim Callaghan's government rather than Thatcher in the crucial vote which led to the 1979 general election. McCusker much preferred the company of Labour MPs at Westminster even while his party leadership courted the Tories. He was often seen having a drink with Dublin officials at the Irish Embassy in London, an anathema for most unionists. McCusker even discreetly engaged with the heirs of the Official IRA and in 1982 gave an interview to *Workers' Life*, the theoretical journal of the Workers' Party in Dublin. He was arguably the most proactive member of the parliamentary party, the rest of whom virtually sleepwalked their way around Westminster. In 1981 he set up a unit inside the UUP headquarters to persuade the European Commission on Human Rights that border security was inadequate and the widows of terrorist victims were suffering from a deprivation of their human rights.

There was, none the less, another side to McCusker's politics which marked him out as distinctly hard-line. After his heartfelt speech to the Commons following the Anglo–Irish Agreement, he argued that Ulster independence might become a realistic alternative given that unionists were being ignored in London. In the event of a future nationalist majority, he hinted, unionists might prefer to repartition Northern Ireland into a zone where they would still have a permanent in-built electoral advantage. A year later McCusker served a short prison sentence for withholding his car tax in protest at the Agreement. To many nationalists, particularly in his own constituency, McCusker's association with the Orange Order confirmed their view that he was an uncompromising loyalist. His playing of the Orange lambeg drum on the Twelfth of July instilled deep distrust in many Catholics given that the drum is still viewed as a menacing, triumphalist instrument designed, in the words of one loyalist marching ballad, to 'fill Fenian hearts with fear'.

Whatever people's perceptions of McCusker, it was fair to say he would be a hard act to follow for any successful UUP candidate in the by-election, which was set for 18 May. One of his closest friends in the party was Jack Allen, a former unionist mayor of Derry and at that time the UUP's national chairman. He said McCusker never told him who should take his seat after he died. However, pressure from sections of the local constituency association soon mounted on his widow, Jennifer, to stand for the Upper Bann seat. The forty-five-year-old mother of three could have been the first female MP from Ulster in sixteen years (the last one had been the radical nationalist Bernadette McAliskey, formerly Devlin). Friends of the family said Jennifer seriously considered applying for the nomination in order to carry on her husband's legacy. At the time she was supported by senior party officers including Ken Maginnis and Frank Millar Junior, and once again Trimble's chances of becoming an MP seemed about to be frustrated by the sympathy vote. As one senior Ulster Unionist put it: 'Jennifer would have romped home if she had decided to stand. No one would have stood a chance against her, even someone of Trimble's ability.'[1]

A number of former Vanguard comrades and Ulster Society colleagues approached Trimble at the end of March to ask him if he would run. They included Fred Crowe, who had only rejoined the UUP the year before. Crowe said he received a phone call from someone high up in the Orange Order who asked to speak to him about the nomination battle. The senior Orangeman was Robert Crane, chairman of the UUP's Edenderry branch, who had considerable influence over the loyal orders in the constituency. Crane made a powerful local ally for Trimble in a constituency that included the historic birthplace of Orangeism.

Crowe recounted the first meeting at which Trimble's name was mentioned:

We met in my car and he asked me, 'What do you think of the people who are putting their names forward?' I said I thought they were unacceptable, that none of them could fill Harold's shoes. I then went on to say that there were only two people capable of doing the job – David Trimble and Frank Millar Junior, who worked in unionist headquarters. Crane contacted me shortly after this and said he thought Trimble could be persuaded to stand. He told me he wanted me to use my influence on him to go for it.[2]

Trimble did not come and seek the job, according to Crowe and others in mid-Ulster; he had to be pressurized into it. One of the main factors that propelled him towards the nomination was his progress, or lack of it, at Queen's University. In 1988 he had failed to win another prestige post at Queen's, that of Professor of Jurisprudence. The successful candidate, Simon Lee, a young left-liberal Englishman, accepts that Trimble's politics worked against him. 'Although he was not the world's best writer – he published less academic work than others – it's true to say Queen's found it difficult to have him as a professor of law given his views.'[3]

There was another motivating factor in that Upper Bann was a safe Ulster Unionist seat – McCusker had had a thumping seventeen-thousand majority in the 1987 general election. Trimble finally agreed to put his name forward following a meeting organized by Fred Crowe at a local unionist activist's house in Donaghmore in the first week of March. According to Crowe some fifty people turned up, enough to convince Trimble that he had more than enough support in the local constituency associations to try for the nomination. On 6 March he finally announced he was in the running. He pledged himself to fight not just on parochial constituency matters but on the wider question of how Northern Ireland was governed.

Most successful politicians depend on a fair degree of luck; Trimble's fortunes, it seems, were now blessed on two fronts. First,

Jennifer McCusker finally decided not to stand just twenty-four hours before the nominations closed. She had confided in Jack Allen that she was worried about the impact of taking the seat on her three sons, one of whom was just off to university; Allen opted to run in her place. Among Trimble's other six opponents were a number of popular UUP Craigavon councillors including Sam Gardiner, George Savage and Arnold Hatch as well as the local mayor, Jim McCammick. Senior figures in Glengall Street who admired Trimble's talents and had promoted his cause contrasted his potential as an MP with the rest of what was on offer: 'He was a bit like Harold. Trimble was first-division material while the others were decent dullards. The opposition were honest, solid but very dull Ulstermen.'[4] Yet despite Trimble's obvious advantages the contest turned out to be a damn close-run thing.

In fact he would never have won the nomination but for another twist of good fortune. At the start of 1990 the Upper Bann Ulster Unionist Association adopted proportional representation as its method for selecting candidates. Had the contest been run on the old first-past-the-post rules, Trimble would have lost. Voting by 250 delegates in the first round of the selection meeting on 19 April put him in second place. The first-preference votes were: Sam Gardiner 91, David Trimble 68, George Savage 37, Arnold Hatch 18, Jack Allen 13, Jim McCammick 12, William Ward 11 and Sam Walker 5. On the third count Trimble eventually gained more second-preferences, defeating Gardiner by 136 to 114 votes.

The next day he played down the narrowness of his victory, attributing it to the fact that he was an outsider from the nearby Lagan Valley constituency. He then confidently predicted victory 'in this the Tercentenary of the Battle of the Boyne and save Ulster for unionism'.[5] Trimble now concedes that, while the old Vanguard cadre and his work with the Ulster Society helped him, there was still residual suspicion of a man regarded as 'not a natural Official Unionist'. He believes his past made it harder for him to win.

The Upper Bann by-election was the first Northern Ireland electoral contest to come under the national spotlight since the hunger strike elections of 1981. The reason was the presence of the Conservative Party – the first time the Tories had stood in a Westminster election in Ulster's history. The Conservatives had broken a national political taboo in October 1989 when the party conference accepted the principle of organizing in the Province. The following month the Tories' National Union accepted the affiliation of the North Down Conservative Association after Tory councillors were elected to the council. Laurence Kennedy, a dental surgeon at the Royal Victoria Hospital in Belfast, led the North Down Tories. Like McCartney and his Campaign for Equal Citizenship, Kennedy believed passionately that grafting the national parties on to Northern Ireland would provide a real alternative to the sectarian politics that poisoned local parties. Just before the by-election the Northern Ireland Conservatives received a welcome boost when Gary Haggan, a councillor for Ian Paisley's Democratic Unionist Party, joined them. The local Tories predicted they could break the mould of Ulster politics at Upper Bann, their first real electoral test. The national news networks and the heavyweights from the press lobby in Westminster flocked to Portadown, Lurgan, Craigavon, Banbridge and the smaller towns and villages of the constituency to gauge the mood and discover whether there really might be a Tory breakthrough. But at the heart of new Northern Ireland Conservatism lay an inherent contradiction – how could self-proclaimed unionists who also wanted to be Tories join a national party which had introduced the much-despised Anglo–Irish Agreement? That question was put directly to Gary Haggan on the day he announced he was defecting to the Conservatives. Unable to provide an adequate answer, he deflected it to Laurence Kennedy who simply berated the press corps for 'asking stupid predictable questions'.

Trimble relished the prospect of taking on the Conservative candidate, Colette Jones. He had never hidden his disdain for the Tories, even when Molyneaux et al. continued to send speakers to the Conservatives' annual conferences while ignoring Labour and the Liberals. The previous November, in front of some of unionism's staunchest Westminster allies, Trimble had accused the Conservatives of being the 'enemy of the union'. He had made his comments at a meeting of the Friends of the Union in Belfast, a Tory ginger group founded in London by his old Vanguard colleague, David Burnside, following the Anglo–Irish Agreement. Trimble told the meeting, which was attended by the late Ian Gow MP and Lord Cranborne (later the Tories' leader in the House of Lords), that the presence of the Conservatives in Northern Ireland had put the relationship between the two political head offices,

Glengall Street in Belfast and Smith Square in London, in jeopardy: 'The Northern Ireland Conservatives are deluding themselves if they think they will make any impact on government policy. The government will use them as a means to build support for the Anglo–Irish Agreement, because local people will be obliged to support government policy.'[6]

It was this contradiction dogging the local Tories that Trimble exploited to the full during the by-election campaign. In Upper Bann (the 'Orange county' to local loyalists) the Anglo–Irish Agreement was loathed. Here was a real opportunity to punish the party which had signed the treacherous document. As the favourite for the seat, Trimble was receiving more national media attention than most front-runners ever dreamed of getting in Northern Ireland elections. He concluded that, with the British media out in force, the UUP needed to trounce the Tories and thus strangle at birth the Conservative challenge to Ulster Unionism in the Province. Tory cabinet ministers including Chris Patten from the Northern Ireland Office and Douglas Hurd, the Foreign Secretary, toured the constituency with Colette Jones. Trimble, meanwhile, went out campaigning with a number of senior national political correspondents such as *The Independent*'s Donald Macintyre, who followed him on a canvass of Lurgan. The by-election presented Trimble with an opportunity to meet high-powered television and newspaper journalists as well as to clash in the local media with cabinet ministers canvassing for the Tory candidate. This experience was to serve him well in the near future.

During the campaign Trimble was clearly associated with his uncompromising attitude towards the Anglo–Irish Agreement, which went down well in the staunch unionist/Orange heartlands of Portadown and Lurgan. His colleagues made no secret of the fact that it was Trimble who had led the rooftop protest at Glengall Street against the visit of Charles Haughey, his first-ever official trip to Belfast, to the nearby Europa Hotel on 11 April. Four hundred loyalists had besieged the hotel during a speech made by the Irish Premier to the annual conference of the Institute of Directors. A number of unionist politicians, including Ian Paisley and his deputy, Peter Robinson, broke through the massive security cordon around the hotel to get to Glengall Street. There was considerable anger among some senior UUP officers when Trimble allowed the new arrivals, particularly Paisley and Robinson, on to the roof with them. Moreover, Trimble found himself on the opposite side of the police lines from another old Vanguard comrade, Reg Empey. At the time of Haughey's visit Empey was the Ulster Unionist Lord Mayor of Belfast, and in this capacity he had to give the opening address to the conference. He came under sustained and severe criticism for agreeing to do so because Haughey had been a hate-figure for most unionists since the 1970 arms trial, when a number of Irish ministers including Haughey, at that time Finance Minister, were accused of running guns to the Provisional IRA.

Throughout the by-election campaign Trimble confidently predicted that rather than achieving a breakthrough, the Tories would be broken in Upper Bann. The result at Banbridge leisure centre on 19 May was a triumph for Trimble and a humiliating disaster for the Tories. He sailed home with 20,547 votes while his nearest rival, the SDLP's Brid Rogers, polled 6698. The Conservatives came in sixth in a field of eleven candidates with just 1038 votes, thus losing their £500 deposit. To make matters worse, Colette Jones got fewer votes than even minor candidates like those of the Workers' Party and the Ulster Independence Party, the Reverend Hugh Ross, an eccentric, toupee-wearing Presbyterian minister who believes in a global Vatican conspiracy aimed at destroying Northern Ireland. Although the Tories limped on after the Upper Bann defeat, Trimble's triumph effectively killed off any chance of the Conservatives breaking the mould. Their hopes of becoming a major force in the Province were dashed.

Another of the candidates ahead of the Tories was the Sinn Fein representative Sheena Campbell. The girlfriend of a prominent Lurgan republican, Campbell had just started a law degree at Queen's and was one of Trimble's students at the time of the by-election. She was shot dead two years later by the UVF inside the York Hotel in Botanic Avenue just a few hundred yards from Queen's law faculty.

In his victory speech Trimble taunted the Tories and said that the primary issue had been the Anglo-Irish Agreement. The Upper Bann electorate had rejected the Accord, he said: 'Surely now Peter Brooke [the Secretary of State] must realise he is defending the indefensible.' After the disappointments of failing to get the Euro nomination, of being the outsider in the party for so long following Vanguard's demise and the professional roadblocks he had faced at

Queen's, election to Westminster was a moment of sweet satisfaction. But there were people to remember in the midst of his long-awaited triumph. He paid tribute to the late Harold McCusker, pointing out that his victory was tinged by sadness because of McCusker's untimely death. Trimble promised to 'carry on his great work'.[7]

After the speech Trimble travelled back to his family home in Lisburn to relax and cut the lawn, which he had neglected during the month-long campaign. The first day of his new life as an MP was largely domestic. He went shopping with Daphne to stock up on food, an activity for which there had been little time while he was canvassing. Trimble then drove his eldest son, eight-year-old Richard, to a Beaver Scouts rally in the town before returning home to prepare a meal for visiting relatives. Celebrations for the Trimble children, Richard, six-year-old Victoria and three-year-old Nicholas, consisted of a sausage-and-chips takeaway from a local café.

There were celebrations of a different kind the next evening when two thousand Orangemen cheered the new MP through the streets of Portadown during a loyalist band parade to mark the tercentenary of the Battle of the Boyne. Trimble walked at the head of the procession with several leading local Orangemen, including the Portadown District Master, Harold Gracey, and the man he had beaten into second place for the Upper Bann nomination, Sam Gardiner. A hero's welcome was given him in the citadel of Orangeism. The Orangemen thought they now had the articulate but hard-line unionist MP they had always wanted. To people like Gracey Trimble was their man, someone who would never sell Ulster out. A few years later some of them would be deeply disappointed with their choice.

Given the high profile at Upper Bann, it did not take long for the London and Dublin press to conclude that Trimble might be unionism's coming man. A day after his win, the London *Times*'s headline over a profile by the paper's Irish correspondent Ed Gorman was: 'Ulster Poll winner a bright light in lacklustre party'. Gorman's prophetic analysis was that Trimble might one day become the UUP's leader. However the article also contained a number of hostile points, such as the reference to his involvement with the UWC strike and 'his appetite for indulging in the kind of hysterical anti-Catholic rhetoric more often associated with Mr Ian Paisley's Democratic Unionist Party than Mr James Molyneaux's

UUP'. Gorman went on to note that there was an uneasy paradox in the heart of Trimble's thinking, 'where reason, moderation and a genuine desire for reconciliation battle the instinctive prejudice and ghetto mentality of the born and bred Orangeman'.[8] Despite the predictions of great things to come, Gorman's references to prejudice and bigotry hurt Trimble so deeply that he lashed out at any available target. At first he thought his academic colleague Simon Lee, a neighbour of Gorman's in the Notting Hill area of South Belfast, was the source and accused him of stitching him up. But when he found out it was someone else he apologised.

A week later, as Trimble prepared his maiden speech for the Commons, the *Irish Times* ran a less controversial profile by one of its Northern reporters, Marie O'Halloran. Her piece too seemed to be touched by the gift of prophecy: 'Among most shades of opinion within the party he is viewed as an articulate and persuasive purveyor of unionism, who could do much to enhance unionism's image at Westminster. . . . Some consider him a potential leader with a close association with the maverick Strangford MP John Taylor.'[9]

What these two correspondents did not know was that senior party officials were looking into their own oracle to see what might become of David Trimble's future. A month after he was elected a leading Glengall Street apparatchik carried out a telephone poll of party officers to determine who might succeed Molyneaux. The result stunned him. Trimble was already making an impact – a large majority said he would be the 'next leader but one' after Wee Jim; a substantial minority even tipped Trimble to take the leadership first time around.

His election delighted that most radical right-wing section of the UUP, the Young Unionists. The party's youth wing, particularly its branch at Queen's, had traditionally been hard-line whereas many of the older Ulster Unionists were liberals. Some of the Young Unionists' critics defined them as the 'Genghis Khan tendency' of the party. Liberals and left-wingers in the UUP pointed to the extremism of the Young Unionists at Queen's, whose programme included establishing fraternal relations with the youth wing of the South African National Party just as the racist regime was crumbling. One of the first of the Young Unionists to rejoice at the Upper Bann result was Peter Weir, a Queen's law graduate and former student of Trimble's who joined the UUP's North Down constituency association in 1990. Weir, one of the most vociferous of a right-wing ginger group inside the UUP known as the 'baby barristers', noted that Trimble's election 'may turn out to be one of the most significant in the history of Northern Ireland. The Ulster Unionist parliamentary team have gained an articulate, ambitious and intelligent new member.'[10] Like the Portadown Orangemen, the new right inside the UUP clearly saw that Trimble might be their man. And even though the extremism of the Young Unionists was well known, in his early years as an MP Trimble did little to discourage them from thinking that he was indeed their new ally.

On his first day in the Commons Trimble generated further controversy. Breaking the tradition that a maiden speech should not be contentious, Trimble launched a bitter attack on the Northern Ireland Conservatives. He told MPs that the margin of his victory over Colette Jones proved that there was no mandate for the Tories' policies. Then he accused the Conservatives of trying to 'divide and diminish' the Unionist voice through its first venture into Ulster politics in seventy years. His comments came under immediate fire from Gerry Hayes, a Tory MP with Irish roots whom unionists thought was too sympathetic to Dublin. Hayes complained that maiden speeches were meant to be non-controversial. In stepped Trimble's parliamentary colleague, the UUP South Belfast MP Martin Smyth, who reminded Hayes that history was on their side: 'He [Trimble] could have reminded the House that a Tory was originally an Irish Jacobite, and in this tercentenary year of the Battle of the Boyne, we are glad that we beat the Tories again in Upper Bann.'[11]

Trimble's first full day as an MP was a highly significant one: it marked the start of the first serious negotiations between unionists and the British government since the Anglo–Irish Agreement. Peter Brooke had persuaded Paisley and Molyneaux that there would be a gap in meetings of the inter-governmental conference if they agreed to round table talks with the SDLP. Although the talks did not open until the autumn, the unionist leadership's acceptance of the discussions signified the end of their ministerial boycott and the effective demise of their five-year-long anti-Agreement campaign.

Within a matter of months, meanwhile, Trimble had burned up the Westminster learning curve. He had been appointed Home Affairs spokesman for the party, even pursuing a number of issues outside the Northern Ireland remit. Trimble shared a room at the Commons with John Taylor, an old Westminster pro who showed him the ropes. Observers back in Glengall Street noted that he had come into his own in the Commons.[12] He easily outshone his fellow UUP MPs in terms of debating skills and work rate. Friends noted that he applied a meticulous lawyer's touch to examining legislation and preparing his speeches. While most MPs headed home at weekends for their constituency surgeries, Trimble preferred to stay at Westminster late into Friday night during the private members' debates when individual MPs had the optimum chance of getting to speak.

Although he relished the cut and thrust of the Commons, Trimble did not hang out with fellow MPs and journalists in the members' bar. His extra-curricular activity at Westminster was confined to his membership of the all-party group on opera. Even in his first year he liked to leave Westminster and melt into the anonymity of London, where he did not want the kind of security protection that every MP is afforded in Northern Ireland. Barry White Junior, his current parliamentary assistant, confesses that Trimble's wanderlust still worries his Westminster team: 'When he comes over here he doesn't have his security minders with him, so he just likes to jump on the Tube and go and buy CDs. Or he'll head off to the bookshops. We don't like the way he walks down Oxford Street in his green mac with two plastic bags full of Elvis and opera CDs and books on Irish history. I suppose it's his way of relaxing.'[13]

White characterizes Trimble as a 'news junkie – someone who never turns Sky News or BBC News 24 off the television screen in his office, who constantly monitors radio bulletins and who scans all the national newspapers'.[14] Even on the journey back and forth from Belfast he will telephone his parliamentary staff and open with the inevitable question: 'Any news?'

In London he renewed his acquaintance with Ruth Dudley Edwards, who would often take him to the Reform Club for dinner after he had finished business at the Commons. Edwards described herself in that early period of their friendship as 'the Virgin Mary interceding for people who wanted to meet David'. Her intercessions included passing on an invitation to Trimble to have lunch at the Irish Embassy. However, he declined because he believed it would send out the wrong signal – that relations between Belfast and Dublin were normal despite the continued existence of the Anglo–Irish Agreement. He also knew that someone like Paisley would exploit such a visit to the full.

While he may have wined and dined with journalists and intellectuals outside Parliament, at all other times Trimble lived quite frugally in the capital. He bought a two-bedroom council flat across the Thames in the less than salubrious Elephant and Castle area, and usually travelled to the Commons by bus. Friends who came to stay with him noted the shambolic state of the flat, with papers and magazines scattered everywhere. One of his circle at Queen's University was David Brewster, who had been a student of his and a leading figure in the Young Unionists. Brewster visited Trimble at Westminster and was startled by the lack of security that he had opted for:

At two or three in the morning he would leave the Commons and walk back to the flat. Here was this middle-aged middle-class specky geezer walking through some of the hardest areas in south London with a couple of bottles of wines banging together in his briefcase. He should have had a 'Mug me' sign pinned to his back. When we got to the flats I thought he was living in very grotty conditions – there were dead rats on the balcony and piss all over the place. I remember thinking to myself on one occasion that it must be a miserable life.[15]

The first six months of Trimble's Westminster career centred on home-affairs issues such as border security. In October 1990 he concocted a public stunt to highlight the lack of security along the Northern Ireland/Irish Republic frontier. He and Jim Nicholson had been asked to speak in Dublin at an Irish Association dinner; the invitation was issued just a month after the IRA had ambushed and murdered an RUC constable travelling over a border crossing point. Trimble and Nicholson refused to make the hundred-mile journey to Dublin by car; instead they each spent £300 on flights from Belfast to London and then on to Dublin (there have never been direct air links between Belfast and Dublin). The two men advised people not to use the the Kileen checkpoint outside Newry, where Constable Louis Robinson had been abducted and killed. 'Anyone in a vulnerable position or who feels they are a target would be foolish to go that way, and that includes normal travellers. Until the authorities make sure that mile and a half of road is safe, either by patrolling or relocating the checkpoint, I won't be using it,' Trimble said.[16]

Earlier, on 24 August, Trimble had taken up another issue which was generating controversy within the unionist community – the case of the UDR Four. Harold McCusker had previously championed the cause of four UDR soldiers who protested they were innocent of murdering Armagh Catholic Adrian Carroll seven years before. Trimble announced that he was satisfied that their conviction represented a miscarriage of justice and joined their campaign group, the Armagh Four Committee. The soldiers – Neil Latimer, Noel Bell, James Hegan and Winston Allen – claimed that the RUC had tampered with their original confessions and that the crown's key witness was unreliable given that she had twice spent time in a mental institution undergoing treatment for a personality disorder. In addition, the group that claimed responsibility for the murder, the UVF, denied that the soldiers had anything to do with Carroll's death. A senior member of the UVF later admitted that the terror unit involved had come directly from Belfast and had received no assistance from the UDR or indeed anyone else in Armagh city.

The campaign to release the UDR Four had received a massive boost when other miscarriages of justice were exposed, in particular when the Guildford Four were freed in 1989. The four in question – Paul Hill, Gerard Conlon, Carole Richardson and Patrick Armstrong – had been convicted of carrying out IRA pub bombings in Woolwich and Guildford in 1974, but they were freed after the Director of Public Prosecutions announced that it would be wrong for the crown to 'seek to sustain the convictions'. Subsequently the convictions of six members of the Maguire family, relations of Gerard Conlon who had been caught up in the original investigations into the Woolwich and Guildford bombings, were quashed. Nationalists, however, regarded the involvement of Trimble, Ian Paisley and other unionist politicians in the Armagh Four campaign as one-sided opportunism. They pointed out that not a single unionist politician had ever spoken up for the Guildford Four, the Maguires or the Birmingham Six (men from Belfast and Derry who spent seventeen years in prison for a crime they did not commit – the IRA bombing of two pubs in Birmingham in 1974 which killed twenty-one people) during their long period in English prisons. The impression was that unionists only cared about their own victims of injustice.

While this charge may be justified when levelled at certain

unionist politicians, it is hardly fair to David Trimble. A year before he took up the UDR Four case he had persuaded the Ulster Unionists' annual conference in Enniskillen to call for an investigation into the Surrey Police's handling of the Guildford Four case. He told delegates that no one should be convicted on false evidence, no matter who they were.[17] And while Trimble was in favour of a robust security policy that included sealing off parts of the Irish border and selective internment, he was opposed in principle to capital punishment and would have been reluctant to see it introduced.

At the end of 1990 Trimble's star was in the ascendant. In the second week of October he accompanied Jim Molyneaux to speak at the Conservatives' annual conference at Bournemouth. He was in no mood to moderate his attitude to the Tories, and his belligerent tone contrasted sharply with the softly-softly approach that Molyneaux employed in the corridors of Westminster. Shortly after the conference – Margaret Thatcher's last as Prime Minister before the coup which ousted her and ushered in John Major – Trimble issued a warning to the Tories: the Ulster Unionists would drive a hard bargain in the event of a hung Parliament following the next election. Trimble's 'shopping list' included the replacement of the Anglo–Irish Agreement. 'At both Westminster and Bournemouth,' he said, 'I have been approached by Tory MPs anxious to know the price of our support if it is required. I think if there is to be any understanding, we should not settle for promises but rather have something concrete on the table.'[18]

He lashed into the Tories again eight days later with the disclosure that the Upper Bann Conservative Association had set up a businessmen's dining club aimed at helping members gain access to government ministers. Trimble wrote to the Secretary of State, Peter Brooke, warning him that this constituted corruption and discrimination against businessmen not holding the £100 membership card.

The end of his first year in Parliament coincided with the first IRA Christmas ceasefire in fifteen years. Trimble was scathing when it broke down after three days. 'I regard the ceasefire as a fraud anyway. The only significant thing about it is the way Peter Brooke seemed to have been taken in by it.'[19]

At the start of 1991 Trimble went to the Maze prison (as Long Kesh had been renamed) to visit the UDR Four; he was accompanied by Ian Paisley Junior, the son of the DUP leader. They discussed a dossier of new evidence which Trimble presented to Peter Brooke the following day in London. The evidence in question related to the police interview notes during the Four's interrogations. Trimble later wrote that, if the notes were subjected to testing by electronic detection analysis (Esda), it would show that the interview was not an accurate contemporaneous record, thus casting doubt on the veracity of the Four's confessions. However, his concerns in Parliament were not just parochial. At the end of the Gulf War Trimble took up the cause of the Kurds fleeing Saddam Hussein's revenge following their failed uprising in northern Iraq. In contrast to the non-interventionism of many Tory and Labour MPs Trimble urged the government to arm the Kurds to enable them to fight back against the Iraqi Army, and wanted British forces in the region to defend Kurdish refugees from attack.

Beneath the glacial surface of Ulster politics, in early 1991 the ice was beginning to crack. The thaw began on 25 March when the UUP, DUP, SDLP and Alliance agreed on Peter Brooke's formula for talks. They would be run on three separate strands. Strand 1 would deal with internal matters within Northern Ireland; Strand 2 would concern cooperation between Northern Ireland and the Republic; and Strand 3 would focus on East–West relations encompassing the entire British Isles. On the same day Richard Needham became the first Northern Ireland Office minister to visit Belfast City Hall since the signing of the Anglo–Irish Agreement. A month later the umbrella body representing all the major loyalist terrorist groups, the Combined Loyalist Military Command, announced a ceasefire for the duration of the talks.

For the first time since he joined the UUP, Molyneaux took Trimble on to the party's high-powered talks team. The UUP delegation was split into three sections to deal with the various Strands. Michael McGimpsey and his brother Chris were appointed to take charge of Strand 2 on the North–South axis. The previous year the McGimpseys had taken a landmark case to the Irish Supreme Court in Dublin in their bid to challenge the validity of the Republic's territorial claim on Northern Ireland. The main significance of the judgement in their case was that Articles 2 and 3 of the Irish constitution were not merely an aspiration but a real claim of legal right and thus a constitutional imperative. The judgement on Articles 2 and 3 was to be a major sticking point in later talks in Belfast and Dublin. Ken Maginnis joined the McGimpseys in Strand 2 talks, while Reg Empey, Jeffrey Donaldson and Molyneaux looked after Strand 1.

Michael McGimpsey could not understand why Trimble wanted to plough the lonely furrow of Strand 3 on East–West relations within the British Isles (though he may have been unaware that Trimble had been a passionate advocate of a Council of the British Isles since helping to write *Ulster Unfettered* for the loyalist paramilitaries).

> To be honest I thought it was a crazy idea at the time. There seemed to me no chance that the Tories would even give devolution to Scotland and Wales, and yet here was Trimble arguing for a Council of the British Isles that would also include the Channel Isles and the Isle of Man. Power at the time was still rushing to the centre through Thatcher and then Major. But it turned out Trimble was spot-on, and I think in hindsight it was very prescient that he was able to work out the way the UK would eventually evolve.[20]

Trimble's enthusiasm for his old concept of a Council of the British Isles led to problems with other members of the talks team, notably Ken Maginnis. The Fermanagh/South Tyrone MP remembers a short, sharp row with Trimble: Maginnis was 'less than lukewarm' about the Council because he believed it would give Dublin even more influence in London, and ended by reminding this relative newcomer to the UUP talks team: 'I don't like being talked down to.'[21] He confesses that the spat coloured their relationship for several years.

Although Trimble was relegated to the third division of the UUP talks team, a number of his colleagues were still impressed by his diligence and attention to detail. Michael McGimpsey admitted that he was not sure where Trimble was coming from politically, but 'David could think on his feet, talk fast and was the most analytical in the team'.[22] However, Trimble never got a chance to submit a paper on Strand 3 because the talks broke down on 3 July. A day later the CLMC announced that the loyalist ceasefire would end at midnight.

The IRA's response to that ceasefire had been to intensify rather than scale down their own violence. Their targets included mainly

Protestant towns and villages such Donacloney and Markethill, which suffered severe damage from huge IRA car bombs at this time. Trimble campaigned for speedy compensation for house-holders and businesses whose property had been destroyed in the blasts. He was angry that one bomb compensation case in every six was taking more than two years to complete. Given the IRA's blatant attempt to blow the talks off the agenda, thus undermining the loyalist ceasefire, Trimble held out little hope of peace or political progress. At the start of 1992 he was still arguing for a military solution to the IRA's campaign. He praised undercover soldiers for killing a four-strong IRA unit during a gun attack on Coalisland's joint Army/RUC base in Co. Tyrone on 16 February.[23] What was needed, he contended, was more of the same.

Political progress in Northern Ireland had also been put on hold since the end of the Gulf War now that the UK was engaged in a phoney political war in the run-up to the 1992 election. Major confounded the pundits with a stunning victory at the polls. The local result in Upper Bann was a triumph for Trimble too: his overall majority leaped from the by-election figure of 13,949 to 16,163. Trimble's re-election to Parliament signalled the end of his career at Queen's University. From the 1990 by-election until the general election Trimble had been granted leave of absence from the law department. Following his return to Parliament Trimble was summoned to see the Vice-Chancellor, Sir Gordon Beveridge, who advised him that the time had come to end the uncertainty and leave the university for good. Trimble hardly needed to be per-suaded.

The national picture was also encouraging for the Ulster Union-ists, who returned to Westminster with nine members. John Major had defied the opinion polls to score a historic fourth win in a row for the Conservatives. Yet while Major had finally seen off Neil Kinnock's challenge, the Conservatives' overall majority had been cut to twenty-one. Trimble's threat the previous year about the UUP driving a hard bargain would soon be fulfilled.

A month later Trimble's fourth and final child, Sarah, was born. She was baptised at Harmony Hill Presbyterian church in Lisburn by a new young minister who was to become a firm friend of the family especially in times of need. The Reverend David Knox was a Bangor man who had attended the same grammar school as Trimble. Knox, who with his beard and John Lennon-style glasses resembles a left-wing intellectual, was immediately taken with the down-to-earth attitude the family displayed despite the fact that the head of the household was a rising star at Westminster. He contrasted the lifestyle of the Trimbles to the sniffy aloofness of the old Anglican establishment that used to run the Ulster Unionist Party, some of whom had their own private reserved pews in church every Sunday.

> David still comes into Harmony Hill like everyone else and sits in the same pew where the Trimbles always sat. The same people sit behind them every Sunday, a working-class Presbyterian family from Lisburn, and they chat before the service. They are simple people who live simple lives, but who seem to like David because there are no airs and graces with him or his family. It's a very Presbyterian thing – everybody is equal in the church. People don't make a difference with him, and David seems to like it that way.[24]

Harmony Hill has a tradition of being a liberal Presbyterian congregation in the sense that it has always reached out to its Catholic neighbours. The Reverend Knox's church, for instance, holds a joint carol service at Christmas with the nearby St Colman's Catholic church. On a number of occasions during the joint seasonal celebrations he has asked Trimble to read one of the lessons. Harmony Hill and St Colman's also organize annual barbecues, Bible readings and charity fund-raising events that the Trimbles often attend. Knox points out that if Trimble cannot get to the functions himself because of his political commitments, the rest of the family will still go along.

Daphne and David ensure that all their children are involved in church activities. Victoria is a member of Harmony Hill's choir while Sarah, Nicholas and Richard belong to the Sunday-night After Eight club. According to Knox, Richard Trimble is highly regarded in the church and was elected on to its ruling committee at the tender age of seventeen. The younger son, Nicholas, he describes as 'a real live wire, full of beans – a great character who likes to slurp Slush Puppies at the back of the church when I'm delivering my sermons'.[25]

Knox is one of the people who have been close to Trimble in times of triumph and turmoil. He describes his most famous parishioner as a 'shy, reticent man who takes time to be comfortable with people'. But is he a religious man? Does he even believe in God? Knox is certain Trimble has not lost his faith.

> All I can say is that when you have your child baptised the question is directly put to you: 'Do you believe in one God, Father, Son and Holy Spirit?' I say that is the core question of your belief. David had no qualms about saying it, so I take his word and I see it by his example. I don't expect my congregation to be perfect, but I see in his family a real living thing. I see them supporting him and encouraging him all the time.[26]

Knox is certain that the Presbyterian ethic of speaking the truth has marked Trimble's style in politics. 'We are people of the Word. Fundamentally, within Presbyterian hearts that means what you say is what you mean. He comes from that tradition, and that means he is not afraid to speak out even if it upsets some people.' His one complaint about Trimble is that 'it's easier to talk to him on a mobile phone on a train to Leicester than it is to see him at home'. The centre of gravity in the household is Daphne, who also works as his secretary in the Upper Bann constituency office. Knox admires her ability to hold the family together when Trimble is at Westminster. 'Daphne is a very warm-hearted and friendly, outgoing person. They are a very solid family and you can see that the kids have their heads screwed on. They don't let their father's position influence their behaviour, except perhaps Nicholas who would sometimes say, "Do you know who my father is?" But he is the only one, and everyone would laugh at it.'[27]

Trimble's long association with his local Catholic church is telling. His politics are firm to hard-line on the union but flexible to the point of benign indifference with regard to someone's religion. A further broad hint of his evolving secular unionism was given two months after Sarah's baptism in a row with the Orange Order. Archie McKelvey, a UUP councillor in Banbridge, was expelled from the Order for attending a number of Catholic services in his role as chairman of the local council. The Orange Order officially forbids its members from attending Catholic mass on theological grounds. Trimble stepped into the furore on 3 July – at the height of the loyalist marching season – to defend McKelvey, whom he described as a 'committed loyalist' of high personal integrity. Risking the wrath of the Orange Order – a powerful force in his own constituency and one which had helped him get the 1990 nomination – Trimble spoke out in the press against the expulsion: 'I am extremely disappointed to see that this action has been taken against him for carrying out what he believed to be his civic obligations.'[28] The row marked his first serious clash with the Orange institution since it had backed Ernest Baird's breakaway faction in the Voluntary Coalition row in 1975. It would not be the last time Trimble fell foul of the sour-faced grey men at the Orange Order's headquarters in Belfast.

The political talks limped on through the summer and autumn of 1992 while both IRA and loyalist violence increased. John Hume continued his dialogue with the Sinn Fein President Gerry Adams, with the SDLP leader predicting that their talks would produce an end to IRA violence. Meanwhile Trimble still languished in the third division of the talks team, which was evident when Molyneaux took the historic step of agreeing to talks with the Irish government in Dublin. It was the first occasion since 1922 that a unionist leader had held discussions with Irish ministers in the Republic's capital. The last such leader, Trimble noted, was his old hero Sir James Craig. He was delighted when he was asked to join Molyneaux's team in Dublin. While Paisley accused the UUP of backsliding on their principle of 'no negotiation with Dublin', the UUP team's task was made easier by the absence of Charles Haughey, the loyalist bugbear, who had been removed from office in an internal party coup in February 1992. His successor, Albert Reynolds, was seen as a pragmatist who was less burdened by republican baggage than Haughey. At their first meeting, on 21 September, the unionists thought Reynolds was someone they might even do business with. Reynolds, though, had one eye on the forthcoming general election and another on the Hume–Adams talks process. In the absence of any change in Articles 2 and 3 of the Republic's constitution, there was little prospect of progress. Molyneaux's team left Dublin with the impression that Reynolds had treated them disdainfully. Their mood was 'downcast and humiliated', especially given that Ian Paisley would gleefully exploit their failure.

The UUP team, however, realized that a renascent Irish Labour Party under Dick Spring was going to have a good election and could possibly end up in government. Molyneaux delegated the

McGimpsey brothers, who had contacts with the Dublin left, to open up a channel with Labour. Though the discussion did not produce any movement, for Molyneaux it did establish the left-leaning brothers as useful conduits for making new friends south of the border. The McGimpseys arranged for the UUP talks team to have dinner with Chris Hudson, a Dublin-based trade unionist and peace activist who ran the campaign against IRA bomb attacks on the cross-border rail link. As a vocal opponent of the IRA in the Republic, Hudson was someone who could be trusted to understand and articulate unionist fears and concerns.

Hudson met four of the UUP team – the McGimpseys, Ken Maginnis and David Trimble – in the Old Connaught restaurant off Wicklow Street. He noted the symbolism of the unionists sitting around a table in one of the Irish capital's less sophisticated restaurants while John Hume was wined and dined by the Irish government in the splendour of Dublin Castle. The peace campaigner also gained the impression that Trimble was still a junior member of the team. Maginnis and the McGimpsey brothers were huddled around the trade unionist, but Trimble was relegated to the end of the table beside Hudson's wife Isabella. Whilst Maginnis and the McGimpseys talked high politics, exploring their chances of a meeting with Fergus Finlay, Dick Spring's chief of staff and special adviser on Northern Ireland, Trimble's conversation centred on opera and classical music. Hudson recalled:

> Isabella's father was in an orchestra and she was delighted to talk to him about music. Trimble talked all night about Puccini and Wagner. I remember afterwards Isabella took me aside and said, 'God, Chris, that man is so knowledgeable about music. He's very cultured – he's not what you expect from the unionist stereotype. He exhausted me for a couple of hours talking opera.' The McGimpseys appeared to be very close to Molyneaux at that time, while Trimble was not as prominent. The seating arrangements at the Old Connaught sort of reflected that.[29]

The upshot of the dinner was a meeting between the McGimpseys and Fergus Finlay at Hudson's home in Blackrock a few weeks later. The spin-off from the Blackrock meeting was a promise by the brothers to introduce Hudson to political activists with loyalist paramilitary connections. This in turn eventually led to Hudson becoming a go-between for the new Irish government and the UVF right up to the 1994 loyalist ceasefire.

The Ulster Unionists were initially encouraged by Dick Spring's statement in early 1993 on the parameters for new talks. The Irish Labour leader and deputy Prime Minister in the coalition government promised 'openness and flexibility', and even assured unionists that Articles 2 and 3 were not cast in bronze. The leader of Ireland's four million Catholics, Cardinal Cathal Daly, even predicted that there would be peace by the end of the year. The facts on the ground, however, still suggested the opposite. In January the UDA threatened to wage war on the 'pan-nationalist front', defined as Sinn Fein, the SDLP and the Irish government. The Hume–Adams dialogue was generating deep anxiety in the unionist community, who believed that a combination of IRA bombs in London and clever manipulation by the SDLP leader with Dublin's backing could force John Major into making major concessions to republicans. This widespread fear was reflected in an *Ulster Newsletter* opinion poll on 1 April, which showed that 42 per cent of Protestants agreed with loyalist violence – an alarming figure for a community which had always prided itself on being law-biding.

Trimble reflected the mood of creeping paranoia within the unionist community when he got embroiled in a bitter public exchange of words with John Hume on 26 May. On the BBC Radio 4 programme *The World at One* Hume insisted he would talk to anyone, including loyalist paramilitaries, in the interest of securing peace. The SDLP leader then re-emphasized his absolute opposition to violence. Asked if he accepted Hume's word, Trimble replied: 'I think a very serious question mark – I am sorry to say – has to be placed against Mr Hume's motives, because he is persisting in talking to republican paramilitaries at a time when other people are anxious to see positive dialogue taking place.' When Hume repeated that he would talk to loyalist killers, Trimble interrupted: 'We draw the line at terrorists.' Hume then exploded: 'I don't need advice from unionist politicians who have not only talked to paramilitaries, they have sat down with them in order to achieve political objectives working together.'[30] The SDLP leader was clearly alluding to Trimble's past connections with Vanguard and the UWC strike.

Trimble's rather foolish and moralistic intervention illuminated a wider problem for unionists who were lecturing Hume on the folly of talking to terrorists. The Upper Bann MP's own chequered political past had seen him mixing with the leadership of loyalist organizations who were engaged in brutal ethnic slaughter. Trimble had been prudent enough to put further distance between himself and the UDA leadership from the time he was first elected as an MP. Nevertheless it seemed a bit rich for Trimble et al. to wag their fingers disapprovingly at Hume when they had very recently sat on Ulster Clubs grand committees and attended meetings with John McMichael, Andy Tyrie, Sam McClure and other leading figures in the loyalist underworld.

Despite the deep differences with the SDLP over Hume–Adams, Trimble backed his party's decision to accept the Secretary of State Patrick Mayhew's offer of a new round of talks in May. It was a measure of Trimble's growing stature in the party that he was cast as the spokesman to confirm that the UUP would enter new talks. 'Dialogue between ourselves and other parties has been under way for some time now,' he said.[31] In contrast to Trimble's flexibility, Ian Paisley's DUP announced on the same day that it was having nothing to do with the new phase of talks.

The relationship in Parliament between the nine Ulster Unionist MPs and John Major's government was critical in this period. Trimble's warning to the Tories that the UUP would use their nine votes to put maximum pressure on Major was not a hollow threat. In November 1992 the UUP fired a shot across Major's bows when all nine MPs voted against his handling of the Maastricht treaty on European integration. It was a sobering experience for Major, who survived by just three votes. Four months later Trimble again threatened to use the Unionists' newly acquired parliamentary muscle in a second Maastricht debate called by leading Eurosceptic Lord Tebbit. Although the UUP had not decided which way to vote, Trimble pointed out that in the past his party had taken its guide from Tory back-benchers who opposed European integration. Trimble's relations with the Tories in the first half of 1993 were raw, to say the least. He even found himself arguing with another old Vanguard comrade, David Burnside, who had left Northern Ireland for a glittering if somewhat controversial career in PR, eventually becoming British Airways' publicity director. Burnside, a convinced Thatcherite with strong links to the Tory high command in Smith Square, suggested that the UUP should merge with the Conservatives. He asserted that the best way to use the nine crucial votes was to rejoin the Conservatives: 'Unionists could, if they returned to the Conservative fold, exert real influence to have the Anglo–Irish Agreement replaced.'[32]

However, Trimble was in no mood to take such advice from an old friend: 'It would be an act of folly as well as a betrayal of our supporters to enter into a relationship with a Conservative Party which is not a unionist party. While the present Tory Government occasionally voices unionist sentiments, we are not convinced they are genuinely unionist.'[33] The UUP's mistrust of the Tories ran so deep that Trimble was eventually despatched to build bridges with the revamped Labour Party under John Smith.

That autumn paramilitary violence reached levels dangerously close to the carnage of the 1970s. October 1993 was particularly bloody – the worst month for casualties in seventeen years. On the 23rd an IRA bomb on Shankill Road killed nine Protestant civilians and the IRA bomber. The device had been intended to kill the UDA leadership, which normally met in an office above Frizzel's fish shop. The IRA's 'mistake' plunged Northern Ireland into a spiral of sectarian strife. A week later the UDA shot dead seven Catholics in a bar at Greysteel, a village just outside Derry city, in revenge for the Shankill massacre. For people living at the sharp end of sectarian violence it was impossible to imagine that progress was being made behind closed doors in Dublin, London and Belfast. But the UVF's secret dialogue with the Irish government via Chris Hudson was paying dividends. UVF envoys told Dublin there could be peace, and in October they even had a direct input into the drafting of Dick Spring's Six Principles which included a promise that there would be no constitutional change without the consent of the unionist majority. British intelligence was telling the British government that the IRA was slowly inching towards a ceasefire.

The reaction within unionism to these developments was confused. On 29 October, during a European summit in Brussels, Albert Reynolds and John Major met to discuss Northern Ireland. The two Prime Ministers issued a joint communiqué aimed as a direct message to Sinn Fein and the IRA. Major and Reynolds said that if violence was given up for good 'new doors could open'. Ian Paisley responded predictably by rejecting the Brussels statement. The UUP, however, took a more positive interpretation. Trimble said the communiqué meant that the Hume–Adams talks were now 'completely off the agenda'.[34] It was a mark of Trimble's growing influence in the party that it was he who had been chosen to deliver a response to the Major–Reynolds statement. The autumn of 1993 was one of the most critical periods in the development of the peace process, and the job of interpreting and responding to the political initiatives had passed to David Trimble.

But at a time when he was fast gaining a reputation in both London and Belfast as a most capable advocate of Ulster Unionism, Trimble set down the first of two political booby-traps for himself which were to blow up in his face just a few years later. On 20 November the *Daily Mail* reported that John Major would offer an amnesty to IRA and loyalist terrorists if there was a total cessation of violence. According to the report, all paramilitaries would receive a 'no prosecution' offer if they handed in their guns and bombs as part of the government's peace initiative. It added that known killers would not be included in any amnesty. Trimble responded by underlining the need for paramilitary murderers to serve the whole of their sentences. 'All those involved in shootings and bombings still have a debt due to society,' he wrote. 'We can't have peace without justice, and justice requires that those who have murdered and maimed will pay for their crimes.'[35] This moral absolutism on the question of paramilitary prisoners would haunt him throughout the rest of the peace process and provide Ian Paisley with lethal ammunition with which to attack the UUP.

The pact between Paisley and Molyneaux that had existed on and off since the Anglo–Irish Agreement was under severe strain at the end of 1993. The relationship between the DUP and UUP reached breaking point on 15 December when the British and Irish governments launched the Downing Street Declaration. The Declaration, which Albert Reynolds said offered a 'historic opportunity for peace', included a clause which stated that the British had no selfish, strategic or economic interest in remaining in Ireland. However, it ruled out republican demands the British should become 'persuaders' and urge unionists that their best option for the future lay in a United Ireland. The Declaration also accepted that constitutional change would only come about with the consent of the unionist majority. The important sections of the Declaration on unionist consent were drafted in concert with the Anglican Archbishop Robin Eames, the most senior Protestant clergyman in Ireland. With advice from Trimble, Molyneaux too was allowed to contribute to the Downing Street text. Although the Declaration was carefully crafted to entice republicans to come in from the cold, its assurances on consent were clearly enough for the Ulster Unionists.

Paisley, on the other hand, launched into a tirade of vituperation. In a letter to John Major written on the day the British and Irish governments signed the Downing Street Declaration, the DUP leader said:

> Before the latest victim of the IRA murder campaign has been buried, you have been making a deal to bring them to the conference table. . . . It is a tripartite agreement between Reynolds, the IRA and you. You have sold Ulster to buy off the fiendish republican scum and you are prepared to do this notorious deed with such speed that time is not even given for the Christian burial of their latest victim.[36]

From the earliest days of the peace process David Trimble and other leading Ulster Unionists had insisted that a ceasefire had to be followed by the surrender of illegal weapons in order to establish former paramilitaries' new democratic credentials. But in fact it was the Irish government in late 1993 that first set the decommissioning standard. On the day of the Declaration, Dick Spring told the Irish Parliament that an end to violence would involve terrorists handing over their arms: 'We are talking about the handing-up of arms and are insisting that it would not be simply a temporary cessation of violence to see what the political process offers. There can be no equivocation in relation to the determination of both governments in that regard.'[37]

Sinn Fein's response (or lack of it) to the Downing Street Declaration coloured Northern Ireland politics in the first half of 1994. The assessment from the UUP camp was gloomy. While Gerry Adams demanded 'clarification' of what the Declaration actually implied, Molyneaux concluded that the IRA had rejected it. In his eyes the Declaration was dead, and Trimble thought on the same lines. As the IRA and Sinn Fein prevaricated, Trimble urged the government to forget the Provos and switch from a political to a military solution. As a pragmatist, he believed that the Declaration was worth trying if it could woo the Provos into ending their violence, but there now seemed little likelihood of that. 'The Government have held the carrot. Now it is time for the stick. Militarily they should clobber the Provos. The Government has gone through the phase of following the advice of John Hume and Albert Reynolds. It was wrong and bad advice, where they are publicly negotiating with terrorists. It is time to quit that.'[38]

Trimble's hostility towards the Tories was bolstered by the revelations that the Conservatives had maintained a 'back channel' to the IRA ever since 1990. He now saw an opportunity to cultivate new links with senior figures in John Smith's Labour Party, including a young MP who had just been promoted to the front bench – Tony Blair. Trimble first came across Blair in March 1994 when the MP for Sedgefield was appointed Shadow Home Affairs spokesman. According to Trimble, Blair spoke frankly about the need to change the Labour Party's pro-nationalist policies on Northern Ireland towards a more balanced position that addressed unionist concerns. Trimble recalls that Blair told him prophetically that changing Labour's Ulster policy would mean sacking Kevin McNamara, the party's avowedly pro-nationalist Northern Ireland spokesman. The first meeting between Blair and Trimble was at the former's request.

I got this message from Blair to come and have a discussion with him about the Prevention of Terrorism Act. I checked with Molyneaux and he said, 'Go ahead.' So I arranged to see him and it became quite clear what he wanted. He said very openly that he wanted to change the Labour Party's stance on the PTA. He couldn't do it immediately but he would focus opposition to the PTA on specific items and ask the government to review them. He told me he had noticed that I had spoken the previous year on the PTA and had criticized some aspects of it such as exclusion orders and the lack of proper judicial procedures. Blair said he had noted these criticisms, which were exactly what he wanted to focus on. He asked me would I support him if he called for a review of the legislation on those matters I had criticized. I told him I would need to check with Jim Molyneaux, and then we chatted a bit. His obvious disapproval of Kevin McNamara came out in that conversation. When I went back to check, Molyneaux said yes.

That led to a meeting with John Smith, Tony Blair, Molyneaux and myself in the Labour leader's office, which was astonishing.

Molyneaux was engaged in one of these elliptical conversations in which he alluded to the Callaghan years, sending out the broad message to Smith that Molyneaux might do for Smith what he did for Jim Callaghan. Smith then sent a coded message back, emphasizing his position as someone from the West Coast of Scotland who understood Ulster Unionists. The thing that fascinated me most about sitting there listening to this was that Molyneaux had never actually spoken to John Smith before! That established a reasonable relationship between Blair and myself.[39]

Trimble and other Ulster Unionists had a growing belief that the Tories would eventually be voted out of power, and that it was wise to forge closer ties to Labour now. Within a year Kevin McNamara was dumped and Labour's oppositional stance to PTA was moderated; for Trimble these were clear signals that Smith and eventually Blair were men the UUP should cultivate.

By the middle of the year Trimble was earning a reputation not only as a formidable speaker in the Commons but also as the Ulster Unionists' most controversial parliamentary spokesman. On 29 May, as he was challenging the government over an alleged lack of action against the Belfast IRA, he used the cloak of parliamentary privilege – a device which goes back to King William's Glorious Revolution of 1688, when a Bill of Rights was issued for freedom of speech and debate within Parliament – to name three men who were alleged to be IRA commanders in Belfast: 'Why have there been no inquiries into these people? Why have they not been questioned? Who grants such immunity?'[40]

Trimble's decision to use parliamentary privilege to 'name and shame' alleged IRA leaders blew up a storm of controversy. His critics noted that Trimble was a trained lawyer who, they claimed, had discarded the due process of law and engaged in 'trial by Parlyvision'. Gerry Adams said naming the names was 'yet another example of unionist politicians hiding behind parliamentary privilege in an attempt to set nationalists up for assassination'.[41] Trimble, however, was unapologetic and threatened to name more alleged IRA leaders in the Commons.

The controversy and publicity generated by such stunts, alongside his prodigious output in both Parliament and the local press, convinced many in the UUP that Trimble was the coming man. For the nationalists, he was a hard-liner who was articulate and adept in Parliament was hardly a welcoming prospect. Even the tight-lipped, cautious conservatism of Molyneaux was infinitely prefer-able to this emerging advocate of robust unionism, they concluded.

Through June and July there were broad hints that the IRA was preparing to call a ceasefire. Their campaign, however, would end not with a whimper but rather with a series of carefully planned bangs. During the summer the Provos, employing a tactic they had not used since the early 1970s, attacked a number of Protestant-owned pubs in North and South Belfast. They also targeted several leading loyalists. On 10 July the IRA fired forty shots at the home of the DUP member for mid-Ulster, the Reverend William McCrea. A day later an IRA unit shot dead Roy Smallwoods, leader of the UDA's political wing, the Ulster Democratic Party. A fortnight after Smallwoods was assassinated the Provos killed two leading UDA men in South Belfast. Loyalist leaders suspected that there was more to the IRA's summer offensive than a simple round of score-settling before they turned off their violence. Using Ulster vernacular – 'Prods' in street slang are Protestants, while 'Taigs' is an ancient term of abuse used by Protestants for Catholics – David Ervine, the spokesman for the UVF-aligned Progressive Unionist Party, best summed up the loyalist analysis of the IRA's summer of provocation: 'Adams and McGuinness wanted to swan the world's stage while the Prods continued to kill Taigs. A loyalist ceasefire would, of course, screw that strategy up.'[42]

The IRA strategy of directly targeting loyalists and unionists in a bid to force them to over-react and not participate in the peace process was a tactic they would employ over and over again. The thinking according to republican sources was that if the unionists excluded themselves from political discussions after an IRA cease-fire, Sinn Fein could negotiate directly with the British government. In the absence of the unionists, Sinn Fein would be in a better position to drive forward a nationalist agenda in the talks and force the British to impose a settlement on unionism. Some unionists fell for the republican bait; others, particularly the loyalist paramilitary leadership, refused to bite.

On 31 August the IRA announced a 'complete cessation of military operations'. Many unionists were caught unawares by the statement. In fact Trimble himself had warned at the beginning of August that the government should not be strung along by rumours of a ceasefire. His attitude to an IRA cessation reflected the wider mood of mistrust inside unionism: 'Even if the IRA did announce one, it would be for purely cynical and tactical reasons.'[43] On the day of the announcement Trimble was driving through northern England on his way home after spending a summer holiday with his family in Europe. The previous night the Trimbles had stayed at their flat in London, where David heard the media speculation of an impending IRA statement. Now he kept the radio on to monitor events back at home. As he boarded the ferry at Stranraer he was anxious to get home quickly to prepare for a round of interviews the next day. It was a measure of his increasing prestige in the party that Glengall Street had selected him to be one of its chief spokesmen and to outline the UUP's assessment of the IRA cessation. According to his diary, Trimble was interviewed on special Ulster Television and BBC Northern Ireland programmes on the Thursday, Friday and Saturday after the IRA declaration.

The ceasefire statement was met with triumphant celebrations in republican strongholds such as West Belfast. To ordinary unionists watching their television screens it must have seemed that the cavalcades of republican supporters beeping car horns and waving tricolours as they drove past Sinn Fein's Belfast headquarters implied that the IRA had secured some sort of victory. Two days after the ceasefire an opinion poll in the *Belfast Telegraph* disclosed that 56 per cent of people in Northern Ireland believed the cessation had come about as a result of a secret deal with the British government; only 30 per cent believed the ceasefire was permanent. The scenes of joy outside Sinn Fein's Connolly House headquarters and the adulation heaped on leading Provos on the platform may have looked and sounded as if the republicans had just won a war, but this was light years from the truth.

In many ways, the triumphalism in West Belfast on 31 August was similar to the 'victory celebrations' of the Serbs in Belgrade following the end of the 1999 Kosovan war. The scenes of joy in both cases were orchestrated by propaganda machines to create the illusion that their respective ethnic wars had been won. The truth, of course, was that the Serbs had been heavily defeated. In the Irish case, the 'war' had simply ground to a halt with no clear victory for either the IRA or their loyalist opponents. The party mood in West

Belfast on ceasefire day was designed to keep the troops happy and mask any possible republican dissent. Illusions, none the less, are dangerous devices in Northern Ireland. In addition to reassuring their own supporters, Sinn Fein's 'victory' parades would also produce among the unionist community confusion and suspicion that John Major was selling them out.

The unionist political leadership was split over their interpretations of the IRA ceasefire. True to form, Ian Paisley was loud in his assertion that it was not permanent: 'The only way you could prove that there would be a permanent cessation is by the surrender of their killing machine, their Semtex stores, their guns, their mortars, and their equipment.' Jim Molyneaux, on the other hand, took a more sanguine view when he met John Major in Downing Street a day after the IRA statement: 'I'm very glad that there has been a halt to the killing in Northern Ireland and throughout the United Kingdom and I hope that those who have influence with the IRA will now be able to persuade them to take the next decisive step and make the halt permanent.'[44]

The different interpretations within unionism of what really lay behind the IRA ceasefire coloured the entire loyalist political landscape. Less than a month after the announcement, John Taylor had provoked a row within the party when he declared his gut instinct that the IRA campaign was over. The Strangford MP's views were highly significant, since he had been on the sharp end of republican violence. Taylor narrowly survived an Official IRA assassination bid in 1972 when he was ambushed in Armagh city and riddled with sub-machine-gun bullets. Some of them shattered his jawbone and he had to have extensive plastic surgery.

While Taylor believed the Provisional IRA's so-called armed struggle too was in effect over, Trimble at this stage was not so sure. A fortnight later he wrote:

Personally my view is that Sinn Fein–IRA are doing this as a tactical manoeuvre and will either resume the war or resume the conflict by different means at a future point. We are being told that the IRA are still recruiting, they're still trying to acquire means of intelligence and targeting people. That underlines the need for being very cautious, but the fact that there is no violence would encourage one to proceed cautiously.[45]

This kind of ceasefire-scepticism was well received in the galleries of the Ulster Unionists' right wing who, like Paisley, regarded the cessation as a sham.

One of Trimble's fellow MPs who was in the optimistic camp was the Reverend Martin Smyth. The member for South Belfast upset many on the right when he suggested that ultimately Sinn Fein would be involved in talks with the UUP. Although Trimble expressed grave reservations about Smyth's prediction, he kept open the door to talks with the IRA's political wing. He already knew there was a historical precedent with the Official IRA which had also declared a ceasefire, had dumped most of its violent nationalist ideology and had long engaged in dialogue with both the Ulster Unionists and Paisley's DUP, even while maintaining a small military wing for self-defence. So in the autumn of 1994 Trimble was urging caution while Smyth was adopting a more pragmatic approach. Yet, within four years the two MPs were to trade places regarding their respective attitudes over the intentions of the IRA and Sinn Fein.

Unionism was not just blinded by the headlights of the IRA ceasefire juggernaut, it was being torn apart all over the road by it. The UUP splits over how to respond to the cessation exposed an even deeper contradiction inside unionist ideology. The two sides can be roughly characterized as a dichotomy between the rational and emotional.

Rational unionism à la John Taylor, the loyalist paramilitary leadership and, much later in the peace process, David Trimble read the ceasefire as the IRA's grudging acceptance that it could not win the war. It concluded that unionists would have to stay inside the peace process, even if that meant sitting down to talks with Sinn Fein. By excluding themselves from the inevitable negotiations, unionist parties would leave the field wide open for Sinn Fein, the Dublin government and the SDLP to dictate the terms of a peace settlement. Rational unionism underpinned the loyalist ceasefire on 13 October 1994. The UVF and UDA took the view that to carry on their violence in the absence of an IRA campaign would only allow republicans to paint Protestants as the aggressors in the Ulster conflict.

The espousers of the new rational unionism had already began to woo the United States, whose involvement in the peace process they had previously regarded as unwelcome interference in Ulster's

internal affairs. Trimble's standing in the party was further en-
hanced when he was chosen, along with Jeffrey Donaldson who
was later to succeed Jim Molyneaux as the MP for Lagan Valley, to
take the Ulster Unionist message to the White House, where they
met Vice-President Al Gore. For Trimble it was the first of several
trips to Washington, and they enabled him to break the public-
relations monopoly long held by Irish nationalists. Observers who
travelled with Trimble on trips to the United States noted his
enthusiasm: 'Trimble is fascinated by America. I've never seen
him so happy and relaxed as much as when he is on Capitol Hill or
just hanging around Washington.'[46] His fascination with the USA
and his recognition of its impact on events in Northern Ireland
prompted him to suggest that Glengall Street should establish a
Unionist Information Centre in Washington as a foil to Sinn Fein's
slick propaganda machine there. This was one Trimble-led initiative to which Molyneaux readily agreed.

Emotional unionism cut across the rival unionist parties' bound-
aries. Its innate scepticism about the IRA ceasefire was driven by
both historical and moral objections. This wing of unionism
included not only Paisley's DUP but also many in the UUP along
with Robert McCartney, the very able and articulate Independent
Unionist barrister who was set to become a thorn in David
Trimble's side. Their historical objections *pace* John Taylor were
based on a view that the IRA would never really change its basic
ideological foundations. The terror group remained intact and was
only taking a breather from the conflict, they argued. Any government concessions flowing from the ceasefire were in reality a result
of the early 1990s' IRA campaign in London that created chaos
there and cost the British Exchequer billions of pounds. To emotional unionists, successive British governments had an ignoble
tradition of doing deals with the republican enemy behind Ulster
Protestant backs that dated to the time of the first Home Rule
crisis, in 1912–14.

Their historical suspicion about Britain's perfidy on the union
was compounded by moral revulsion at having to sit down with the
political representatives of IRA terrorism. Many emotional unionists had had family members, close friends or constituents murdered by the IRA. Evangelical Protestants in particular found the
prospect of looking across a negotiating table at Gerry Adams and
Martin McGuinness stomach-churning. For them to sit down with

Sinn Fein on the basis of what they saw as a tactical IRA ceasefire was an anathema to every principle they held dear. These unionists found it next to impossible even to enter the same discussions as the IRA and Sinn Fein leadership.

However, emotional unionists' principles only applied, it seemed, to republican terrorists. Throughout the present Troubles mainstream unionist politicians from all parties have sat down in smoke-filled rooms with the leaders of loyalist terror groups. They did so with Vanguard in 1972. They used loyalist terrorist muscle effectively in the UWC strike two years later and less successfully in the strike of 1977. DUP and UUP councillors attended the funerals of loyalist killers, in some cases carrying their coffins. Unionist MPs also shared platforms with loyalists known to be murderers, such as Billy 'King Rat' Wright, yet simultaneously denounced others for talking to IRA and Sinn Fein representatives. Their hypocrisy was at times quite extraordinary.

It is hard to discern exactly which side of the rational/emotional unionist divide David Trimble stood on in late 1994. The answer, probably, is that he was rather wisely keeping his options open. He was now leading the UUP from the front in their campaign for a new Northern Ireland Assembly. In the wake of the IRA ceasefire, Trimble still appeared to want to keep the door open for republicans. During a keynote speech to the Young Unionists' annual conference in Fivemiletown, Co. Tyrone, he said Sinn Fein could have a peaceful role in a new Assembly: 'It would be a major step forward for the peace process if Sinn Fein took their place in an Assembly alongside the constitutional parties. It would also sidestep the difficulties that are bound to occur if any attempt is made to insert them too quickly into some talks process.'[47] It was obvious that Trimble saw the Assembly as a means of putting a brake on Sinn Fein's entry to talks leading to an overall settlement. He clearly believed the Assembly would be an ideal testing ground to gauge Sinn Fein and the IRA's commitment to peaceful methods. His 'wait and see' approach was located somewhere between the rational and emotional unionist camps. Moreover, he was still seen as a man on the right of the party. The fact that the Young Unionists, who included many of the active cadres of right-wing Ulster Unionism, had invited him to give the main address at their conference proved that Trimble was regarded as a hard-headed, no-compromise, not-an-inch-further politician. Trimble the pragmatist versus Trimble the champion of the new right: would the real David Trimble please stand up?

There was another new issue that he latched on to after the IRA ceaesfire – paramilitary disarmament. This was to give him greater grief than even his earlier, rather absolutist statement about convicted paramilitary murderers having to serve out their full sentences. Just over a week after the IRA called off their 'armed struggle', Glengall Street gave Trimble the vital task of outlining the Ulster Unionists' response to this historic development. Trimble's critical position paper in the *Belfast Telegraph* was in part designed to reassure nervous unionist voters that there was no secret sell-out: 'Our judgement is that as things stand today there is no deal involving the British Government and the IRA, but there clearly is a deal between Adams, Hume and Reynolds'. Drawing from the pool of rational unionism, Trimble urged people not to be worried about the ceasefire: 'Peace is not a threat to us. If anything it is an advantage. The ceasefire, of course, is not peace but every peaceful day is a gain and the IRA will find little popular support for a return to violence, if loyalists do not give them an excuse.' His assertion that the Major government had not concocted a secret deal with the IRA in return for a ceasefire seems in hindsight to have been correct. Throughout the Hume–Adams discussions Sinn Fein had sought a commitment from Britain that it would act as a 'persuader' for Irish unity. But at no point did it appear that the Major administration would give that commitment or even comply with Gerry Adams's newly found support for joint London/Dublin authority over Northern Ireland.

Trimble, the assiduous student of Irish history, must also have noted that the IRA ceasefire and Sinn Fein's peace-speak of the mid-1990s were subtle shifts away from their United-Ireland-or-nothing pronouncements of the not so distant past. (At the 1986 Sinn Fein Ard Feis, for instance, Martin McGuinness told his fellow republicans at the party conference: 'Our position is clear and it will never, never, never change. The war against British rule must continue until freedom is achieved.' In the 1990s 'freedom' no longer necessarily implied a United Ireland, but rather some vague notion about cross-border bodies with executive powers as well as parity of esteem for nationalist culture inside Northern Ireland.) Trimble seemed to acknowledge that the Provos had retreated slightly from the Holy Grail of armed struggle. He claimed that the

IRA's prevarication over whether their ceasefire was permanent 'may be intended to conceal from their supporters that the IRA have abandoned their campaign without securing any of their core demands and have, as Bernadette McAliskey appears to believe, been defeated'.[48]

Yet the central thesis of Trimble's highly significant post-ceasefire analysis contained a demand for the IRA to be disarmed and run down. He wrote:

> Deeds include not just the continued absence of violence but, more importantly, dismantling the IRA military machine. One has not established a commitment to exclusively peaceful methods if one maintains a secret army. Soon the IRA arsenal must be effectively disposed of or surrendered. It is estimated that 50 to 60 tons remain of the Libyan shipments including some 700 submachine guns plus all the other material smuggled from the US and elsewhere. The best way of proving that there is a permanent cessation is to give these up. Until that happens, no one can honestly say they are confident that there has been a permanent cessation.[49]

In short, there had to be IRA decommissioning. This, for Trimble, was the test of the IRA's and Sinn Fein's peace credentials. His stance in the immediate post-ceasefire situation was that, without decommissioning, unionists would not engage in talks with republicans on Northern Ireland's future.

In his first four years as an MP Trimble had soared through the ranks of the Ulster Unionists to the point that, with the exception of Jim Molyneaux, he had become the party's chief spokesman on vital constitutional matters, especially important at this most unsettling of times for unionism. He was now very definitely a star in the ascendant. Yet his article laying down the condition of IRA decommissioning before talks had tied him to the rock of post-ceasefire politics. More than any other controversy, decommissioning would cast a spectral shadow over David Trimble's political career right up until the eve of the new century.

A Man for All Factions

It was a student revolt on his old campus that indirectly led to David Trimble taking control of the Ulster Unionist Party, for the plot to dethrone Jim Molyneaux was first mapped out over a table in the Cloisters restaurant at Queen's University Students' Union just before Christmas 1994. The impatient radicals planning Molyneaux's demise were Young Unionists who, just like their counterparts twenty-three years earlier, were fed up with what they saw as an inept and pedestrian leadership unable to cope at a time when unionism was in crisis. In their eyes, history was repeating itself. The new rebels included a politics student who belonged to the Young Unionists but, unknown to Glengall Street, was also a member of the Ulster Democratic Party – the UDA's political wing. Lee Reynolds was one of the new breed of Young Unionists who believed Molyneaux had surrendered too much ground, from the Anglo–Irish Agreement onwards, and would have to go. Every lunch hour Reynolds held court at what became known as 'the Unionist table'. The students' discussions centred on rumours of a British–Irish initiative which would give the Republic more say in Northern Ireland than even the hated Anglo–Irish Agreement. These right-wingers felt that Molyneaux had placed too much faith in John Major; that in reality the British government would grant major concessions to Dublin as a pay-off for the IRA ceasefire. They agreed that after sixteen years at the top Molyneaux would not exit the stage voluntarily – he would have to be pushed.

Reynolds recalls that one of the informal meetings at the Cloisters spilled over into the evening and the group of students retired to 103 Dunluce Avenue, home of one of their number, Graham Craig. There they hit upon the idea of a stalking-horse candidate, someone unlikely to defeat Molyneaux in a leadership challenge but who could deliver enough votes to embarrass the leader into early retirement. The plotters already had a model to work from. The beginning of the end came for Margaret Thatcher in November 1989 when a back-bencher, Sir Anthony Meyer, challenged for the Tory leadership. Although Meyer only received the votes of thirty-three MPs, his audacious attempt undermined her apparent invincibility and paved the way for a successful coup a year later. Reynolds agreed that he would put himself forward as the Irish stalking-horse if there were no other contenders – a bold step for a twenty-one-year-old newcomer to the political scene.

Politically speaking, Molyneaux had been limping along since the signing of the Anglo–Irish Agreement. His diplomatic, soft-spoken approach had simply not worked; Thatcher's government ploughed ahead with the Accord regardless of him. The Conservatives' next big constitutional move in post-ceasefire Northern Ireland cut the ground from beneath Molyneaux's feet and provided the opportunity for the radicals at Queen's to accelerate their assault upon his authority. On 1 February 1995 the *Times* published early extracts from the Irish and British governments' *Frameworks* document. The paper's claim that 'The British and Irish Governments have drawn up a document that brings the prospect of a United Ireland closer than it has been at any time since partition in 1920' set off alarm bells within the broad unionist family. *Frameworks* was finally launched publicly by John Major and the new Irish Prime Minister, John Bruton, on 22 February in Belfast. Although the actual document was not as bad for unionists as the extracts printed in the *Times* story three weeks earlier had suggested, some aspects of it genuinely frightened Ulster loyalists. A proposed North–South cooperation body would not come under the control of a Belfast-based Assembly but would emerge free-standing out of legislation in both Dublin and Belfast. In addition, the range of areas over which the cross-border body would have executive powers was enormous, including agriculture, fisheries, industrial development, consumer affairs, transport, energy, health, trade, social welfare, education and economic policy. Further areas would be examined in the near future and considered for incorporation. To many unionists this looked like a United Ireland in embryo form.

Although the wide range of areas covered by the cross-border institution suggested a take-over, the truth was that the two governments had not met Sinn Fein's key demand for a British timetable for withdrawal. Moreover, quite a number of the areas would have been impossible to harmonize in practice given the different taxation systems, organization of health and education expenditure, and competing industries in North and South. Yet, as always, impressions counted in the paranoid politics of Northern Ireland; and the impression amongst the unionist community was of a process designed to nudge the Province towards Southern control. A day after *Frameworks* was introduced, an acerbic graffiti writer left a message on a wall in the loyalist Ravenhill Road area of East Belfast: 'The Union is Safe – Ha Ha Ha.' It was an allusion to the Combined Loyalist Military Command's assertion the previous October that the union with Britain had not been tampered with as a reward for an IRA ceasefire. A growing number of unionists no longer felt the union was safe after 22 February.

One of the first people outside the student circle the Young Unionists at Queen's consulted was Gordon Lucy, Trimble's old friend and colleague from the Ulster Society. Reynolds was encouraged: 'Gordon was favourable to it. So we went out and canvassed opinion and the response that came back was favourable. There also seemed to be a lot of resentment against Molyneaux that stemmed from the time of the Anglo–Irish Agreement.'[1] Reynolds then leaked his decision to stand for the leadership at the 15 March AGM of the Ulster Unionist Council to an old Queen's acquaintance, Darwin Temple, a reporter on the local *Sunday Life* newspaper.

The Reynolds roadshow was launched on 14 March at a business centre off Belfast's Shankill Road and was chaired by Gordon Lucy. The youthful challenger ran his campaign on a shoestring. His parents bought him a suit for the press conferences and his girlfriend paid for a mobile phone. The contrast between Reynolds, the weedy, fresh-faced, bespectacled student with the sinister connections to the UDA's political wing and Molyneaux, the seventy-four-year-old World War II veteran with the tight lips, the sombre visage and the steady-as-she goes attitude to politics, could not have been greater. Party luminaries including MPs, councillors and the Glengall Street bureaucracy rallied around the much-respected leader who had been forced to face this humiliating contest with someone whom they regarded as an extremist upstart. On the other hand, Reynolds had managed to attract several figures on the UUP's hard right as well as a number of unionist intellectuals. His allies included Nelson McCausland, an ambitious councillor from North Belfast with hard-line Protestant fundamentalist views.

The presence of Gordon Lucy on the platform planted the idea in some minds that the secret hand of David Trimble lay behind this stalking-horse ploy. A number of Belfast UUP councillors, including Jim Rodgers, have accused him of orchestrating the leadership challenge. Reynolds, however, said the idea that Trimble masterminded his move was 'an absolute and total myth'.[2] In fact Reynolds has confirmed that Trimble tried desperately to get the leadership challenge stopped before the AGM:

> There was a famous telephone conversation where Trimble looked at the *Frameworks* document and told Gordon that Molyneaux was our last hope. He said to Gordon that if we had any chance of digging ourselves out of this hole then it would be done by Molyneaux – that we had to stick with Molyneaux. He played the loyalty man. I talked to Gordon the same day and I told him to convey a message to Trimble, which was basically 'Fuck off'. I thought it was a joke – he [Molyneaux] was the man who had just been done over and Trimble was telling us he was our last hope.[3]

Reynolds is unsure if his blunt answer to Trimble's plea for the stalking-horse to stay in the stable was ever conveyed to him. However, Gordon Lucy too is adamant that Trimble did his utmost to try to make Reynolds pull out.

> I had just come home after Lee's press launch and the phone rang. It was David, and he asked me if there was anything interesting in the news. I said, 'Yes, there's been a riot in the Maze prison – the UVF have been burning the place down.' Then David said to me, 'Is there anything else you want to tell me about, Gordon?' It was clear he was unhappy with what I had done. He accused me of a lack of political wisdom over the whole episode. He still claims Molyneaux would have gone anyway, and he also said that if anything we extended the period of his

rule. I don't accept that. Quite simply we thought that James Molyneaux had done it wrong twice – he'd got it wrong in 1985 and he'd got it wrong again over the publication of the *Frameworks* document. If you'd attended the Ulster Unionist conference in Carrickfergus at the end of 1994 there was Molyneaux saying that everything was all right and there were going to be no cross-border bodies. The one thing I'd like to stress is that Lee's campaign did not enjoy the support or backing of any senior Ulster Unionists I know, including David Trimble.[4]

Despite the absence of political heavyweights punching for his side, Lee Reynolds polled relatively well in the leadership contest. He was never going to win, but the 88 votes he received astonished party members and impartial observers alike. While Molyneaux had a massive majority with 521 votes, it was an inescapable fact that 15 per cent of the UUP's ruling body had voted for a complete outsider in defiance of their leader, all nine of the party's MPs, hundreds of councillors and the entire Glengall Street apparatus. Molyneaux tried to gloss over the surprising vote for Reynolds by claiming that those who had supported the stalking-horse were 'taking a kick at John Major through me'. Trimble may have thought that the whole exercise had been a wasteful and embarrassing distraction for the party. However, the reality was that Lee Reynolds had unintentionally kicked open a door for the Upper Bann MP. Molyneaux was now even more damaged. Within a few months of the challenge, Wee Jim was to get a visit from the men in suits at Glengall Street. Then he would be given the option to jump with grace before being pushed with ignomiy.

Trimble was well aware of the damage that the *Frameworks* document had inflicted on the UUP, particularly since Molyneaux had placed his trust in Major. On the day of its launch Trimble's reaction was one of fury because, like the other UUP MPs, he felt a deep sense of betrayal: 'It could not possibly be worse. I feel absolutely sick. I would almost have preferred that there was legislation for a United Ireland. At least we would know where we stood.' His temper grew worse throughout the day and reached boiling point during a discussion of *Frameworks* on Channel 4 news. Trimble, SDLP deputy leader Seamus Mallon and Tory MP Andrew Hunter sat around the table with a journalist in Westminster. Suddenly Sinn Fein's Martin McGuinness appeared on a television screen from an up-link in Derry to join the debate. Trimble, his face puce with rage, gathered up his papers, tore off his microphone and stormed out of the studio, shouting: 'You know, or should have known, that the policy of the Ulster Unionists is very clear; we do not share platforms with Sinn Fein/IRA.'[5]

It was a day when various unionist politicians interviewed about *Frameworks* had thumped tables in studios in Belfast, London and Dublin. Trimble's temperamental walk-out seemed to sum up the mood of anger infecting the entire unionist community. For viewers outside Northern Ireland it seemed to underline a widely held belief that all unionist politicians were hot-headed rabble-rousers who ran away from rational debate. Storming out of TV studios to avoid debate with Sinn Fein was counter-productive and only added grist to the republican propaganda mill.

Trimble's tough line – no negotiations with Sinn Fein until it was established that the IRA ceasefire was permanent – continued through the spring of 1995. By this stage he had been elevated to Molyneaux's top table, accompanying the leader to several key Downing Street meetings. At these discussions Trimble emphasized his hard-line stance that the UUP would not even talk to the Northern Ireland Political Development Minister, Michael Ancram, if the minister continued his ground-breaking dialogue with Sinn Fein. Ancram had agreed to hold talks with Sinn Fein leaders at Stormont on 10 May, much to the disquiet of unionists. Following the meeting, Trimble referred to Ancram as having been 'contaminated' by contact with Sinn Fein.

Molyneaux was still welcomed in Downing Street and constantly reassured by Major that no deal could be done without him. Nevertheless his grip on the reins of power inside the UUP had been slipping ever since the stalking-horse contest. His hold was further weakened at a by-election a month after the first British government–Sinn Fein negotiations.

The MP for North Down, the Independent Unionist Jim Kilfedder, had died just two days after Molyneaux, a long-time friend, had survived Reynolds's challenge, and his death provided an opening for one of Trimble's old adversaries to re-enter unionist politics. Bob McCartney, the brilliant barrister and former champion of the Campaign for Equal Citizenship, joined the fray. McCartney had once been the scourge of emotional unionism, arguing in a 1983 paper that the UUP needed to reach out to

Catholics and convince them that their economic and social future would be best served by the union. For McCartney, this entailed ditching the party's traditional link with the Orange Order as a vital first step in building a new secular unionism. The articulate and combative QC had also attacked Paisleyism. In 1981 during a unionist rally at Belfast City Hall he denounced the DUP leader as a 'fascist' and a 'fourth-rate Calvin trying to run a fifth-rate Geneva'. (Calvin established a base for fundamentalist Protestantism in Geneva.) McCartney was accusing Paisley of trying to do the same with Ulster. Fourteen years later, Paisley's party graciously stepped aside in North Down to enable McCartney to win the seat. The rapproachment came about because the former maintained a deeply sceptical line on the peace process. McCartney, an ardent integrationist, interpreted the IRA ceasefire as a purely tactical ploy. In his eyes, any concession was a reward for terrorist violence, particularly bombs in the City of London. While the UUP's response to the ceasefire wavered between accepting it as the genuine article and rejecting it as purely strategic, McCartney was in no doubt that the entire peace process was built on shifting sand.

Glengall Street feared and loathed McCartney. They knew that, unlike Paisley, he could reach middle-class Ulster Unionists and play on their genuine fears. In a record low turn-out of 38.8 per cent, at the by-election on 15 June McCartney won the seat with 10,124 votes; the Ulster Unionist candidate, Alan McFarland, came second. Defeat was bad enough, but Molyneaux's reaction was even worse. The UUP leader caused outrage among many middle-class unionists by attributing the low poll in North Down to the fact that it had 'suffered least from terrorist savagery and [the local electorate] can afford to forget people in the frontier counties'.[6] This gaffe would precipitate Molyneaux's retirement, but before he was forced to step down the whole of Northern Ireland was to be engulfed in a more serious controversy – the 'siege' of Drumcree.

The stand-off between Orange marchers and the security forces on the slopes of a hill beside an Anglican church on the outskirts of Portadown would propel David Trimble into the international spotlight. It began on 9 July after the RUC Chief Constable, Sir Hugh Annesley, decided to reroute a Portadown Orange Order parade away from the mainly nationalist Garvaghy Road area. Local Orangemen, who claimed this was the first time in two hundred years that they had been prevented from marching along their traditional route back into Portadown following a church service, refused to accept Sir Hugh's ruling. Thousands of fellow Orangemen rushed to Drumcree or organized impromptu protest rallies across Northern Ireland in solidarity. Loyalists blockaded main roads and even managed to shut down Larne, Northern Ireland's busiest sea port. The scenes of mass disruption were reminiscent of the UWC strike in 1974. And, as at the time of the UWC strike, one of the first and most robust supporters of loyalist direct action was David Trimble, who played a central negotiating role on behalf of the Orange Order at Drumcree. His involvement, including his call for Orangemen to stay put, went down well with the loyalist ultras in his constituency but angered senior RUC officers. Several of them privately labelled the local MP as irresponsible and claimed he had increased the tension by urging the protestors to remain on the Drumcree hill. When the march was first blocked, Trimble delivered an uncompromising message at a loyalist protest rally in the nearby Corcrain estate. The Orangemen, he told the meeting, would never surrender their right to march. He added that more demonstrators should 'muster' at the church – a clear call for the intensification of a potentially violent stand-off.

In the face of an imminent loyalist uprising, the government attempted to broker a compromise between the Portadown Orangemen and the Garvaghy Road Residents' Coalition led by former IRA prisoner Brendan McKenna. By 10 July there were some ten thousand Orangemen and their supporters facing a thousand police and troops. Twenty-four hours later, with Portadown having reached boiling point, a deal was hammered out. Five hundred local Orangemen would be allowed down the Garvaghy Road, but unaccompanied by the usual marching bands. In return the Portadown Orange Order agreed not to press for a second march scheduled to take place on the Twelfth – loyalism's most sacred day.

The relatively peaceful end to Drumcree in 1995, however, turned out to be as controversial as the original RUC decision to ban the parade. Trimble had informed Harold Gracey, Portadown's District Master, that he would not walk with them down the Garvaghy Road since he did not belong to the local Orange Order. Ian Paisley, who too had stood in solidarity with the Portadown Orangemen, was not entitled anyway, as he was not a member of the loyalist institution. Instead, Trimble drove back into the centre of Portadown to greet the five hundred marchers in their bowler hats and orange sashes when they completed their ten-minute walk down Garvaghy Road. At this stage Trimble did not want to do anything that might scupper the local agreement between the Orangemen, the RUC and local nationalists. He was not a Portadown Orangeman, and if he walked with Gracey nationalist residents would accuse them of breaking the compromise arrangement. If everything went according to plan, Trimble thought, the deal could become a paradigm for future contentious marches. Then, just as the parade passed under a colourfully decorated arch at the start of Carleton Street, the headquarters of the Portadown Orange Order, Trimble did something extraordinary.

The five hundred Orangemen were given a hero's welcome by their supporters in the narrow, terraced Protestant streets leading up to Carlton Street Orange Hall. As the parade was breaking up, a number of Orangemen and loyalists standing on the kerb shouted at Harold Gracey to come forward to be applauded for getting them down the disputed route. Then the bystanders started baying for Trimble and Paisley to follow him.

Trimble walked on to the street and grabbed Paisley by the hand. The Upper Bann MP lifted the DUP's leader's arm together with his and raised them in the air. The sight of the two rival unionist MPs walking, their arms held aloft, between two lines of wildly cheering and clapping loyalists was transmitted by television cameras around the world. This triumphal image caused deep resentment among nationalists across Ireland. Many in Portadown who had reluctantly agreed to a parade through their area were angry that Trimble and Paisley appeared to be rubbing nationalist noses in it: there was a widespread belief that the two unionist politicians were dancing a jig of victory on the Drumcree deal. That single victorious gesture compounded local nationalist determination that under no circumstances would any parade get down their road the following year.

The Paisley–Trimble 'dance down Carlton Street' was played over and over again on television in the aftermath of Drumcree. In the minds of the media, it had planted an idea of Trimble as someone every bit as hard-line and belligerent as Ian Paisley. The fall-out included Trimble being depicted in the UK press as a bigot in a bowler hat, an image used by a number of political cartoonists, particularly the *Guardian*'s Steve Bell, and replicated constantly throughout the peace process. The constant replaying of the Drumcree dance may seem slightly unfair to Trimble when compared to the treatment of other Northern Ireland politicians. Gerry Adams, after all, carried the coffin of Thomas Begley, the young IRA man who placed the bomb that killed nine Protestants, including several young children, at a fish shop on the Shankill Road just three years earlier. However, the presence of Adams at Begley's funeral was treated with less severity in the media than Trimble's Portadown walk with Paisley.

Some of Trimble's closest aides now stress that he looks back on this episode as a major blunder. So why did he risk the local agreement with nationalists and decide to walk hand-in-hand with a man who had been his enemy since his Vanguard days? Only now has Trimble finally explained that he simply wanted to protect his own electoral patch against Paisley. 'I'm afraid I was having some rather inglorious thoughts at the time. I was thinking, "This is my constituency and I'm not having that fella walking in front of me." So I thought to myself, "How do I make sure he doesn't walk in front of me?" So I grabbed his hand to keep him in his place. The images were a trifle unfortunate, but there we are.'[7]

Unfortunate or not, the affair sent shivers down the spines of the UUP's liberal wing. John Taylor believed it had been a gross mistake, describing it as 'counter-productive' and telling Trimble privately that he had made a serious error. 'I told him that when you achieve something you should not overplay your hand. You should sit back and keep quiet. David got carried away by Paisley.'[8]

A fortnight after Drumcree Trimble was embroiled in a second controversial march, this time involving republicans. On 30 July a thousand or so loyalists attempted to block a Sinn Fein march entering the centre of Lurgan, the second-largest town in his constituency. The loyalist counter-demonstration degenerated into violent clashes with the RUC. Although Trimble condemned the violence, he said the degree of it had been exaggerated; he defended his presence at the rally, insisting that he had tried to stop things spiralling out of control. His remarks drew him into a public row with one of his parliamentary colleagues. The MP for Fermanagh and South Tyrone, Ken Maginnis, who had served in the security forces, dismissed Trimble's claim that the violence had been insignificant, asserting that those who had organized the protest had played into the IRA's hands – an indirect jibe at Trimble. Maginnis accused the organizers of helping republicans to 'portray it as a denial of civil rights to Catholics. Internationally, it will go a considerable way to fostering support and sympathy for our enemies in the IRA.'[9]

Trimble, however, was unapologetic and accused Maginnis of being unaware of the facts on the ground in Lurgan. The public tiff between the two Ulster Unionist MPs shone light into a wider chasm within the party a year after the IRA ceasefire. Maginnis was the public face of the liberal wing of the party, while Trimble increasingly found himself on the harder edge of Ulster Unionism. The test as to which wing represented the majority thinking within the party was about to be set. On 28 August, one day after his seventy-fifth birthday, Jim Molyneaux finally resigned as leader of the UUP. His remaining few months at the helm had looked more like a stay of execution than someone enjoying the twilight of his political career. During Drumcree Molyneaux had been visited by a number of senior party officers, including the MEP Jim Nicholson and the UUP's honorary president Josias Cunningham, who had pressed Molyneaux as to when he might retire. He was left in little doubt that it was time for him to go.

Thanks to Drumcree, after Molyneaux and Paisley Trimble was now arguably the best-known unionist face in Westminster and among the parliamentary press corps. Three days after Molyneaux's resignation Trimble was invited by *The Independent* to write a unionist analysis of the IRA ceasefire one year on. In his article, coloured by his scepticism about the Provos' true intentions, he contended that there was a 'difference between the current uneasy, uncertain ceasefire and a permanent peace'. The mere fact that he had been commissioned to write the UUP's response emphasizes his growing stature in both Northern Ireland and London: speculation was rife that he would throw his hat into the leadership contest. But Molyneaux's departure had actually taken Trimble by surprise. He still believed the party needed Molyneaux, with all his parliamentary experience, to lead it.

On the day Molyneaux retired Trimble had a chance encounter which made him think that he should go for the job – up until then he had not been prepared to stand.

I went down into Lisburn just to go into Eason's to buy my newspapers. On the way in and out I was stopped by two delegates from the Lagan Valley constituency. One of them stopped me at the door, the other walked back with me to the car park. They both asked me if I was standing. Now I did not change my mind immediately, but I sort of thought, 'Whoops, maybe I could get the votes.' I then started to think about it seriously over the next few days, and then the phone calls started.[10]

The first person Trimble confided in was his wife, warning her, with an audacious display of confidence, that if he went for the leadership he would win. As with all his endeavours, Daphne pledged 100 per cent support, even though she later admitted that if he won life would never be the same again.

A day after his *Independent* article appeared, Trimble confirmed that he was in the leadership race. At a press conference in Belfast he revealed that he had been influenced to stand not only by his supporters but also by comments in the *Times* and the *Daily Telegraph*. Trimble quoted a *Telegraph* editorial, which said he had 'the highest national profile and the greatest gifts of presentation' of all five candidates. While Trimble was seen as the candidate riding in late from the right, there was also a broad hint during his campaign launch of the flexibility and pragmatism that he would display much later. If elected, he said, one of his first priorities would be to hold informal talks with the Irish Prime Minister, John Bruton.

Despite the complimentary remarks of the two English national newspapers, Trimble faced some formidable opponents. His main rival was John Taylor, his old room-mate at Westminster. Taylor, MP for Strangford and a former Stormont minister, was the most experienced political operator after Molyneaux. With his reputation for being both tough and flexible, he was seen as a man who could unite the liberals and hard-liners in the UUP. Party members, journalists and even the bookmakers tipped him as the likely winner. They also regarded Taylor's most dangerous challenge as coming from the left in the person of Ken Maginnis. The Fermanagh/South Tyrone MP was seen as the acceptable face of unionism internationally – someone who could sell the party's message in the Republic and on mainland Britain. Unlike Trimble,

Maginnis had not been tainted in the media's eyes by the Drumcree disturbances. The final two candidates were South Belfast MP Martin Smyth and Willie Ross, the MP for East Londonderry.

On the first weekend of the leadership battle, Taylor's odds were 7/4 favourite with Maginnis at 5/2, Trimble and Ross at 3/1 and Martin Smyth at 9/2. But Trimble, the dark horse, had one important advantage over his rivals – a well-run, slick and highly motivated campaign team. One of the first to offer his services was Gordon Lucy, who stressed that the key strategic move was to talk to as many as possible of the 860 delegates on the Ulster Unionist Council who were entitled to elect the leader. The vote was scheduled for 8 September so the team had to move fast to build their support base. Trimble acknowledges that the Young Unionist cadres he had trained in the Ulster Society were the shock troops of the battle. The team, headed by Lucy, included John Hunter and his brother Gareth, along with a number of students from Queen's. Interestingly, Lee Reynolds decided not to back Trimble and canvassed for Taylor.

Lucy found a list of all the delegates, including their home telephone numbers. To their surprise, the campaign team discovered that their man was not an outside bet. Lucy said:

> By ringing people up you are able to get a sense of where things would go. One of the things that came out most strongly from the telephone polling was that people were saying it's either Taylor or Trimble. More importantly, quite a few of them weren't telling us which one they were going to vote for. Early on we got a clear sense that this was a two-horse race, with Taylor still slightly in front. The ones that did tell us who they were voting said, 'We'll vote for Taylor this time and Trimble the next.' There was a lot of support for Trimble, but we didn't know whether it would translate into votes.[11]

Taylor's aide-de-camp for the contest was Steven King, an English-born Queen's politics graduate on the left of the party. King contrasted the Trimble team's ability to reach down to the party grass roots with their own operation, which concentrated on MPs, party officers and councillors. Trimble himself was prepared to talk directly to the electorate, which King believes the Taylor campaigners should have done too: 'They just had the nerve to call people up and say, "Hello, my name is David Trimble or Daphne Trimble." We didn't get involved in that. Taylor believed that if he could get the opinion formers on his side the rest would follow like sheep.'[12] The Taylor-waverers were in fact to play a vital role in determining the outcome. Although Trimble had a reputation in all sections of the party as a great communicator, as well as the admiration of hard-liners for his stance at Drumcree, good fortune played a key part in his triumph: two unexpected events helped propel him to victory in Belfast's Ulster Hall.

The first was a televised gaffe by Taylor. On the eve of the poll BBC Northern Ireland's current-affairs programme *Spotlight* devoted its entire slot to the leadership contest. During the debate among the candidates John Taylor took a side-swipe at Trimble, commenting about people prancing on the streets. Gordon Lucy could not believe their luck: 'I had a nagging suspicion that remark didn't do Taylor's campaign any favours. I just think it was too snide.'[13] Taylor's second blunder occurred behind closed doors, but almost everyone who was there on Friday, 9 September agrees it blew his chances of becoming leader. Stephen King had prepared a speech for Taylor to deliver on the night: 'It was very similar to Trimble's – there was the need to modernize the party, to safeguard the union, to draw out some points where Molyneaux had got it wrong, to broaden the party's appeal internationally by setting up offices in London and Dublin as well building up links with Christian Democrats in Europe.'[14] But just as he set off for the meeting Taylor ditched King's speech and told him he would rather speak to the delegates from the heart. His impulsiveness proved to be disastrous.

Since its inception the UUP has been a broad church made up of farmers, business leaders, trade unionists, young professionals, religious ministers, Orangemen, academics, housewives and students. The broadest spectrum of this alliance was represented at the Ulster Hall – a historic venue for loyalists given that this was where the Conservative leader Lord Randolph Churchill had launched the first campaign against Home Rule for Ireland in 1886. The loyalist battle cry of 'Ulster will fight and Ulster will be right' was first coined here. Regardless of the disparate backgrounds of the delegates, there was a consensus that Friday night that it was John Taylor's speech that squandered his chance of becoming leader. Supporters complained that he 'talked down to delegates and was very aloof'.[15] Taylor kept referring to newspapers which supported him, ranging from the *Times* to the *Ulster Newsletter*. There was a chink in his propaganda armour just waiting to be exploited. The nationalist Belfast daily the *Irish News* also recommended that the delegates should vote for Taylor, so when Trimble got up to speak he reminded delegates of that paper's support for his main rival. This reference played well with the delegates in the Ulster Hall, particularly the waverers because they reasoned that if northern nationalists à la *Irish News* wanted Taylor to win then Ulster Unionists had something to worry about.

Strategically placed near the stage, Stephen King cringed in his seat. He knew that Taylor was alienating waverers who were contemplating voting for him but then changed their minds midway. King commented: 'A lot of people came up to me afterwards and said they went to the Ulster Hall to vote for John Taylor and were insulted that he hadn't prepared anything. During the question-and-answer session with the delegates John was asked a question about women which he didn't seem to take seriously – I think that probably upset a number of people in the hall.'[16]

When the first round of votes was counted, prominent party members and journalists waiting outside for news were stunned. Trimble led with 287 votes, Taylor came second with 226, Maginnis polled 117, Ross got 116, and Smyth was eliminated having received just 60 votes. On the second round Trimble still led with 353 to Taylor's 255. Ross was then eliminated on 91 and Ken Maginnis bowed out. The third and final ballot confirmed the inevitable – Trimble was elected leader with 466 votes to Taylor's 333. Some delegates shook their head in disbelief. But Trimble's confident, perhaps even arrogant, prediction to his wife at the start of the contest had not been unfounded. There was something almost unnerving about his bravado.

Some of Taylor's shell-shocked supporters looked for excuses for why their man had been so decisively beaten by the outsider. The UUP's treasurer Jack Allen, having lost a Westminster nomination to Trimble, now had to swallow defeat once more. One of Taylor's chief advisers during the campaign, he is adamant that his candidate was double-crossed to the point of sabotage. 'I knew a lot of Young Unionists who said officially they were working for us but in reality were in the Trimble camp. I don't think David knew anything about this, but I suspect there was a lot of sabotage. For instance, our mail went out late and did not reach all the delegates. I have my suspicions, because a lot of those allegedly in our camp were closely associated with Trimble afterwards.'[17] There is no way now of proving or disproving Jack Allen's allegations, but they reflect the utter bewilderment that their candidate, the bookies' and pundits' favourite, was routed.

The prospect of David Trimble as leader was not a happy one for many on the liberal wing, such as Chris McGimpsey. 'My first reaction to his victory was deep disappointment and concern. Trimble had a lot of friends on the loony right.'[18] Yet the divisions in the Ulster Hall were not easily reduced to a simple left/right split, because scores of liberal members also voted for Trimble. They did so either as a reaction to Taylor's alienating speech on the night, or simply because they felt Trimble was a potential modernizer who could articulate the unionist cause better around the world. Ken Maginnis admits that he was 'completely stunned' by Trimble's win, but comforted by the fact that Taylor had been vanquished. Maginnis, firmly on the party's liberal wing, actually preferred Trimble to Taylor. 'I was very concerned that John Taylor would get it,' he said. 'I felt that he would be totally unpredictable, and did not have the intellectual energy to stay with the problem.'[19] Maginnis believes that many of his own supporters switched to the Upper Bann MP's camp when he himself looked likely to lose.

How important in pushing him towards victory was Trimble's presence at the siege of Drumcree? He believes it was the work of the cadres from the Ulster Society that really won the day. Among some factions of the UUP, the sight of Trimble hand-in-hand with Paisley (who is deeply disliked within many quarters of Ulster Unionism) played against him.

The antecedents of Trimble's present internal troubles lie partly in his victory that night at the Ulster Hall. He was seen as a man for all factions. On the one hand he could be the right wing's champion, whether at Drumcree or Lurgan: here at last was a unionist leader who was prepared to get his hands dirty and join in the fight. Some, on the other hand were impressed by his pragmatism and his willingness to go to Dublin, even to countenance talking to former IRA members. They pointed to the fact that the first leader of any political party, north or south of the Irish border, whom Trimble invited to Glengall Street was Proinsias De Rossa. The leader of the small Democratic Left Party had once been a member of the Official Sinn Fein and the Official IRA. The message Trimble transmitted to the world through his invitation to De Rossa encouraged rational unionism. To its followers, Trimble seemed to be saying that if De Rossa and the Officials could change, the new leader of Ulster Unionism could consider the prospect of other republicans following suit. Trimble acknowledges the symbolism of the De Rossa meeting, and has confirmed that it was designed not only to reach out to Dublin but also to send a message to the Provisionals that there were circumstances in which he would meet them. The conflicting signals that the new leader was sending out from Glengall Street encouraged some on the right to purge leading liberals and left others deeply suspicious about Trimble's long-term agenda.

Beyond the Byzantine intrigues of Ulster Unionism there was widespread concern, especially in the British and Irish media, at Trimble's election – was it a signal that the party was retreating into extremism? Their fears were compounded when, the day after his victory, the Orange Order awarded him a medal commemorating the siege of Drumcree. (For Ulster loyalists – the 'People of The Word' – there was major embarrassment when it emerged that a critical word on the medal had been misspelled as 'seige'.) The two main liberal/left British broadsheets, *The Independent* and the *Guardian*, threw their hands up in horror at the sight of the hero of Drumcree taking over from Molyneaux. Much of the Southern Irish media also expressed fears about the implications of Trimble's triumph. The Dublin *Sunday Business Post* said his victory 'has confirmed the fundamentally extreme nature of the politics favoured by the party's activists'.[20] In Northern Ireland there was panic among nationalist opinion. Jesuit priest Father Brian Lennon, who for years had campaigned for nationalist residents' rights in Portadown, described Trimble's election in the *Irish News* as 'deeply depressing' given that he was 'the least desirable candidate from a nationalist viewpoint'.[21] One of the few commentators to take a more balanced attitude to Trimble's win was not a journalist but Northern Ireland's leading chat-show host. Gerry Kelly, who fronted Ulster Television's *Kelly Live* show, praised Trimble as a 'pragmatic man who knows that he cannot rely on ranting on in the traditional anti-Dublin way of old'. Writing in the *People* newspaper Kelly, a Catholic, also noted the import of the Trimble–De

Rossa meeting. The TV star rounded on those sections of the press who had painted Trimble as simply a bigot in a bowler. 'It goes to prove that we can all too easily get trapped into perceptions given by the media.'[22]

The reaction among the Dublin political establishment was less benign. A senior official in the Irish Department of Foreign Affairs said Trimble's elevation to the leadership 'sent shivers down my spine. It brought me back to the old days of no-surrender unionism.'[23] The main opposition party, Fianna Fail, admitted it was disappointed at the outcome, having expected Taylor to come out on top. One Fianna Fail source described Trimble's style as 'somewhat extreme to say the least'.[24] Even in London there was exasperation in some Tory quarters that Trimble would be 'less amenable' than Molyneaux.[25]

In the midst of all these reactions Ruth Dudley Edwards received a letter from Trimble. It was sent in response to an article that she had written urging the new UUP leader not to purge the party's liberal wing and shift Ulster Unionism back to no-surrender politics. Trimble's reply was the clearest indication yet of his true intentions in the critical negotiations ahead – being prepared to do a deal with Irish nationalism. The letter, which Dudley Edwards keeps in her private collection, ends with a prophetic note: 'Don't worry, Ruth, all will become clear soon.'

Whatever Trimble's private reassurances to Ruth Dudley Edwards, the early months of his leadership were marked by growing militancy on the party's right-wing. Their first targets were Chris McGimpsey and Hazel Bradford – two of the party's honorary secretaries – who were seen as dangerously liberal and, in the former's case, had given away too much to the Republic during the Brooke–Mayhew talks. Within a matter of months McGimpsey and Bradford were voted out of their positions, thanks to the efforts of the hard-liners. McGimpsey was genuinely shocked at the language and posture of right-wingers in his own East Belfast Unionist Association: 'There was one Trimble supporter who quite publicly stated at a party meeting that the only people who should get on inside the UUP are those that hate Taigs. It was appalling stuff. They broke poor Hazel Bradford. She died a year after they voted her out. And Trimble didn't seem to want to know what was going on.'[26]

In North Belfast the sitting Ulster Unionist MP, Cecil Walker, faced a serious attempt by a right-wing caucus to deselect him from the seat. One of the front runners to replace Walker was Nelson McCausland, who described himself as a 'Trimble man'. Walker's allies, concerned that the North Belfast Unionist Association was retreating into extremism, branded the new right 'Trimble's Militant Tendency'[27] after the tactics of the British far left who infiltrated branches and purged liberals. Although McCausland's campaign was eventually seen off, those loyal to Walker were furious that the party leader had made no attempt to intervene, publicly stating that he would not interfere with the internal running of the North Belfast Association. It seemed to them that Trimble had given the new right the green light to oust Walker.

Trimble's right-wing friends were encouraged to position themselves to take over seats from those who had been his parliamentary enemies in the leadership battle. David Brewster has confirmed that two of Trimble's closest aides, the lawyers John Hunter and Drew Nelson, were being groomed by the leader for Westminster. According to Brewster, Trimble wanted Hunter to run against Willie Thompson for the nomination in the West Tyrone constituency; while Nelson was picked to deselect Martin Smyth, the MP for South Belfast. Brewster was even asked if he was interested in challenging Willie Ross for the East Londonderry seat, but declined. John Hunter was a key player for Trimble in his first year in the top post. Ever since he was elected to Parliament Hunter had tried to refashion the shy, awkward academic and give him a more common touch with his constituents. Trimble knew virtually nothing about sport, particularly soccer, so Hunter took him to a number of Irish League derby matches in his constituency. Although the two local teams, Portadown and Glenavon, were supported mainly by Protestants in mid-Ulster, the rivalry between the clubs has always been intense. Oblivious to the rivalries generated by football, Trimble would spend the first half of matches sitting with the Portadown directors and the second half with the Glenavon bosses. A man truly for all factions, even in a football stadium!

While circumstances would eventually destroy Trimble's close working relationship with both Hunter and Nelson, it is clear that in the early months of his leadership the rising sons of the UUP right were on the march. One of the first to face the wrath of the new right was Jim Wilson, the party's general secretary. Rumours were leaked to the newspapers that Trimble would dispense with Wilson's services given his ties to the *ancien régime* of Jim Molyneaux. Allegedly a P45 form, signifying the end of a contract of employment, was sent anonymously through the post and arrived on Wilson's desk at Glengall Street a few days after Trimble became leader. But Trimble stuck loyally with Wilson, despite having been on opposite camps in the Vanguard split nearly twenty years earlier.

The best that can be said about Trimble's role in all of this was that it exposed a major weakness in his style of leadership. His critics claim that he has a crippling inability to put down factions and suppress tendencies. His preference is to try to unite disparate wings of the party, which is seen as a fatal flaw by both left and right. He certainly did next to nothing to puncture the right's newly found confidence that he was their man and that they could now do what they liked. Here there are striking similarities with John Major, another politician beset by party factionalism. Major was initially marked out as the right wing's candidate, the man who could stop the hated Michael Heseltine becoming leader after Thatcher's fall. But Major the great white hope of the right ended up being a disappointment. The subsequent bitter insolence of the Euro-sceptics on the back benches flows from that sense of let-down. And, like Major, Trimble would find out soon enough that his old right-wing allies would become his most troublesome opponents.

Trimble's note to Ruth Dudley Edwards about all being revealed later was not just a throwaway remark to make a Dublin liberal sleep well at night. A mere twenty hours after his elevation to the leadership the right had failed to notice what were surely more dangerous signs of liberalism from Trimble's own lips. In an interview with BBC Northern Ireland Trimble hinted that he wanted to see an executive government with nationalists formed in the Province. Referring to his support for the Voluntary Coalition in 1975, he said:

It's something I'm quite comfortable with and will stand over and regard it as not being significantly different from the current policies of the Ulster Unionist Party, which are to adopt a system of proportionality in any future Assembly. Indeed, in theory you could argue that our present policies of proportionality are closer to power-sharing than the Coalition proposal that Bill Craig and I espoused in 1975 are.[28]

Trimble may have baulked at using the explicit term 'power-sharing', but in effect this was what he was suggesting as the way forward. Many on the UUP right clearly did not recognize the import of his remarks.

Only one unionist politician in the 'peace-sceptic' camp had an early appreciation of the possibility that Trimble might compromise on core principles. A week after the leadership election Trimble drove to Bob McCartney's home in Cultra on the North Down coast for a private meeting. He was interested to discover whether McCartney would come back into the UUP fold, and was keen to hear the MP's views on the political process. McCartney told Trimble that he would wait and see what differences emerged in their respective approaches to talks before considering rejoining the UUP. Then, as Trimble was leaving, the ever-eloquent and deeply secular McCartney drew a parallel from the Gospels to warn the UUP leader about the pitfalls ahead. McCartney compared the flattery that Trimble was inevitably going to receive from powerful forces around the world to Satan's temptation of Christ in the wilderness.

As we both stood on my doorstep I remember telling him, 'David, you are the leader of the largest party in Northern Ireland. There are people in London, Dublin and Washington who will take you to the top of the temple and say all this can be yours if you do what we want.' And given what has happened since, this is one piece of advice that David Trimble has never taken or even considered.[29]

One of unionism's core principles was not to speak directly to the Dublin government until the Irish Republic removed its territorial claim on Northern Ireland. On 2 October Trimble broke that taboo. Accompanied by John Taylor and Ken Maginnis, the UUP leader had lunch in government buildings with Irish Premier John Bruton. Although Trimble and Bruton disagreed over the early prospect of all-party talks including Sinn Fein, the two leaders opened up a regular channel of communication. Ian Paisley condemned the ground-breaking meeting, but Trimble defended it with a back reference to Sir James Craig. If Craig could negotiate Ulster's future with active IRA strategists like Michael Collins in the 1920s, then Trimble could hold discussions with the leader of the major Irish party (Fine Gael) probably most sympathetic to unionist fears seventy years later. On the same day as his historic lunch with Bruton, the *Irish Times* published a piece by Trimble that outlined the need for decommissioning. 'The reality is,' he wrote, 'that unionists after 25 years of bombing and shooting, do not trust IRA/Sinn Fein and will not sit down to discuss any constitutional proposals, so IRA/Sinn Fein have the ability to leave the table and begin murdering again when they do not get their way. Surely no one in their right mind would sit down to talk under these circumstances.' In other words – no guns, no talks. Unionists in the 'peace-sceptic' camp would hold David Trimble to these words over the next three years.

Towards the end of 1995 there were ominous signs that a return to violence was possible. Leading republicans, including Gerry Adams, warned of this reality if Sinn Fein demands for all-party talks were not met. Indeed, even during the build-up to President Clinton's visit to Belfast – aimed at putting a seal on the peace – the IRA in South Armagh was building the huge bomb which would usher in the end of the first ceasefire. Nationalist commentators have blamed the resumption of IRA violence on John Major refusing to move quickly to meet republican requests for round-table peace talks. They make the charge that David Trimble used his disproportionate parliamentary strength to exercise a veto over British government policy given Major's slender majority in the House of Commons. So was there a secret deal between Trimble and Major aimed at propping up the Tories and slowing down the pace of the peace process?

In the last Major cabinet unionism had an important ally in the Tory leader of the House of Lords, Viscount Cranborne. Given his family connections to the British establishment, which stretched back to the sixteenth century, Cranborne generated deep suspicion in nationalist quarters that he had used his influence on the unionists' behalf on the Major government. Cranborne, however, believes that Trimble did not need to hold a parliamentary gun to John Major's head; the Prime Minister's own back-benchers would have done that for him. In Cranborne's eyes, the reason for Major's caution on issues like all-party talks was actually more ideological than opportunistic:

> My feeling was that there was a strong Orange tinge which affected a substantial proportion of the Tory back-benchers in the House of Commons, and the presence of people like me was an inhibitor against more wholesome concessions. There was a hard core of strongly Orange/Unionist sympathisers, about sixty MPs at the core. But it took in everybody – there was widespread sympathy for the unionist cause.[30]

(Cranborne makes some telling comparisons between Jim Molyneaux's and David Trimble's styles of leadership. The former Tory cabinet minister describes Molyneaux as 'secretive, more in control and someone with the manners of a gentleman'. Trimble, however, is 'more unashamedly emotional but cleverer'.)

Ever since the autumn of 1995 the IRA ceasefire had been in danger of collapsing. The catalyst for a resumption of republican violence was the British government's response to an international report on decommissioning. The respected leader of the United States Senate, George Mitchell, headed the international body set up to explore the decommissioning question. His report, delivered on 24 January 1996, side-stepped the unionists' key precondition that guns had to be handed over before Sinn Fein and the loyalist parties were allowed into all-party talks. The Mitchell Report argued instead that decommissioning might take place during negotiations. Republicans had always viewed the unionist demand for decommissioning as tantamount to seeking the IRA's surrender. Unionists, on the other hand, saw disarmament as a central confidence-building measure to assure Ulster Protestants that the IRA's so-called war was well and truly over.

Nationalists were angered when John Major, speaking in the House of Commons in response to the Mitchell Report, stated that he accepted the report but saw no reason why the paramilitaries could not begin disarming. He then met a major demand that David Trimble had been making since the UUP leadership battle – legislation to hold Province-wide elections in the summer. John Hume could barely contain his anger, accusing Major of doing a back-door deal with Trimble and effectively binning the Mitchell Report. 'It would be utterly irresponsible for any party to play politics with the lives of those people in Northern Ireland. It would be particularly irresponsible for a government to try to buy votes to keep themselves in power.'[31] Outside Westminster, Gerry Adams claimed that John Major had simply swapped one precondition for another.

Trimble firmly rejects the notion that he extracted a heavy price from John Major for propping up the Tories. Observers inside his government feel that Major wanted to put the peace process on a slow track due to his innate caution, especially given recent RUC intelligence assessments that the IRA was reactivating terror units and was involved in a series of murders of drugs dealers in Northern Ireland. And if we are to believe Lord Cranborne, it seems the Prime Minister's reluctance to push the process too quickly would have been coloured more by the attitudes of his own back-benchers than by those of the Ulster Unionists, who were unreliable allies in Parliament. Senior government figures indicate that Major was worried about the loyalty of an estimated sixty Tory back-benchers who threatened to rebel if he pushed the Ulster Unionists too far. (The UUP's record in voting for the Major government was actually not that encouraging. While Molyneaux had secured nine UUP votes for Major in the crucial Maastricht debate in July 1993, the Ulster Unionists voted against the Tories on two other critical issues: VAT on fuel in December 1995, and BSE in 1996.)

One of the more encouraging signs for Trimble during the Mitchell Report debate was the attitude of the new leader of the Opposition, Tony Blair, who had become Labour leader following John Smith's death the previous May. Blair appeared to back Major's position despite the reaction of Labour's sister party in Northern Ireland, John Hume's SDLP. The new Labour leader told the Commons:

> At heart of this issue is how we move to all-party talks. For that to happen, there must be confidence – in particular, confidence among all the parties – that violence has gone for good and been replaced by democratic debate. May I therefore reiterate our support for the view that confidence cannot arise unless there is tangible evidence of the commitment to democratic means. We remain of the view that the simplest way of providing that tangible evidence is indeed the decommissioning of weapons.

It is right in itself. People of all communities want it. It will strike any reasonable person as sensible. Senator Mitchell says that it will not occur, in his view, before talks. May I stress that if that is so, it is incumbent upon those making it so to engage with other means of confidence building.[32]

The last section of Blair's response is important, given his implication that Major's decision to hold elections to a new Forum was a means of establishing that much-needed confidence. Trimble's aides noted Blair's speech and concluded that here was a man with whom they must start to do business. They concluded that, unlike the electorally weak and vacillating Major, the new Labour leader might act decisively and, like his predecessors in the 1970s, take a more robust line with republicanism.

The New Year of 1996 was to be the most testing time for David Trimble since becoming an MP. Two pivotal events put his leadership under severe strain: the end of the IRA ceasefire in February and the second siege of Drumcree five months later. In between, Trimble's UUP had to fight a Forum election and fend off criticism from his opponents inside unionism that he was preparing to bend on the issue of guns-before-talks with Sinn Fein.

The huge IRA bomb at London's Canary Wharf tower block on 9 February only confirmed unionist suspicions that the ceasefire had been nothing but a tactical sham. The end of the ceasefire caused maximum embarrassment for one of Trimble's rivals in the leadership contest, Ken Maginnis. The Fermanagh/South Tyrone MP generated controversy in his party by taking part in a face-to-face BBC television debate with Sinn Fein's national chairman, Mitchell McLaughlin, on the eve of the Canary Wharf attack. The next morning, just before the explosion, it was reported that Sinn Fein councillors were to be invited to Downing Street the following week as part of a local government delegation holding talks on the economy with Major.

On the night of the ceasefire breakdown, disaster had been averted on the loyalist Shankill Road when a Protestant man refused to hand over his car to a number of masked men. They were part of a freelance loyalist murder squad that was planning to carry out a number of sectarian assassinations in retaliation for the deaths caused by the IRA blast in London. The bravery of one individual gave the loyalist paramilitary leadership vital time to take control of their organizations and ensure there were no revenge attacks. The loyalist political parties called on the UVF and UDA not to retaliate and hence play into the IRA's hands. It was with this in mind that Trimble held his first public round of talks with the political representatives of loyalist terrorists just over a week after Canary Wharf. In two meetings with the UVF-aligned Progressive Unionist Party and the UDA-backed Ulster Democratic Party, Trimble urged their military wings not to respond. These discussions drew the inevitable and understandable charge of hypocrisy from nationalists. On the one hand, it made sense for the leader of Ulster Unionism to hold face-to-face talks with the loyalists if it helped secure their ceasefire. On the other, Trimble's refusal to meet Sinn Fein, a party with a large electoral mandate, because the IRA held on to all its weapons smacked of double standards.

While Trimble had scored a victory at Westminster by persuading Major of the need for elections in the summer, he suffered a major setback in Washington less than a week after Canary Wharf. During a visit to Capitol Hill on 12–13 February, which included a White House meeting with Bill Clinton, representatives of the US administration told Trimble that the President intended inviting Gerry Adams into the Oval Office. Trimble had argued that the Americans should refuse Adams a visa and ban Sinn Fein fund-raising activities in the USA as a result of the IRA ceasefire being broken. The President's spokesman, Mike McCurry, said Clinton would still meet Adams on the 14th because 'It is hard to imagine a process making progress towards peace without the active involvement of Sinn Fein'.[33] The White House was now in the unusual situation of being closer to Sinn Fein than even the Irish government, which had blocked more official meetings with Adams until the IRA ceasefire was restored.

Despite the 13 February rebuff Trimble continued to try to woo opinion formers on Capitol Hill. Although the importance of American influence on the peace process has been wildly exaggerated in some quarters, Trimble felt that unionism had always undersold its message in the United States. His brainchild the Unionist Information Office in Washington, staffed by an English-born party supporter, Anne Smith, is seen as a counter-balance to the slick PR machine that Sinn Fein runs. The UUP leader has also found financial backers among a number of American millionaires who have become sympathetic to the unionist position. Winning new friends in the United States business lobby is regarded as one of the main fruits of his research in the Ulster Society, which set out to demonstrate that there are probably as many Americans with Ulster or Scottish Protestant roots as there are with Irish Catholic antecedents.

Lobbying the White House seemed to have paid off a month later, when Clinton invited Trimble to the President's St Patrick's Day party. Gerry Adams was now the odd man out, with the doors to the Oval Office remaining closed to him. The previous year the roles had been reversed, with Adams inside the White House and the Ulster Unionists smouldering in isolation back in Belfast. Journalists who gathered at the White House saw Trimble arrive holding a Marks and Spencer's bag. It contained a gift for Clinton and his wife Hillary – His and Hers Ulster-made bathrobes. One of Trimble's entourage, Jeffrey Donaldson, who was coordinating the UUP's North American operation, said the present went down well with the Clintons. 'It beats a bowl of shamrocks any day,' Donaldson was heard to say. White House aides reported that Clinton asked for the robes to be taken up to his and Hillary's bedroom so that they could be used later that evening.

The promised elections to a Northern Ireland Forum were scheduled for 30 May. During the campaign Trimble's personal security was tightened considerably after RUC intelligence reported that the IRA considered him a high-profile target. Before the collapse of the IRA ceasefire his security had been scaled down and it took the personal intervention of John Major to make the RUC provide Trimble with a bullet-proof escort vehicle following the Canary Wharf bomb.

While Trimble might receive armed and armoured protection against the IRA, politically he was defenceless against rival unionists who accused him of being too soft on Dublin interference and naïve in his reliance on Major. Ian Paisley charged him with being 'in cahoots with the Dublin government'. The DUP were deeply suspicious, given Trimble's relations with John Bruton which included meetings at the Irish Prime Minister's home in Co. Meath. The allegations clearly hurt the UUP in the Forum elections: their overall share of the vote had dropped from 29.4 per cent in the 1993 local government elections to 24.2 per cent in the Forum. The DUP increased their overall vote and ended up with twenty-four seats, just six short of the UUP. The Forum result provided cold comfort for peace-optimists as extremist parties performed better than expected. While middle-ground parties like Alliance faltered, Sinn Fein continued to soar despite the breakdown of the IRA ceasefire. Sinn Fein's 15.5 per cent share was its best-ever performance in a Northern Ireland election. The Forum election set an alarming trend for Ulster Unionism over the next three years. The UUP's vote continued to decline in subsequent elections as an increasing number of unionist voters flocked to parties seen as more robust on the union and deeply sceptical about the entire peace process. The startling performance of Ian Paisley's DUP was a warning light to Trimble that his room for manoeuvre was heavily restricted. Unionist confidence in the peace process was ebbing away. Emotional unionism was gaining ground.

The divisions within rational and emotion unionism were publicly exposed on 13 June when Trimble engaged in a televised spat with the DUP's MP for Mid-Ulster, the Reverend William McCrea. Trimble had agreed that George Mitchell could act as independent chairman for the all-party talks (excluding Sinn Fein) scheduled for the end of the month at Castle Buildings in Stormont. As Trimble left the austere, razor-wire-ringed offices to meet the world's media, McCrea heckled him in front of the cameras. 'Ulster is not for sale,' McCrea cried out as Trimble gave an on-camera interview outlining why he could accept Mitchell. Trimble then characteristically lost his composure, went red in the face and told McCrea to 'calm down'. The DUP MP hit back: 'I am very calm. It is you that has the guilty conscience.' Trimble found himself coming under fire from two different fronts that day. Robert McCartney later attacked the UUP leader for being the 'union's weakest link' after accepting Mitchell as talks chairman.

Just two weeks after this public bickering, however, an unsolved dispute raised its ugly head again and temporarily united the feuding unionist family. The events at Drumcree in July 1996 were another blow to peace prospects in Northern Ireland, for loyalist marchers and nationalist residents staged a replay of the siege which had engulfed the entire Province in sectarian violence the year before. On 6 July the RUC had announced it was rerouting the Drumcree parade away from the Garvaghy Road. Nationalists viewed the decision as a litmus test of the RUC's alleged impartiality, while most unionists regarded it as a sop to violent republican agitators in Portadown. After the previous year's triumphalist scenes, including Trimble's merry dance with Paisley, nationalist residents were determined not to compromise – the RUC would simply have to hold the line. As early as April Trimble had warned that he intended to back the Portadown Orangemen. His defiance over Drumcree seemed to fly in the face of his stated intention to re-forge the historic link between the Ulster Unionist Party and the Orange Order as a means of making the party more acceptable to Catholics. This contradiction illuminates a central problem for Trimble in trying to reach out to Ulster's Catholics while main-taining his traditional support base, particularly in his Orange-dominated home constituency. In a sense Trimble's dilemma is similar to Tony Blair's – both are politicians who want to reform their parties and broaden their electoral bases, yet at the same risk losing their loyal supporters who feel betrayed by the changes the leaders have to make to win new voters.

At Drumcree in year II Trimble was being pulled so far back by the forces of traditional emotional unionism that he was spotted negotiating with extreme loyalists. For three days after the RUC Chief Constable's banning order, loyalist mobs went on the ram-page across Northern Ireland. The Orange Order, meanwhile, held impromptu protest marches all over the Province to show solidar-ity with the Drumcree brethren and attempt to stretch police and army resources to breaking point. Catholics living in vulnerable areas were attacked and expelled from their homes. The violence reached a crescendo on 8 July when the mid-Ulster UVF, defying the orders of their Belfast-based leadership, shot dead a Catholic taxi driver, Michael McGoldrick, in nearby Lurgan. The man who orchestrated much of the disturbances and gave the order for the murder was Billy Wright. Nicknamed King Rat, Wright was the leader of the UVF in Portadown and had headed one of Ulster's most notorious murder gangs. Articulate as well as hard-line, Wright played a central role at Drumcree, marshalling hundreds of young loyalists to face police lines on the hill outside the church. (McGoldrick's murder prompted the UVF's national leadership to expel Wright and his associates from the organization a matter of months after Drumcree. They had defied their own leadership and broken the ceasefire.)

The atmosphere on the hill during the second Drumcree siege parthy resembled that of a summer carnival, with tea stalls, hamburger and ice cream vans and pop tunes as well as Orange anthems blaring out from a turntable inside the church hall. But the other aspect was of a battleground, with menacing young loyalists facing razor wire, armed troops and barricades. Ruth Dudley Edwards travelled to Drumcree with Trimble during the siege to see for herself what the stand-off meant to the average unionist. She recalls the incongruous sight of Trimble's youngest child, Sarah, standing beside her father playing while he spoke to the *Daily Telegraph* on a mobile phone; he was warning the paper's chief leader writer of the dire consequences if the British government ordered police and troops to clear the Drumcree hill.

Trimble was concerned that the Orange Order was rapidly losing control of the situation. His fear was that Billy Wright and his cohorts were planning to attack police and troops. In his mind there was only one course of action – to talk to Wright. The UUP leader was well aware of who Wright was, since he had first met him in the Ulster Clubs movement in the mid-1980s. (It must be stressed that Wright was a minor figure in the movement with no direct links to the organization's leadership at the time.) Wright had also sought Trimble's assistance when he was elected as Upper Bann's MP. The Portadown UVF boss had gone to Trimble's constituency office to inform his local MP that a British Army battalion in Co. Armagh had put a bounty on his head. Naturally, at first Trimble did not believe the allegation, but he went to great lengths to find out if it was true. In the end it does seem there was substance to Wright's claims, although there was little that Trimble could do about the matter.[34]

At Drumcree on 10 July Trimble met with Wright inside the church hall, where the UVF commander warned him that loyalists would turn their guns on the Army and police if the security forces moved forward towards the Drumcree hill to clear it. Panicked by Wright's prediction, Trimble phoned the Secretary of State, Sir Patrick Mayhew, to tell him of the threat: 'I asked him to lower the temperature by stopping army manoeuvres in the area. By 7 p.m. or 8 p.m. there was a lowering of the police profile, and we believe army movements were down too.'[35] The UUP leader also tried to dampen down passions by approaching RUC lines close to the graveyard, where riot squad officers with helmets, visors, shields and guns were within eyeball contact of lines of Orangemen. A number of policemen had their guns loaded with plastic bullets, trained on the loyalists. Trimble walked through the graveyard, yelling at a senior officer to rein in his men. He later justified his action in the cemetery by claiming that the truculent stance of some of the riot squad was in danger of provoking the Orangemen further.

His justification for talking with Billy Wright was harder for nationalists to swallow. Trimble stresses that he told Wright over and over again that the Orange Order wanted no violence at Drumcree. 'To ignore his [Wright's] presence and impact on the situation would have been irresponsible and this against a background where the loyalist paramilitaries are on a ceasefire,' he explained.[36] Trimble may have been in an invidious position, but his parley with Wright would have been easier to understand if the Drumcree dispute had not centred on the Orangemen's refusal to talk to former terrorists. The Portadown Orange Order would not hold discussions with Garvaghy Road residents because their chief spokesman was Brendan McKenna, a former IRA prisoner. Yet the local MP, who was working on the Orange Order's behalf, was sitting down at Drumcree with Billy Wright, a known loyalist killer who had also served a prison sentence for loyalist terrorism. Trimble said that the reason he talked to Wright but not to McKenna was that the IRA ceasefire had been broken while the loyalist one remained intact. Yet in reality the loyalist ceasefire was not intact, but had been breached in Trimble's own constituency with the McGoldrick murder. Everyone who gathered at the Drumcree stand-off knew that the local Portadown UVF had been responsible for the killing just two days before Trimble met Wright. The UUP leader was probably duty-bound to speak with Wright if it meant calming things down at Drumcree. But doing so prompted nationalists once again to contrast his willingness to enter into dialogue with loyalist terrorists while refusing to meet Sinn Fein because of IRA violence. Even Ian Paisley and Robert McCartney said they would have avoided talking to Wright, recognizing that such a meeting would only be a propaganda coup for republicans. (Probably the best defence in favour of Trimble came from the lips of Billy Wright. The former loyalist prisoner said SDLP attacks on his MP were hypocritical given the three-year dialogue between John Hume's party and Sinn Fein, which had taken place while IRA violence intensified. Wright also claimed that he had met local SDLP councillors and had even held talks with Dublin government officials.)

The threat of loyalist violence at Drumcree and beyond forced the British government into an embarrassing U-turn. One day after the Trimble–Wright meeting, the RUC Chief Constable announced that the Orange parade would be allowed down the Garvaghy Road. One of the biggest considerations for Sir Hugh Annesley was advice from British Army representatives, who told him that troops could only stop the massed ranks of loyalists on the hill if they fired live rounds. In other words, the prospect of an 'Orange Bloody Sunday' loomed on the horizon. The subsequent reversal, which included forcing nationalists off the Garvaghy Road, with riot police battering protestors and firing plastic bullets at Catholic residents, provoked anger across Ireland. There were several days of vicious rioting in nationalist parts of the Province. On 13 July the SDLP withdrew from the Northern Ireland Forum in protest and John Bruton, a man seen as sympathetic to unionists, accused the British government of backing down in the face of loyalist threats. The two communities were more polarized than they had been since the 1981 hunger strike. Nationalist confidence in the RUC was at an all-time low. And on top of everything else, in Catholic eyes David Trimble emerged from the 1996 stand-off as the chief demon of Drumcree. Even John Major was understood to be furious with Trimble, who he thought had been 'weak and unreliable' in the crisis.[37]

On the day the SDLP walked out of the Forum Trimble spoke at a rally in Edenderry, a loyalist village in his constituency. He told several hundred Orangemen and their supporters that Drumcree marked a reverse in the years of retreat, concessions and surrender to republicanism. But while loyalists at Drumcree 1996 had won the battle, the upshot of their famous victory was defeat on the wider and more important fronts of Ulster's political war. Trimble had been winning new friends and gaining real influence in Washington throughout the spring. Following Drumcree, his Ulster Unionists lost the credibility they had patiently built up on Capitol Hill. For instance Congressman Bill Gilman, chairman of the International Relations Committee of the House of Representatives, wrote to Trimble warning him that he would not meet the UUP leader again until he called for an end to enforced Orange marches. More importantly, the pan-nationalist front which had split apart following Canary Wharf was pieced back together in response to Drumcree. Up until the stand-off Sinn Fein was reeling from a series of negative publicity blows, first over the Manchester bomb during the Euro '96 soccer tournament and then over the IRA murder of Irish police officer Jerry McCabe during a bungled bank robbery in Co. Limerick. However, the sights of Trimble talking to Billy Wright; of Orangemen marching defiantly through a Catholic area; and of the local residents being battered off the road by RUC riot police reversed opinion in the Irish Republic. During Drumcree, Sinn Fein was invited back to discussions with the government in Dublin, while the SDLP's Mark Durkan shared a platform with Martin McGuinness in Derry during a debate on the marching season. The underlying historical theme of unionism squandering its long-term advantages in pursuit of short-term gains was replicated at Drumcree in 1996. The IRA had been on the ropes after Canary Wharf, but Unionism rescued the Provos via the Orange antics in Portadown six months later. And David Trimble cannot be wholly exonerated for this dramatic reversal of fortunes.

Yet even as he was being berated in the British and Irish press as the hard-liners' hero at Drumcree, Trimble was planning a daring move that would lead to a decisive break between the UUP and the Tories. At the end of the summer he had been making tentative approaches to the Labour Party through the New Dialogue pressure group. New Dialogue is an alliance of Labour, Tory and Liberal Democrat MPs, left-wing activists, writers, academics and peace campaigners who set out to challenge Labour's traditional pro-United Ireland stance and tilt party policy towards a more balanced position. Trimble knew several of the group's leading figures including Gary Kent, a parliamentary researcher for the Labour MP Harry Barnes who had had a long interest in Northern Ireland affairs. Kent had organized several fringe meetings on Ulster at Labour conferences, to which speakers from the Orange Order, the Ulster Unionist Party and even the parties connected to loyalist paramilitaries had been invited. His aim had been to present the other side of the Northern Ireland story to counter the dominance of the pro-republican/nationalist tendency within Labour. However, until 1996 no Unionist leader had ever spoken at a Labour conference.

Ironically, the prime mover in the initiative to invite Trimble was one of the losers in the contest for UUP leader, Chris McGimpsey. The Belfast UUP councillor was a long-standing member of the

Unionist Labour Group inside the party. McGimpsey had friends across the British and Irish left and was ideally suited to put Trimble's name forward. McGimpsey and Kent approached the *New Statesman* magazine to ask them to sponsor a fringe event at which Trimble would make a historic address to Labour in Blackpool during their party conference. The *New Statesman*'s Ian Hargreaves agreed to co-host the meeting if there were a range of other speakers on the platform, while the magazine's PR company, Hobsbawn/Macauley, booked a room at the Imperial Hotel. McGimpsey then asked UUP headquarters to put up some money to pay for food and drinks at the fringe meeting; he was so exasperated when the party refused to give him the £240 requested, that the meeting was nearly cancelled.

> I knew that Labour would be in government within six months, and I thought that Trimble should go to Blackpool while Labour was still in opposition. It was important to take Labour seriously before Blair took power, but the Ulster Unionist Party took a very lazy attitude to this meeting. At first they were not even prepared to pay our bills at what I regarded as the most important party conference visit for a Unionist leader in more than twenty years.[38]

Trimble set out for Blackpool on 2 October from Belfast City Airport accompanied by a number of local reporters (including myself) and Richard Gordon, the head of one of Northern Ireland's leading lobby/PR agencies. The two men – Trimble the unionist and Gordon the representative of private business – personified the changing nature of New Labour. As he boarded the plane one of the journalists commented to Trimble on the red tie that he was wearing – a sop to Labour, perhaps? The remark drew no response. Hugh Jordan from Ireland's leading tabloid, the *Sunday World*, butted in to remind Trimble that New Labour had ditched 'The Red Flag'. 'You'd be better off with a grey tie at Labour conferences these days, David,' Hugh quipped.

On the approach to Blackpool a fog bank descended over the Lancashire coast, blotting out the town so that only the top of the resort's famous tower poked out of the clouds. The plane circled for almost fifty minutes, giving the reporters on board a chance to probe Trimble. One of the articles he was reading in the *Daily*

Telegraph predicted that the Tories were poised for an 'autumn of recovery' and that the Conservatives would dramatically cut Labour's huge lead in the opinion polls. Trimble was asked if he believed it. Shaking his head, he replied: 'Not a chance. The Tories look doomed.' Although confident that Labour would win the general election, Trimble dodged other questions about his courting of Blair. Instead he steered the conversation towards opera, vigorously denying that Richard Wagner was an anti-Semite. As the plane continued to circle precariously close to the tower, one of the reporters whispered to his colleagues: 'Oh God, it's the *Ring* cycle over Blackpool.'

With no sign of the fog lifting, the pilot diverted to Liverpool Airport. When the plane finally landed and the passengers disembarked, Trimble's mobile phone rang. The journalists huddled up close to him to hear the answer-message tone. Their suspicions were confirmed when a female voice was heard announcing: 'This is the Orange answer service. . . .' Trimble just grimaced when one of the reporters asked him if his choice of mobile-phone company was deliberate.

The fog over Blackpool was indeed a metaphor for Trimble's precarious foray into New Labour country. There was great uncertainty as to how his message might go down in a party on the verge of power. He was unsure how Labour would react to the UUP's years of courting the Tories and the recent hard-line reputation he had earned at Drumcree. He was clearly taking a gamble which Molyneaux and his predecessors would never have risked. As he walked into the Blackpool conference centre to pick up his pass delegates' jaws dropped at the sight of the first unionist leader ever to attend a Labour conference. Yet his visit seemed to pay further dividends. Unionist liberals like Chris McGimpsey were delighted with Trimble's speech during a debate with the SDLP's Denis Haughey, which he described as 'balanced and pitched perfectly to ordinary Labour members'. Gary Kent thought Trimble's address had shattered a number of myths widely believed by senior Labour MPs. 'They thought he was terribly right-wing – they only saw the images at Drumcree and not the other side to his personality.' In addition Trimble was able to network with a range of opinion formers at the conference, in particular the former editor of *The Independent*, Andrew Marr, who took a more sympathetic position towards unionism than most national editors.

After the debate there were photo-calls with *New Statesman* proprietor Geoffrey Robinson and Shadow Chancellor Gordon Brown at the Imperial Hotel before a wine reception hosted by Tony Blair. During the photo-call with Robinson outside the Labour conference centre Trimble was asked by a female police officer to move on to the pavement as he was blocking the road. Gary Kent remembers that Trimble immediately turned to the policewoman and said: 'Where I come from we're used to blocking the road.'[39] Kent hoped the Labour hierarchy was not in earshot for that remark.

Trimble drew most comfort from Blair's keynote speech the following day. Blair angered Sinn Fein representatives attending the conference when he warned republicans that 'as members of the human race' they should take the path of peace. Moreover, the Labour leader vowed that if the IRA did not call a ceasefire he could carry on the search for peace 'without you'.

Trimble's trip to Blackpool had laid the foundations of a new relationship with the Labour Party. After more than a century of being umbilically connected to the Conservative Party, Trimble had finally cut the last tentative link between Smith Square in London and Glengall Street in Belfast. He had many people to thank for the success of his ground-breaking visit, but Chris McGimpsey, in particular had kept the Unionist Labour torch alight for decades while his party leadership fawned all over the Tories. Yet as he was leaving the fringe meeting to attend Blair's party Trimble demonstrated characteristic inattention towards those who had helped him most. He walked out of the room accompanied by David Burnside (the malleable Tory spin doctor now also urging Trimble to woo Blair!) and hardly even acknowledged McGimpsey's role: 'I remember as David was leaving I called to him and said, "Leader, you were fucking brilliant – that was a perfect speech. All he said was "Thanks very much", and he and Burnside just walked out the door and I never saw him for the rest of the conference.'[40]

Despite his overtures to Labour, right up to the late winter of 1997 Trimble's parliamentary team failed to deliver the knockout blow to John Major's government. The UUP MPs abstained in a crucial vote on 17 February when Labour attempted to censure Agriculture Minister Douglas Hogg over his handling of the BSE crisis. John Hume accused Major of doing a secret deal with the

Ulster Unionists, although there is little evidence of what exactly Trimble had extracted from the Prime Minister as a price for abstention. Downing Street believed Hume had his own party-political reasons for putting about the rumours, given the imminent general election. As in 1992, the election had put political progress in Northern Ireland on hold. It was clear by early spring that Labour would be swept into power with a massive majority. Observers had the evidence of heavy Tory defeats in by-elections to convince them that there would be no hung Parliament. Ken Maginnis contrasted Trimble's relationships with Major and Blair. According to Maginnis, Trimble 'got on tolerably but very well' with Major, whereas his friendship with Blair was 'much closer'. Maginnis believes that Trimble's decision to open a dialogue with New Labour was one of his better pieces of judgement.[41]

It was the young man whose audacious challenge to Molyneaux had inadvertently helped Trimble become Ulster Unionism's leader who pointed up his chief mistake in the dying months of Conservative rule. 'He didn't kick the Tories out when we had the chance, and that was stupid. The UUP threatened to do it but failed to do anything, and that made us look weak. If Trimble and co. had moved quicker and forced an early general election then Labour would not have had such a massive majority in Parliament. The party would have had more leverage.'[42] Lee Reynolds's assessment of the UUP's parliamentary strategy was insightful, since Trimble would soon have to deal with a Prime Minister with the largest majority in British political history.

Whenever Reynolds's right-wing coterie tries to annoy him, they remind him about his role in leading Trimble to power in the party. He confesses that sometimes even he too wakes up at four o'clock in the morning and wonders how he managed to get rid of one weak leader, James Molyneaux, only to pave the way for another one, David Trimble.

Towards a Long Good Friday

Around 11.45 on the morning of 16 June 1997 two community policemen, Constables John Graham and David Johnston, were walking through the centre of Lurgan in Co. Armagh chatting to local shopkeepers. As they passed by Church Walk, just yards from the town's RUC station, a number of gunmen approached them. Two masked terrorists fired several shots into the officers' bodies, and according to eyewitnesses the killers then pumped more bullets into them as they lay on the ground dying. The clinical nature of the double murder clearly indicated that the IRA was responsible, and many in the Northern Ireland media were bewildered. This was just over a month after Tony Blair's landslide victory over the Tories. Blair had offered Sinn Fein a chance to join his 'peace train' if the IRA declared a second ceasefire. All the signals emitted by republicans throughout May and early June suggested that the Provos were on the brink of calling a new cessation. And then, inexplicably to some observers, came the Lurgan murders.

Some commentators put the murders down to local difficulties between a young Lurgan republican and the RUC in Co. Armagh, alluding to a grudge that the man had harboured against police officers in the town for several years. But the real reason had more to do with cynical strategy than with personal revenge. These killings had to be seen in the context of the IRA ceasefire almost a month later. For the main political target of the IRA on that hot day in Lurgan was actually David Trimble. The location for the murder, after all, was hardly a coincidence. The officers were gunned down in the heart of his constituency, at a time when the Ulster Unionist leader was ruminating on whether to enter talks with Sinn Fein in the event of a renewed IRA ceasefire. Trimble himself was certain that the killings were designed to sicken the unionist community so much that the UUP would find it practically impossible to move into discussions with republicans. He remains convinced that the murder of Constables Johnston and Graham was another blatant example of armed propaganda: 'Those killings were no accident, no accident at all. Sinn Fein's game plan with regard to the talks was based on the assumption that unionists would walk out. The murders were to make it harder for us to remain inside the political process.'[1]

His analysis of the IRA's motives was shared by a former Provo who has since become his key independent (and unpaid) adviser on Irish republicanism – Sean O'Callaghan. The killer-turned-police-agent first met Trimble just a month after leaving Maghaberry jail in December 1996. O'Callaghan was introduced to him by Ruth Dudley Edwards in a central London wine bar following a Unionist Information Office meeting at Westminster. Although O'Callaghan sensed that Trimble was initially very suspicious of him, their discussion had been cordial and centred on how the ex-Provo could help the Ulster Unionists interpret republican strategy. Even while in jail O'Callaghan had forged relations with an unlikely band of historians, journalists, MPs and grandees of the Conservative Party. Before his release he had corresponded over several years, for instance, with Lord Cranborne, promising the Conservative leader in the Lords that he would do all he could to thwart Sinn Fein and the IRA's political aims. Dudley Edwards arranged a series of meetings between Trimble, Jeffrey Donaldson and O'Callaghan in the spring and early summer of 1997. The Unionists met O'Callaghan at Westminster as well as in London restaurants, hotels and bars to work out what moves the Provos were planning next. Following the murder of the RUC constables in Lurgan and the revulsion it provoked throughout the unionist community (at Constable Graham's funeral the Presbyterian Moderator, Dr Sam Hutchinson, called on Tony Blair to rethink his policy of wooing Sinn Fein back to the talks), O'Callaghan was concerned that the UUP was falling into a carefully laid republican trap.

About a fortnight after the murders he sent Trimble a fax. O'Callaghan recalls:

I basically urged him not to walk out of the talks, because at that time he was on the edge of going. It was getting very difficult for him to remain, even though he didn't want to go. In the fax I told him that he couldn't allow himself to be stampeded into doing something rash – he had to take control of the situation. He should stay in the process and open up dialogue with the Catholic Church, have consultations with his own party and other unionists and nationalists. My advice was to have a stalling strategy, to take time out to consult.[2]

Senior UUP allies of Trimble's admit that O'Callaghan's advice, which came shortly before the IRA declared their second ceasefire on 20 July, was invaluable. O'Callaghan's idea of a consultation process bought time for Trimble to persuade his party to stay in the talks even if Sinn Fein was invited by Blair to join them. He is in no doubt that the Lurgan killings and the ceasefire a month later were part of a carefully honed plan to flush all the unionist parties out of the talks.

O'Callaghan was adamant that, if Trimble stayed in, the republican game-plan would be seriously compromised:

The whole republican project is based on the assumption that the unionists would all walk out together once Sinn Fein entered the negotiations. Trimble didn't walk out, and they have been caught ever since. Knowing the Provo leadership, I think this has come as a shock to them because what they really want is unionists out of the equation so they can negotiate with the British and force London to impose a settlement on the unionists. Republicans have a very clichéd programmatic vision of unionists. With a few exceptions like Tom Hartley and Jim Gibney [a Sinn Fein councillor and a leading republican strategist] they think the unionists are political Neanderthals. Martin McGuinness, for instance, has no experience of unionists given that he comes from Derry, and Adams, while having some contact with them, patronizes unionists. I told Trimble that he must get in there and negotiate with them. He would find out they are not super-strategists after all.[3]

Unionists of all hues could have been forgiven for dismissing the chances of a second IRA cessation in early July. Trimble himself was sceptical that the IRA would declare another ceasefire in an atmosphere of mounting sectarian tension; in fact when the British government suggested that another ceasefire might be in the offing he actually dismissed the idea as 'wishful thinking' less than a week before it was actually announced.[4] After all, the third Drumcree stand-off had ended with the RUC forcing the Orange march down the Garvaghy Road by sealing off the nationalist enclave. The security operation in Portadown had culminated in violent clashes between nationalist residents and RUC riot squad officers. As the Orangemen passed through the mainly nationalist road, some residents, penned into their streets by RUC Land Rovers and squads of riot police, had chanted: 'No ceasefire! No ceasefire!' For several days republican areas had erupted in anger, with IRA gun attacks on the police and widespread destruction of property in towns like Derry. It seemed that the entire republican community was against another ceasefire.

A week later Northern Ireland appeared to be edging towards wider communal violence as a result of a number of contentious marches scheduled for the Twelfth of July. There were threats that, if the government banned an Orange march from the Lower Ormeau Road, the entire Belfast Twelfth demonstration would converge on two bridges leading to the Lower Ormeau Road, where loyalists would confront RUC lines blocking their route. The prospect of thousands of Orangemen and their supporters gathering at both entrances to the Lower Ormeau was potentially disastrous. But on the eve of the most important day in the loyalist marching calender, in the interests of peace and stability the Orange Order unilaterally called off all its contentious parades. In places like the Ballynafeigh Orange Hall in the Upper Ormeau Road, that decision was enforced by mainstream loyalist paramilitaries, who protected local Orangemen from loyalist ultras who wanted outright confrontation. The Orange Order's surprising move prevented widespread violence on the Twelfth and, paradoxically, made it easier for the IRA to declare their ceasefire a week later. Trimble was also relieved because the prospect of Province-wide disturbances with Orangemen getting injured or killed would have made it impossible for any unionist leader to join all-party talks that included Sinn Fein.

Once again the UUP leader had Sean O'Callaghan to thank for giving critical strategic advice. Lord Cranborne and O'Callaghan had travelled to Northern Ireland at the beginning of the 1997 marching season to hold secret meetings with Orange Order leaders: Denis Watson, head of the Order in Co. Armagh, the Reverend William Bingham, chaplain to the Order in that county, and Robert Saulters, Grand Master of the Orange Order through-out Ireland. As with Trimble, O'Callaghan warned the Orangemen that they would be falling into a complex trap if they refused to compromise on the parades issue. While he failed to achieve any breakthrough on Drumcree, it was partly O'Callaghan's counsel which prompted the Orange Order to cancel their other contro-versial marches planned for the Twelfth.

O'Callaghan also collaborated during the marching season with that arch-sceptic of the peace process, Robert McCartney. He said McCartney had contacted him and asked for a meeting, during which the UK Unionist leader showed O'Callaghan an article about Drumcree that he had written.

> His proposal, which was published in the *Belfast Telegraph*, was that once the right to walk down that road was upheld the Orangemen should not exercise it. They should walk away having established the principle that they were entitled to march. I have to admit Bob was very straightforward and helpful. He said to me, 'Here's the piece I've written. If you think it's rubbish I'll throw it in the bin.' I read it and told him this was the kind of thing we were looking for.[5]

Twenty-four hours after the IRA ceasefire was restored, Trimble gave his strongest public hint yet that he would not walk away from the talks. As he went into 10 Downing Street to meet Tony Blair, Trimble even declined to rule out the possibility of facing Sinn Fein across the negotiating table. At that stage he still regarded the IRA ceasefire as a tactical sham but added prophetically: 'We are not going to walk out, but we'll continue to try and find an agreement. We'll continue to do that'.[6]

The second IRA ceasefire had placed Trimble in a precarious position. He was aware that the balance of forces at Westminster was now heavily realigned against unionism. The UUP leader no longer had any parliamentary leverage over the British govern-ment, given Labour's unprecedented 287-seat Commons majority. And despite his warm relationship with Blair, dating back to the days of John Smith's leadership, Trimble realized that the new Prime Minister was in a strong enough position to gamble on the IRA ceasefire. Blair was clearly going to grant Sinn Fein the benefit of the doubt and, in the light of these new political realities,

Trimble concluded that there was no point fuming on the sidelines and crying sell-out like Paisley and McCartney.

He took the same attitude with regard to political changes in the Republic. The outgoing Irish Premier, John Bruton, had been traditionally viewed in Belfast as a man who genuinely tried to understand unionist fears and concerns. Bruton's Rainbow Coalition had contained the Democratic Left leader Proinsias De Rossa, whom Trimble had long admired as someone who appreciated the unionist position. Yet by late spring it had become obvious that Bruton's government was heading for defeat in the forthcoming general election. Trimble had therefore moved fast to court the man certain to replace him as Taoiseach, the Fianna Fail leader Bertie Ahern. In public Ahern may have sounded more partisan and pro-Northern nationalist, but Trimble suspected this Dublin-born political fixer was a non-ideological pragmatist in private.

On the surface, the election of Ahern's government on 28 June fuelled the widespread belief among nationalists and republicans in Northern Ireland that things were moving in their direction in Dublin. Apart from having their first Irish MP elected to the Dail since the hunger strike, Sinn Fein's leadership believed they had a reliable new ally in the Irish government, which they felt would push for a pan-nationalist stance at future talks with the British and unionists. In short, Sinn Fein believed Bertie was their man. Some republican sceptics, however, cautioned against Gerry Adams's enthusiasm for him. They pointed out that Fianna Fail, despite all its republican rhetoric, was historically more ruthless and duplicitous in repressing the IRA and Sinn Fein than was the more unionist-friendly Fine Gael. After all, had it not been the Fianna Fail Premier Eamon de Valera who had executed IRA volunteers, in league with Nazi agents in Ireland, when they challenged the authority of the Southern state during World War II?

Trimble knew his Irish history too. Through an intermediary in Dublin, he set up three secret meetings with Ahern before the Irish general election to outline unionist fears about a future Fianna Fail government. The meetings, held in Armagh city, established a pragmatic working relationship between the two men. While Ahern made no promises to the UUP leader, Sean O'Callaghan recalls that, when he asked Trimble in the summer if he could do a deal with republicans, he replied: 'I can definitely do a deal with Bertie.'[7] (In public, however, Trimble stalled on the question of a meeting in Dublin with the new Irish Prime Minister. Illusions had to be maintained if Trimble was to calm a nervous and suspicious party.)

Unionists had been seething with resentment towards the government since 16 July (before the IRA ceasefire), when it was disclosed that the Northern Ireland Office had sent a secret letter to Sinn Fein and had two telephone calls with its leaders despite the ministerial ban on contacts with republicans that had been put in place after the Lurgan murders. Trimble was coming under intense pressure to quit the talks as it became clearer that Blair and his new Secretary of State, Mo Mowlam, were intent on bringing Sinn Fein into the Stormont talks. The Orange Order spearheaded the campaign to persuade all five unionist parties to boycott the negotiations. Once again Trimble found himself on the opposite side of the Orange Order, just as he had in 1975 when the Order opposed Bill Craig and his plans for a Voluntary Coalition. From the other end of the Protestant spectrum, the Church of Ireland urged Trimble to take risks for peace and enter the talks with Sinn Fein. According to those closest to him during the interregnum between the ceasefire and the all-party talks, Trimble already had his mind made up. He was going into the discussions regardless of what Paisley, McCartney or the Orange Order thought.

However, his intentions were almost torpedoed at the end of August when Mo Mowlam made one of her characteristic gaffes to the Northern Ireland media. The Secretary of State appeared to suggest that a 51 per cent majority vote in a referendum on the Province's constitutional status would not be sufficient to maintain partition. One of Trimble's lieutenants, David Brewster, accused Mowlam of not respecting the majority wishes in Northern Ireland in the same way as her government did in England and Wales. Brewster accused her of rigging the ballot box in favour of nationalists. The upshot of this faux pas was decreasing confidence in the Northern Ireland Secretary among unionists – a confidence that had not been restored by the time of her replacement by Peter Mandelson on 11 October 1999.

What made matters worse for the Ulster Unionists was that Mowlam's injudicious remarks were made in the same week that she accepted the IRA ceasefire as unequivocal and set 15 September as the opening date for all-party talks including Sinn Fein. Although Trimble seemed in control of the party as they entered the talks and faced republicans across the negotiating table for the first time since 1922, there were warning signs of what lay ahead. The Ulster Unionists' Graduate Association, which contained many of the party's rising young stars, advised the leader not to treat Sinn Fein as a normal political party. The Association's chairman, Drew Nelson, a close colleague of Trimble's while at Queen's, sent a letter to him cautioning that the UUP should not enter into bilateral negotiations with Sinn Fein. From the hard-line viewpoint, Trimble was to do even worse in the near future.

One of the few to raise a voice of dissent about entering the talks was David Brewster. 'I told him to get out,' he said. 'We had a meeting and five of us said to him to get out, because once these people [Sinn Fein] are in the door and you're in the door with them they are suddenly respectable and you will never, ever get them marginalized no matter what they do.'[8] Brewster believed that Trimble was setting the party up for attack in the near future by Paisley and McCartney, whose unlikely alliance had been forged in 1995 when the DUP stood aside to help McCartney win the North Down seat in a straight by-election fight with the Ulster Unionists. But Trimble had more room to move inside the UUP than Brewster and his comrades assumed. One week before the talks opened, a survey found that 82 per cent of the party's 110-strong ruling executive believed that Trimble should attend the talks with Sinn Fein.[9]

Exactly a week after the survey Trimble finally announced that he would attend the talks, which were scheduled to start the following day. Accompanied by Ken Maginnis, John Taylor and Jeffrey Donaldson, he duly walked through the razor-wired gates of Castle Buildings at Stormont. Behind them came the political representatives of loyalist paramilitaries – David Ervine of the UVF-aligned Progressive Unionist Party and Gary McMichael of the UDA-linked Ulster Democratic Party – whose presence at the talks would have been impossible had Trimble refused to go. Trimble and his party were no longer the sole unionist voices at Castle Buildings.

Throughout the build-up and during the early stages of the talks Sean O'Callaghan kept in close contact with Trimble and his team. Every week they either talked on the phone or met in London. 'Sometimes these meetings lasted up to four and five hours,' said O'Callaghan. 'At that stage he was convinced he could do a deal with the SDLP.' From his own experience the former IRA man supplied Trimble with close personal profiles of the republican leaders he was facing across the floor in Stormont. O'Callaghan told him he should focus on Martin McGuinness, Sinn Fein's chief strategist and one-time chief of staff of the IRA. 'I told David . . . that McGuinness was a straighter character and he was the person the unionists needed to deal with.'[10]

O'Callaghan had warned Trimble that the IRA would do everything they could to make him press the eject button and push the UUP out of the talks forever. A day after the negotiations began the centre of Markethill, a mainly Protestant town in South Armagh, was devastated in a huge car bomb. The blue Ford transit van that had carried the 400lb device had been stolen in Dundalk in the Republic on 5 September. At first it was thought the bombing was the work of republican dissidents from the Continuity IRA, Republican Sinn Fein's military wing, but senior Irish police officers now suspect it was down to the mainstream Provisional IRA. Although the terrorist unit which planned and executed the attack later left the Provisionals and formed the Real IRA in November 1997, at the time of the Markethill bomb they were still under the control of the PIRA's leadership. The only conclusion to draw is that the bombing was a sanctioned operation which fitted a pattern that flowed from the murder of the RUC constables in Lurgan – kill and destroy to force unionists to walk from the talks.

In the autumn Trimble had to clear two internal hurdles in order to remain inside the talks. The first and easier one was the Young Unionists' annual conference in Belfast on 4 October. The only criticism from the floor of the conference came from a usual suspect, the North Belfast UUP councillor Nelson McCausland, who told delegates that Trimble had failed to deliver the 'new vision' expected of him. McCausland, who just a year earlier had seen Trimble's election as the green light for a right-wing take-over of the North Belfast Ulster Unionist Association, was not happy that his former messiah was staying put at the talks. It was McCausland's gut reaction that the UUP should have walked out along with Paisley and McCartney. At the time of this diatribe, Trimble was flying to Washington for another White House meeting with Bill Clinton. But he need not have worried about dissenters such as McCausland, who were seen in the party as isolated on the far right. At this early stage, Trimble's inter-party talks strategy was to shed leaves from the Ulster Unionist tree rather than break any branches.

On 25 October he faced his second and more serious obstacle, the annual party conference at the Slieve Donard Hotel in Newcastle, Co. Down, a seaside resort at the foot of the Mourne Mountains. Here he won the overwhelming backing of the delegates to stay in the Stormont talks, with all but a dozen of the five hundred delegates giving him a standing ovation at the end of the conference. Trimble had assured them that he would not sign anything similar to the Sunningdale Agreement he had helped bring down twenty-three years earlier. 'We will not agree anything that undermines the rights of the people of Northern Ireland, still less than any Trojan house that would be, in the fateful words of Hugh Logue in 1974, a vehicle to trundle us into a United Ireland,' he said.[11] (Trimble's obsession with not repeating the errors of Sunningdale, particularly Faulkner's acceptance of the Council of Ireland, was to weigh heavily on his mind throughout the negotiations. Some allies say he was so determined to reduce the power of cross-border bodies in Strand 2 of the talks that he lost out on other critical issues relating to the internal governance of Northern Ireland covered by Strand 1.)

But the rumblings about his strategy were louder now than at the Young Unionists' conference. Willie Thompson, the West Tyrone MP, was open in his opposition to the talks or indeed to any form of power-sharing arrangement with the SDLP. While Nelson McCausland now refrained from attacking Trimble, his fellow North Belfast delegate Ian Crozier bitterly criticized the UUP talks team. Crozier accused the party negotiators of entering a process 'based on a lie'. He claimed Dublin, London and Washington were engaged in a three-pronged assault to lead the UUP into a sell-out. In a barely concealed warning to Trimble, Crozier added: 'For those men who would take us down this road, mark my words well, those who sow the seeds into the wind will reap the whirlwind'.[12] John Hunter, who clearly did not share David Brewster's concerns about remaining in the talks, gave the most important pro-Trimble/leadership speech of the conference. Hunter admitted that there were grave risks in entering into talks with Sinn Fein, but 'you get nowhere unless you take risks'.[13] Within seven months Hunter would eat his words and Crozier's prophecy, in right-wing eyes at least, would come to pass.

Five days after the Slieve Donard meeting Trimble travelled to the Conservative Party's first annual conference at Blackpool since their colossal defeat on 1 May. At a Friends of the Union fringe meeting he gave Tories his most explicit defence yet of why he was prepared to sit in negotiations with Sinn Fein. 'I am going to see that the rights of the people of Northern Ireland are protected. I am going to see that the consent principle is maintained and strengthened. If it meant sitting in a room with some rather nasty people I would do so and make no apology for it.'[14]

Ever since he had been elected UUP leader, one of Trimble's key concerns had been to unify the disparate and often warring forces of unionism. He had often repeated the need, in theory at least, for a single unionist party, given that nationalism was coalescing as never before at the Stormont talks. In practice the likelihood of a united unionist party was a far-off prospect in the post-Paisley future. Unionism's friends in Britain, too, were concerned about the fractiousness afflicting the unionist parties in Northern Ireland. Sean O'Callaghan had maintained contact not only with Trimble but also with Robert McCartney and key Friends of the Union members such as David Burnside and Lord Cranborne. During the British party conference season O'Callaghan hit upon the idea of a pan-unionist think-tank to explore the possibility of a common strategy at the talks. The former IRA commander was worried about the gradual loss of confidence in the peace process throughout the unionist community. He persuaded Cranborne to help him organize a pan-unionist conference, for which Cranborne offered his family's stately home, Hatfield House in Hertfordshire, as a venue on 28–29 November. Kate Hoey, the Northern Ireland-born Labour MP for Vauxhall who was sympathetic to the unionist cause, was brought on board in order to refute criticism that the Hatfield House talks were a Tory-inspired initiative with the Conservatives once more seeking to play the Orange card.

Yet Trimble, the keenest advocate of a single unionist party, was also the most sceptical about the unity conference. Two weeks before the conference took place he warned that the event might degenerate into an 'inter-unionist squabble'.[15] This drew criticism from Robert McCartney, who had accepted Cranborne's invitation. 'If David Trimble has any "ifs" about expressing his views in the presence of others, that is his problem.'[16] The organizers refused to invite any of the loyalist politicians who were standing shoulder-to-shoulder with Trimble at Stormont. Davy Adams, a spokesman for the UDA-aligned Ulster Democratic Party, condemned the exclusion of both his party and the Progressive Unionists, which he claimed made a mockery of Trimble's commitment to unionist unity.

The exclusion of the PUP and UDP also exposed the moral double-think of Friends of the Union. The DUP and UK Unionists, along with Cranborne and others in Friends of the Union, objected to the UDP and PUP being present because of their links to loyalist terrorism. Yet they ignored the fact that the conference had been the brainchild of Sean O'Callaghan, a former IRA killer with Ulster Protestant blood on his hands.

The presence of the UDP and PUP side-by-side with Trimble's team at the talks was vital for the Ulster Unionists. Any decisions emerging from the talks would only be put into practice if there were cross-community support. The UUP on their own did not command the support of a majority of unionists. However, the combined vote of the PUP and UDP pushed the figure of popular support for unionists who stayed at Stormont to over 50 per cent. The two loyalist-linked parties therefore had a crucial role to play at the talks, yet Trimble and his party failed to protest at their exclusion from Hatfield House.

Trimble's pessimism about the usefulness of the Hatfield House discussions was confirmed as Ian Paisley and his deputy Peter Robinson spent most of the conference attacking the UUP leader. The eighty delegates included representatives from the three main unionist parties and the Friends of the Union as well as journalists, academics and leading members of the loyal orders. But the two-day think-in produced little of substance. It was a measure of the disunity in loyalist ranks that the Reverend William Bingham initially refused to attend the meeting because of the presence of Ian Paisley. (As O'Callaghan later observed: 'Bingham dislikes Paisley probably more than Brendan McKenna.'[17] He was referring to the former republican prisoner convicted of bombing a British Legion hall in Portadown, now the spokesman for nationalist residents opposed to loyalist marches through their area in that town.) While Trimble thought the weekend conference had been worthwhile, he added that it was quite ironic that his fellow unionists had concentrated their energies on criticizing the Ulster Unionists. So much, he said, for the reunification of unionism.

For Trimble, one positive by-product of the Hatfield House

conference was the coalescing of a number of his supporters and admirers in the London and Dublin media. They included John Lloyd of the *New Statesman* and Eoghan Harris, the former Workers' Party strategist (he was a central intellectual influence in the evolution of Official Sinn Fein to the Workers' Party in the 1970s and 1980s) and Radio Telefis Eireann television director, and now *Sunday Times* columnist. Lloyd continued to steer the *New Statesman* away from supporting a pro-SDLP-nationalist line on Northern Ireland. He was also someone who Tony Blair and the New Labour establishment listened to on Northern Ireland. However, Harris confesses that he despaired for the UUP when Trimble was elected leader in 1995, believing that the two-step with Paisley at Drumcree sent out the wrong message to the rest of the world. Yet Harris admits that within a matter of months he was converted, particularly after Trimble invited Proinsias De Rossa to the UUP headquarters. Harris, who helped run Mary Robinson's media campaign during the 1990 Irish Presidential election, was to become a key adviser to Trimble, second in importance only to Sean O'Callaghan. Trimble can at least go down in history as the first unionist to unite former members of the rival wings of the Irish republican movement in the cause of Ulster Unionism.

Since the summer of 1997 Harris had been sending Trimble position papers on everything from Drumcree to decommissioning. He was also trying to reshape this stiff, media-awkward unionist leader into a commodity that could be sold around the world. Harris claims he is the man who 'reinvented Trimble', particularly in the Irish Republic, and changed his image from the sash-wearing triumphalist holding Paisley's hand aloft in Portadown to someone who could reach out beyond the narrow confines of the Orange Order, the UUP and Protestant Fortress Ulster. 'One of my position papers told Trimble to reach out to civil society in Northern Ireland. I told him to use this concept of civil society in his speeches,' Harris recalls.[18] Drawing on his years of experience in television, Harris also advised Trimble on changing his image on screen. He urged Trimble to control his temper with interviewers, which he saw as one of the leader's major weak points.

If his relations with rival unionist parties were fraught, the atmosphere in talks that autumn between Trimble and Mo Mowlam was worse. At one stage he even accused Mowlam of trying to drive the UUP out of the talks – effectively claiming the Secretary of

State was working to a republican agenda. In a temperamental outburst on BBC1's *On the Record*, Trimble asserted: 'I got the feeling she was trying to drive us out of the talks in September. I've got that feeling again in terms of the way she has constantly over the last few days handed concession after concession to Sinn Fein.'[19] In fact relations were so bad between Mowlam and Trimble that he ensured he would be able to bypass the Secretary of State and speak directly to Tony Blair about substantive issues at the Stormont talks.

Mowlam was not the only person at the talks to be the victim of Trimble's ire. Remarks by the Irish Foreign Minister, David Andrews, that any cross-border structure which emerged from the negotiations would 'not be unlike a government' prompted Trimble to demand his resignation. He felt the Irish had let him down following earlier reassurances by Dublin officials that there was no question of imposing an embryonic all-Ireland government on unionists. 'Now Andrews is proposing that,' Trimble protested. 'Certainly it would cause very great problems for us to continue a dialogue with the Irish government if they were to support the Andrews line.'[20]

His anger with Andrews reflected his central concern about a repetition of the Council of Ireland fiasco in 1974, which was the weakest link in Brian Faulkner's historic compromise with Dublin and the SDLP. With no faith in Mo Mowlam and outright hostility to her Dublin counterpart David Andrews, the prospects of Trimble cutting a deal at Stormont looked remote. In fact by the end of the year Trimble had still to engage directly with Sinn Fein. In addition there was a growing rebellion inside his own party over the policy of staying at Stormont. Three days before Christmas four UUP MPs formally withdrew their support for the party's participation in the talks. Willie Ross, Willie Thompson, Roy Beggs (MP for East Antrim) and Clifford Forsythe (MP for South Antrim) sent Trimble a letter via the party's parliamentary whip, Martin Smyth, informing him of their opposition to the negotiations. The gang of four were increasingly disillusioned with the British government's attitude to the peace process, in particular the granting of concessions to republicans under the guise of 'confidence-building measures' such as troop withdrawals. Tensions between Trimble and the four MPs were building at Westminster.

According to one UUP staff member close to all sides in the

debate, meetings of the party's nine MPs were growing more divisive:

> Some of the meetings were getting very fractious by the end of that year. When the MPs got together with Trimble in his room in the Commons it degenerated into a shouting match. Willie Ross would remind everybody that he had been in the Unionist Party for most of his adult life and had never joined any other political movement – a jibe at Trimble's Vanguard days. You could sense the atmosphere between the sceptics and those loyal to Trimble was deteriorating.[21]

Even those loyal to Trimble questioned whether the talks could achieve a lasting settlement. On the day the four MPs' revolt was exposed, John Taylor let it slip that he thought the talks had only a 4 per cent chance of succeeding.

Five days later matters were made worse when two prisoners from the Irish National Liberation Army wing of H-Block 6 in the Maze prison assassinated Billy Wright, the founder of the anti-ceasefire Loyalist Volunteer Force. His murder, in what was supposedly the most secure jail in western Europe, sparked a two-month revenge murder spree by loyalists. The killings, initiated by the loyalists but later drawing in both the INLA and the IRA, were to have a direct bearing on the talks at Stormont. On 20 February Sinn Fein was suspended from the talks following the IRA murder of South Belfast UDA leader Robert Dougan and a Catholic drug dealer, Brendan 'Bap' Campbell. The party had been found guilty of breaching the rule set down by the talks chairman, George Mitchell, that none of the parties would use violence or the threat of violence to influence the outcome of the negotiations. It appeared that the entire talks process was becoming increasingly irrelevant as violence returned to the streets of Northern Ireland. On the day Sinn Fein was ejected from Stormont, a Continuity IRA bomb ripped through the centre of Moira, a mainly Protestant town not far from Trimble's home in Lisburn. Three days later another huge car bomb exploded in the centre of Portadown – an even more direct message to Trimble from republicans determined to blow up the entire talks process.

How did Trimble cope personally with the rumblings in his own party, the lack of progress in the talks at Stormont, the renewed sectarian attacks on the ground and the enormous pressure piling up on him from government quarters in London, Dublin and Washington? Ken Maginnis, who was close to him in the autumn and winter of 1997–8, attributed Trimble's staying power and enormous energy throughout the negotiations to his ability to slip back into stable family life. Maginnis singles out his wife as the real tower of strength in his leader's life. 'Daphne is a class act, a real gem,' Maginnis said. 'I saw situations where she was able to calm David down and take the pressure off him. David is never more at ease and in control than when Daphne is there.'[22]

Eoghan Harris too praises Daphne's skill in bringing Trimble back to earth. Harris, who has long experience of making and breaking politicians in the Republic (witness his successful management of De Rossa in the 1989 Euro elections and of Mary Robinson a year later), believes Daphne is not just there to be a pillar for Trimble to lean on:

> Daphne is classic middle-Ulster – she has an enormous feel for what the ordinary people think, and that is something which has affected Trimble's politics. I would often send her a position paper or a speech before it went to David just to sound her out. The thing I like about Trimble is he has a rich home life, which he doesn't neglect. The worst kind of politicians are those that hang about in bars after work with journalists. But journalists are generally out of touch with society, whereas women who run homes like Daphne are more in tune with what ordinary people are thinking. So when David comes home in the evening the first thing he encounters is the reality of middle-Ulster through his wife, through the children. Good politicians should stay away from bars after working, talking shop with journalists and the like. Trimble copes with the pressure because he can go back to reality every night.[23]

Both Maginnis and Harris note that Trimble seems infinitely more relaxed in female as opposed to male company. As Maginnis puts it: 'David is least at ease in the macho situation, with the boys. He is happier being surrounded by women.' There is more than a degree of truth in this perceptive observation of Trimble's more cultured, almost feminine side compared to the more testosterone-driven politicians and terrorists in Northern Ireland. Harris puts it down to family life outside the cut and thrust of Ulster politics. For the party, the downside of that aspect of his character is the risk that at any time Trimble might forsake the leadership in order to maintain his other life beyond politics.

However, even at the height of the loyalist and republican murder campaigns of early 1998 Trimble did not appear ready to quit. According to close aides in the party, he seemed determined to tough it out and do everything possible to reach a political settlement. At the end of January he attended a lunch at Belfast's Ulster Reform Club, which had been organized by John Laird with a view to fostering ties between Trimble's talks team and local religious and business leaders. The guests included Archbishop Sean Brady, the leader of Ireland's four million Catholics, and a number of prominent Catholic business figures from the city. Throughout the lunch Trimble went around the tables chatting with the other guests, noting their views and listening to their concerns. It went on well into Friday afternoon, with Trimble and Ken Maginnis staying on to polish off the remaining few bottles of wine. Laird recalls:

> Trimble was sitting there in the middle of about eight people, including Ken and myself, and he suddenly burst into life. For no apparent reason he said to us, 'You know, I think I will be the first Unionist leader who will survive Paisley. And I am the only Unionist leader who has got the official credentials to deal a deal. And I'll tell you one thing – that when I do this deal I will stick to it.' I realized only then that he knew there was some kind of deal on the table.[24]

The Stormont talks actually seemed to be moving Trimble's way in January, particularly after the two governments produced their *Heads of Agreement* document on the 12th. The document was clearly a coup for Trimble and a major headache for Sinn Fein. Ed Moloney, the Northern editor of the Dublin-based *Sunday Tribune*, reported on republican uneasiness over the paper. 'When I saw Trimble on the box last Monday,' seethed the Belfast republican, 'it was like that day in Portadown when he danced down the street with Paisley, fist clenched, after their victory at Drumcree. Pure triumphalism.'[25] So why was Trimble triumphant about *Heads of Agreement*?

Moloney, a sceptic of peace process propaganda but also an extremely astute commentator on Northern Ireland affairs, pointed to the fact that the paper stressed that any political settlement must be rooted in consent – in other words, the unionist majority had a veto over constitutional change. Crucially, this meant that any future cross-border bodies would require unionist assent in order to function. As Moloney highlighted, this entailed a revision and indeed a retreat from the *Frameworks* document of three years earlier, which had envisaged cross-border bodies as free-standing and not under the control of a unionist-dominated government in Belfast. The cross-border structure laid out in *Heads of Agreement* was a far cry from David Andrews's assertion that these bodies would be 'not unlike a government'.

For Sinn Fein, this marked a defeat. The republican movement's leadership had welcomed *Frameworks*, particularly its cross-border dimension, and attempted to sell it to the IRA grass roots as containing the dynamic towards Irish unity. Trimble's behind-closed-door discussions with both Tony Blair and Bertie Ahern in late 1997 and early 1998 had clearly paid dividends. In the days leading up to *Heads of Agreement* Trimble received six calls from Blair at the G7 summit in Tokyo and four calls from Bertie Ahern's home in Dublin, during which the two leaders outlined their ideas for the way forward. Trimble had undoubtedly persuaded both men to roll back the more 'republican' aspects of the *Frameworks* document. Even his four rebels at Westminster stayed their hand when the UUP parliamentary team met on the day that *Heads of Agreement* was published. The MPs had been planning to call for Trimble to withdraw from the talks, but instead kept silent. Why, after all, should Trimble pull the plug when he had just achieved a major victory and set the tone for negotiations on Strand 2 of the talks at Stormont?

On the Saturday following the publication of *Heads of Agreement* Trimble took a pot shot at the Paisley/McCartney camp for walking away from Stormont. Stressing that the paper had been 'partitionist' in make-up, Trimble said it was 'a pity that some can only carp at progress'.[26] In addition, the paper had recognized the need for the replacement of the Anglo–Irish Agreement. He drew further comfort from the fact that Gerry Adams's ally in the United States, the publisher Niall O'Dowd, had written in the *Irish Times* that the two governments' document gave Sinn Fein 'very little satisfaction'. O'Dowd complained that the governments had moved away from the *Frameworks* document. This was music to Trimble's ears.

The rough shape of a possible peace settlement had already been in Trimble's mind since the late autumn. Much of this was discussed in a book published in early October 1997 by Professor Paul Bew, along with Henry Patterson and Paul Teague from the University of Ulster. Trimble was particularly impressed with Chapter 8 of *Between War and Peace: The Political Future of Northern Ireland*, which contained a blueprint for political progress based on the renegotiation of the *Frameworks* document. The authors argued for a revision of Articles 2 and 3 (which made it a constitutional imperative of the Irish state to regain or take over Northern Ireland from the UK) and limited cross-border cooperation. They contended that this would be enough to allow Northern nationalists to accept the principle of consent, while at the same not creating the impression in unionist minds that they were in a halfway house towards a united Ireland. In fact the book foreshadows much of what would later become part of the Good Friday Agreement. Trimble was so impressed with the authors' arguments that he gave copies of the book both to the Prime Minister during a visit to Downing Street and to Sir John Holmes, the only senior Foreign Office diplomat whom Blair kept on from Major's administration. Sir John, now Britain's ambassador to Portugal, was Blair's principal civil service adviser and regarded as highly influential on Northern Ireland affairs. Trimble later told Bew that every time he went to Holmes's office in London he saw *Between War and Peace* on his desk.

Yet whatever achievements and intellectual influence Trimble was exercising in his talks with Blair and Ahern, the entire political process was coloured by the ongoing sectarian violence outside the confines of Castle Buildings. Relations between Trimble and the British government went sour in late February when Mo Mowlam announced that Sinn Fein would be allowed to re-enter the talks on 9 March following their temporary suspension caused as a result of IRA violence in Belfast. Before he flew off to the United States for a break from the talks George Mitchell imposed a deadline for the discussions – Thursday, 9 April. Mitchell said he had been studying the calendar to find an appropriate date: 'Easter weekend leapt out at me. It had historical significance in Ireland. It was an important weekend in Northern Ireland, a religious society. If there were an agreement by Easter there could be a referendum in late May and an assembly election in late June.'[27] However, any agreement seemed a remote possibility while the killings continued. On 3 March news came through of a double murder in Poyntzpass, a village on the border between Trimble's Upper Bann constituency and Newry/Armagh, the area that Seamus Mallon represented in Parliament. The Loyalist Volunteer Force – the terror group originally formed by Billy Wright – shot dead two lifelong friends in a local pub. One of the victims, Phillip Allen, was a Protestant; the other, Damien Trainor, a Catholic.

The following day Mallon and Trimble, two political rivals, went to the village together and visited the Allen and Trainor families. Trimble told reporters he was ashamed that Protestants had been responsible for the killing. Friends of the UUP leader claimed that Trimble was particularly touched by the killings given that the victims' friendship had survived nearly thirty years of sectarian terror and bigotry. On the day of the funerals the *Belfast Telegraph* editorial stressed the import of Mallon's and Trimble's joint visit to the border village. 'By going together to the homes of the bereaved families to express their sympathy, they sent a powerful message to the world that, despite our differences, the people of Northern Ireland have so much in common', the paper's leader writer wrote.[28] The editorial hoped that the display of unity in tragedy augured well for the talks at Stormont. Indeed, many commentators saw Trimble and Mallon as the new axis on which a lasting political settlement could be based.

Ten days later Trimble and John Taylor flew to Washington for a series of meetings with Bill Clinton, members of Congress and the US media. Although determined to reach a deal at Stormont, Trimble warned Americans on St Patrick's Day that there were serious problems to overcome. Addressing the National Press Club in Washington, he spoke of the need for a strong vote in favour of any settlement that might be produced in the talks. He even suggested that the deal might require 85 per cent majority support in the May referendum. This reflected his long-held anxiety about a deal being imposed without unionist consent. Trimble had helped bring down the last major constitutional settlement, the Sunningdale power-sharing initiative in 1974. One of the reasons he had opposed that agreement was that its content had never been put to the electorate of Northern Ireland in a referendum. This time he was determined that any long-term deal would be anchored in a referendum which commanded the support of most unionists. His speech also focussed on his other major concern – not to repeat Faulkner's mistake of accepting a Council of Ireland outside the control of a Northern Ireland Assembly. 'We will not have a third centre of government on the island of Ireland. This is the rock upon which things might founder,' he warned the gathering.[29]

Trimble's visit to the United States illuminated the changing nature of Ulster Unionism's attitude to foreign interference in Northern Ireland. Jim Molyneaux would never have accepted any American involvement in political initiatives to solve the Irish question. However, his successor now had a well-run Unionist Information Office in Washington and was winning new friends and financial backers across the USA. Trimble even took time out to visit the one American politician who had promoted Irish nationalist interests on Capitol Hill since the early 1970s and had consequently become a bugbear for unionists, Senator Edward Kennedy. It was clearly a sign of changing times if the leader of the Ulster Unionist Party and his deputy were prepared to hold discussions on talks at Stormont with a man whom unionists had once loathed and regarded as interfering, partial and partisan.

When he walked into the White House to shake Clinton's hand Trimble had a present for the President. This time it was a book on the IRA by Malachi O'Doherty, a journalist who has been deeply critical of armed republicanism. *The Trouble with Guns* casts a sceptical eye over the IRA's peace strategy and deconstructs many of the myths surrounding Irish republicanism. Republicans detest this highly acclaimed book because they see it as an intellectual challenge to their most precious ideological assumptions. When Trimble handed it to Clinton he informed him that this was the key work on the modern IRA, adding that he hoped the President might learn from it a few home truths about the IRA – such as their continuation of so-called punishment beatings and shootings – beyond the misty-eyed, romantic lionizing of Gerry Adams et al. in the Irish-American press. The upshot of the White House meeting was that Clinton managed to persuade Trimble and later John Hume to hold face-to-face discussions on the talks when they returned to Northern Ireland. The two party leaders had not met for over three months and during separate meetings with them

Clinton expressed concern that this was sending out negative signals to the public back home. Overall, the Washington trip had been reasonably successful from Trimble's viewpoint. Bertie Ahern was also in the US capital for St Patrick's Day, and during his address he bluntly told Sinn Fein that there was going to be an Assembly in Belfast despite their objections. Privately, Trimble and his talks team were pleased that Ahern's remarks caused even more discomfort for Sinn Fein.

But on his return to Belfast Trimble had to face an increasingly restless party which was worried about the government acquiescing to pressure from the SDLP and Dublin to allow Sinn Fein to return to Stormont following their temporary expulsion. On 21 March he squared up to his internal critics at the annual meeting of the UUP's 860-strong ruling council in Belfast. The opposition to his policy of remaining at the talks was again routed. Two of the four Westminster rebels were known to have privately distanced themselves from their letter urging him to pull out of the negotiations. Meanwhile, Nelson McCausland's attempt to establish a right-wing caucus to change the party's direction had faded away. No one suggested a vote of no confidence in the leader should be taken, and there was no attempt from the floor to reverse policy. Trimble was even confident enough to announce the establishment of a joint UUP/Orange Order commission to explore the future of the link between the party and the loyalist marching institution. His proposed changes were on the lines of Tony Blair's reforms of the connections between the Labour Party and the trade unions. Being somewhat mesmerized by the New Labour spin machine, to the horror of some traditionalists Trimble even called on the party to set up a Blairite-style 'rapid rebuttal unit' in London.

Two days later Trimble sought to have the issue of decommissioning put back on the agenda of the all-party talks. He had earlier sidelined the controversy into a sub-committee of the talks, allowing Sinn Fein to remain at the table without a single bullet being surrendered. However, with the talks deadline looming, Sinn Fein re-entering the negotiations and his political opponents on the unionist side crying sell-out, Trimble had no choice but to resurrect the disarmament question. Speaking outside Castle Buildings as the Sinn Fein delegation were about to walk back into the talks, Trimble said it was inconceivable that the negotiations could be completed without having addressed decommissioning. He also continued to rule out face-to-face talks with Sinn Fein. Mo Mowlam's assertion on the same day that she was 'stubbornly optimistic' that an agreement could be reached seemed to have been made in hope rather than expectation.

By the beginning of Holy Week Trimble's allies were far from optimistic. In a characteristically off-the-cuff remark to the media at Stormont, Trimble's deputy, John Taylor, rated the chances of success at between 4 and 7 per cent; during the last round of discussions he had earned the sobriquet 'Mr something per cent' because of his tendency always to put the prospect of progress in percentage terms. Trimble, too, was guarded about any breakthrough. He warned against making foolish predictions, emphasizing that there were two key problems: the design of the Assembly and the nature of the relationship between that body and Dublin via cross-border bodies.

Trimble's talks team for the last lap of the negotiations represented every wing of the UUP's broad church. On the left were Ken Maginnis, Steven King and Dermot Nesbitt, the latter having a reputation for being soft on issues such as power-sharing since his time as a key Brian Faulkner supporter in 1974. In the centre were Reg Empey, his old Vanguard comrade, and John Taylor. And on the centre-right were the so-called 'baby barristers' David Brewster, John Hunter and Peter Weir. Brewster depicts the UUP's handling of the last week of the talks as a 'shambles'. In particular he singles out Trimble's leadership style:

> The trouble with Trimble was he was trying to do everything himself. We, particularly Reg Empey and I, said, 'Look, you are the field marshal, so you should sit in your room in splendid isolation and the guys who are fighting on the various Strands can come to you and say, "Here is our position." That will give you an overview.' Instead of which the stupid bugger was doing everything himself.[30]

The shambolic UUP organization at Stormont stood in stark contrast to the cold control of Sinn Fein, who marshalled their representatives at the talks with military precision. Unlike the UUP, Sinn Fein is run on Bolshevik lines with a politburo-type leadership enforced with army-style discipline.

The pivotal figure for Trimble in that final week was John

Taylor. Trimble knew he would not be able to sell a deal to his party, and ultimately to the wider unionist electorate, without the support of this wily, highly experienced if somewhat mercurial politician. On Tuesday morning it appeared that the deal was dead. Trimble and Taylor received the first draft of the Agreement, which had been presented by George Mitchell's team although Strand 2 was actually drafted by Irish and British government officials. On his first reading of the document Taylor told Trimble he could not support it. (Interestingly, Mitchell now admits that he knew at the time that Trimble would reject the document. The Senator has been at pains ever since to distance his team from the section on cross-border bodies, emphasizing that it was the work of Irish and British civil servants.) Taylor wanted to study the paper in private before he made a public statement:

> I took my copy away to one of the rooms in Castle Buildings and locked the door in order to read it again on my own. By lunchtime I contacted David and I said to him, 'David, I am not going to support this document.' His reply was, 'John, I fully understand and I am going to get on to Downing Street and tell them that this is not acceptable.' That was fine by me, because otherwise I would not have stood with David on that one. Half an hour later David came back and said, 'John, don't tell our colleagues, this is strictly private between you and me, but the Prime Minister is coming over.'

During his telephone conversation with Blair, Trimble had told the Prime Minister 'that there had to be a willingness to consider fundamental change, and in the absence of that willingness, then we would prefer not to get involved in negotiations and to say, "Well, that's it." '[31] As Mitchell noted, without this commitment the talks were doomed. Blair was flying to Belfast to save the entire process from collapse.

Taylor was delighted when Trimble told him Blair was arriving the following day, because he had wanted to attend a concert and party in London that evening. Realizing that nothing further would happen that day, he decided to drive to Belfast International Airport to catch a late afternoon flight. Around half past two he walked out of Castle Buildings and uttered some of the most infamous remarks of a historic week. As the representatives of the world's media who had been camped outside the gates of the building approached, Taylor said: 'I'm away. I wouldn't touch this thing with a forty-foot pole.' By the time he reached London his comments had made national news, and people rushed up and shook hands with him before the concert. 'They had all recognized me from the television,' he recalled. 'I couldn't believe it.' During the intervals Taylor kept in contact with Trimble and the talks team, and at 7 a.m. next day he took the shuttle back to Belfast.

> I strolled into Stormont at nine o'clock, as if I had been there all night, just as the Prime Minister arrived. By that time my remark about the barge-pole was making the headlines on most of the national newspapers. So David and I went into the room to meet the Prime Minister, and of course Mo Mowlam was put out of the room before the meeting. Blair was sitting on the table and then he said to me, 'John, what is this forty-foot thing people keep talking about?' And I said, 'That's on all the front pages, Prime Minister,' and he laughed.[32]

Trimble's and Taylor's prime concern with the original Agreement document was the section on North/South bodies. The first draft shown to them on the Tuesday included a chapter on cross-border institutions, naming a hundred of them, drawn up by the two governments. Taylor had advised Trimble that this grandiose scheme would produce a United Ireland in all but name. Both men urged Blair and later Bertie Ahern to renegotiate this section of the Agreement and radically reduce the number. George Mitchell has since confirmed that Trimble's friendly but firm influence on Blair, and Taylor's blatant hard-line stance – a kind of nice cop, nasty cop routine – persuaded the two governments to change this critical element of the agreement. The number of cross-border bodies was drastically cut to six. For Taylor this marked real progress, even though he still had reservations about the early release of prisoners (a key concession to Sinn Fein and the IRA) and, of course, decommissioning. On Strand 2 the Irish government effectively backed down in the face of threats by Trimble to pull the entire process down. Bertie Ahern, the man with whom Trimble had built secret links even before he had been elected Taoiseach, gave the UUP leader a lot to be thankful for. As Mitchell points out, had Ahern stood firm on the need to retain the hundred cross-border bodies an agreement would never have been reached. Ahern, who was in mourning following the death of his mother that week, sought a trade-off in relation to the early release of IRA prisoners. But the essential selling point of the *Frameworks* document, the large number of free-standing cross-border institutions, was sacrificed by Ahern to keep Trimble and his team in the talks. Mitchell's description of Ahern's handling of the Strand 2 controversy as a 'superb demonstration of leadership'[33] must surely be seen even by Trimble's team as justified.

Throughout Holy Week the Ulster Unionists were unable to form any common front with their fellow loyalists at the talks, the PUP and UDP. In fact the relations between Trimble's party and the loyalists were at times both frosty and mutually suspicious. The UUP's mistrust of fellow unionists even extended to some in their own party. At one stage Roy Garland, a UUP member on the left of the party with close links to loyalist paramilitaries, was turned out of the Ulster Unionists' negotiating room because the talks team thought he would leak information to the PUP. David Brewster recalled serious disagreements with the PUP over the make-up of the Assembly:

> Trimble said at one stage he needed volunteers to talk to the PUP and UDP. So John Hunter and I volunteered, even though we weren't part of the Strand 1 talks team – we were focussed on Strand 2. It was around three o'clock in the morning when he went to see David Ervine and Dawn Purvis of the PUP. We were opposed to the idea emerging from the talks that there would be six seats per Assembly constituency. Six seats would mean more nationalist members but the PUP seemed in favour of it, especially since in at least one constituency they would be guaranteed the sixth seat. When Ervine challenged Hunter and myself to let us show him our calculations about the way the seats would work out, we simply didn't know. We had been dropped in it too quickly – we simply had no brief. Ervine was quite sharp about this and sent us packing by saying, 'Look, guys I appreciate you coming down and telling me this, but you people had a chance to talk last September and you didn't.' It was obvious Trimble never tried to form a common front. There was no coordination among the unionists and loyalists at the talks.[34]

The UUP team, however, did consult some unlikely independent advisers both inside and outside the Stormont negotiations. Sean O'Callaghan, in weekly communication with Jeffrey Donaldson, continued to second guess the strategy of his former comrades in the Sinn Fein leadership and then conveyed his thoughts on their next moves. Trimble, meanwhile, sought the counsel of Brian Garrett, even though he was part of the small, disparate labourite coalition at the talks. Garrett was consulted over the redrafting of Articles 2 and 3 (on the Republic's territorial claims over Northern Ireland) during the Strand 2 talks on Thursday evening. There had been some anxieties in the UUP that the articles were only going to be revised rather than dropped completely from the Irish constitution. Garrett reassured Trimble when he read the new draft: 'I told David I thought the rewriting of the articles was masterly and that I would rather see them rewritten than simply dropped. As far as I was concerned, the revised articles were an end to the Republic's constitutional claim over Northern Ireland.' At the end of their discussion Trimble turned to Garrett and, laughing, said: 'I agree with your analysis, but would you tell some of my colleagues that.'[35] Garrett then spoke to Ken Maginnis and Steven King to calm their fears over the revision of Articles 2 and 3. The intervention of an outsider seemed to unsettle several of the UUP talks team, particularly Trimble's legal advisers.

John Taylor, the veteran of marathon political negotiations and back-room dealing, observed that Trimble seemed to be coping well with the enormous pressure piling upon him. 'David is a pretty excitable person and I know, having shared an office with him for so long. The back of his neck gets redder and redder as he gets more annoyed about something. He can get very bad-tempered with people. At one stage he lost his rag with a British official whom he turned on very quickly.'[36] Since Trimble had held the party together for most of the week while under severe personal strain, Taylor insisted that he go to bed on Holy Thursday evening while he himself stayed up for the overnight negotiations.

But Trimble's short fuse blew again during the final hours of the talks on Good Friday. He turned on Steven King, who was working on the nature and role of the cross-border bodies. The Dublin civil servants whom King was dealing with had managed to slip in an extra cross-border body aimed at promoting the Irish language, even though it was not to have been included in the overall agreement. Trimble gave King a dressing-down in front of almost the entire UUP talks team, accusing him of not being sufficiently wise to the ways of Irish civil servants. The unfortunate King went out of the door and straight into another room reserved for the Irish officials. King then verbally attacked the civil servant, claiming he was exhibiting the worst qualities of his race by duping him over the Irish-language body. The spat was immediately conveyed to Bertie Ahern, who held a short discussion with Trimble about the issue. The upshot was that the language body was initially removed from the Agreement.

It may have seemed a petty point over which to provoke a row with Ahern and his officials, but Trimble later reminded King that the last thing he wanted was to be trying to sell an Irish-language body during his campaign for the subsequent referendum. Most unionist voters would have been repelled by the sight of Trimble offering them a package that included an all-Ireland body promoting Gaelic, since in many unionist minds it was the language of republicans. (Later the Irish-language body was put into the Agreement, but only on condition that Ulster Scots – a dialect spoken by Protestants in the east of the Province – be given parity of esteem.)

Trimble needed all the strength he could muster on Good Friday morning, because a fresh rebellion was about to break out in the ranks. Two of the three 'baby barristers', John Hunter and Peter Weir, ran for cover, walking out before a final deal was reached. He also lost the services of David Brewster, who had to take the ferry to Scotland that morning because he was getting married. Even if he had stayed, Brewster is adamant that he too would have deserted Trimble owing to the nature of the deal on offer. Jeffrey Donaldson, meanwhile, was getting increasingly nervous about the absence of a link between the early release of prisoners and decommissioning. There were fears that he too would jump ship. The Young Turks whom Trimble had promoted – to the detriment of older, more loyal and reliable figures, some in the party said – were running away when the leader needed them most. Stephen King describes the atmosphere inside the party's talks room as they gathered that morning as 'very poisonous'.[37] King said years of bad feeling between the different wings of Ulster Unionism were bubbling to the surface as two UUP delegations, the talks-team and the party officers, went off to separate meetings.

Shortly after lunch Trimble came into the talks-team room to announce that the party officers were seriously split on the Agreement. He received the final draft of the Agreement that morning and distributed copies among his team for examination. There were two major sticking points: the release of terrorist prisoners, and the question of whether Sinn Fein would be allowed to serve in an executive government in the absence of IRA decommissioning. The other parties at the talks had already accepted the final draft and there was some irritation that the Ulster Unionists were prevaricating.

As the UUP were debating among themselves whether or not to accept it, a delegation from the liberal Alliance Party burst through the door with their leader, Dr John Alderdice. The Alliance leader started to berate several senior UUP members, including Jeffrey Donaldson, for holding up the peace accord. An altercation broke out between Alderdice and Donaldson before John Taylor intervened. Taylor stood in Alderdice's way and told him to get lost, while other UUP members screamed at the Alliance leader that it was all very easy for him to agree to this deal. Taylor reminded Alderdice that if they had to stay up all night debating the agreement they would do so. (One UUP insider at the talks said it was hilarious to watch those paragons of liberal virtue in Northern Ireland, the Alliance Party, trying to throw their weight around. 'It reminded me of that remark of Denis Healey's after he was "attacked" in the Commons by Geoffrey Howe, about the experience feeling like he had been savaged by a dead sheep.')[38]

At that moment Donaldson, Peter Weir and David Campbell, another personal ally of Trimble's, walked out. Campbell, the director of the Somme Commemoration Centre in East Belfast and a close friend of Trimble's since the Ulster Society's formation, left with tears in his eyes. The emotion of that historic afternoon and the punishing talks schedule were too much for a number of the UUP delegates. Arlene Foster, another of the 'baby barristers', whose father had nearly been killed in an IRA gun attack on her family's farm in Co. Fermanagh in the 1970s, was rumoured to have fainted, probably due to exhaustion.

At the meeting, Trimble had taken soundings from the party about their concerns on prisoners and decommissioning. They had asked for a meeting with Blair, even though the fine detail of the Agreement had been put into print. Blair was alarmed that the UUP might reject the document following a telephone conversation that afternoon between Trimble and a newspaper magnate. The latter had relayed to Downing Street that Trimble's party was on the verge of walking out of the discussions and that several of his team had already defected. A mid-afternoon meeting between Blair and Trimble was then set up. According to David Kerr, Trimble's youthful-looking, dour but extremely witty press officer, the party leader asked the team what they wanted from the Prime Minister. Kerr said Jeffrey Donaldson was adamant that Blair should provide safeguards over decommissioning:

> Jeffrey kept saying, 'I want linkage, explicit linkage to say these people will decommission before being allowed into the executive.' He was coming under tremendous pressure. He told me he was getting threats on his answering machine from LVF [Loyalist Volunteer Force] types. People were phoning him up and threatening to kill him.[39]

Trimble's meeting with Blair was, as usual, extremely cordial, but the Prime Minister was firm in his view that at this late stage he could not change the text of the Agreement. The UUP leader had tried to impress upon the Prime Minister that decommissioning was an issue for Strand 1 and thus under the British government's control: Blair could make changes if he forced his hand. But the Prime Minister refused to budge, arguing that modifications of the text would precipitate a crisis with the Irish government. However, he would give them personal reassurances about IRA disarmament in a letter. Trimble and his colleagues returned to Castle Buildings to brief the talks team and wait for Blair's letter. There was a moment of low farce in this high political drama when the Prime Minister's chief of staff, Jonathan Powell, arrived at the door of the UUP delegation with the missive. Since the fracas with the Alliance Party the UUP had kept it locked. Powell could not get in and started to bang on the door. It took several minutes for someone inside to hear him. When the letter was finally handed over, Trimble read it through and then handed it straight to John Taylor. It stated, over Blair's signature:

> I understand your problem with paragraph 25 of Strand 1 is that it requires decisions on those who should be excluded or re-

moved from office in the Northern Ireland Executive to be taken on a cross-community basis.

This letter is to let you know that if, during the course of the first six months of the shadow Assembly or the Assembly itself, these provisions have been shown to be ineffective, we will support changes to these provisions to enable them to be made properly effective in preventing such people from holding office.

Furthermore, I confirm that in our view the effect of the decommissioning section of the Agreement, with decommissioning schemes coming into effect in June, is that the process of decommissioning should start right away.

The Agreement would now live or die, depending on whether or not Trimble's team believed Blair's promises. Taylor admits that the letter was 'a bit of a fudge'[40] but that Trimble had to make a judgement in the round, to balance the UUP's achievements in rolling back the cross-border bodies and securing the union on the basis of consent. Taylor nodded to Trimble and said he could live with it. Next to speak was Ken Maginnis, who gave arguably the most impassioned address to the assembled UUP team on why they must back the deal. Maginnis insists that it was he rather than Taylor who was the first member of the talks team to support Trimble on the Agreement. The Fermanagh/South Tyrone MP described those final few hours in Castle Buildings as 'the most traumatic event of my political life. I never looked around a room and saw so many people on the verge of tears. I think David Trimble himself was on the verge of tears.'[41] But Jeffrey Donaldson was now slowly backing away from the leadership. For him, Blair's assurances were far too vague and woolly; the deal had, in Donaldson's mind, already been done, and the Prime Minister's promises were not in the fine print of the Agreement. He would not sign up.

This eleventh-hour desertion deeply pained David Trimble. He was much more disappointed with Donaldson's defection than with John Hunter's or Arlene Foster's. As one aide put it: 'The break with Hunter was complete that day. Hunter and he had been great mates, and now there was this mutual loathing. But David expected more from Jeffrey. Even after Good Friday he still didn't have the heart to put Jeffrey down.'[42] David Kerr believes his leader felt hurt and deeply let down by Donaldson. The Lagan

Valley MP had worked closely with Trimble on many aspects of the negotiations, and now he was walking out on him with minutes to go before the parties voted on the Agreement. John Taylor feels Donaldson was motivated mainly by the emotional pull of personal history – two of his relatives, both members of the RUC, had been killed in IRA attacks in South Down during the Troubles. However, David Kerr spotted something more coldly logical about Donaldson's refusal to support the Agreement:

> His rationale, his argument to our group that afternoon was that the people out there would reject the document because of issues like prisoners, because of decommissioning, because of proposed changes to the police. He was saying that he was not sticking with Trimble because the people were going to reject it, and he didn't want to be part of the ship when his leader fell overboard.

Kerr said his sense of relief and elation that a deal was going to be done was tempered by Donaldson's attitude: 'When I shook Trimble's hand on Good Friday I knew we were doing the right thing, but it was with a heavy heart. I felt so unhappy that Jeffrey had gone.'[43] (Trimble in fact did not learn about Donaldson's exit from the team until he went outside to speak to the media. He said he was 'very surprised, very shocked' when he heard.)

Despite Donaldson's late rebellion, Trimble rang George Mitchell at a quarter to five that afternoon to inform the talks chairman that they were ready to do business. The entire UUP delegation, led by Trimble and Taylor, then went upstairs to a larger room where Mitchell had held the plenary sessions involving all the parties. The atmosphere inside crackled with anticipation as the UUP filed in to face their enemies in Sinn Fein along with Mitchell, Tony Blair and Bertie Ahern. Trimble and Taylor sat in the front row, flanked by Reg Empey and Ken Maginnis. Mitchell asked each party leader in turn whether he supported the Agreement document. The UUP were the last to be asked, and when Trimble answered 'Yes' Taylor recalls: 'I whispered into his ear, "David, you need to get out of this building and talk to the media quick before the other parties work against us politically on this one. We need to seize the initiative." So David got up and said to me, "You take over." He would go outside and talk to the press.' As Trimble got to the door he stopped himself, turned around and marched back to the table where Taylor was seated. 'He just leaned over my shoulder and said, "By the way, John, many thanks – because if you hadn't supported me this would have collapsed." I thought that was very big of him.'[44] The importance of Taylor's support for Trimble cannot be overstated. Stephen King regards Taylor as the pillar on which the entire Trimble project rested on Good Friday: 'If John had gone against the Agreement it would never have reached the Ulster Unionist Council. Unlike David, John Taylor has always been a party man. David is seen as very accomplished and very intelligent but in the end he is not really of our Ulster Unionist flesh.'[45]

Another of those who stayed loyally at Trimble's side was David McNarry, his old comrade from the Devolution Group of the 1980s. McNarry remembers that at one stage close to the end, with defections all around him, Trimble turned around and said: 'I'm going ahead with this. This is what leadership is all about.' McNarry has also confirmed that the road to the Blair letter started around noon with a telephone call from a 'powerful newspaper magnate'.

> A call came through to our office and the newspaper man said, 'Can I speak to David?' I remember the room very well – everyone was hungry because there were no staff to make lunch. The newspaper man said, 'What's the problem?' and David outlined his difficulties. Then the newspaper man said, 'Leave it with me.' He must have telephoned Blair, because ten minutes later the phone rang again and it was the Prime Minister on the line. Blair asked Trimble for ten minutes, and the phone went again. This time it was Bill Clinton on the line. I was standing next to Trimble when he took the call from the President. He told Clinton what his problem was and Clinton also said, 'Give me ten minutes.' The end product of all these phone calls was Blair's letter.[46]

McNarry also reveals that, prior to the first call from the newspaper magnate, Trimble had drafted a note to Blair stating that the UUP would not accept what was on offer because there was nothing in the letter of the Agreement linking decommissioning to Sinn Fein in government. 'High noon was the crisis point, and the only thing that stopped Trimble from walking away was that series of phone calls.'[47]

In the euphoria that followed the announcement of the deal, many commentators and experts missed an essential fact about Sinn Fein's attitude to what quickly became labelled 'The Good Friday Agreement'. SDLP and Irish government sources have since confirmed that up until the last moment Sinn Fein expected the Ulster Unionists to reject the package in its entirety and thus plunge the entire political process into crisis – a crisis, republicans hoped, which would be blamed on the UUP. Now that Trimble had accepted the Agreement and they were locked into an essentially partitionist solution, Sinn Fein found itself in the difficult situation of having to overturn its century-old constitution barring the party from entering a Northern Ireland Parliament. Sinn Fein was as lukewarm about the outcome as some in the UUP but far more adept than Trimble's team at masking dissent and, in public at least, repressing their own anxieties.

Snowflakes fell on David Trimble's head as he stood outside Castle Buildings in an unseasonal storm to address the world's media. He informed the press that the delay in signing the Agreement had been justified given the party's serious concerns about the proposed Assembly and the necessary link with decommissioning and holding office. Trimble then declared: 'I have risen from this table with the Union stronger than when I sat down.' And then he alluded to the reservations of many of his colleagues about the deal that had been hammered out behind the gates at Castle Buildings: 'It's not perfect, it's the best we can get at the moment.'[48]

The deal could be summarized in six main points:

(1) A Northern Ireland Assembly with 108 seats, elected by proportional representation, would be established.

(2) The Assembly would elect a twelve-strong executive committee of ministers. Given their electoral support, Sinn Fein would be entitled to two ministers on an executive run on power-sharing lines.

(3) The Assembly's first task would be to set up a North–South ministerial council within one year.

(4) This Council would be accountable to both the Assembly and the Dail – a key concession to the Ulster Unionists given that the Parliament in Belfast would exercise a considerable veto over all-Ireland social and economic bodies.

(5) Articles 2 and 3 of the Irish Constitution would be amended to establish the principle of change only by the consent of the

unionist majority in the North and the repeal of the British Government of Ireland Act.

(6) An inter-government Council of the British Isles would be set up with members drawn from the Dail, the Assembly, the House of Commons and the new Parliaments in Edinburgh and Cardiff.

Several months before the Agreement was signed, Seamus Mallon predicted that any settlement would be on the same lines as the 1974 peace deal between Brian Faulkner and Gerry Fitt. Mallon colourfully characterized the new deal as 'Sunningdale for slow learners'. In reality, the Good Friday Agreement was 'Sunningdale minus one' – the 'minus' being the absence of a free-standing Council of Ireland. As he left Castle Buildings on 10 April Trimble felt he had scored some considerable achievements. So what for him were the main differences between the Agreement and Sunningdale? He explained:

> At Sunningdale the constitutional changes proposed in the Republic were smoke and mirrors – there was no substance to them at all. The Agreement ensured Articles 2 and 3 would be changed – that was a big, big difference. Secondly, the North–South dimension is now radically different, because the Council of Ireland in Sunningdale was quite clearly a third government in Ireland quite independent of the Parliament in Belfast. This time we got accountability because cross-border bodies would derive their authority from the Assembly.

Astonishingly, he also now admits that he might have accepted the power-sharing concept in 1974 if the cross-border arrangement had been closer to the model laid out in the Good Friday Agreement. And he claims the Agreement's arrangements for power-sharing, with the prospect of Sinn Fein ministers, were not as good as the plan envisaged in the Voluntary Coalition he drew up with Bill Craig in 1975. Trimble confesses he was not initially keen on the idea of First and Deputy First Ministers for Northern Ireland. He had proposed the concept of secretaries instead of ministers. 'I was surprised at the SDLP because I thought they would want to get away from the old Stormont language of ministers and deputy ministers, but they wanted it.'[49]

Many members of the UUP talks team now look back on Good Friday as the day they won on the core issues of constitution but lost on the emotional peripheral issues such as prisoner releases. Trimble accepts that he and his colleagues spent so much time rolling back the pan-nationalist project on Strand 2 that it was probably to the detriment of the prisoners issue. On reflection, Trimble now realizes he should have worked harder to force the government to build safeguards into the early release scheme: 'I must confess that perhaps I didn't treat the prisoners question with the same attention. I didn't realize the psychological impression that would be made by the appearance of terrorists walking free, partly because we knew that the government was always going to do something on the prisons issue regardless of what we did.'[50]

The Agreement had hinged on Trimble's willingness to trust the promises in the Tony Blair's letter. Even some non-unionists watching from the sidelines nursed concerns that Trimble might have invested too much faith in the Prime Minister. Amid the euphoric scenes inside Castle Buildings on Good Friday, Brian Garrett stopped to wonder if Blair could really be relied on to keep to his word:

> I got the feeling when the Agreement was signed that this was the Last Chance Saloon. I was very concerned that Tony Blair might be putting too much pressure on David. I was aware of this, because David and I had spoken about Blair given my Labour connections. He obviously liked Blair a lot. But I hoped at the time that Blair wasn't doing what Bob McCartney predicted he would do – that he was taking David up to the top of the temple and saying, 'Look, this can all be yours', and maybe entrapping Trimble with the grandeur of it all. I think you have to remember that David, like many other people, is vulnerable to flattery. I saw that as a danger even on the day.[51]

On his way back home to Lisburn Trimble stopped off at a cash dispenser. He had promised Daphne and the children he would take them to London for an Easter break as soon as the negotiations were over at Stormont, and said that he would get the necessary cash. But as he slipped his card into the machine, Trimble could not remember his PIN number. He tried several times to punch in the number but without success. 'It was pure stress – I just couldn't get the digits in the right order. I was totally stressed out, and it wasn't until Monday that the number came back to me.'[52]

Here was the man on whom the entire world had waited to give his assent for an historic peace agreement, and he was going home to his wife and children without a penny in his pocket!

Even before he had signed the Good Friday Agreement, Trimble was denounced by unionist ultras as the worst traitor since Governor Lundy. Every day of the talks he had had to drive through a gauntlet of DUP supporters waving placards denouncing him as a renegade. The debate on whether Trimble had sold out was in essence the old intellectual struggle between rational and emotional unionism. Shortly after the Agreement was announced, Trimble told the world that the deal was 'as good as it gets'. This was his clearest admission yet that unionism would have to swallow unpalatable compromises on prisoners, arms and eventually Sinn Fein in government as the price for changing Articles 2 and 3, forcing nationalists to accept the principle of consent and the curbing of cross-border integration.

A forensic analysis of the Agreement seemed to support the contention that Trimble had achieved a great deal on the North–South dimension of the talks. Rational unionism's assertion that Trimble had repelled the pan-nationalist front's attempts to turn cross-border bodies into another Trojan horse with which to trundle unionists into a United Ireland is confirmed by Sir David Fell, one of the chief architects of the *Frameworks* document and former head of the Northern Ireland civil service. In a speech, made three months after the Agreement, and not reported at the time, Sir David compared and contrasted the *Frameworks* document and the Strand 2 element of the Good Friday deal, claiming that the Agreement posed less of a threat to unionists than *Frameworks*. He accepted that many unionists were terrified that the North–South body envisaged in *Frameworks* would assume quasi-governmental functions. In other words, it would be a nascent third government leading to a United Ireland by the back door. Fell outlined how the Agreement was radically different in two important respects:

The Framework also envisaged that the North/South body would 'oversee delegated executive, harmonising or consultative functions'. This terminology, which so frightened unionists, has disappeared in the Agreement, which requires the North/South Ministerial council to 'develop consultation, co-operation and action within the island of Ireland – including through implementation on an all-island and cross-border basis – on matters of mutual interest'.

A further element of the Framework which frightened unionists was the section which indicated that the North/South body should have a 'clear institutional identity' and its own 'dynamic', thus further heightening unionist paranoia that this was indeed a one-way street to a United Ireland. I find no such language in the Agreement; which says in terms, that any further development of the initial arrangements of the North/South Council will be subject to the extent of the competencies and responsibilities of the two Administrations.[53]

Fell's conclusion was that, overall, the changes that Trimble managed to win between the *Frameworks* document and the Good Friday Agreement were 'favourable to the unionist position'.[54] He also noted the significant omission from the *Frameworks* document of 'aspects of industrial development'. Its absence confirmed his view that attracting inward investment to the whole of Ireland was problematic, given the different taxation and grant regimes between North and South coupled with the regional and institutional jealousies. Fell posed this dilemma, which Trimble's advisers have characterized as the 'North Tipperary question'. Put bluntly, it juxtaposes the republican rhetoric of Southern political parties with the reality of economic competition between the two states in Ireland. Would the Fianna Fail TD for North Tipperary be happy to let a free-standing cross-border body decide that a German car manufacturer should set up a factory in David Trimble's Upper Bann constituency instead of his own? Trimble is well versed in the vagaries of economic cooperation on the continent and the way conflicting regional and national rivalries can sometimes complicate the grandiose designs for European unity in Brussels.

(A measure of how much Trimble had achieved in the North–South element of the negotiations can be gauged by the standard that Gerry Adams originally set out as his bottom line in the run-up to Good Friday. On 8 March he wrote in *Ireland on Sunday* that Sinn Fein wanted cross-border bodies operating independently of the Assembly; the retention of Articles 2 and 3 of the Irish constitution; and policing and courts coming under the remit of new all-Ireland institutions. The end product, however, was a reduced number of North–South bodies, under the Assembly's

The young David Trimble (back row, centre), 'a wee quiet lad, gangly, wearing glasses', a keen member of the Air Training Corps, with Leslie Cree (back row, far left) and Alan McKillen (back row, second left). RAF Wittering, Gloucestershire, 1959.
Private Collection.

Trimble (in glasses) and fellow air cadets enjoy some dormitory larks while on summer camp in England. Lying on the bed beside him with RAF cap is Allen McKillen. Leslie Cree is also lying on the bed (fourth from left).

Trimble (fourth from left), the young Orangeman, and fellow marchers photographed in their sashes, Bangor, 1965. Leslie Cree is third from the left, with his brother Winston (far left). *Private Collection.*

The young politician, David Trimble photographed for his first election as North Down Vanguard Party candidate in the 1973 Northern Ireland Assembly elections. *Victor Patterson Archive / Linen Hall Library.*

Trimble marries his former Queen's student Daphne Orr in Warrenpoint, County Down, August 1978. Trimble's brother Ian is best man, and the bridesmaids are Daphne's twin sisters, Caroline and Judith. *Courtesy of the Down Recorder.*

Trimble's first meeting with John Major after succeeding James Molyneux as leader of the Ulster Unionist Party. They pose for photographs beneath a portrait of Winston Churchill before talks at 10 Downing Street, 19 September 1995.
Photograph by Greg Bos / Reuters / Popperfoto.

Trimble the tireless campaigner. The Ulster Unionist leader protests against hospital closure in his Upper Bann constituency, July 1996.
Kelvin Boyes Photography.

The Drumcree stand-off.
Trimble, the hardliner in sash,
walks in an Orange march in
Portadown town centre,
July 1996.
Kelvin Boyes Photography.

The Easter Peace talks. David Trimble passes Sinn Fein leader Gerry Adams as he is interviewed outside the Stormont buildings, Belfast, 8 April 1998.
Photograph by Dan Chung / Reuters / Popperfoto.

Give peace a chance. Yes campaigners, SDLP leader John Hume (left), Prime Minister Tony Blair (centre) and David Trimble take a break before holding a press conference at a hotel in Antrim to promote the Yes vote in the Irish Referendum, 21 May 1998. *Kelvin Boyes Photography.*

Trimble gestures to John Hume beside a stack of Yes ballot papers during the count for the Irish Referendum at the King's Hall in Belfast, 23 May 1998. *Photograph by Dylan Martinez / Reuters / Popperfoto.*

The Omagh bombing. David Trimble, First Minister of the Northern Ireland Assembly, walks through the scene of the Omagh bomb on 17 August 1998. Twenty-eight people died in the massive car-bomb attack in the town's centre on Saturday 15 August. *Photograph by Dan Chung / Reuters / Popperfoto.*

David Trimble and John Hume campaign for the Yes vote in the Irish Referendum, 21 May 1998. *Kelvin Boyes Photography.*

The Nobel Peace Prize. John Hume (right) and David Trimble display their shared Nobel Peace Prize during the awards ceremony in Oslo's City Hall, 10 December 1998. *Photograph by Tor Richardson / Reuters / Popperfoto.*

Home Rule for the first time in twenty-five years. First Minister David Trimble and his Deputy Seamus Mallon (left) address journalists in the Great Hall at Stormont in Belfast on the eve of the handover of power from London to Belfast, 1 December 1999.
Photograph by Paul McErlane / Reuters / Popperfoto.

David Trimble, Northern Ireland's Trade and Industry Minister Sir Reg Empey (left), Irish Taoiseach Bertie Ahern (back right) and Minister for Foreign Affairs David Andrews (back left) before the first meeting of the North/South Ministerial Council in Armagh, 13 December 1999.
Photograph by Paul McErlane / Reuters / Popperfoto.

control, the end of Articles 2 and 3 and no provision for all-Ireland police and courts services. The Sinn Fein's President's losses were, of course, Trimble's gains.)

Although in Sir David Fell's eyes Trimble had scored several key victories in the negotiations, particularly in Strand 2, none of this seemed to have any impact on those tied to the emotional wing of unionism. They accused Trimble of going too far on prisoners and of asking for far too few guarantees to link decommissioning with Sinn Fein entering government. Trimble has now accepted that he underestimated the depth of revulsion that prisoner releases would provoke inside the unionist community. Eight days after he signed the Agreement, the mother of one of the RUC constables murdered in his Upper Bann constituency almost a year earlier gave her reaction to the peace deal. Pearl Graham directed most of her anger at Trimble for his part in the historic accord:

> I find it disgusting that any democratic politician would even sit down with murderers and those who would support murder. I cannot understand how people like David Trimble can sleep in their beds at night. This agreement has been built on people's blood. It can only be bad for any society to elevate murderers and their co-travellers. I do not know anyone in this country who does not have equal rights like me. I will absolutely be voting against this.[55]

Mrs Graham's revulsion at the prospect of the IRA's political wing entering a Northern Ireland government was shared by thousands of ordinary unionists. Trimble now had to sell the Agreement not only to his party but also to the very people who had elected him and his colleagues. The Agreement would survive or falter on his ability to persuade a majority of unionists to back the deal. As he reflected on one of the most demanding weeks of his life, the UUP leader must have felt he was embarking on a second Sisyphean journey – pushing the dead weight of emotional unionism, with all its historical baggage and bitter memories, up the mountain in an attempt to reach the summit of a new power-sharing government at Stormont.

A Longer Hot Summer

It had been a bad afternoon for rejectionist loyalism. On Saturday, 18 April Cliftonville FC, the North Belfast soccer side which is mainly supported by the city's Catholics, won the Irish League for the first time in eighty-eight years. Hard-line loyalists including the future leader of the anti-ceasefire terror group, the Orange Volunteers, who were standing outside the Ulster Unionist Council annual meeting in the Europa Hotel that afternoon were outnumbered and out-shouted by a large crowd of rival pro-Agreement loyalists. RUC officers had to intervene to separate the two groups, who bayed at each other across the driveway of what was once the most bombed hotel in the Western world. Several of the pro-Agreement loyalists carried placards praising the Ulster Unionist leader. 'David Trimble peacemaker not peace breaker', one read. Among their number were known associates of Johnny 'Mad Dog' Adair, leader of the UDA's most feared terrorist unit in Belfast and a Maze inmate.

The divisions engendered by the Agreement within loyalist paramilitarism were laid bare outside the Europa Hotel on that afternoon just one week after Good Friday. But worst of all for the Protestant ultras, Trimble had triumphed inside. At seventeen minutes past two Jim Wilson, one of the Vanguard old boys, had emerged from the banqueting hall to tell the waiting reporters, cameramen and photographers that a motion in favour of the Agreement had been passed by 540 votes to 210. After a tense five-hour meeting in front of 860 delegates Trimble had scored a resounding victory over his internal opponents: 72 per cent of the Council had voted for the Good Friday Agreement, despite the opposition of MPs Willie Ross and Willie Thompson and the Orange Order in Trimble's Upper Bann constituency. It was round one to Trimble.

The victory convinced him that the party would now rally around his line, and he predicted:

> Even those who were unhappy with the Agreement and voted against, made it absolutely clear that they had no recriminations of the talks team as a whole, or the leadership in particular. I think that's an indication that now the vote is over, the party is going to unite around the line that the council has adopted, and we proceed into the next round on that basis. We will not have a split unionist party.[1]

However, his vision of a party united behind the Agreement was wildly optimistic. In any normal political party in the democratic world a 70 per cent-plus vote in favour of a given policy would have bound almost the entire membership to that position. But the UUP has never been a normal political party. Although it had run Northern Ireland on the lines of a one-party state for almost seventy years it was now the most fractious, disorganized political movement in western Europe. Paradoxically, the party itself was run on the lines of a hyper-democracy – it was less a party than a loose alliance of conflicting interests ranging from the Young Unionists to the Orange Order. The party's disparate nature was and still is in many ways oddly similar to old Labour when it was umbilically tied to the trade unions and the cooperative movement. Stephen King best summed up the nature of this anachronistic beast slouching across the late twentieth-century political landscape when he defined the UUP as a party 'run on the lines of Presbyterian anarchy with a whiff of Anglican arrogance'. The UUP's character meant there would always room for internal rebellion to grow. The disaffected 30 per cent who lost on 18 April were not going to limp away and accept defeat meekly.

The rebels were split into two factions which sometimes overlapped. The larger group consisted of five of the UUP's nine MPs, a majority of the Young Unionists and the Orange Order. The balance included Jeffrey Donaldson who, while speaking against the Agreement at the Council meeting, was careful not to say he opposed David Trimble. In this early stage of the Referendum campaign Jim Molyneaux was lumped in the latter camp: he had opposed the Agreement but, initially at least, declined to join platforms with Ian Paisley and Robert McCartney. Donaldson's opposition to the Agreement was qualitatively different from that of Ross or Thompson. The older MPs were viscerally opposed to any form of power-sharing with nationalists, let alone republicans, whereas Donaldson recognized what he believed was the fatal design fault in the Good Friday deal – the absence of a link between decommissioning and Sinn Fein entering a government in Belfast.

Trimble's troubles with his dissenters were not made any easier by events south of the border on the same weekend as the Ulster Unionist Council vote. The Sinn Fein leadership who had signed the Good Friday Agreement still had an enormous task to sell the deal to the republican grass roots. Gerry Adams, Martin McGuinness, Gerry Kelly et al. had built their revolutionary reputations in the 1970s by accusing the Official Republicans of selling out on basic principles. The Officials had embarked on a more reformist path that entailed the *de facto* recognition of partition and their willingness to enter a Stormont-based administration. Twenty-odd years later Adams's group, whether they liked to admit it or not, were following the same course. Every ideological retreat could be dressed up as a strategic move to wrong-foot unionism. When the news came through at their party conference (the Ard Feis) that the Ulster Unionist Council had supported Trimble's line, Adams hailed the decision. 'We welcome it. Well done, David,' he told delegates. When one of Trimble's closest aides heard Adams's remark on the television news that evening he shuddered: 'I could just imagine all those ordinary unionists out there, uncertain as to whether they should support the Agreement, watching Adams smiling and him saying, "Well done, David." They were bound to be asking themselves why Adams was praising Trimble. Why would the political wing of the IRA be so enthusiastic about this deal?'[2] Yet there was worse to come for Trimble and his campaign team a month later, when Sinn Fein held a second Ard Feis to overturn their constitutional ban on entering a Stormont Parliament.

In the first fortnight of the Referendum campaign the No unionist alliance was setting the pace. Twelve days after Trimble's victory, the anti-Agreement unionists took the fight to his own constituency. A United Unionist coordinating committee consisting of the DUP, the Orange Order, the Ulster Clubs and several anti-Agreement members of the UUP set up an office in Portadown, in the heart of Upper Bann. From the outset the No campaigners played the emotional card with unionist voters who were horrified at the prospect of terrorists walking free from jail. While Trimble could call on the support of intellectuals and academics, the United Unionists played on the real fears of ordinary unionists. In these circumstances it seemed pointless to allow the campaign to become simply an intellectual struggle between rational and emotional unionism. Trimble soon realized that without positive imagery, in what was fast becoming the most highly televised political campaign in Irish History, his Yes unionist camp would lose the war.

The United Unionists attempted to soften their image with the somewhat crass slogan 'Have a heart for Ulster'. Heart-shaped lapel pins in the colours of the union flag were sold in their thousands to raise finance for the No campaign. The central thrust of their assault on the Agreement was to play on the raw emotions of Protestants who had endured thirty years of terrorism. The extreme wing of the No camp (the LVF, along with some of the loonier Ulster Independence faction and so on) employed dirty tricks and downright intimidation. Trimble's offices in Portadown were attacked by vandals, and his party workers in Upper Bann faced a constant barrage of verbal abuse down the telephone. Leaflets distributed in the constituency contained the home telephone numbers of Trimble and some of his more loyal local lieutenants. Under the banner head 'Trimble embraces the IRA', another leaflet printed the constituency office numbers of David Trimble, John Taylor, Ken Maginnis and Cecil Walker. The text repeated the line, peddled for more than a year, that Trimble was an agent of the British security services. 'Why is David Trimble taking this course of action? Is he an MI5/6 agent – recruited during this Vanguard days – as some allege?' Yet another leaflet showed a picture of bomb-damaged Portadown and below it the words: 'If you want some good to come of this destruction of our town make yourself this promise. I WILL NEVER VOTE FOR DAVID TRIMBLE AGAIN!' One of the more subtle propaganda ploys was the overnight appearance of a series of fly posters in mainly Protestant areas of the Province. They depicted an Irish tricolour with the slogan: 'Vote Yes.' The UUP is convinced that the tricolour posters were the work of elements in the No camp, designed to make Protestants see the Agreement as an exclusively republican/nationalist project.

Every successful modern politician needs a professional spin doctor – preferably someone who comes from outside the ranks of his or her party such as an experienced journalist or PR professional. Trimble hit upon the idea of hiring an outside media campaign director for the month-long battle ahead. The choice was a bearded, gregarious, Southern-born journalist called Ray Haydn. After working for nearly a decade as Ulster Television's industrial correspondent, and with with more than twenty years' experience of covering the Northern Ireland conflict, at the time of the Agreement he was running a successful PR and media training agency business in Belfast. Haydn had known Trimble since the mid-1980s when, as one of the producers of BBC Northern Ireland's *Inside Politics* programme, he often invited the then UUP spokesman on constitutional affairs to take part in radio debates. There was another important advantage for the UUP in hiring Haydn – he strongly believed in the merits of the Agreement and its benefits not only to Ulster Unionism but to Northern Ireland society in general.

One of the first things Haydn wanted to change in the Ulster Unionists' campaign was Trimble himself. He knew how the camera could easily distort a politician's public image, and was worried that his boss's hair appeared greasy and unkempt on television. 'No one else would touch the subject in Glengall Street, so I said it. I told him, "David, you've a problem with your hair. You are going to have to wash it every day." He actually took my advice and for the first few days of the campaign he washed his hair every morning.'[3]

Haydn then insisted on further radical improvements to Trimble's image. When his new PR informed him that there was a problem with his clothes, especially his tendency to wear the same suit and tie two or three days running, Trimble was at first quite indignant. Eventually Haydn persuaded him to do something about it. The two of them walked the short distance from Glengall Street to Parsons and Parsons in Wellington Place, one of the best-known traditional menswear shops in central Belfast. When they returned an hour later, Haydn made Trimble model several new suits in the UUP boardroom. At one stage the leader lifted up a pile of suits and shirts that they had bought. Haydn recalled: 'He turned to me and said, "Are these non-iron shirts?" I said to him it didn't really make a difference – he would have to wear them. But he was worried about his wife's reaction. "I can't ask Daphne to iron shirts." I was insistent that he had to wear them, even though he huffed and puffed about it.' Despite Trimble's reluctance to have his image modernized Haydn claims the UUP leader was an easy client to manage: 'Whenever you argued your case he always accepted it. I don't think throughout the campaign I was over-ruled once. No one in the party would dare say the things I said to him.'[4]

There were two main handicaps facing Trimble and his shrinking band of party loyalists in the campaign. First, only half of the Ulster Unionist Party appeared to be with him – the majority of his MPs, scores of local councillors, the Orange Order, most of the Young Unionists and some of his closest friends had joined the No camp. This was compounded by the lack of women he could call upon for press conferences and publicity shots. His daily briefings with the media were by and large male-dominated affairs. Even before the Agreement was signed he had lost arguably the most telegenic and articulate woman in the party, Arlene Foster, who had sided with John Hunter and the rest of the 'baby barristers' in the No camp. Haydn made up for the dearth of support among party stalwarts with a strategically planned PR offensive. He and his core, which included Patricia Campbell (one of the most senior Catholic members of the UUP), Reg Empey, David Kerr and Jim Wilson, drew up a table prioritizing the media. At the top of their list were the local newspapers and broadcasters in the Province; behind them came the Southern papers, radio stations and RTE; then there were the UK national papers; while at the bottom of the pile was the foreign media. This was to be the most professionally run unionist media campaign in history. On any given day of the Referendum campaign Haydn and his colleagues took on average a hundred requests for interviews with Trimble, Taylor, Empey and others in the Yes camp. Never before had the UUP been given such international media attention.

Trimble's herculean task involved fighting on two fronts – against Paisley and McCartney, and against his own dissidents. His problems were underscored on the eve of his campaign launch. Jeffrey Donaldson led a delegation of No Ulster Unionists to

Stormont, where they pressed the Secretary of State for legal safeguards on the Agreement. Donaldson said the Agreement 'blurs the line between terrorism and democracy'[5] and demanded that paramilitaries begin to decommission before prisoners were freed and Sinn Fein entered office. Twenty-four hours later Trimble opened his campaign by admitting that the UUP had to 'get off our knees' for the fight ahead. He told a large press conference in Glengall Street that he was angered by the 'cheap, misleading, negative No campaign that wants to consign the country to another thirty years of misery'.

Two days later Trimble set out his goal for the Referendum: in order to survive, the Agreement needed to be backed by around 70 per cent of the electorate. In an interview with the unionist daily the *Ulster Newsletter*, Trimble demonstrated his legendary self-confidence: 'I'm quite sure we are going to get a very substantial vote, and I think a lot of people who in the past haven't bothered voting, because politics seems to be unable to do something, will now see the referendum means something and thus it opens the door to new politics.'[6] His appeal to this great swathe of voters, particularly those living in prosperous middle-class redoubts east of the Bann, was an important indication of the Trimble strategy ahead. At an early stage the campaign team concluded that the only way to get a 70 per cent Yes vote was to persuade this normally indifferent band of affluent Protestants, who usually regarded elections as no more than sectarian head counts and stayed at home, to take time out from the garden, the boat and the golf club and vote on 22 May.

The day after his *Ulster Newsletter* interview the No camp were handed the greatest propaganda weapon of the campaign so far. Sinn Fein's special Ard Feis, called to allow Gerry Adams and Martin McGuinness to change the party's constitutional ban on entering Stormont, degenerated into a Nuremberg-style rally. The stars of the show were the four members of the IRA's Balcombe Street gang who had caused havoc and committed murder in London during the 1970s. The four, who had been transferred to jails in the Republic, were granted temporary release to attend the conference. At the RDS conference centre in Dublin they were greeted with wild cheers and a standing ovation. The triumphalist scenes of IRA killers being hugged by Sinn Fein politicians on the platform and the general heroes' welcome they were given outraged unionist opinion in the North. The No faction could justifiably argue that pictures like these would be constantly replayed with different actors each time IRA prisoners walked free from jail without completing their sentences. Only by voting No could this nauseating prospect be prevented, they asserted. To many ordinary unionists the sight of killers being feted only seemed to confirm Robert McCartney's contention that the Agreement was all about appeasing terrorists.

A number of prominent IRA figures in the Maze, too, were granted weekend parole to attend the Ard Feis in order to urge delegates to back the Agreement. They included Padraig Wilson, the IRA's commanding officer in the Maze. The British government's logic in allowing Wilson and his comrades out was that the prisoners' arguments would be pivotal in swaying Sinn Fein to drop its policy of abstentionism in Northern Ireland and thus strengthen the Agreement. Up until 1986 Sinn Fein also boycotted the Irish Parliament, the Dail. They refused to recognize the legitimacy of the Dail because they argued it was set up as a result of the partition of Ireland in 1921. The upshot, however, was that the picture of the smiling IRA killer Hugh Doherty being embraced on the Sinn Fein platform, with his hand held aloft in triumph, threatened to become the dominant image of the Referendum campaign.

To his closest colleagues, Trimble was visibly despondent. He realized the damage that the Balcombe Street gang's welcome-home party had inflicted on the Yes Unionist camp. The decision to allow IRA prisoners in the Maze leave to speak at the Ard Feis put the relationship between Trimble and Mo Mowlam under even greater strain. He claimed her approval for the weekend releases tied in 'with a lot of similar actions in which she has shown considerable indulgence to republicans but considerable insensitivity towards unionists'.[7] Low morale in the UUP was rapidly becoming fatalistic pessimism. On a canvass in Armagh city, two days after the Ard Feis, only three supporters came out to pound the pavements with Trimble. At one stage he was overheard talking into his mobile to Glengall Street: 'I think we may have lost it,' he whispered. For once his famous self-confidence seemed to be slipping away.

His feeling was confirmed by the results of an *Irish Times* opinion poll the same day, which found that 56 per cent of the Northern Ireland electorate would vote Yes. Although it was a technical majority in favour of the Agreement, the figure meant that only a small percentage, certainly a minority, of Protestants would back the deal. Trimble would surely be finished if an overwhelming number of unionists voted No.

The people closest to him during these dark days were furious with those who they believed had stabbed Trimble in the back. Ken Maginnis was unforgiving in his attitude to the rebel UUP MPs, and in particular Jeffrey Donaldson. 'I once berated David for spending too much time with individuals who turned out to be treacherous. David confessed to me that he found it hard not to be loyal to his friends. The difference was that I would find it hard to forgive anyone who deserted me in a time of need.' Maginnis is also scathing about John Taylor's performance during the Referendum: 'John Taylor disappeared off the scene. He did not campaign and instead went AWOL.'[8] This is a view shared by many at the heart of the campaign team, though not by Trimble himself.

Trimble took a less sanguine view of the other deserting MPs, Smyth, Forsythe, Beggs, Ross and Thompson, whom he saw as short-sighted rather than treacherous. According to Stephen King, Trimble referred to them as 'the wooden tops'. Trimble's unwillingness to dismiss Donaldson as he did the other parliamentary rebels is seen by even his closest supporters as the fatal weakness of his leadership. During the campaign Eoghan Harris continually urged Trimble to slap Donaldson down:

> I told David that Donaldson should have been despatched on the principle that if people commit treachery then they should go. I used to quote what I call 'Leonard's law' to David, which is named after the Dublin writer Hugh Leonard. Hugh said that if you do somebody a favour in Dublin you make an enemy of them for life. I told David it would be very wrong for him to forgive Donaldson, because he would do it again in the future. Every great politician needs a chip of ice in his heart. It's probably the only down side to David's character as a politician that he can't put people like Donaldson down.[9]

But in the penultimate week of the campaign there were more optimistic signs that the unionist grass roots were not as vehemently opposed to the Agreement as were some of the UUP sceptics in the No camp. Trimble was given a standing ovation by Pro-Agreement delegates in Lagan Valley at a private meeting organised by Lisburn councillor Ivan Davis, days after the Balcombe Street gang debacle. The packed meeting of almost a hundred UUP delegates in Hillsborough cheered Trimble following a heated question-and-answer session. Donaldson sent an apology for being unable to attend.

The Yes unionists then suffered a second major setback on 14 May when the convicted UDA killer Michael Stone was given a massive hero's welcome by thousands of loyalists in the Ulster Hall. The UDP-organized rally in favour of the Agreement turned into a public-relations disaster as pictures were beamed around the world of Stone, the loyalist who had launched the lone gun and bomb attack on the funerals of the three IRA members killed in Gibraltar ten years earlier, being treated like a pop star by his adoring fans. One banner strewn across the upper balcony of the hall where David Trimble had been elected UUP leader three years earlier read: 'Michael Stone says Yes.' And while Paisley and McCartney were lampooned on stage by speaker after speaker, the two No unionist leaders must have relished the scenes inside the Ulster Hall. One senior Trimble aide called Michael Stone's adulation a 'fucking disaster. We now had D.T. lumped in the same camp as the Balcombe Street gang and the Milltown murderer. Paisley and McCartney would exploit that to the hilt.'[10] In private Trimble was furious with Mo Mowlam for allowing Stone out for the evening. David Kerr recalls, 'We thought that image of Stone combined with the Balcombe Street gang had finished us off.'[11]

Although the loyalist killer would claim to have been fighting for the union, the overwhelming majority of unionists never supported the UDA or UVF throughout thirty years of conflict. The derisory number of votes cast for the two terror groups' political wings during the Troubles was testimony to this. What made matters worse for Trimble was that the UDA rally took place in the same week that the No unionists launched an emotive media blitz via poster and newspaper advertisements. One of them showed a young woman wiping away a tear a year after the Referendum, and asking: 'How did I bring myself to vote SF/IRA into government?'

On the streets Trimble was getting a rough ride from opponents of the Agreement. On the morning of 16 May DUP supporters in Lurgan jostled him. During his walk-about they had stalked him with placards denouncing him as a traitor. At one stage Trimble's two armed police bodyguards put themselves between him and an angry group of protestors. The No unionists screamed 'Judas' as

Trimble attempted to speak to the media. Ray Haydn, who walked through lines of baying loyalists with Trimble, actually thought this spectacle had helped their cause. He believed that 'middle Ulster' would be repelled by the sight of the mild-mannered UUP leader being harangued and threatened by a group of over-excited fundamentalists, that Trimble might in fact have gained some sympathy among those unionists who had still not made up their minds about the Agreement.

Later that day, however, Trimble came under fire from a new and more damaging quarter – his predecessor Jim Molyneaux. The ex-UUP leader stood on a United Unionist platform in Lurgan and affirmed his support for the No campaign. The former Irish cabinet minister and one-time editor of the *Observer* Conor Cruise O'Brien joined Molyneaux on the rostrum. O'Brien received an enthusiastic welcome from the 1500-strong audience, which included all factions of No unionism including members of the Loyalist Volunteer Force. In 1995 O'Brien had welcomed Trimble's election as UUP leader, but he had since joined McCartney's party and, like the North Down MP, regarded the Agreement as a sop to the IRA.

(Many Irish intellectuals, writers and peace campaigners who admired O'Brien's laser-sharp critique of violent republicanism felt utterly disillusioned with his involvement in the No unionist camp. Chris Hudson, the Dublin peace activist and go-between with the UVF and the Irish government, accused O'Brien of retreating on his liberal principles by aligning himself with Ian Paisley. David Trimble, who held O'Brien in high esteem for many years, regarded his defection to the Paisley/McCartney axis as a 'sad mistake'. A close friend, also disappointed that O'Brien had backed the No camp, put it down to his infatuation with Robert McCartney: 'The trouble with Conor is he needs heroes, and McCartney is obviously one of them.')

In those difficult days Ray Haydn probably got closer to Trimble than many of his political colleagues had done over two decades. 'Up close and personal I witnessed a man with enormous courage. I did not see somebody who was rude or arrogant. He had time for people, and yet he was terribly absent-minded.' At the 8.30 a.m. daily meeting in Glengall Street (nicknamed 'prayers' for the campaign's duration) Trimble would open his personal organizer and have the morning papers sprawled across his desk. Haydn said that one second he would be engrossed in his Psion or the papers and the next he would look up and nod in agreement to whatever was being said. 'He was so lost in that computer that some of us had to haul him back to reality. Ken Maginnis did it very well. One morning Maginnis shouted at him, "David, for God's sake would you put that f***ing thing away. This is serious." Trimble blushed and replied, "Yes, sergeant major, sir." These were nervous moments and there was a lot at stake. We needed to keep him focussed.'[12] Another of Haydn's main functions was to tear Trimble's mobile phone from his ear, where it seemed to be permanently stuck.

With just a week left to polling day, Trimble's advisers were alarmed that the tide had not turned in his favour. A *Daily Telegraph* opinion poll on 16 May found that, while 61 per cent now favoured the Agreement, the Protestant community was still uncertain about how to vote. Among unionists, 43 per cent said they would vote for the Agreement while 27 per cent said No. Crucially, large numbers of Protestants – 27 per cent – were still wavering as the campaign entered its final week.

Sean O'Callaghan was worried that Downing Street was treating the Referendum like a mainland election campaign. In particular he thought that the language of the campaign had to change in order to give the unionist community reassurance on issues like prisoners, decommissioning and Sinn Fein in government. Over that weekend he got in touch with Jonathan Powell, the Prime Minister's chief of staff, through a third party. O'Callaghan suggested that Powell should talk to an Orangeman in Co. Tyrone whom he regarded as a good touchstone of grassroots unionist opinion. The Orangeman in question was a waverer who, though in his head he wanted to support the Agreement, in his heart was sickened at the prospect of IRA and loyalist prisoners walking free without having served their full sentences. The former IRA commander believed that, if Powell listened to this Orangeman's concerns and then conveyed them to Tony Blair, the language of the campaign could change radically in the last week.

According to O'Callaghan, Powell was scathing about the decision to free Michael Stone and its subsequent negative impact on the Yes campaign. He also tried to repair the fractured alliance between Trimble and Donaldson. O'Callaghan claims the two men almost did so, but allies on each side ensured that they remained apart.

O'Callaghan then worked on Lord Cranborne who was sceptical about the Agreement, especially the rather vague promises on decommissioning. However, he managed to persuade Cranborne and Labour MP Kate Hoey to travel to Northern Ireland and canvass with Trimble. The Northern Ireland-born Hoey was an important addition to Trimble's team because she had been a close ally of Robert McCartney's during the days of the Campaign for Equal Citizenship.

There was third person whom O'Callaghan sought to influence in the last week of the Referendum campaign – the chaplain of the Orange Order in Co. Armagh, the Reverend William Bingham. O'Callaghan played on Bingham's dislike of Paisley:

> William was definitely going to be a No voter, a soft No. But then I spoke to him and said, 'So you are going to work with Paisley.' I knew that William would not like that, since he disliked what Paisley stood for. Bingham was very important to get on to Trimble's side. He was respected throughout the rank and file of the Orange Order and the wider Protestant community. Jonathan Powell, who once told me that 'William tells me what to say and I write the script', also held Bingham in high regard.[13]

O'Callaghan's personal crusade to persuade this motley crew to come to Trimble's aid proved an invaluable contribution to the UUP's flagging Yes campaign. Cranborne and Hoey travelled to Northern Ireland on 18 May to accompany Trimble on a canvass of Derry city centre. For Trimble it was a return to the home of his forebears. He and his entourage were taken on a tour of the historic walls under which the townspeople had sheltered during the 1689 siege. As he passed that section of the walls overlooking the republican strongholds to the west which included Free Derry corner, the original entrance to the Bogside which assumed legendary status when nationalists held back Stormont's security forces there in August 1969, Trimble declared: 'As Mitchel McLaughlin [Sinn Fein's national chairman] acknowledged last week, this Agreement is one in which the Irish government, nationalists and republicans are recognizing the legitimacy of Ulster. They are saying that Londonderry and the Bogside here behind me are as British now as Bangor or Bournemouth.'[14] Cranborne then told the raft of reporters following the group that unionists could vote Yes and show they were prepared to take a chance for peace and prosperity. Hoey then attacked her old comrade Robert McCartney: 'I think he set out to make sure he could not agree with the Agreement, and now has to say some ridiculous things.' As they were leaving, the Trimble team were nearly caught out by a disastrous photo opportunity. One of the accompanying photographers spotted a headstone marked 'Trimble' in the graveyard inside the walls and asked the UUP leader if he would pose beside it given his own connections to the siege. His media minders went apoplectic and quickly ushered their man away. The last thing they wanted was a picture of Trimble beside a gravestone bearing his name, which would have been quickly exploited by the No camp as an image of a man whose political career was about to be buried.

The O'Callaghan–Cranborne–Hoey axis played an important part in helping to steady nerves and shore up the Trimble campaign. But the critical moves in its final days were made by four other radically different players. They were Glen Barr, Bono, Tony Blair and the former RUC Chief Constable Sir Jack Hermon.

Although Barr personally opposed the Good Friday Agreement he still held some residual loyalty to Trimble. The former UWC spokesman and old Vanguard comrade had been appointed to the British government's Parades Commission – the quango charged with taking decisions on controversial loyalist parades – as one of two loyalist representatives on the body, the other being Tommy Cheevers from the UVF-aligned Progressive Unionist Party. In the middle of the Referendum campaign the Commission was scheduled to deliver its preliminary verdict on whether the Drumcree 1998 parade would be allowed to pass through the Garvaghy Road. (As it turned out, the Commission recommended – despite opposition from both Barr and Cheever – that the Orange march be rerouted away from the Garvaghy Road. The verdict, however, did not make the light of day until after the Referendum.) Barr realized that during the campaign Trimble's unionist opponents would exploit the ban and dress it up as just one more sop to violent republicanism. He contacted Trimble and informed him that the Parades Commission was about to ban the Drumcree March. Trimble then relayed to Downing Street his concern about the impact that this would have on the Yes campaign. Tony Blair agreed with Trimble's analysis and intervened to delay the Commission's report.

Barr, a faithful adherent to Ulster independence who actually disagreed with the Agreement, had saved his former Vanguard colleague. The Parades Commission had a remit to take controversial decisions on Orange marches out of the hands of politicians and police officers. And yet Trimble was able, via Barr and ultimately Blair, to compromise its political independence in the wider interests of saving the Good Friday Agreement.

Eight days before the vote, with things starting to slip badly for the Yes camp, a group of SDLP campaign workers met at the party's headquarters on the Ormeau Road in South Belfast. Tim Attwood, an SDLP activist since his time as President of Queen's University's Students' Union, suggested that what was needed to boost the Yes campaign's flagging fortunes was a major event that could capture the public's imagination. Attwood knew that John Hume had been a close friend of the band U2's lead singer Bono for over a decade. If Bono could be invited to Belfast in the final week of campaigning, the fortunes of the Yes camp might turn. During an early morning meeting at the SDLP HQ Attwood proposed that Hume and Trimble should be seen together with Bono – the leaders of unionism and nationalism united by one of the world's most famous pop stars. The SDLP, concerned that Trimble needed help, sent Attwood and the party's press officer, Connail McDevitt, to seek out David Kerr, Trimble's press secretary.

In the meantime Eamon McCann, one of Ireland's premier pop-concert promoters, was asked to help set up an event at Belfast's Waterfront Hall, the flying-saucer-shaped venue on the river Lagan which had come to symbolize the spirit of reconstruction in post-ceasefire Northern Ireland. McCann told the SDLP he might be able to get rock band Ash to join U2 at the peace concert. This group of young Protestants from Downpatrick, he said, would be a perfect counter-balance to the Dublin-based super-group. Bono telephoned the SDLP office and told Attwood he thought the peace concert was a great idea. Around five o'clock that day Attwood and McDevitt met Kerr. 'Kerr was delirious,' Attwood recalls. 'He kept saying to us, "What? Bono? You can get Bono?" He thought it was a brilliant move.'[15]

(To their credit the SDLP generally fought a non-triumphalist, politically neutral Yes campaign designed not to cause panic in the unionist community. In contrast Sinn Fein, usually among the most energetic and proactive parties in Ireland, were noticeable by their absence. The party hardly canvassed at all on the streets of republican heartlands such as West Belfast. Republican sceptics said this was due to the overall lack of enthusiasm for the Agreement amongst the Provisionals' rank and file. Indeed, on the Referendum day itself the electorally insignificant Workers' Party had a more visible presence outside polling booths in parts of Belfast and seemed to have put up more Yes posters on lamp-posts than any other non-unionist party.)

When Kerr returned to Glengall Street that night he told Trimble about the proposed concert. Trimble's first reaction was: 'Who's Bono?' Ray Haydn, who had hardly left Trimble's side that day, burst out laughing. He recalled:

> About sixty million people around the world knew who Bono was – except David Trimble. I suppose if it had been Pavarotti or Domingo he would have known. But I jumped at the idea, even though there was huge reluctance initially from many of the old guard – the ones with the Neanderthal attitudes in Glengall Street. I was trying to drag the party into the twentieth century, never mind the twenty-first, and this was the perfect opportunity to do that.[16]

As with almost every decision, Haydn made Trimble agree. 'That's great, that's great,' he kept repeating in order to convince his media director that he was taking the whole thing seriously.

Attwood's small team at the SDLP worked tirelessly with Eamon McCann over the weekend to organize the concert, which had been scheduled for Tuesday, 19 May. On Saturday morning Bono confirmed that his entire band would return from various parts of the world to be there. One of the main logistical problems was distributing the two thousand free tickets. Attwood was concerned that some of them could fall into the hands of DUP supporters, who might disrupt the gig with a publicity stunt of their own. The best way to hand out the tickets was through the Province's schools. That weekend Attwood and his fellow SDLP workers contacted the principals of hundreds of schools to offer tickets to their sixth-formers. A smaller number were reserved for the youth wings of the political parties in the Yes camp. The announcement that Hume and Trimble were to unite with U2 and Ash was made that Monday. It helped steal publicity away from what was meant to have been a major coup for the No camp – Jim Molyneaux holding a press conference to call for a No vote on Referendum day. Molyneaux's public rebuff of Trimble was drowned in the deluge of media coverage of the forthcoming concert.

Party headquarters at Glengall Street played little part in all this. Chris and Michael McGimpsey rang up to obtain tickets for their sons. The party had been given two hundred tickets but did not know what to do with them. Chris put that down to the Young Unionists' hostility to Trimble:

> Michael rang his son Gareth and asked him how many of his mates would like free tickets for the U2/Ash gig? Gareth told him he could give out at least thirty in half an hour. You couldn't give them to our youth wing, as they were all in the No camp. But even despite that there were plenty of councillors and party members with teenage children. Yet no one in Glengall Street could be bothered to spend an hour ringing them up to ask them if their kids would like to see U2 for nothing. It was the Ulster Unionist Party at its worst – they just couldn't be bothered.[17]

The next morning Ash agreed to attend a press conference with Trimble at the Waterfront Hall, just hours before the concert, to urge a Yes vote. Haydn claimed it was the most enjoyable press conference of the entire campaign. 'We needed a young Protestant image to urge first-time voters in the unionist community to come out and vote,' he said. The band got on exceptionally well with Trimble, although the UUP leader confessed to the group that 'I know nothing about your music – I'm more an opera person'. Tim Wheeler, the band's lead singer, turned to Trimble and said: 'Don't worry – we'll educate you.' The massive media interest in this unique meeting of politics and pop included live broadcasts from MTV, which beamed out hours of coverage from the Waterfront Hall including the Ash/Trimble press conference. How did Trimble, the stuffy, hyper-intellectual, wine-drinking, opera-loving academic, react to suddenly finding himself a world celebrity on MTV? Haydn claimed his client was thoroughly enjoying it. 'He actually thought it was great *craic* [fun]. He even brought some of his older kids along for the concert.'[18]

An hour before the concert Trimble shook hands with Bono outside the Hall and then went in for a meeting with the singer and

John Hume. They chatted about politics and the importance of building a future for the next generation. Ash was first on stage. Tim Wheeler, the son of a local high court judge, told the crowd he wanted to bring on 'some special guests'. Bono and U2 guitarist The Edge then joined Ash in a rendition of the Beatles' song 'Hey, Jude (Don't Let Me Down)'. After a few choruses of John Lennon's 'All we are saying is give peace a chance', Bono addressed the audience. 'This is a great gig, this is a great band and it's great to be in Belfast in a week when history is being made,' he told them. 'I would like to introduce you to two men who are making history, two men who have taken a leap of faith out of the past and into the future. We want them to join us on stage.'

The two party leaders, who had discarded their suit jackets, appeared relaxed as they strode on to the stage in front of a backdrop which proclaimed: 'YES – Make Your Own History'. The crowd, mainly of teenagers, went ecstatic. Bono then grabbed Hume's and Trimble's arms and held them aloft. The incongruous sight of this gesture of camaraderie between the the world's most famous lead pop singer and two middle-aged, slightly overweight Ulster politicians turned out to be the dominant image of the campaign, eclipsing the triumphalist hero-worship of the Balcombe Street gang and Michael Stone. This public demonstration of unity between constitutional Irish nationalism and Ulster Unionism at the Waterfront Hall was in complete and utter contrast to the last time Trimble had presented such an image in public – with Ian Paisley at Drumcree in 1995. His televised journey from demon to peacemaker in the space of only three years was truly remarkable.

Yet the Bono–Trimble–Hume triple act almost never happened. According to Tim Attwood, the original plan had been for the two party leaders simply to be seen in the audience. It was Bono's idea on the day to bring both of them on stage during the concert. After the ovation for Trimble and Hume had died down, Bono called for a moment of silence for the victims of the Troubles. Then Tim Wheeler joined U2 on stage to play their anthem, 'One', followed by the last number of the historic gig, 'Stand by Me'.

(Although the U2/Ash gig was an astounding success, Trimble has yet to thank the principal organizer of the event, Tim Attwood. Friends and foes alike complain about Trimble's absent-mindedness, particularly towards those who have granted him favours. But then he does, after all, have a lot on his mind.)

However, it would take more than prancing about on stage with pop singers to sell the Agreement to a sceptical and nervous unionist population. Trimble needed another political superstar to convince the unionist community, or at least a majority of it, to buy the deal. As with Good Friday, Tony Blair rode into town again to rescue Trimble. The Prime Minister made a number of visits to the Province during the campaign but the most important was his last, on the eve of the poll. Blair was scheduled to meet Trimble and Hume at the Dunadry Hotel on the outskirts of Belfast, not far from the airport. He arrived shortly before nine o'clock in an RAF Wessex helicopter whose rotor blades created a mini-dust-storm around journalists and TV crews as it landed in the car park. Blair flew in to announce five pledges to the people of Northern Ireland. Following a photo-call with the UUP and SDLP leaders under a tree in the hotel's gardens, he hailed David Trimble as a brave leader 'who has shown courage, tenacity and leadership that has been missing from the politicians of Northern Ireland for a long time'.[19] His pledges, in his own handwriting, were enlarged and then splashed over a mobile advertising hoarding. Each of them was intended to reassure doubting unionists. Those pledges, which would come back to haunt both Trimble and Blair, were: no change in the status of Northern Ireland without the express consent of the people; power to take decisions to be returned to a Northern Ireland Assembly, with accountable North–South cooperation; fairness and equality guaranteed for all; those who used or threatened violence to be excluded from the government of Northern Ireland; and prisoners to be kept in jail unless violence was given up for good.

The Prime Minister then travelled with Trimble to Coleraine, 'capital' of East Londonderry, the constituency of Willie Ross, the UUP No campaigner. With Trimble on his right, Blair told another batch of reporters that he reaffirmed his support for the union. 'I am proud to speak to you as the Prime Minister of the UK. I value that union.'[20] At this stage the UUP still regarded Blair as a vital asset in their campaign. Since his party's election the previous year Blair had underlined his belief in the union and the principle of consent. Most unionists appeared to trust him even if they had little or no faith in his Northern Ireland Secretary. (Mo Mowlam was curiously absent for most of the Referendum campaign. Her only big public appearance was on the same day as the U2 concert, when she went walk-about in Belfast city centre with Virgin boss Richard Branson – another public figure who flew to the Province to back the Agreement.)

Trimble's campaign team had one more ace card to play before he went into two head-to-head contests on television with Paisley and McCartney on the eve of the poll. One of the most nervous constituencies inside the wider unionist community comprised the thirteen thousand members of the Royal Ulster Constabulary and their families. They were deeply concerned about Chris Patten's commission on the RUC's future which was envisaged in the Agreement, and what it might entail for policing. What the Trimble team needed was an experienced, well-respected policeman to assuage those fears. Unlike their opponents in the No camp, the UUP were blessed with support from non-party-political allies in civil society. One of Trimble's strongest supporters was Trevor Ringland, the former captain of the Ireland rugby team and a one-time member of the British Lions. Ringland, who strongly supported Trimble and the Agreement, had extensive contacts throughout the RUC including its former Chief Constable, the doughty and combative Sir Jack Hermon. Sir Jack had guided the force through troubled waters, including the shoot-to-kill controversies and the subsequent Stalker investigation. He had been at the helm when the RUC endured some of the worst years of terrorist violence and when officers came under attack not only from their traditional enemies in the IRA and INLA but also from loyalists during the early years of the Anglo–Irish Agreement. Ringland, who kept in constant contact with Trimble and his colleagues during the Referendum, believed he could deliver Sir Jack to the Yes camp. Ray Haydn was overjoyed at the prospect, for Hermon was still highly respected inside the force.

Ringland rang Hermon and asked him if he would accompany Trimble on an eve-of-poll walk-about in Belfast city centre. Sir Jack agreed, and around mid-morning on 21 May he joined the UUP leader outside Belfast City Hall. The media interest in the event was beyond Haydn's wildest dreams, with thirty-five camera crews and some seventy reporters following the pair as they crossed Donegall Place into Royal Avenue, the main shopping thoroughfare. The two men found it next to impossible to press the flesh of early-morning shoppers given the media scrum around them, but the pictures of Trimble and Hermon together on the Yes trail were an invaluable propaganda coup. Haydn insists that the walk-about may have been even more important than the Bono concert, though he was relieved that the media failed to pick up on a remark made by Sir Jack. He said he was there to canvass not for the UUP but for the Agreement. Had the SDLP asked him to walk down Royal Avenue with them, he would have obliged.

Later that afternoon Trimble's final canvass of the campaign took him into the loyalist heartland of the Shankill Road. In the strongholds of the UVF and UDA (both terror groups supported the Agreement) he was greeted warmly. During another walk-about along the Shankill Trimble passed a series of huge wall murals depicting armed and masked UVF men. As Trimble stopped to talk to shoppers a car drove by with its loudspeakers blaring out an anti-Paisley message. 'God votes Yes but his main disciple votes No,' it boomed. Many of the loyalist terrorist leaders whom he had known in his Vanguard and UWC days also came out to support him in the last twenty-four hours of the campaign. Andy Tyrie spoke publicly in favour of the Agreement, while Sam McClure also backed the deal. The Shankill – at the height of the Troubles one of the most dangerous roads in western Europe – was arguably the safest place for Trimble to be that week. It was a measure of the depth of support he still commanded within working-class loyalism that Trimble was able to walk freely there even though he had signed up to a historic compromise with Irish nationalism. One UDA man who came out of a loyalist prisoners' aid centre to give the thumbs-up sign to Trimble as he walked past summed up these new times: 'If Brian Faulkner had come up to this road after signing Sunningdale in 1974 he would have been lynched. Trimble can come up here any time he wants. He did a good job.'[21]

His first televised clash with McCartney was recorded later that afternoon for BBC Northern Ireland's flagship politics programme *Hearts and Minds*. On the way to the studio Kate Hoey advised Trimble to laugh off McCartney's jibes. But the UKUP leader clearly landed a number of severe blows on Trimble, particularly on decommissioning. McCartney berated Trimble so much that the UUP leader made a damaging gaffe, calling disarmament 'irrelevant'. The head-to-head then degenerated into a squabble over who was the more adept lawyer. When Trimble left Broadcasting House for the short journey to Glengall Street he confided that he might have lost the clash. 'Oh well, you can't win them all,' he confessed afterwards to Ray Haydn. His spin doctor was furious at Trimble's handling of the scrap. He kept apologising to Haydn for being too tense on air: 'Next time I'll make sure I'm a bit more relaxed.' 'Next time' was less than three hours away, when Trimble was scheduled for his first live television debate with Ian Paisley on BBC Northern Ireland's early evening news programme *Newsline 6.30*. At a final strategy meeting in Glengall Street Ken Maginnis urged Trimble to play hard with Paisley. He was blunt with his advice: 'We are trying to find a polite way of saying, "Look, you arsehole, the decent people don't want your politics, so piss off!" '[22]

Haydn armed Trimble with a secret weapon to produce during the debate – a series of photographs of Paisley and party colleagues wearing the red berets of Ulster Resistance in 1986. When Paisley accused Trimble of supping with the paramilitary devil by signing the Agreement, Trimble pulled out the pictures. 'What about these, Ian?' he kept shouting at the DUP leader, who sat impassive as a colossus. Haydn was delighted with his client's performance. Trimble had listened to his advice and the photographs had turned out be an effective shield against Paisley's line of attack. Although he was still shaking slightly from his encounter, Trimble seemed happier when he walked out of Broadcasting House for the second time that day. He had kept his notorious temper under control, avoided getting bogged down in legalistic detail and exposed Paisley to charges of hypocrisy regarding links with paramilitaries.

As Trimble went off early the next morning to vote at his local polling station, Harmony Hill primary school in Lisburn, people were reading a profile in *The Independent* by one of the first national political correspondents to track his career. Donald MacIntyre had followed Trimble on the hustings during the 1990 Upper Bann by-election, when the quiet-spoken academic was an unknown quantity in Westminster. So it was appropriate that MacIntyre should return to the Province eight years later to rejoin Trimble on the campaign trail, this time in the most important political contest in Northern Ireland since partition. He had frequently been at Trimble's side during the campaign, travelling with him to places like Coleraine and Portstewart, Protestant middle-class redoubts that were home to many of the unionist undecided. MacIntyre was impressed by Trimble's political journey from phlegmatic hard-liner to soft-spoken compromiser. At the end of a rather glowing profile, he quoted Louis MacNeice, the Northern Irish Protestant poet who wrote about his impatience with the bigotry that blighted his land:

> Your hope must wake
> While the choice is yours to make,
> The mortgage not foreclosed, the offer open.

MacIntyre ended his piece by reminding readers in Britain that if Northern Ireland accepted the offer now on the table – the Good Friday Agreement – 'it will owe a large debt to the brave, complex and sometimes prickly man who leads the Ulster Unionist Party'.[23]

With only hours to go before polling closed, Ray Haydn laid several wagers with key figures in the UUP camp. He predicted that the Yes vote would be around 71 per cent – in line with the Ulster Unionist Council vote the previous month. Trimble's praetorian guard – Ken Maginnis, Jack Allen, Jim Wilson, Reg Empey and party chairman Denis Rogan – all estimated that the vote would be slightly lower, perhaps around 65 per cent. Haydn bet each of them £5 that his figure would be the closest to the actual vote.

The next day Ray Haydn was £25 richer. Shortly after lunch Northern Ireland's chief electoral officer, Pat Bradley, announced the result: 71.12 per cent for Yes and 28.88 per cent for No. There were cheers and chants of 'Easy! Easy' from scores of pro-Agreement loyalists in the UDP and PUP, many of them ex-prisoners who had served long sentences in the Maze. The turn-out was perhaps as important as the result – at 81 per cent it was the highest in Northern Ireland's history. The great indifferent mass of middle-class and young Protestants who normally did not bother to vote had done so this time – the UUP strategy for arousing the indifferent affluent from their slumber had worked.

A simultaneous vote in the Republic on the same day produced a startling 90 per cent in favour of the Agreement. The people there were sending a clear message to Northern Ireland that a peaceful settlement meant more to them than constitutional imperatives about taking back the Six Counties.

The breakdown of the Yes vote in the North's seventeen parliamentary constituencies seemed even more promising for Trimble, especially since he now had to fight a second election campaign for the new Northern Ireland Assembly proposed in the Agreement.

Bob McCartney's constituents in North Down voted 70 per cent in favour of the Agreement. Even a narrow majority (52 per cent) in Jeffrey Donaldson's Lagan Valley constituency voted for the Agreement. The only constituency with a majority No vote was Ian Paisley's in North Antrim, where 55 per cent said No.

The expression on Trimble's face as the vote was announced was a mixture of elation and relief. 'The people want to go forward,' he declared. 'They cannot be held back any longer.'[24] Then he turned to Sinn Fein, calling on the republican movement to disarm their war machine and promise there would never be a return to violence. The No unionist leaders tried their best to put a brave face on a bad defeat. As he left the count centre Robert McCartney insisted that a majority of the pro-union people had actually voted No. (In fact a *Sunday Times*/Coopers and Lybrand survey published a day after the result showed that 96 per cent of Catholics voted Yes, while a smaller majority of Protestants, around 55 per cent, also backed the Agreement.) Behind McCartney came Ian Paisley and his DUP entourage, who had to run the gauntlet of jeering loyalists including several ex-UVF and ex-UDA men who had once regarded the Free Presbyterian preacher as the father figure of modern unionism. As Paisley and his colleagues were bundled through a melee of cameramen, photographers and journalists the loyalists chanted: 'Cheerio, Cheerio, Cheerio . . . Cheerio, Cheerio, Cheerio!' An English journalist remarked perhaps too optimistically: 'A sad end for Paisley.' One of the DUP leader's younger admirers heard the comment and shouted back: 'Oh, don't worry – we'll get Trimble in the Assembly elections. We'll be back!'

Less than a fortnight later Trimble attempted to heal the wounds afflicting the party when he invited Jeffrey Donaldson to join him and Ken Maginnis at a meeting with the Prime Minister in Downing Street. But the pictures of a scowling Maginnis a few paces behind Donaldson as they entered No. 10 only illuminated the bitter divisions caused by the Agreement and the subsequent bruising Referendum campaign. Maginnis had been appointed director of elections for the Assembly contest and was adamant that Donaldson would not be allowed to stand. It was a view shared by the pro-Trimble bureaucracy in Glengall Street. The UUP had strict rules about double jobbing: no MP could serve in another chamber, such as the European Parliament or a local Assembly. While the leader and deputy leader of the party were granted special dispensation to stand for the Assembly elections on 27 June, Glengall Street imposed a blanket ban on all the other MPs; they included the chief dissenters during the Referendum – Donaldson, Thompson, Beggs, Smyth and Ross.

Trimble refused to intervene on Donaldson's behalf, although he personally did not revel in the exclusion of the Lagan Valley MP from the list of Assembly candidates. He still sought a reconciliation with his former protégé, even while others such as Maginnis were counselling their leader to discipline him for his desertion the previous month. Eoghan Harris was even more savage in his assessment of Donaldson, and before the election campaign began urged Trimble to cut him down to size. 'I told Trimble that he should have treated Donaldson like a dog with mange – he should have put him down.'[25]

Once again Trimble was entering a bruising political battle under fire from two fronts. He had one advantage, however, over his unionist opponents: control of one of the most sophisticated media machines in Northern Ireland's history. The party's election broadcasts were regarded as among the best ever seen or heard in the Province. Trimble was able to call on influential sections of society for visible support during the month-long campaign. One of the broadcasts included on-camera messages of support for Trimble from public figures such as rugby star Trevor Ringland and Northern Ireland's leading cancer specialist, Roy Spence, at Belfast City Hospital. Haydn hired one of the North's most prestigious independent production companies, Visionworks Television, to shoot and edit the two broadcasts. Their style was reminiscent of Peter Mandelson's classic 'Kinnock-the movie' for Labour's 1987 general election campaign.

'Trimble-the movie' started off in a bucolic sequence on the Fermanagh lakes, showing the UUP leader at the helm of a power-boat with Daphne at his side as he steered the vessel through the water past Enniskillen Castle. The subliminal message was clear – a safe pair of hands at the wheel. His critics in the DUP and UKUP jibed that the direction of Trimble's boat was telling – southwards towards the border with the Republic. Yet the Fermanagh segment of the film was important in terms of shoring up the confidence of UUP voters.

Harry West, party leader at the time of the UWC strike in 1974, came out of retirement to back Trimble in the run-up to the election. West even made a fleeting appearance in the first broad-cast, urging sceptical Ulster unionists to support their leader in these trying times. West's endorsement was all the more important given the tensions and divisions that were now surfacing from inside the UUP. This intervention demonstrated that Trimble still had some supporters in the Ulster Unionist old guard.

Jeffrey Donaldson's constituency association agreed with Glen-gall Street's view that the party's MPs (with the exception of Trimble and Taylor) should be barred from standing for the Assembly. So on 26 May the Lagan Valley Ulster Unionists delivered a snub to their MP by refusing him permission to stand. Donaldson's supporters were furious and pledged to support other No unionist candidates in the election instead of official UUP candidates. Arlene Foster suffered a similar fate in Fermanagh and South Tyrone, Ken Maginnis's parliamentary constituency. Maginnis, director of elections for the Assembly campaign, ensured that Foster was not selected as a candidate. The Fermanagh and South Tyrone Ulster Unionists had been solidly loyal to Trimble during the Referendum. Many were angry at Foster's defection to the No camp and were determined to pay her back.

However, the pro-Trimble tendency did not get its way entirely in other constituencies. Peter Weir was selected as the third Ulster Unionist candidate in North Down, while Trimble's old comrade turned adversary John Hunter won one of the UUP nominations for South Antrim. In those areas where anti-Agreement candidates had been prevented from standing, Ulster Unionists in the No faction pledged to support Bob McCartney's UKUP candidates instead. The mutiny was growing, and on 4 June the most senior Orangeman in Co. Armagh decided to run as an Independent Unionist against the official UUP candidates in Trimble's Upper Bann constituency. Denis Watson, the Co. Armagh Grand Master, was actually a member of the UUP's ruling executive when he opted to stand against his own party's selected list. Watson insisted that he did not want his candidacy to be seen as a personal attack on Trimble, even though that is exactly how most party members perceived it.

(The day before Watson's defection Trimble had attempted to placate the Orange vote. At a press conference in Belfast he suggested that the marching season could be turned into the most colourful folk festival in western Europe. When pressed on what he was doing to ensure that the disputed marches did not threaten tourism, Trimble rather naïvely replied: 'This is something we should be able to turn to our advantage, something the entire community would benefit from in terms of tourism.'[26]

Trimble tried to quell the new rebellion by adopting a hard-line attitude towards republicans at his manifesto launch on 9 June. He was adamant that there would be no government in shadow form set up in Belfast until the 'democratic credentials' of republicans were well and truly established. Denying journalists' suggestions that he was already moving away from the Good Friday Agreement, Trimble set down five conditions that had to be met before he was prepared to set up the Shadow executive. These were: a clear and unequivocal commitment that the 'war' was over; an end to targeting, training, weapons procurement and punishment beatings; a progressive abandonment and dismantling of paramilitary structures; disarmament to be completed within two years; and the disclosure of the whereabouts of the Disappeared (a number of IRA victims, all Catholics, who had been kidnapped, killed and buried in secret in the 1970s).

In the middle of the election campaign Trimble's attentions were diverted to the other side of the Atlantic, where a book by the Northern Ireland-born journalist Sean McPhelimy had just been published. *The Committee* contains allegations of the existence of a sinister coordinating committee of Protestant businessmen, politicians, clergymen, police officers and loyalist paramilitaries. This committee is supposed to have directed loyalist terrorism for more than a decade, particularly in mid-Ulster, where high-grade intelligence is said to have been passed via the security forces, businessmen and political leaders to the UVF and UDA. McPhelimy alleged that Trimble was one of the political leaders directing loyalist terrorism. In a legal action ongoing at the time of publication McPhelimy subsequently withdrew the specific allegation against David Trimble.

Although Trimble had long-standing connections with loyalist leaders from Vanguard, the UWC and Ulster Clubs, there is no evidence to implicate him in any terrorist activities. He may have given the late John McMichael and Andy Tyrie advice on constitutional matters, he may even have briefly held membership of the legal but menacing Vanguard Service Corps, but there is no trail leading to Trimble's direct involvement in the terror campaigns of the UDA and UVF.

None of this has prevented McPhelimy's publishers, the Colorado-based Roberts Rinehart, from printing twenty thousand copies of *The Committee* in the United States. While some commentators have dismissed them as exaggerated, the allegations made in the book have created the impression in politically naïve sections of Irish-American opinion that David Trimble is somehow linked with terrorism and that his party holds on to and controls Protestant guns in Northern Ireland. With just over one week to go before the Assembly elections Trimble sent Roberts Rinehart a fax demanding an apology over the allegations made in the book. The publishers declined his request and now face legal action from the UUP leader. Trimble has subsequently sued Amazon Books Ltd, the Internet bookshop, for selling *The Committee* on the World Wide Web.

Leaving aside whether the Committee in fact existed or not, as far as Trimble is concerned there is no question that he had any knowledge of or involvement in such an organisation. McPhelimy's book has given rise to a number of legal actions, some of which are ongoing, but some loyalist paramilitaries dismiss the suggestion that they would answer to a high-powered body including politicians and clergymen, whom they deeply distrust. The second-in-command of the UVF in Northern Ireland said the allegations 'read like something from *The X Files*. If we had half the information McPhelimy claims we were given, then there would have been hundreds more dead IRA men in graves all over the place.'[27] McPhelimy continues to defend the veracity of the allegations in his book.

This legal action was not the only distraction Trimble had to contend with at this time. In the same week that Trimble warned Roberts Rinehart about a possible libel action, Phillip Black, a close ally in Upper Bann during the 1970s and 1980s, turned viciously on his old Vanguard comrade. The two men were now on opposite sides of the chasm dividing unionism. When Black was asked on Irish television what Trimble should do now after backing the Good Friday Agreement, he urged the UUP leader to kill himself for selling out the union: 'The traditional remedy is to leave him alone in a room with a loaded revolver and a whiskey bottle and hope that he takes the decent way out. I hope that he will take the decent way out, so that unionism can heal the scars and divisions that he has caused and set us back on the unionist road again.'[28] Trimble was taken back by the verbal attack: 'Phillip Black and I were in Vanguard. Vanguard split in the autumn of 1975 over the idea of having a coalition with the SDLP. Phillip Black and I were on opposite sides then, and it took the best part of eight or nine years to restore our relationship. We've split again. I wonder is it going to take another eight or nine years to put us together again.'[29] These last comments demonstrate another weak trait in Trimble's political judgement – his tendency to seek reconciliation with those who desert him. Expecting as uncompromising a hard-liner as Black to kiss and make up with him after such a public assault was hopelessly naïve. There are parallels here with John Major, who, in the interests of Tory Party unity, indulged some of the right-wing critics who were stabbing him in the back during the dying months of his administration.

With half his party in revolt, things were starting to slip for Trimble in the last ten days of the election campaign. On 10 June the government published its Northern Ireland Sentences Bill to allow the early release of terrorist prisoners. The legislation was deeply flawed in unionist eyes, including Trimble's, because it did not appear to link decommissioning with the early release pro-gramme. Even Trimble voted against its second reading in the Commons. His opponents complained that the lack of a connec-tion between disarmament and prisoner releases illustrated the folly of putting too much faith in Tony Blair. The government attempted to assuage Ulster Unionist fears a week later when Blair suggested changes to the Bill. The amended clause, which went into the Bill on 18 June, provided for the Secretary of State to take into account whether a terrorist organization is 'cooperating fully' with the independent body set up to encourage decommissioning and headed by Canadian General John de Chastelain. However, Trim-ble and his party had no faith in Mo Mowlam's ability to act robustly over the prisoners issue. They perceived her to be soft on that issue and elastic in her interpretation of what constituted a breakdown in a ceasefire.

Trimble's failure to force Blair's hand and establish clear con-nections between prisoner releases and paramilitary disarmament provided his internal opponents with another opportunity to undermine their leader. On the same day that the government published its amendments to the Sentences Bill the UUP parlia-mentary team issued a statement – without Trimble's prior knowledge, let alone approval – accusing Blair of making a 'fig leaf' response to decommissioning and prisoners. In their letter the MPs warned that 'We would like to caution the people of Northern Ireland against accepting at face value the statements of spin doctors which are designed to produce an atmosphere of euphoria which is quite unjustified by the actual situation.'[30] It was not the first time that the UUP (or at least a section of the party) had clashed with Blair's infamous spin doctors, but to rattle the door of No. 10 Downing Street over prisoners and decommissioning in the middle of the Assembly election campaign was highly significant. It signalled that Tony Blair was no longer regarded as a prize asset in the Trimble campaign.

Trimble's riposte to his 'wooden tops' was that, even if there had been no Good Friday Agreement, the British government would have moved to release terrorist prisoners early as a means of securing the IRA and loyalist ceasefires. Unionists had to take control of those things which were in their hands to shape. His problems were compounded that week when the Parades Commission (minus Barr and Cheevers, who had resigned) finally published its decision about the 1998 Drumcree march. The Commission announced that it would not be allowed down Garvaghy Road. While Trimble protested at the decision, arguing that the ban threatened peace and stability in the Province, his rivals now had more ammunition to fire at the pro-Agreement unionists. They painted the ban as a government-inspired plot to appease republicans. And given that Trimble was on the same side as Tony Blair, he too could be associated with the appeasement. An increasing number of unionists and loyalists were growing disillusioned with the Agreement. They believed that the only people to benefit from the new order were republicans, who were getting their prisoners out and Orange marches banned.

Even as he was losing ground in his traditional support base in the last week of campaigning, Trimble sought to reach out again to wider sections of society, especially to those who had come out for the first time in decades to vote for the Agreement on 22 May. Three days before polling he delivered the most important speech of the campaign to a gathering of two hundred business leaders, trade unionists, community workers and peace activists at a lunch at Malone House in South Belfast. In the audience were some of the Catholic businessmen who had attended John Laird's lunch at the

Ulster Reform Club in February, including Jim Fitzpatrick, the owner of the nationalist daily, the *Irish News*. In his address Trimble sought to broaden the appeal of the UUP and redefine unionism for the twenty-first century – in short, to make the union more appealing to Ulster's Catholics. Borrowing language from Ulster's parades dispute, Trimble told the guests that the long march to peace and stability was a march that could not be banned. He urged tolerance between unionists and nationalists: 'Each tradition must strive and earn the respect of the other and, in turn, give respect to the other.' He called for the creation of a new civil society which would 'raise up a new Northern Ireland in which pluralist unionism and pluralist nationalism can speak to each other with the civility that is the foundation of freedom'.[31]

In many ways his critics such as Ian Paisley Junior were right when they claimed that his vision of the future sounded like a classic John Hume lecture on tolerance and cooperation. Paisley Junior claimed Trimble's message was designed to appeal to SDLP voters to lend the ailing UUP second-preference votes in the election. However, the Malone House speech was more than a cheap ploy to get Catholic second-preferences; it marked a retreat from equating all things unionist with all things Protestant. Trimble's new unionism would be secular and culturally neutral. It would mirror the socio-cultural changes within the UK, which was becoming more openly a multi-faith, multi-cultural society. No one could doubt Trimble's sincerity in wishing to invent a different kind of unionism from the traditional dismal vision of a 'Protestant Parliament for a Protestant people'; whether or not he could sell his new vision to his party was a matter of doubt.

Lenin once warned the Bolsheviks that the revolutionary party should be one step ahead of the masses, but only one step ahead. The elections on 25 June showed that Trimble's new unionism was in fact ten steps ahead of grassroots unionist opinion. As the results came in from across the Province Trimble grew more and more despondent. The party's dream figure was between thirty and thirty-five seats, and at one stage it appeared that they were heading for just twenty-four. This would have meant that Trimble was imprisoned in a new Assembly with a majority of unionist members against the Agreement – exactly the same position in which Brian Faulkner found himself twenty-four years earlier. Critically, the turnout – 68.8 per cent – was down more than

10 per cent from that of the Referendum a month earlier. Many traditional non-voters who had turned out then had reverted to their customary apathy for the Assembly elections. Given that the total nationalist vote had increased, it was evident that those who stayed away from the polling booths this time around were unionists living east of the Bann – the type of people David Trimble needed to shore up his party. In addition, a number of UUP seats were lost thanks to the shredding of the unionist vote between rival unionist parties. West Belfast was a typical case. There appeared to be enough unionist votes to enable a unionist candidate to take the sixth seat in the otherwise nationalist/republican-dominated constituency, and Chris McGimpsey, a UUP councillor for loyalist West Belfast, was the favourite to take it. In the event it went to the SDLP, due to the four-way unionist split in the constituency with the UUP, UKUP, DUP and PUP fighting amongst themselves. The loyalist heartland of the Shankill Road how had no one to represent it in the new Northern Ireland Assembly.

However, Trimble's legendary luck did not let him down. Although the UUP received its lowest-ever share of first-preferences, 142,858 (21.3 per cent), it was still the largest party in the Assembly, ending up with twenty-eight seats. The vagaries of proportional representation resulted in the SDLP getting the largest first-preference share (172,225) but ending up with four seats fewer than Trimble's party. It had been a close call, but he had squeaked home again. And while the loyalist parties had failed to achieve a historic breakthrough the two Progressive Unionists elected to the Assembly (the former UVF prisoners David Ervine and Billy Hutchinson), combined with Trimble's twenty-eight members, ensured that a narrow majority of unionists in the chamber supported the Agreement.

The narrow win, though, provided no comfort for Trimble. Stephen King said his leader took the result very personally, particularly the bad first-preference figure. 'I tried to console him and said, "Look, David, it's not your fault, – it's not that bad." He wouldn't have it. He replied, "Oh, come on, Stephen, don't give me that. It *was* my fault." '[32] Ray Haydn took a more benign interpretation of the result: 'He was fighting the contest with one hand tied behind his back and yet he managed to get twenty-eight seats. I kept telling him he did remarkably well given the circumstances.'[33] His closest aides blame others for the record low first-preference vote, namely the rebel MPs and in particular Jeffrey Donaldson. The Lagan Valley MP caused further outrage on the night of the results when he turned on Ken Maginnis over his handling of the campaign. Live on BBC Television's *Newsline* Donaldson tore into the UUP's director of elections, calling for him to 'hold his head in shame today. He has presided over one of the biggest electoral disasters for the Ulster Unionist Party in recent years.'[34] Maginnis exploded with rage, accusing Donaldson of being disloyal and partly responsible for the drop in the UUP vote.

This publicized division highlighted the fragile nature of Trimble's leadership of the UUP, and his problems were exacerbated by the fact that several anti-Agreement Ulster Unionists and sceptics had been elected to the Assembly. Peter Weir was open in his opposition to the Agreement, while several others, including Roy Beggs Junior (son of the anti-Agreement East Antrim UUP MP) and the East Londonderry Assembly member Pauline Armitage, were known to be lukewarm about the Agreement. Ian Paisley's and Bob McCartney's key strategy for the forthcoming Assembly, which was scheduled to meet for the first time on 1 July, was to persuade enough UUP waverers to defect to the combined anti-Agreement benches. If Paisley and McCartney could alter the balance in the Assembly and produce a majority of unionists opposed to the Agreement, the entire project would collapse. The process was predicated on the central condition that the Agreement must have cross-community support in the Assembly, but once a majority of unionists had voted against its implementation the entire arrangement would have been deemed unworkable. With such a wafer-thin majority Trimble now had to appease his sceptics, thus limiting his room for manoeuvre in negotiations with nationalists and republicans.

Curiously, those who now gathered around Trimble to support him were the figures whose careers had seemed to be over or at least on hold when he was elected leader three years earlier. He and Reg Empey had been on opposing sides of the Voluntary Coalition fall-out in 1975. They were at odds again in 1990 when Trimble led the rooftop protest at Glengall Street against Empey's welcome for Charles Haughey. Jim Wilson, too, had been an opponent on the rival wing of Vanguard in 1975, and had been the target of pro-Trimble activists at the time of the leadership election. The McGimpsey brothers had been frozen out of the centre of power following Trimble's triumph in 1995. And yet Empey, Wilson and Michael McGimpsey were now his praetorian guard inside the new Assembly while former friends such as John Hunter, Drew Nelson, and Peter Weir were actively working against him inside the party. One UUP insider caustically summed up the changing nature of support for Trimble: 'Sometimes you find out too late who your real friends are!'[35] Denis Rogan, the party chairman and former colleague from Queen's University, was frustrated that Trimble and the party machine did not take a tougher line on the UUP rebels. In a letter to Assembly members, Rogan urged Trimble to act: 'We simply cannot afford to destroy our electoral chances in the future by allowing mavericks to dictate the agenda. The relaxed attitude that we have taken towards dissidents within our own ranks over the last few weeks will have to be tightened considerably.'[36] Trimble, however, preferred to indulge rather than discipline the 'mavericks', especially Jeffrey Donaldson.

The old debating chamber inside Stormont was still being restored after a fire in 1994, so the inaugural meeting of the new Assembly took place in the austerely functional surroundings of Castle Buildings. It was held in the same room where George Mitchell had gathered all the parties to the Good Friday Agreement in the final plenary session. Now Ian Paisley faced Gerry Adams across a narrow strip of carpet in this cramped, strip-lighted room. There had been rumours that the DUP and UKUP would walk out *en masse* when Sinn Fein representatives started to speak. Instead, the anti-Agreement unionists talked amongst themselves or simply sniggered when Gerry Adams and Martin McGuinness took the floor. There were two moments of humour in the debate, which punctured an otherwise tense and febrile atmosphere on the first day. Adams began his speech with a few sentences in Irish. When one member complained that they couldn't hear the Sinn Fein President, Ian Paisley interjected: 'We can't even understand him.' During McGuinness's speech to the Assembly he pointed out that he had never seen many of his unionist rivals in the flesh before – though he said he was particularly glad to see Sammy Wilson with his clothes *on*. This remark produced gales of laughter on both sides of the room (with the exception of the DUP and UKUP). Wilson had been severely embarrassed by nude photographs of himself and his girlfriend published in the Irish tabloid the *Sunday World*.

The main business of the day was to elect a First and Deputy First Minister for Northern Ireland. Earlier that morning Trimble had characteristically played down the significance of the date, of the fact that he was stepping into the shoes of Sir James Craig, Terence O'Neill and Brian Faulkner. It was hardly surprising for a man so influenced by Popper's *Poverty of Historicism* to deny the nature of the occasion. 'It's not an historic day,' he insisted as he arrived at Castle Buildings. 'It's another step.'[37] There was, however, a genuine and unprecedented display of warmth between Trimble and Seamus Mallon when the two men were elected First and Deputy First Minister (John Hume had turned down the offer of becoming Trimble's deputy).

Mallon had been an adversary of Trimble's, particularly over law and order issues, from the time of the shoot-to-kill controversies; now they were united in a critical axis on which the entire political process rested. Mallon told the 108 Assembly members that he looked forward to working with Trimble in a partnership government. Acknowledging Trimble's internal troubles, Mallon said he was sure the UUP leader's back was 'sore enough at the present time that he wouldn't appreciate it any other way . . . a man who has to take responsibility for his people and the place he lives. He has done that with courage, dignity and integrity.'[38] These were generous words from a nationalist politician who had long been a bitter opponent.

However, there was also a thinly disguised warning to the UUP that the SDLP would not engage in the politics of exclusion – that is, cut a deal with the Ulster Unionists at the expense of Sinn Fein. On the other hand, Trimble told the Assembly that his party would not sit in a government with 'unreconstructed terrorists'. In his mind, decommissioning was the ultimate test of a commitment to democracy. The public display of unity aside, Mallon and Trimble still held two radically different interpretations of the way ahead.

In his speech Trimble remembered his murdered friend and colleague Edgar Graham. Addressing republicans directly, Trimble said that there were some members sitting in the Northern Ireland Assembly who had done terrible things in the past. However, he accepted that these people could change: 'We are not saying, nor have we ever said that, simply because someone has a past, they can't have a future. We have always acknowledged that people can change.'[39]

What kind of man had the Northern Ireland Assembly chosen to succeed Craig, O'Neill and Faulkner? John Taylor had served in one capacity or another under two of them and was better positioned than most Assembly members to contrast them with Trimble. 'Faulkner was a hard Ulster businessman and a man of the people. In contrast O'Neill was slightly aloof and aristocratic and totally detached from people. Trimble stands shoulders above them all in terms of intellectual ability.' Taylor is aware of the various weaknesses in his political character. First, he believes Trimble has taken on too many burdens – as First Minister, UUP leader, UUP parliamentary leader, MP and Assemblyman for Upper Bann. Secondly, he feels Trimble's academic qualities also make him slightly aloof from the unionist masses. In the middle of the Assembly contest Taylor, a dedicated follower of the Northern Ireland football team, decided to take Trimble to an important international game as part of his efforts to bring his leader closer to the people. But Trimble, on the verge of becoming First Minister of Northern Ireland, still could not display even superficial enthusiasm for the fortunes of the national team.

[It was] a European championship match between Northern Ireland and Germany. He was greeted very warmly in the directors' box and by many of the supporters in the ground. David had never been to an international before and he showed absolutely no interest in the match. It was very funny because he sat and fidgeted throughout the ninety minutes, looking at his watch all the time. He didn't say it to me, but I got the indirect message that he couldn't wait for the game to end. David was just not at ease – he would have been happier being back home listening to his opera CDs.

Taylor, a true charmer on the campaign trail, has attempted to humanize Trimble on the canvass but to no avail: 'I try to get him to kiss the ladies and the babies, but he finds that terribly difficult.'[40]

Those closest to him in the two campaigns found that he only relaxed when he had a set of headphones on and was listening to a classical CD in the back of his chauffeur-driven car. Throughout May and June he hummed constantly at meetings, canvasses, press conferences and photo-opportunities, all to mask his visible nervousness – like a child whistling in the dark to ward off the fear of the night. He was also prone to mood swings which took him from the depths of despair to an upbeat cheerfulness, particularly when his opponents appeared in trouble. David Kerr says Trimble is at his best when he is on the ropes fighting to stay alive. It is a trait noticed by other more objective observers, such as BBC Northern Ireland's erudite political editor Stephen Grimason. Kerr recalls that Grimason once told him during the elections that Trimble was at his most impressive when he was battling to survive – when he picked himself up from the floor just as it seemed he was down and out. Ray Haydn, too, testifies to Trimble's enormous powers of recovery, both political and physical. The latter is all the more remarkable because Trimble does not work out or play any sport to keep fit. During the Referendum campaign he put on a stone in weight, although the subsequent pressures of the new Assembly, his elevation to First Minister and the looming Drumcree crisis were absorbed with a fresh burst of nervous energy – enough, it seemed, to allow him to burn off the excess pounds.

Unlike any other unionist leader before him, Trimble can call on the advice of an eclectic array of intellectuals and writers from Belfast, Dublin and London. Anthony McIntyre, a former IRA prisoner and one of the sharpest intellectual republican critics of the peace process, paid Trimble a backhanded compliment when he said that the UUP leader had 'more catholic advice' than Gerry Adams. McIntyre argues that, while Trimble can listen to voices outside his own party (O'Callaghan, Harris, Dudley Edwards, Bew and so on), the advice given to Adams is generally one-dimensional, coming as it does almost solely from the republican community. Bew and shares McIntyre's analysis, although he cautions that this does not necessarily imply that Trimble will win in the end. Both Bew and Taylor fear that sometimes Trimble listens more to his external advisers and supporters than those inside his own party, thus risking the alienation of his traditional support base. Taylor is impressed that Trimble's new unionism has won back old allies, but warns that he must not go too far.

We're back where we were in the 1920s when the main newspapers in London were writing editorials supporting the unionist case. Fifteen years ago at the time of the Anglo–Irish Agreement we were being ridiculed in the national press. I think he has done a lot for Ulster Unionism in gaining this influence and respect but he must be careful. He has to bring his own people with him because at the end of the day we depend on the people of Northern Ireland to elect us.[41]

Much of Trimble's traditional base in Upper Bann was already alienated from the UUP leader. As the marching season began he was warned to stay away from the hill at Drumcree. Death threats from newly emerging loyalist terror groups were conveyed to his security staff in the weeks leading up to the annual march in Portadown. On the day he was elected First Minister Trimble acknowledged the danger to his personal security if he attended the Drumcree protest. 'I have to consider that because unfortunately there are elements on the loyalist side – not the Orange side – who have uttered threats against me too. It may be that my presence would provoke violence amongst loyalists and I would have to consider that as well.'[42] This was a remarkable turnaround – Trimble the hero of the Portadown Orangemen in July 1995 had become the Lundy-like villain of 1998.

Having lost the Agreement referendum and failed to relegate him to the status of a minority unionist leader in the Assembly, many in the extreme wing of the No camp regarded Drumcree as their last stand. The stand-off there could unleash enough civil disorder and sectarian violence to destabilize the new order in Northern Ireland. Anti-Agreement loyalists burned down ten Catholic churches on 2 July as part of their strategy to heighten tensions just before the banned march. (The loyalist ultras were no doubt outraged next day at the sight of Trimble visiting one of the damaged churches, St James's near Belfast International Airport. He went there with the Reverend James Dickson, the Presbyterian Moderator and the Catholic Bishop of Down and Connor, the Reverend Patrick Walsh, in a show of solidarity with beleaguered Catholics in the area.) Four days later, with the ban still in place, there had been four hundred attacks on the security forces in loyalist parts of Northern Ireland, including twelve shootings and twenty-five bombings.

There was also renewed pressure on Trimble from inside the party. One of his Assembly team, Pauline Armitage, indicated in the second week of the crisis that she would have difficulty sitting at Stormont while Orangemen continued their protest at the field in

Drumcree. Moreover, one-third of his Assembly members were Orangemen too. With a majority of just two inside the unionist bloc at Stormont, Trimble knew that if Drumcree spun out of control defections to the No camp would leave him as a minority leader in the Assembly, just as Brian Faulkner had been twenty-four years earlier.

One of the abiding fears of the pro-Agreement unionists during the Drumcree stand-off was the possibility of an 'Orange Bloody Sunday'. Trimble and his allies were terrified that, if loyalists massed in their thousands at Drumcree and threatened to break through army and police lines, British soldiers would have to be used to repel them. To prevent a breach of their line, the troops might open fire, possibly resulting in deaths among Orange pro-testors which would lead to the eruption of widescale violence across Protestant parts of the Province. Given these concerns, Trimble tried desperately to broker a compromise between the Garvaghy Road residents and his former comrades in the Orange Order. Once more Sean O'Callaghan was approached to give wise counsel to the Orangemen. A few weeks before Drumcree Trimble had asked him to travel secretly to Portadown to meet a number of senior Orange figures from Co. Armagh. The former IRA killer claims that he met the Reverend William Bingham at the home of the Presbyterian Moderator, the Reverend William Dickson, to discuss the opening of proximity talks between the Orangemen and the nationalist residents. The subsequent talks, however, failed to produce any deal, although O'Callaghan was on call throughout early July, on Trimble's behalf, to contact the Orange Order and attempt at the eleventh hour to dissuade them from pushing Northern Ireland over the edge.

Trimble monitored the increasingly dangerous events at Drum-cree from his new office at Castle Buildings. One of the few positive developments emerging in the crisis was the first sign of a close working relationship between Trimble and his new Deputy First Minister, Seamus Mallon. The two former political foes worked tirelessly together to find a last-minute deal during the stand-off. They held joint press conferences, including one during which Mallon defended Trimble against charges from journalists that the UUP leader could have done more to stop the loyalist violence at Drumcree. When Trimble was elected UUP leader in 1995, Mallon had expressed grave concerns that he had won thanks to his triumphal march with Paisley following the first Drumcree stand-off. Yet three years later here was Mallon shielding Trimble from awkward questions about his past involvement with the Orange protests.

As the 1998 Drumcree siege entered its second week there appeared to be no way out of the deadlock. During its worst days Trimble was, according to close friends, a bundle of nerves, never off the telephone. He realized that everything that had been achieved since Good Friday was in jeopardy. However, once again an external event came to his rescue. Around 6.20 on the morning of 12 July Trimble received a phone call from one of his aides, who told him that a few hours earlier three young Catholic brothers, Richard, Mark and Jason Quinn, had been killed in a petrol bomb attack on their home in Ballymoney, Co. Antrim. The arson was just one in a series of sectarian attacks on isolated Catholic families during the second weekend of the Drumcree crisis. The Orange Order may have condemned the murders and sought to distance their protest from the sectarian arsonists, but it was clear that the credibility of their stand-off had been shattered. As the Reverend William Bingham said at a Sunday service just a few hours after Trimble was given the news: 'No road is worth the life of three young children.' Thousands of ordinary Orangemen heeded Bingham's advice. The siege at Drumcree and the Orange protests throughout the Province were over. On first hearing what had happened in Ballymoney, Trimble whispered to his aide: 'Oh, that's the end of the Orange.'[43]

Nobel, No Guns, No Government

Ray Haydn was relaxing at home on the afternoon of Saturday, 15 August, happy in the knowledge that the gruelling last three months of Referendum, elections and Drumcree crisis were finally over. He was thinking about his summer holiday in Vancouver, where he was flying that coming Monday, when a news flash interrupted normal television programmes shortly before half past three. The announcer said there were reports of a bombing in Omagh, and it was understood there were casualties. Haydn sat up and waited for more news. A few minutes later a second news flash said there were four confirmed dead and the death toll was expected to rise. He knew immediately that Trimble would have to be called home from his holidays. Haydn phoned several UUP Assembly men and party officers, but no one seemed to know where their leader was. David Kerr and Ken Maginnis did not even have a contact number for Trimble, who was known only to be somewhere in Germany. Kerr suggested Haydn should get in touch with David Campbell, who had been appointed Trimble's chief of staff following his election as First Minister. The trouble was that Campbell himself was also on holiday, in Canada. It took Haydn over an hour to track him down in Toronto, but fortunately Campbell had the telephone number of Trimble's guesthouse in the Mosel valley.

It was eight o'clock that evening before Haydn finally relayed the bad news to Trimble: there were now more than twenty people dead and hundreds injured as the result of a massive car bomb in the centre of Omagh. He would have to come back home as soon as possible. Until then Ken Maginnis would hold the line, conducting a marathon session of television and radio interviews and visiting the blast scene.

The problem for Haydn was the logistics of getting Trimble home: 'David agreed right away to come back but he said to me, "Ray, I can't leave my wife and kids here." I told him we would whisk them out of Europe as fast as we could and that the Northern Ireland Office would pick up the tab for it,' Haydn recalled. He then opened negotiations with the NIO, which turned into a shouting match between him and Ken Maginnis on one side and a senior civil servant on the other. The following morning Haydn and Maginnis met the NIO official in the restaurant of the Europa Hotel and demanded a jet to bring the First Minister back home. The NIO official refused, and suggested instead that if Trimble drove from Germany to one of the Channel ports and took the ferry they would provide an RAF jet at the nearest air base in southern England. When the RAF subsequently announced that they did not have any spare transport, the NIO reluctantly agreed to charter a plane from the Isle of Man to go to a rendezvous point near Dover. Haydn was furious with the NIO's lack of help: 'I found them most unhelpful and I laid into a couple of them during the negotiations. I told them that David was the f***ing Prime Minister of Northern Ireland, and I couldn't understand why they found it impossible to get him back to respond to one of the worst atrocities of the Troubles.'[1]

Trimble drove the family to Calais through the early hours of Sunday morning. When they arrived at Dover he was taken by car to a small airfield nearby while Daphne drove the children to London where they stayed overnight in Trimble's flat. The irony was that the Trimble family hardly ever went to the continent for their summer break. After the strains of coping with Drumcree and the Quinn murders the Trimbles had spent a few days cruising on a canal boat in the English Midlands. On the Warwickshire canals Trimble remembered his shares in Eurotunnel that entitled them to free tickets through the Channel Tunnel, so he seized the opportunity to visit the Mosel valley in north-west Germany for a fortnight of wine-tasting, river-cruising and spectacular scenery. They found a guesthouse in a quiet village where they could cut themselves off from the wider world. The Trimbles were actually packing to come home when the daughter of the guesthouse owner told them there was a phone call from Toronto. Trimble recalled:

It was fortunate that Ray Haydn got through to me, because the next day I would have left Germany en route home via France and London. Between eight o'clock the next morning and late that evening I would have been incommunicado – the radio would have been switched off. I would have known nothing about what happened until I reached the flat in London in the early hours of Monday morning. I remember thinking when I heard about Omagh that it was horrendous – that when we all thought we had peace there were over twenty people dead in a major bombing incident.[2]

The chartered light aircraft took three hours to reach Belfast. Haydn met him off the plane and whisked him to his home in Lisburn to allow him to freshen up. After showering and changing his clothes, Trimble was driven to nearby Hillsborough Castle where Haydn, Kerr and Maginnis briefed him before a meeting with the Prime Minister. His discussion with Blair centred on the security response to the atrocity. Trimble and Maginnis insisted that the two governments had to have a coordinated cross-border strategy to catch the Omagh bombers. Blair agreed immediately.

Trimble recalled that the Prime Minister appeared to be in a state of shock, having just returned from Belfast's Royal Victoria Hospital where he had visited some of the injured. Ray Haydn, who had thought his work for Trimble was over after Drumcree and the Quinn murders, was also emotionally overwhelmed by the experience. It was three o'clock on Monday morning when he finally left Trimble and went home to pack for his flight to Vancouver later that day. 'I got home, sat down and cried,' he said. 'On the way to the airport to get a connecting flight to London I never issued one word to my wife.' Trimble too was taken back by the scale of the carnage and the fact that the casualties included young children and pregnant women. 'David was devastated,' Haydn recalled. 'He never thought there would ever be another terrorist incident like it again.'[3]

The brutal truth about Omagh was that Northern Ireland was spared massive loyalist retaliation due to the fact that more than half the victims were Catholics, some of whom actually came from republican strongholds such as Carrickmore in rural Tyrone. Omagh, a town with a Sinn Fein-controlled district council, was a cross-community atrocity, the victims ranging from the niece of a

DUP councillor to the wife and children of a prominent GAA referee. If the bomb had exploded in another town, such as those recently targeted by the Real IRA like Banbridge (the town was attacked by this terror group a fortnight before Omagh) or, worse still, Portadown, in the middle of Trimble's constituency, almost all the casualties would have been Protestant. The ferocity of the loyalist paramilitary response would have been unprecedented, and the entire peace project, along with Trimble's tenure as First Minister, would have been rapidly destroyed as the Province slid towards widespread civil conflict.

On the day Haydn left Northern Ireland, Trimble went to Omagh accompanied by the local MP and anti-Agreement Ulster Unionist Willie Thompson. The two men put aside their differences to visit twenty-three of the injured at Tyrone County Hospital, where the 'good spirit of the people who were plunged into this tragedy' touched Trimble deeply. 'It was heart-warming to hear how they have coped with their injuries,' he said.[4] At the bomb scene Trimble called for a robust security response to the atrocity from both the British and Irish governments.

Three days after the bombing Trimble travelled to Dublin for an emergency meeting with Bertie Ahern. He was encouraged by the Taoiseach's remarks that the Irish government would ruthlessly suppress those responsible. Trimble recalled a telephone conversation with him shortly after the outrage which illuminated the close personal and professional relationship between the two men.

At an early stage of the inter-party talks I recall a meeting with Bertie and saying to him, 'Suppose we get an agreement. In the nature of things the agreement is not likely to have 100 per cent support – there are likely to be splits, splinter groups continuing violence. In the event of that happening, are you going to defend the agreement we have entered into?' He assured me that would be his position. After Omagh, I came home on Sunday and went down there with Willie Thompson. My mobile went off. On the other end of the phone was Bertie, and he just wanted to say he remembered my question. He remembered what he had said and he just wanted me to know that he was going to deliver.[5]

Yet although the British and Irish governments changed their anti-terrorist legislation to abolish a suspect's right to silence, Trimble's other demands such as selective internment of Real IRA members were in the end not met. It is a measure of the effectiveness of Blair and Ahern's promises to repress the Real IRA that by the first anniversary of the Omagh bombing only one person had been charged with offences connected to it.

Twenty-four hours after a cordial and businesslike meeting with Ahern Trimble crossed the border into the Irish Republic again, this time to attend the funerals of three children from Buncrana in Co. Donegal who had died in the bomb. There was a moment of powerful symbolism at the beginning of the service, when Trimble walked into the requiem mass hand-in-hand with the Irish President, Mary McAleese. Trimble was now united with his former nationalist foe from Queen's University in opposition to the Real IRA bombers and in solidarity with the victims. The image of the leaders of the two states in Ireland walking together into the church sent out a powerful message of reconciliation to the world. In the atmosphere following the bomb it was tempting to conclude that out of the Omagh tragedy came new hopes for harmony between the two traditions on the island. The Catholic Bishop of Derry, Dr Seamus Hegarty, noted the import of Trimble's presence during his homily. He told mourners that the sight of Trimble and Seamus Mallon together alongside the Irish President was extremely significant. The congregation burst into spontaneous applause as Dr Hegarty said Trimble was 'particularly welcome' in Buncrana, the place where his mother had grown up. Addressing Trimble directly, the Catholic bishop said: 'We wish you well and a fair wind in all your endeavours in the autumn.'[6] What was not widely reported at the time was that Trimble also attended another requiem mass for Catholic victims in Omagh itself. He remembered that mourners in the nearby graveyard where the victims were buried gave him an equally civil reception.

Not everyone, however, was impressed with Trimble travelling to Donegal or Omagh to pay his respects to murdered children. Extremists within the Orange Order demanded that Trimble and Denis Rogan, who accompanied his party leader to Buncrana, be expelled: they argued that the two Orangemen had broken the Order's rule forbidding members to attend Catholic services. It seemed incredibly insensitive to be arguing for the expulsion of Trimble and Rogan on the grounds that they had attended a requiem mass for children killed in the Omagh bombing. The move against Trimble and Rogan by Orange ultras underlined how distanced from reality the Order had now become, with its never-ending Drumcree protests and its stubborn resistance to any political reforms in Northern Ireland. The Orange Order was not just opposed to Sinn Fein in government; it was against any Catholic in government.

Some of his party colleagues wondered why Trimble remained in an institution that was so disconnected from the world at the end of the twentieth century. He could have reminded the geniuses in the House of Orange that two of his predecessors, Sir Edward Carson and Sir James Craig, both Orangemen, had attended a requiem mass for their old enemy, the Irish nationalist parliamentary leader John Redmond, at Westminster Cathedral in March 1918. The records show that the twin founders of twentieth-century Ulster Unionism were not threatened with expulsion. Indeed, as the young Cambridge historian Colin Armstrong has pointed out, unionist leaders including Dawson Bates and Sir James Craig continued to attend requiem masses for Catholic members of the Stormont Parliament until the early 1960s. Armstrong's contention is that it was not until Ian Paisley burst on to the political scene with his crusade against ecumenism that the Orange Order enforced the ban, probably in panic at the rise of the Paisleyite tendency.

But Trimble did not bother to draw the historical analogy when the modern-day Orange ultras set upon him for his 'treachery' in attending a mass for murdered children. The reason Trimble stays in the Orange Order is similar to his unwillingness to clamp down on dissenters in his party like Jeffrey Donaldson: he shies away from decisively severing the links with his traditional Orange/loyalist past, despite his newly found project to redefine unionism as secular and non-sectarian. And he may also have a pragmatic reason for keeping his Orange sash, given that the Order's seventy thousand membership makes it the largest Protestant movement in the Province. The Order had, however, stood against him during the Referendum and the Assembly elections. Trimble had promised to re-form the link between his party and the loyalist cultural institution but he has yet to break the historic connection, much to the disappointment of more liberal, forward-thinking members in the party who constantly wonder why Trimble indulges them.

Although Sinn Fein leaders were unprecedented in their condemnation of the Omagh atrocity, the carnage only bolstered

Trimble's determination to keep decommissioning on the agenda. In an interview with the *New Statesman* a fortnight after Omagh, he warned that the creation of a power-sharing executive was in doubt unless IRA arms were handed over. 'We cannot work with them if they are not prepared to decommission,' he said. His firm stance on arms was in all probability aimed not only at republicans but also at dissenters in the UUP, particularly as the party-conference season was coming up. Rather optimistically he looked to the SDLP to apply pressure on Sinn Fein and consequently the IRA: 'They [the SDLP] must argue with them, make the case for decommissioning. They have tended to draw back from doing so, reluctant to make a breach in nationalism. But I hope we can work with moderate nationalists on a front against paramilitaries and terrorism.'[7] Perhaps Trimble saw Omagh as the opportunity to change the SDLP's attitude to decommissioning. John Hume's party always regarded the decommissioning question as irrelevant as long as the guns were silent and there was relative peace on the streets. Trimble hoped Omagh had changed all that, given that the explosives used to detonate the bomb had come from old Provisional IRA arms, but he severely underestimated the strength of the pan-nationalist consensus on disarmament. In his *New Statesman* interview he also walked unwittingly into another trap. He called for Gerry Adams to declare that the war was over and said that Sinn Fein and/or the IRA should appoint a representative to sit on the International Decommissioning Commission. Within a week of the *New Statesman* article appearing republicans were preparing to seize the moral high ground by obliging him.

On 2 September Sinn Fein announced that Martin McGuinness had been appointed to liaise with the International Decommissioning Commission – one day before President Clinton was scheduled to arrive in Belfast on a flying post-Omagh visit to bolster the Agreement. On the same day, in an article in the *Irish Times* Gerry Adams wrote that his party believed 'the violence we have seen must be for all of us now a thing of the past, over, done with and gone'.[8] The Adams–McGuinness double-whammy clearly wrong-footed unionists. It created the impression that republicans had finally answered Trimble's demand that they say their war was over for good without any physical hand-over of weapons and explosives. A negative response from the Ulster Unionists would seem begrudging.

President Clinton addressed all 108 Assembly members in the conference chamber of Belfast's Waterfront Hall, on the same stage where Trimble and Hume had stood with U2's Bono five months earlier. Just before he made his speech there were small signs of a thaw in relations between Ulster Unionists and Sinn Fein. The UUP's Sir John Gorman was seen on camera chatting and laughing with Sinn Fein's mid-Ulster Assembly man Francie Molloy, an unthinkable sight only a year before. Trimble, however, adopted a cautious approach to the Adams–McGuinness initiative of the previous day. During his speech he borrowed an infamous sectarian phrase from former Northern Ireland Prime Minister Lord Brookeborough and refashioned it for the lexicon of new unionism. Trimble promised he would set up 'a pluralist parliament for a pluralist people' instead of Brookeborough's 'Protestant parliament for a Protestant people'. With Gerry Adams, Martin McGuinness, Gerry Kelly and the rest of the Sinn Fein leadership in sight in the audience, Trimble said that he welcomed every move made by those 'crossing the bridge from terror to democracy'. He added, however, that he could not reconcile positions in government with a failure to dismantle terrorist organizations. In other words, no guns, no government for Sinn Fein.

Four days after President Clinton left the Province Trimble sounded optimistic about Martin McGuinness's appointment to liaise with the international arms body. He believed the move made it inevitable that the IRA would decommission. On the BBC's *Breakfast with Frost* programme, Trimble said McGuinness's new role 'has put the republican movement on a conveyor belt which will lead to actual decommissioning or it will be very clear, very quickly that they are refusing, in which case the other parties will draw the appropriate conclusions'.

The net result of the Adams–McGuinness initiative was a historic meeting between the Sinn Fein President and Trimble the following Thursday. In an interview with the *Observer* Trimble revealed that he would not shake Adams's hand on this occasion. Pedantically, he chose to explain the history of the handshake to justify this stance: 'Martin Smyth [the UUP MP for South Belfast] would add that the origin of the handshake is to show that there is no weapon in the other person's hand. You offer your hand to show there is nothing in it. But, of course, in Gerry Adams's hands is three tons of Semtex, six hundred AK47s, hundreds of other rifles ready to strike. He doesn't have an open hand to hold out to people.'[9] Adams might justifiably have retorted that David Trimble was happy to extend his hand to loyalist political leaders in whose own hands were hundreds of weapons and tons of explosives.

In the same interview, Trimble said he would tell Adams that if he were pushed into any further compromises on decommissioning he would 'fall off the ledge'. He repeated his view that Martin McGuinness's appointment as a link to the decommissioning body was highly significant. 'McGuinness once said, "I know we'll have to banjax the weapons." So I am quite sure it's going to happen.' But others in his party were not so sure and regarded the Sinn Fein move as a tactical ploy to paint republicans in a good light during Clinton's visit and so pile pressure on the Ulster Unionists to grant even more concessions.

While there were no handshakes at the first UUP–Sinn Fein bilateral in seventy-five years, the forty-five-minute meeting had taken place in a 'very good atmosphere', according to Sinn Fein's Bairbre de Brun. Some members of each delegation addressed each other on first name terms, and the discussion did not degenerate into a shouting match. Trimble justified the meeting by pointing to the example of his old hero, Sir James Craig, who spoke directly with Michael Collins while the Belfast IRA were still active in the city before the two fledgling governments in the North and South agreed to the 1921 peace treaty. Yet unlike the ground-breaking 1998 meeting, subsequent ones were, in Trimble's opinion, much more strained. Trimble's contrasting impressions of the two main republican players, Gerry Adams and Martin McGuinness, are interesting:

> We find it easier to talk to Martin McGuinness than to Adams. Now McGuinness is short-tempered, but on the other hand he says something to you fairly straight, whereas in my opinion Adams is always playing games. Very frequently Adams is indirect in his language while McGuinness is more direct. It doesn't mean I'm going to agree with McGuinness, but he is a bit more clear about where he stands.[10]

He is not sure, however, what exactly Adams's intentions are, and is convinced the Sinn Fein President has a long road to travel to reach the position of historic compromise as advocated by past republican leaders such as Proinsias De Rossa. 'What the position is within Adams's own mind I do not know. I still haven't made up my mind if he is on the road to total peace or not, whereas I think McGuinness has the possibility of being more pragmatic. He is more actually capable of going down the De Rossa road than Adams is,' Trimble adds.[11]

Following its summer break, the Northern Ireland Assembly resumed on 14 September with more attacks on Trimble's leadership from without and within. After twenty-six years of direct rule and three decades of terror, the representatives of Ulster unionism, loyalism, constitutional nationalism and violent republicanism were sitting in the same chamber for the first time in Northern Ireland's history. The day opened with a message from Trimble that devolution provided 'an historic opportunity to govern with honour and the responsibilities of history. If we pass this, we pass one of the remaining historic tests of centuries.'[12] The mood was lightened somewhat by Trimble's colleague John Taylor, who welcomed the Sinn Fein members to Stormont. Taylor even made Gerry Adams laugh when he congratulated the Northern Ireland shooting team for winning a gold medal at the recent Commonwealth Games. Taylor reminded Adams that the guns used on that occasion were of the legal variety. Behind the smiles, though, lay deep divisions not only between unionism and nationalism but also within the UUP. Denis Watson, a former Ulster Unionist Party member and one-time ally of Trimble, had formed another anti-Agreement party, the United Unionists. It was comprised of him and two other former UUP members. In addition, a band of disgruntled UUP members still inside Trimble's party were plotting to block their leader from making further compromises.

A fortnight after the Assembly opened, the Union First group held its first press conference in the Stormont Hotel just across the road. It mainly comprised Young Unionists like Peter Weir and David Brewster, both former Trimble protégés, but also attracted support from four of the UUP's Westminster MPs, William Ross, Roy Beggs, Clifford Forsythe and, critically, Jeffrey Donaldson. Its chairman, Peter King, called for Trimble to ballot all nine hundred members of the Ulster Unionist Council on whether the party accepted that Sinn Fein should enter government – regardless of whether or not the IRA would decommission. This position drew accusations that Union First was not only trying to box Trimble into a corner over IRA disarmament, but that its real aim was to oppose power-sharing in any form.

Trimble, who was in the United States on an eleven-city tour on behalf of Northern Ireland's Industrial Development Board in an attempt to attract American investment to the Province, claimed that Union First was trying to rewrite the entire Good Friday Agreement. Through his spokesman he said: 'The Ulster Unionist Party will not countenance Sinn Fein taking up executive positions without handing in weapons. But if, on the other hand, this group is saying it never wants Sinn Fein to hold positions in government, regardless of whether it complies with the conditions laid down in the Agreement, then that is an extreme and unrealistic view.'[13]

His troubles were mounting back home, with rumours of a new alignment of unionism minus both Paisley and Trimble. Party members in the South Down area have confirmed that they were approached informally and asked how they felt about a new super-unionist party headed by Jeffrey Donaldson and the DUP deputy leader, Peter Robinson. Although Donaldson strenuously denied ever taking the idea of a new merged unionist party seriously, there were and are many both inside and outside the UUP, particularly in the No camp, who see the Lagan Valley MP and Robinson as hard-line unionism's dream ticket. These elements were certainly taking the prospect of a united unionist front opposed to the Good Friday Agreement extremely seriously during this period. Unease within Trimble's own Assembly team was reflected in a *Belfast Telegraph* survey of the twenty-eight members who still held the party whip at the beginning of October. It found that nine Assembly members would desert him for the No benches if he compromised too far. The nine – Pauline Armitage, Billy Armstrong, Roy Beggs Junior, Robert Coulter, Ken Robinson, Derek Hussey, Tom Benson, Esmond Bernie and one unnamed Assembly member – all said they would withdraw support for their leader if Sinn Fein entered government before decommissioning had begun.

Supporters of Trimble outside the UUP were furious with Donaldson's backing of the Union First group. Eoghan Harris continually urged Trimble to crush his internal enemies, but the leader recoiled at the idea of a Stalinist-style purge. Alluding to Harris's Marxist past, Trimble said:

I am a wee bit doubtful about a line of thought that comes directly from Lenin's mode of operation. We are a democratic party; we don't behave like that. Nor do I really want to. Maybe it's fair criticism to say I indulge my critics too much, but I hope I never rid myself of an academic view of things, which treats other points seriously. I wouldn't be comfortable in a situation where no other views are tolerated. One thing I must bear in mind is that it's possible I might be wrong, I don't have a monopoly on wisdom. Criticism is not something that should be immediately squashed or crushed – it's possible the critic might be telling me something useful.[14]

The last sentence is characteristic of a true disciple of Karl Popper – someone who is prepared to accept refutations of his own thesis, whether in politics or academia.

Trimble would dearly love to have the type of PR machine that New Labour has deployed under Blair, but without the rigid control that the Prime Minister exercises over his party. There is also perhaps in Trimble's approach to dissenters within his ranks a trace of the Presbyterian mistrust of absolutist authority, a sense that no one holds the Holy Grail of wisdom. Whether he can afford to be so generous to his critics in the modern political age is another question. What is certain is that some of his unionist critics would certainly not be so tolerant of him – if Trimble found himself in a minority position his voice would be quickly silenced.

Some non-unionists, too, acknowledged Trimble's growing problems with his dissidents in the autumn of 1998. Maurice Hayes, the Catholic former Ombudsman of Northern Ireland and a key member of Chris Patten's Policing Commission, was one of the few commentators outside the unionist community to recognize how precarious Trimble's position was becoming: 'It is clear that Trimble is in considerable trouble and needs the support of non-unionists as much as that of his own party. The argument is that Trimble should stop whinging and get on with the job. Which is all very fine but not of much practical use if he is left standing there on his own, his troops having deserted him,' Hayes wrote.[15]

While Trimble was telling North American audiences that decommissioning was inevitable, his alleged partners in a new Northern Ireland government, the SDLP, were refusing to listen to

Maurice Hayes's advice. Instead of shoring up the beleaguered UUP leader, SDLP spokesmen were lining up to take pot shots at him. Joe Byrne, the SDLP Assembly member for West Tyrone, said Trimble's insistence on the decommissioning of IRA guns before Sinn Fein entered government was unrealistic. 'No leader in the North of Ireland, in my opinion, has any right at this juncture to demand actual decommissioning on a plate. That smacks of political arrogance and does not contribute in a constructive and positive way to the development of political trust,' Byrne said.[16] Worse still, at the end of September a damaging rift had emerged between Trimble and his Deputy First Minister, Seamus Mallon, and it showed no signs of healing even as the two travelled together on the investment tour. As the deadline approached for the establishment and inaugural meeting of the North–South Ministerial Council, there was no hint of agreement between Mallon and Trimble on decommissioning. The SDLP deputy leader had proposed that, if Trimble allowed Sinn Fein into government before guns were handed over, he would personally call for the republicans' expulsion from the executive if the IRA had not began to decommission by the May 2000 deadline. It was a measure of the mistrust that Trimble harboured, not so much of Mallon personally but rather of his party, that he would not buy his Deputy First Minister's plan.

The show of warmth between the two men at the Assembly's first sitting on 1 July was not to be taken at face value. Colleagues of both complain that the chemistry between them is not right. Perhaps this is because they are of a similar nature. A close aide of Mallon's defines the First and Deputy First Ministers as 'two prickly pears, with a hard, spiky exterior that's always on view but inside they are quite soft, although rarely to each other'.[17] Mallon, like Trimble, is a straight talker who means what he says and is not prepared to mince his words in the interests of diplomacy. Although Mallon has been at the forefront of doggedly defending democratic nationalism from revolutionary republican assaults for three decades, he is also prone to lose patience with his opponents. Trimble's inner circle also worry that their own leader may get so fed up with the squabbling and irrational obsessions of Ulster politics that he might abandon public life.

A major concern for Trimble's staff is the lack of cooperation between themselves and Mallon's ministerial team. David Kerr points out that the two teams rarely socialize or eat together in the Stormont Parliament's canteen. Almost all the joint work between the First and Deputy First Ministers' offices is conducted by civil servants. The political appointees rarely meet – hardly a model for partnership government as envisaged in the Good Friday Agreement.

Trimble greatly admires Mallon for his opposition to the IRA in the republican stronghold of South Armagh during the Troubles. He is angered, however, by Mallon's allocation of blame for lack of progress in the peace process. The SDLP deputy leader blames Sinn Fein and the Ulster Unionists equally for the political stalemate, whereas Trimble, perhaps naïvely, believes democratic parties should stick together and demand the decommissioning of terrorist weapons. Twenty-four years after the collapse of Sunningdale, Trimble still finds it hard to put his faith entirely in the SDLP.

(On the North American investment tour Trimble and Mallon even clashed over the promotion of tourism in of Ireland. Speaking in New York, Mallon said he believed it was nonsense that there were two separate tourism bodies in the North and South of Ireland. He called for the creation of a single tourist promotion agency, which clearly irked Trimble. The UUP leader said, while there could be certain joint marketing initiatives, he was concerned that Northern Ireland would lose out through some tourists' reluctance to cross the border if the North was not promoted separately. There was more minor discord during the New York leg of the tour when Trimble objected to a joke during a reception at the Waldorf Astoria. One speaker, an Irish-American businessman called Jim McCann, made a reference to keeping the WASPs (White Anglo-Saxon Protestants) away. Earlier, at the same venue, Trimble had stood outside the ballroom while the Irish national anthem, 'The Soldier's Song', was played before entering to take his seat.)

It was while Trimble was in the United States with Mallon that the news broke back home that the UUP leader had been awarded the 1998 Nobel peace prize jointly with John Hume. The announcement of the award, which carries a cash prize of £630,000, was made in Oslo on the morning of 16 October. For several hours, however, Trimble was completely oblivious to the fact that he had now been elevated into the pantheon of international statesmen alongside the late Yitzhak Rabin, Nelson Mandela, Henry Kissinger, Lech Walesa and Mikhail Gorbachev. When the announcement was made it was 3 a.m in Denver, Colorado; Trimble was asleep and had ordered his aides not to wake him until six in the morning. Exhausted by the gruelling tour, Trimble slept on while his press team worked through the early hours and set up an impromptu press centre in their hotel. The Irish tabloids had a field day with the story the next day, one paper referring to the new Nobel laureate as 'Rip Van Trimble'.

When he finally emerged, a groggy Trimble spoke down a telephone line to BBC Northern Ireland's morning news and current-affairs programme, *Good Morning Ulster*. He was typically reserved, perhaps even a little suspicious, about the international accolade: 'We hope that is merited because there is an element of prematurity about this. We know that while we have got the makings of the peace, it's not wholly secure yet. I hope that it does not turn out to be premature.' No doubt Trimble was mindful of the fate of the last Nobel peace-prize winners from Northern Ireland, Betty Williams and Mairead Corrigan. The founders of the short-lived Peace People movement were awarded the prize in 1976 for their role in organizing mass cross-community protests, mainly of women, against IRA and loyalist violence. Within two years the Peace movement had disintegrated over internal disagreements, particularly in relation to their attitude towards the H-Block hunger strikes.

At home Daphne Trimble was visibly taken back by the award and confessed that it had yet to sink in. While Tony Blair praised the Nobel committee's decision, others in the unionist community saw the award as another example of Trimble being taken to the top of the temple and shown the riches and flatteries of the world in order to tempt him to sell Ulster out. Peter Robinson, the deputy leader of the Democratic Unionist Party and MP for East Belfast, said the award was 'for those who struck a deal to satisfy the vile murderers of the IRA'.[17]

Trimble was scheduled to fly back to Belfast the following day, and arrangements were made for the local media to meet him at the airport. Ray Haydn took charge of the operation and clashed with Northern Ireland Office officials over the itinerary. The NIO wanted Trimble to go straight to a conventional press conference at Stormont, but Haydn, who has a shrewd eye for a photo-opportunity, argued that the media should meet Trimble as he got off the plane to greet his family. In the end Haydn won and the press and broadcasters descended on the airport to await Trimble's return. As he walked into the arrivals lounge he was given a hero's welcome from his wife and party supporters. The dominant image of the day was that of his youngest child, Sarah, running into her father's arms as he faced the cameras. He used the occasion to repeat his insistence that an executive would only be formed with Sinn Fein if a start was made on IRA decommissioning. Trimble rejected suggestions from journalists that the peace prize actually put pressure on him to alter his stance on IRA disarmament. The single issue that had stalked the peace process for more than four years, decommissioning, had not evaporated in the euphoria over the Nobel award.

On the streets of his own constituency Trimble still risked being beaten up or worse by loyalist ultras. Loyalist protestors in Portadown had barracked him on 23 September when he left a meeting of Orange Order leaders at Carleton Street Orange Hall – the very place where he had marched in triumph with Paisley three years before. Trimble was also the target of a new hate campaign by a fledgling loyalist/Protestant fundamentalist terror group called the Red Hand Defenders. A magazine which supports this group, *The Wright View* (named after the murdered LVF leader Billy Wright) was produced by an extremist Protestant pastor from North Belfast who had a long history of involvement with far-right loyalist groups dating back to the early 1970s. In the autumn edition of *The Wright View* the pastor targeted Trimble, printing the telephone number of his constituency office and urging 'true loyalists' to ring up and 'make sure he gets the message'. He characterized the First Minister as 'traitor Trimble' and accused him of entering a government with the IRA Army Council. The man behind these attacks is also the spiritual head of the Red Hand Defenders/ Orange Volunteers movement, which mixes Protestant fundamentalism with loyalist terrorism. In meetings with his tiny band of deranged supporters, the pastor has called for Trimble to be executed.

The threat to Trimble's life was taken extremely seriously by the RUC. Security around his home and constituency office and at Stormont was stepped up considerably to thwart any potential attack. The pressure on the Trimble family has been compounded by a series of protests outside their home by supporters of the DUP and other No unionist groupings. The abusive phone calls and cries of 'traitor' from the moronic fringe of unionism increased dramatically towards the end of 1998.

Oddly, the terror group founded during the Drumcree stand-off in 1996, Billy Wright's Loyalist Volunteer Force, did not participate in the anti-Trimble campaign. In fact the LVF had called a ceasefire shortly after the Good Friday Referendum and on 8 August issued a statement to the *Observer* claiming that their 'war' was over for good. In addition the LVF promised that they would start to decommission some weapons and explosives. From the outset Trimble took a keen interest in the LVF's position, which had moved from hard-line anti-Agreement killers to the first terrorist group in Irish history to surrender weapons voluntarily. He seized on the chance to create a decommissioning precedent for the bigger terrorist movements to follow.

In order to persuade the LVF via their mediator, the former UDA killer turned pastor Kenny McClinton, Trimble called on Sean O'Callaghan. O'Callaghan knew a senior prison official who had been close to McClinton while he was still in jail serving his life sentence. The former IRA commander asked the prison official to speak to McClinton about what was needed to convince the LVF to surrender some arms. Their key demand was that, if their ceasefire held and they decommissioned, their prisoners could be brought on to the early release scheme.

At first there was some resistance within the upper echelons of the Northern Ireland Office. They argued that only paramilitary groups which supported the Good Friday Agreement qualified for early release – the LVF were just calling a ceasefire and promising to give up guns simply to get their prisoners out. Trimble, however, believed it was worth the gamble – that the sight of guns being destroyed and explosives put beyond use, no matter how few, would shatter the myth that armed groups never surrender their arsenals. He argued that the British government should recognize the LVF ceasefire, which would in turn lead to the first act of decommissioning. Mo Mowlam stalled on the issue, and Trimble expressed his fears that there was a hidden agenda to prevent the LVF from surrendering arms. In an interview with the *Observer* he said:

I am also concerned that even though the LVF offered to decommission, no response was made. It has got to a point where some people, I am not saying myself, but there is a belief in some quarters that the Government's delay is because they wish to avoid embarrassment for other parties. Once somebody starts decommissioning, no matter who it is, no matter what it is, it will be like a pebble on a slope, it will start movement.[19]

O'Callaghan's role in the matter was critical for Trimble. He used his connections with Jonathan Powell in Downing Street and his sources in the State Department in Washington to enable the LVF to disarm. The Americans were used to providing money via a third party for Kenny McClinton's Ulster American Christian foundation, keeping the ex-UDA man focussed on achieving LVF decommissioning. Powell, meanwhile, was urged by O'Callaghan to exert as much influence as he could on Downing Street to recognize the LVF's ceasefire. The initiative involving O'Callaghan and McClinton was an obvious demonstration of Trimble's pragmatism – using a convicted republican terrorist killer to persuade a loyalist killer to convince other loyalists to surrender their guns, ammunition and explosives. (McClinton was in fact totally opposed to the Good Friday Agreement and had actively worked for a No vote in Trimble's own constituency several months before.) The efforts paid off: on 18 December the LVF handed over nine guns, 350 bullets, two pipe bombs and six detonators to General John De Chastelain's International Decommissioning Body. However, most of the weapons were either home-made machine guns or out-of-date World War I rifles including a Steyr from the arsenal sent by Kaiser Wilhelm to the original UVF, set up by the founding father of the Ulster Unionist Party, Sir Edward Carson. No one on the unionist side for fifty years, republicans pointed out to Trimble, had ever decommissioned the guns of Carson's army.

The LVF, the terror group which Trimble had denounced during his poignant visit to Poyntzpass in April with Seamus Mallon, had broken the decommissioning taboo. In doing so the organization which had killed to stop Trimble's Agreement only a few months before was now objectively helping his cause. Conversely, the two mainstream loyalist paramilitary forces to which Trimble had given political and constitutional advice in the 1970s and 1980s now stood against him on the decommissioning question. Trimble wanted both the UVF and UDA to decommission unilaterally a small but symbolically important amount of weapons. His thinking was that, if loyalists were seen to be taking the first step on surrendering arms, it would put massive moral and political pressure on the republican movement to follow suit.

Once more he sent O'Callaghan to Belfast to open discussions with a number of loyalist leaders, including one of the most senior UVF commanders in Northern Ireland. This time, however, O'Callaghan came back empty-handed. The UVF, through their political representatives the PUP, firmly rejected any unilateral decommissioning. At one stage the PUP's North Belfast Assembly member Billy Hutchinson even asserted that the Ulster Unionists, by insisting on decommissioning as a precondition to Sinn Fein entering government, were endangering the peace process. Trimble was reported to be furious about the remark.

The large number of so-called punishment beatings carried out in Protestant areas by both the UVF and UDA further polluted the atmosphere between the two parties. By the end of November 1998 the tally of reported loyalist beatings was 109, thirty more than the number for which the IRA was responsible in Catholic areas. The UVF's and UDA's stubborn refusal to surrender even a token quantity of weapons and their continued savage beatings and maimings left Trimble bitter and frustrated. He was angry that the increase in such behaviour was deepening the antipathy of the law-abiding Protestant middle class towards the Agreement. The Good Friday deal was meant to herald a new era of peace, but the facts on the ground in loyalist working-class areas said otherwise. 'David could not believe how stupidly the loyalists were behaving,' a close aide remarked. 'He could not understand how they didn't seem to realize they were letting Sinn Fein and the IRA off the hook. They had every chance to pile the pressure on republicans with a token gesture, and they never did. Our relations with the PUP in particular were at rock bottom.'[20]

In the late autumn the deterioration in relations between Trimble's party and the mainstream loyalists was eclipsed by a more serious problem. The negotiations between the UUP, the SDLP and the Irish government over North–South bodies were threatening to endanger the entire Good Friday project. On 30 November John Taylor warned that the SDLP was seeking to extend the number of cross-border institutions, which he and Trimble had cut down before the Agreement was signed. Ominously, Taylor compared the actions of the SDLP to their behaviour during the Sunningdale talks: 'I see history beginning to repeat itself as Dublin and the SDLP aim too high in their ambitions for the new North–South council. The issue could collapse the Agreement.'[21]

The threat to the Agreement prompted Blair to fly to Belfast on 2 December on another rescue mission. The negotiations were stuck on the issue of a proposed cross-border body for all-island economic development, something that Trimble had successfully resisted in the lead-up to the Agreement. The relationship between Trimble and Mallon in particular was severely strained. As the talks on the cross-border dimension stalled, his back-benchers issued a warning to Trimble. The day after Blair arrived almost all of Trimble's Assembly team stated their opposition to the all-Ireland economic body. Trimble decided to play for time and on 4 December left Northern Ireland with John Hume to pick up an award in Washington a few days before the Nobel ceremony in Oslo.

On 11 December he received his award in Oslo in front of an array of international guests including two other famous Irishmen – another former Nobel laureate, the poet Seamus Heaney, and the flautist James Galway. In line with his policy of seeking 'catholic' advice from different quarters, part of his address was written with the aid of Eoghan Harris. The former television producer even wrote camera directions for Trimble on the script, enabling him to be at ease as he spoke. Instructions such as 'Look up at the camera', 'Look down at the lectern', 'Smile' and 'Turn to the audience' were marked on it in block capitals.

Harris also had a hand in the content of the speech itself, particularly Trimble's references to the eighteenth-century Irish philosopher and writer Edmund Burke and the US ambassador to Moscow during the 1960s, George Kennan. Yet the address reflected Trimble's own philosophical and political beliefs as well – mildly conservative/liberal, cautious, a child of the European Enlightenment but fearful of the many grandiose social experiments it later spawned. There was, too, a hint of his Presbyterian upbringing in the text. At the beginning of the speech he reminded his global audience about the importance of words to his Ulster Protestant tradition:

The tradition from which I come, but by which I am not confined, produced the first vernacular Bible in the language of the common people, and contributed much to the scientific language of the Enlightenment. It puts a great price on the precise use of words, and uses them with circumspection, so much so that our passion for precision is often confused with an indifference to idealism.

Trimble then called upon three writers from the eighteenth and twentieth centuries to justify his own political philosophy: Edmund Burke, the Israeli novelist and peace activist Amos Oz, and George Kennan. He referred to Burke partly because he was a pluralist Irishman, born of a Catholic mother and a Protestant father, but also because he was in Trimble's mind 'the best model for what might be called politicians of the possible . . . politicians who seek to make a working peace, not in some perfect world that never was'. In his Nobel speech Trimble deployed Burke's anti-revolutionary philosophy to attack the abstract certainties of Protestant fundamentalist loyalism and extreme armed republicanism. Like the British empiricist that he is, Trimble excoriated Rousseau's concept of the noble savage corrupted by society. He agreed with Burke that the pursuit of Rousseauesque perfection, the creation of the new revolutionary man, led and would continue to lead 'to the gibbet and the guillotine'. Modern-day intellectuals have noted that Trimble's Burkean mistrust of the abstract search for perfecting man is a central plank of the UUP leader's philosophy. Dr Arthur Aughey, a politics lecturer and writer at the University of Ulster, borrows a line from the novel *The Leopard* by the Italian writer Giuseppe di Lampedusa to define Trimble's paradoxical conservatism: 'There is a wonderful contradictory phrase from that novel that if you want things to stay basically the same then certain things must change. I think that is precisely the bargain that Trimble wants. Some things are going to have to change in Northern Ireland in order that the big thing, i.e. the union, stays the same.'[22] In other words, the concessions on policing, power-sharing, limited cross-border bodies and so on are needed in order to maintain the status quo, namely the union.

Although Trimble rejected the notion of the Irish peace process mirroring other peace initiatives across the world, he came close to linking the Northern Ireland conflict with the Middle East. When he referred to Amos Oz's definition of a political fanatic as 'someone who is more interested in you than in himself . . . he may not be able to change your race, so he will eliminate you from the perfect equation of his mind by eliminating you from the earth', Trimble could have been talking about the ultra-fundamentalists at Drumcree or the bombers at Omagh. There was a clear indication in his reference to George Kennan's hawkish attitude to the Soviet Union that Trimble feared the peace process could be turned into an appeasement process for terrorists. Perhaps it also pointed obliquely to his own scepticism about whether the IRA was really serious about peace:

> It worries me that there is an appeasing strand in Western politics. Sometimes it is a hope that things are not as bad as all that. Sometimes it is a hope that people can be weaned away from terror. What we need is George Kennan's hard-headed advice to the State Department in the 1960s for dealing with the state terrorists of his time, based on his years in Moscow. 'Don't act chummy with them; don't assume a community of aims with them which does not really exist; don't make fatuous gestures of good will.'

Was Trimble really thinking about the republican movement and the Irish cold war when he quoted those remarks?

There was, however, a message to his own community that certain concessions had to be made in order to preserve the union. He accepted that his critics would say that compromises like those contained in the Agreement were a sign of weakness. Again, though, he drew on Burke for inspiration, referring to the great thinker's view that 'Magnanimity in politics is not seldom the truest wisdom; and a great empire and little minds go ill together'. The 'little minds' Trimble was hinting at were those No unionists unable to sell their message to a new, regionalized, multi-faith, multi-cultural UK.

While the Nobel speech contained messages to republicanism that he was ready to compromise, there was also a repetition of his demand for decommissioning. He was not interested in precise dates, quantities and modalities of disarmament: 'All I have asked for is a credible beginning. All I have asked for is that they say that the "war" is over. And that is proved by such a beginning. That is not too much to ask for. Nor is it too much to ask that the reformist party of nationalism, the SDLP, support me in this.'

These last words coloured much of the media coverage of the Trimble speach. Pro-nationalist writers and journalists accused Trimble of subverting the Nobel ceremony for narrow party-political purposes, as a global platform to beat Sinn Fein. They contrasted his highly politicized speech with the 'statesman-like' address delivered by John Hume, which contained all the usual references to 'our divided people' and 'spilling our sweat, not our blood' and named European unity as the model for peaceful co-existence in Ireland.

(The hysterical reaction to Trimble's address may in part be due to the fact that many journalists simply did not understand a great deal of it, especially the references to Burke, Oz and Kennan. One Irish academic who watched the speech in the BBC Northern Ireland studios was flummoxed when a young journalist listening to the Nobel speech asked him: 'Who the hell is Edmund Burke?' The question said as much about the state of sound-bite journalism in the English-speaking world as it did about the innate hostility towards Trimble in certain sections of the media.)

Yet in their indignation, those who ganged up on Trimble over his Nobel address failed to focus on his important acknowledgement of unionism's historical faults. As the speech drew to a close, Trimble referred to unionism's maltreatment of Catholics during four decades of one-party rule: 'Ulster unionists, fearful of being isolated on the island, built a solid house, but it was a cold house for Catholics. And northern nationalists, although they had a roof over their heads, seemed to us as if they meant to burn the house down. None of us are entirely innocent.'

For decades unionist leaders had maintained the fiction that Northern Ireland had been a 'lovely wee place' up until 1969, arguing that the roots of the subsequent years of terror could be traced exclusively to conspiratorial armed republicanism. In union-ism's Arcadian vision of pre-1969 Northern Ireland there were no state repression, job discrimination, gerrymandering or blatant bigotry. Trimble had now become the first Ulster Unionist leader since partition to accept that the state had sinned against the Catholic minority. It was a belated confession, but an honest confession all the same. Trimble still defends his 'cold house for Catholics' reference in the face of ultra-loyalist criticism: 'Well, it was true. There were reasons why you could justify it – you could look back over history and say that Protestants also felt under siege, but it was true. We can argue how that came about, but the hope I still have with the Agreement is that we can actually produce a society here where everybody feels comfortable.'[23]

Critics such as Robert McCartney saw the Nobel award as the ultimate example of Trimble being taken to the top of the temple to be tempted into selling Ulster to the republican devil. Did Trimble ever think himself that the peace prize was flattery leading to deception? His press officer David Kerr believes that there was one over-riding positive outcome from Trimble standing on the podium in Oslo and receiving his medal from the Nobel committee. 'Up until 10 December 1998 the only image the rest of the world had of unionism was Ian Paisley shouting and screaming in Belfast, London and Strasbourg. Now the world had a different image of unionism in the shape of David. To me that was the most important result of the Nobel prize for us,' Kerr said.[24] Trimble's natural reticence and scepticism had made him feel that the award might have been premature, not just because the ceasefire had only resulted in an armed peace: 'I had a question in my mind then and I still have it now as to whether the developments in Northern Ireland were so important compared to what else was happening in the world. I was pleased that the Nobel committee had balanced the award and recognized the unionist population of Northern Ireland for the first time.'[25]

While John Hume decided to hand his prize money over to two charities working with the poor in Ireland, the Salvation Army and the Society of St Vincent de Paul, Trimble dithered about what to do with his. He admitted that he used a small portion to treat his family to a holiday in Italy. Following the Oslo ceremony he took Daphne and the children to Venice, justifying the trip by pointing out that 'You know, we have not had many benefits from the political events of this year, in fact very few'. It gave him an opportunity to praise Daphne for her role during a tumultuous year. 'I don't I think I would have done this otherwise. It's as simple as that.'[26] Since then Trimble has decided not to hand over the cash to charities, preferring to fund a unionist political think-tank on the lines of the Thatcher and Gorbachev foundations. It was typical of Trimble that he brushed off suggestions that diverting the prize money to a political cause was a bad PR move and that a massive charitable donation would have enamoured him more to the public.

Back home, his party colleagues were getting bogged down with their SDLP opponents in the mundane detail of the aspect of the Agreement that dealt with cross-border bodies. However, by 18 December the UUP had managed to fight off SDLP attempts to increase the number of cross-border institutions radically and extend their remit. The SDLP and UUP now agreed to the creation of six North–South implementation bodies and six areas of cross-border cooperation. The six implementation bodies were inland waterways; food safety; trade and business development; special EU programmes affecting all of Ireland; the Irish and, significantly, the Ulster Scots language; and aquaculture and marine matters. Crucially for Trimble, his team had successfully resisted the abolition of the Northern Ireland Industrial Development Board in favour of an all-Ireland investment body. Trimble arrived back in Belfast safe in the knowledge that his colleagues, including the legal advisers he employed during Easter week had done their job, particularly in the UUP's negotiations over North–South bodies with the Irish government. Trimble was pleased that his legal team had succeeded in limiting the constitutional scope of these cross-border bodies.

December 1998 had been a personally and politically fulfilling month for David Trimble. Four days before his party and the SDLP signed up to the cross-border deal, serious divisions were emerging inside Robert McCartney's UK Unionist Party. Trimble had always regarded the North Down MP as his most dangerous unionist opponent. Now McCartney appeared to be at odds with his own party over his insistence that UKUP members must withdraw from the Assembly in the event of Sinn Fein taking up their ministerial positions prior to IRA decommissioning or strong cross-border bodies being established. McCartney's four Assembly colleagues – Cedric Wilson, Norman Boyd, Roger Hutchinson and Patrick Roche – refused to accept their leader's conditions, and by Christmas the UKUP was on the verge of a serious split.

The party's morale had been severely dented two months earlier when their most esteemed member, Conor Cruise O'Brien, dropped a bombshell on them. Extracts from O'Brien's autobiography, *Memoir*, were published in the *Observer* on the last Sunday of October, during the UUP's annual conference. In his usual lucid style O'Brien outlined a new option for unionists, given that he believed the British government was disengaging from

Northern Ireland. From a position of strength, O'Brien argued, unionists should embrace a United Ireland but on their own terms. They should negotiate with the Dublin government now and ensure they exercised a new veto over political arrangements on the island. Moreover, a large unionist bloc voting in the Irish Parliament could perpetually hold the balance of power in Dublin and extract major concessions for the Protestant community in the North.

One motivation for this rather strange conversion to a United Ireland was that O'Brien worries deeply about Sinn Fein's growing influence on both states. In his mind the unionists holding the balance of power in the Dail would weaken the power of a resurgent Sinn Fein and save the Irish Republic and democracy from the IRA and their political allies. But many in the UKUP, especially those who were emotionally tied to the idea of full integration with the rest of Britain, recoiled from O'Brien's proposal.

His advice, though, was not new. Desmond Boal, Paisley's former ally, had argued something similar back in the early 1970s. One of those who had countered Boal's call for a federal Ireland with strong Protestant voting powers was an unknown young academic lawyer called David Trimble, who wrote a detailed riposte of the QC's arguments. Two decades later, when he was shown Conor Cruise O'Brien's similar call for unionists to embrace a United Ireland, his response was briefer than his youthful counterblast at Desmond Boal. As he sat having lunch in the White Horse Hotel on the outskirts of Derry, preparing for his annual address to party delegates, Trimble perused the important extracts from O'Brien's book and then simply burst out laughing.

There was more amusement for Trimble five days into the new year when the UKUP finally split apart. The four dissident Assembly members formed their own political force, the Northern Ireland Unionist Party. This meant there were now six rival unionist parties represented in the Stormont Assembly.

While Trimble and Mallon had finally agreed to a deal on cross-border bodies, the divisions between them over the pivotal issue – decommissioning – surfaced in the first week of 1999. Mallon wanted the UUP leader to set up the power-sharing executive before the IRA handed over weapons. His logic was that once Sinn Fein was in government the IRA would come under irresistible pressure to decommission. Trimble, however, stuck by his pre-condition of 'no guns, no government'. The atmosphere was soured further on 7 January when the IRA issued a hard-line New Year message, urging the British government to 'face down' unionism. The Provos also warned of 'growing frustration' in their ranks over Trimble's attitude towards the executive. Ominously, the IRA reminded everyone that it was unionism's refusal to accept 'forward political movement' that had fatally undermined the first IRA ceasefire of 1994. Trimble was now taking flak from all sides. Three days after the IRA issued their threat, Billy Hutchinson of the PUP publicly accused him of endangering the peace process by insisting on republican and loyalist decommissioning. The UUP were taken aback by Hutchinson's intervention; it seemed that the UVF-aligned PUP had ganged up with nationalists and republicans to flay Trimble. 'David felt deeply let down by Hutchinson's remarks. He was amazed that a unionist would be allying himself with Sinn Fein to attack a fellow unionist. From that day on our relations with the PUP were never the same again,' said one Trimble aide.[27] John Taylor made matters worse when he an-nounced on 18 January, the day the Assembly debated the agreed UUP/SDLP report on North–South structures, that the Agreement had only a 50 per cent chance of survival. On the same day Peter Weir voted against the report and subsequently had the party whip withdrawn from him in the Assembly. Taylor's gloom and Weir's rebellion created further tension in an already nervous UUP.

In an effort to calm fears inside the party, Trimble decided to embark on a Blair-style tour of party branches around Northern Ireland. In the last week of January he held five private meetings in various parts of the Province to explain his position and underline his determination that he would not establish an executive unless the IRA began to disarm. There were rumblings of a new leadership challenge, possibly around the time of the Ulster Unionist Council's AGM in March. The backdrop to Trimble's meet-the-people tour was not promising.

Paramilitaries on both sides intensified the practice of so-called punishment beatings in working-class Protestant and Catholic areas. Although beatings, mutilations, knee-cappings and expul-sions did not impact on the British or Irish governments, to the average unionist voter, particularly those who supported the Agreement, these actions represented clear breaches of the ceasefires. Violence was continuing, despite promises that the Agreement would usher in a new era of peace on the streets. As a result, unionist confidence in the Agreement was again severely dented. January turned out to be the worst month in ten years for paramilitary beatings and shootings. In response Trimble issued an invitation to Amnesty International to investigate the issue of punishment attacks, and the human-rights group later agreed to the request.

His invitation was another first for unionism. For thirty years it had been republicans and nationalists who made persistent claims of human-rights abuses at the hands of the security forces. Priests such as Father Denis Faul had exposed the use of torture by the Army and police in detention centres. Faul and other local human rights activists called in global watchdogs like Amnesty to probe their claims of torture and abuse. Unionists often reacted defensively to these allegations, believing that they were part of a sophisticated propaganda campaign to undermine the security forces and provide the IRA with a shield to protect its activists from police questioning techniques.

Now Trimble was turning the tables on his republican opponents. He was aware that Amnesty's remit had changed in the early 1990s to cover human-rights abuses not only carried out by states but also by armed insurrectionist groups around the world. It was a clever tactic for Trimble to employ, if belatedly, and illuminated his ability to think strategically rather than viscerally. No other unionist leader would have dreamed of doing it! And for a short time the tactic worked – the number of beatings, shootings and expulsions fell dramatically within a month of his invitation to Amnesty. Yet the ongoing social terrorism in nationalist and loyalist areas, combined with the paramilitaries' stubborn refusal to decommission, gave Trimble no cause for optimism at the start of the year. Prophetically, he warned on 24 January that the political process might have to be 'parked' if decommissioning did not take place, adding: 'What we don't want is for the peace process to have a crash-landing where it is seriously damaged.'

He was encouraged, however, by the comments of Bertie Ahern in the *Sunday Times* two weeks later. The Taoiseach told the paper that being part of a Northern Ireland executive would not be possible 'without at least a commencement of decommissioning, and that would apply in the North and in the South'.[28] Sinn Fein leaders were disconcerted by Ahern's remarks; Trimble, on the other hand, was delighted. Indeed, the relationship between the two men remained very good throughout the first half of 1999. Trimble often speaks warmly of his friendship with Ahern; both men had been seen laughing and chatting together the previous month at Dublin's Lansdowne Road ground when the Ulster rugby side won the European Cup. He is more mistrustful of Ahern's party, Fianna Fail, which he suspects has been recently playing the republican card in a bid to claw back electoral ground lost to Sinn Fein in the Republic:

> We are a wee bit worried about whether some other factors are affecting Bertie's approach. There is a feeling that Fianna Fail – and I'm saying his party, *not* Bertie – are making some adjustments to their policy in the light of Sinn Fein's gains down south. But Bertie is basically pragmatic and personal relations with him are good. He has always been straight with us. Some of the meetings we have in Dublin have been over a meal; we've had a few drinks together. Those encounters have been very friendly.[29]

Trimble's relationship with Ahern was probably more cordial than with some of his own back-benchers. Two days after Ahern's *Sunday Times* interview the First Minister managed to avoid a second rebellion in the Assembly team's ranks. Roy Beggs Junior had threatened to vote against the report into future government structures drawn up by Mallon and Trimble. After receiving a private letter from Trimble, the sceptical Assembly member voted in favour. The report was passed by 77 votes to 29 but the breakdown in the unionist vote only drew attention to Trimble's wafer-thin majority. Twenty-nine unionist members of the Assembly (including the two PUP representatives) backed the Mallon–Trimble report, but exactly the same number voted to reject it. Ian Paisley kept up his barrage against Trimble. 'I never thought I would live to see the day when unionists would destroy the union,' he thundered in the chamber.[30] Trimble was visibly relieved at the result; another hurdle in the race towards a power-sharing government had been cleared.

The final hurdle, decommissioning, still seemed insurmountable. Sinn Fein's national chairman, Mitchell McLaughlin, had warned that even a token gesture of decommissioning threatened to split the IRA. In their bilateral talks with Trimble and his team, Sinn Fein leaders told the Ulster Unionists that a rupture in the republican movement was risked if the First Minister pressed too hard. Moreover, the continued attacks on nationalist homes and businesses by dissident loyalists were making it harder for the republican leadership to hold the line. Conversely, Trimble pointed out to the republicans that he faced being deposed if he agreed to establish the executive before guns were handed over.

On the actions of dissident loyalist terrorists, Trimble had a message for Gerry Adams and Martin McGuinness: 'At one meeting I told them that the strategy behind the pipe bomb attacks was in fact to stop the IRA decommissioning. The republican movement was playing into the hands of these dissidents by not disarming. The dissidents did not want decommissioning because that would lead to real political progress and an executive which they want to destroy.'[31]

Trimble suspects that groups such as the Red Hand Defenders and the Orange Volunteers may be working to someone else's agenda, specifically some politicians in the No camp. There is some evidence to suggest that his suspicions may be justified. In the period between the LVF declaring that their war was over and the terror group handing over weapons to General John de Chastelaine's international arms body, a politician from the No unionist side tried to dissuade the organization from decommissioning. The political figure visited the Portadown home of Mark Fulton, a close friend of the late Billy Wright, who had taken over the LVF after his leader's assassination. The politician asked Fulton not to let the LVF hand over weapons because this would only help David Trimble's cause. Fulton ignored this advice and gave the go-ahead for a token surrender of arms. Although the politician who had links to Billy Wright's mid-Ulster UVF in the recent past had failed, his efforts demonstrated how desperate some in the No camp were to thwart Trimble at any opportunity.

Trimble's own connections to loyalist paramilitarism resurfaced shortly after his victory in the Assembly. His former mentor, Bill Craig, emerged from his self-imposed exile to defend his infamous 'liquidate the enemy' remarks made at the Vanguard rally nearly thirty years before. Craig had agreed to be interviewed by the veteran BBC broadcaster Peter Taylor for a documentary on Ulster loyalism. In his first interview in over a decade Craig stood by his comments. 'I did mean to liquidate the enemy. Not in terms of personalities, but in terms of organization. I didn't expect them to be interpreted in any other way than the normal meaning.' On the same programme Trimble dismissed Craig's comments as simply 'over the top'. Trimble had not seen Craig for more than three years and, given the latter's concern over his protégé's new departure, it was unlikely that any meeting would be convivial. Vanguard's founder stubbornly refuses to talk about his disciple's recent strategic shift, but close friends of Craig's say he thinks Trimble has surrendered far too much to nationalism in the Agreement. Trimble, too, finds it hard to comment on his old guru, stating rather blandly that he regrets not having had the time to see him over the last three years.

The deadline for devolving power to Northern Ireland was set as 10 March, but there were very few in the political class at Stormont who believed that this date could be met. The impact of the IRA's hard-line New Year message, coupled with the intensification of punishment beatings, was a collapse of faith in the Good Friday Agreement within the Protestant community. The results of a BBC opinion poll published on 4 March showed that 41 per cent of unionists now supported the Agreement, a drop of 14 per cent from the day of the Referendum the previous May.

As Trimble prepared for the Ulster Unionist Council's AGM he knew that the pro-Agreement tendency in his party had been severely weakened by events on the ground. The mood of disillusionment was reflected in the reception he received at the meeting on 20 March. The previous year he had won a standing ovation from his party; now a small but vocal minority of delegates was heckling him from the floor. Trimble faced a series of questions from delegates over their concerns about decommissioning. Veteran Shankill Road Ulster Unionist Jean Coulter asked him: 'Will you still keep the promise you made, and pull the plug on this if we don't get decommissioning?' When he refused to answer, several members shouted 'Shame' and 'Fudge'. Trimble tried to strike a balance in his speech, insisting on the delivery of arms without at the same time sounding too truculent to the IRA. He simply said that decommissioning would prove that republicans really wanted the Agreement to work, adding that there was no alternative to the Good Friday deal. As the shouts of dissent grew louder those on the top platform stood up and urged delegates to sing the National Anthem. The cries of 'Shame' and 'Fudge' were drowned in a chorus of 'God Save the Queen'. However, the results of the elections to the UUC were even more disturbing than the chants of malcontents in the audience. Anti-Agreement candidates did so well that some of Trimble's allies admitted that the UUC was now evenly split between pro- and anti-Agreement factions. A year before, the pro-Agreement wing had received a resounding 70 per cent of the vote.

Meanwhile the clandestine relationship between Trimble and Sean O'Callaghan was partially exposed. The Belfast-based *Sunday Life* revealed that the First Minister had been drinking in the company of O'Callaghan in the House of Comons bar shortly after leaving a Downing Street meeting with Tony Blair. The paper did not realize the extent of the collusion between the two men, and Gary Kent, the Labour Party activist and spokesman for New Dialogue, a cross-party British–Irish pressure group compaigning for peace and the restoration of a devolved government in Northern Ireland, managed to pass off the incident as mere coincidence. 'It is no great secret that Sean meets with a variety of politicians, including members of the SDLP, the Orange Order, MPs and peers of all persuasions,' Kent told the *Sunday Life*.[32] What Kent did not reveal was that O'Callaghan did not proffer the same advice to people in the SDLP as he gave to Trimble on a regular basis.

By now the former IRA killer's friendship with Trimble was blossoming. O'Callaghan recalled:

I think Trimble would rather have a meal and a beer with me than with most people. I like to take the piss out of him from time to time, especially about his Vanguard days. We were sitting one night in the Reform Club after a meeting at Robert Cranborne's place and there was Paul Bew, Trimble, John Lloyd, Gary Kent, Ruth Dudley Edwards, young Barry White and me. I remember looking around and saying, 'This is really interesting. Here is John Lloyd, who worked secretly with Peter Mandelson against the Militants; here is Gary Kent, a supposedly left-winger who is more right-wing; there's Ruth Dudley Edwards, a lapsed Catholic who is still fond of John Hume.' Then I turned to Trimble and said, 'The curious ones in this company, David, are you and I. We had one thing in common – we both tried to bring Sunningdale down in 1974, me in the IRA and you in Vanguard.' Trimble laughed and said, 'Yes, but we were more effective than you.' To which I replied, 'And David, we were glad that you were effective.'[33]

Now, in the spring of 1999, O'Callaghan was playing a key role in shaping Trimble's strategy. The ex-IRA man was to become a pivotal behind-the-scenes player in a new political initiative aimed at jump-starting the flagging talks process and ultimately leading to decommissioning and devolution. As the devolution deadline passed, the two Prime Ministers, Irish and British, agreed to travel to Belfast and reopen the talks. The venue this time was Hillsborough Castle, where the Anglo–Irish Agreement had been signed by Margaret Thatcher and Garret Fitzgerald fourteen years earlier.

While Trimble's team engaged in new talks with Sinn Fein, Tony Blair and Bertie Ahern, O'Callaghan worked quietly in London on a formula which he would then put to Jonathan Powell. The plan became the backbone of a joint communiqué from the two Prime Ministers on 1 April which Ian Paisley later termed the 'April Fools' Day charter'. The statement said that on a set date the parties would set up the executive. Within one month, on a date set by General de Chastelaine's commission, 'a collective act of reconciliation will take place. This will see some arms put beyond use on a voluntary basis, in a manner which will be verified by the Independent International Commission on Decommissioning'. In other words the IRA and the loyalists would destroy some weapons themselves, or at the very least seal bunkers full of arms in the presence of international observers. In addition, during the act of decommissioning there would ceremonies on both sides of the border to commemorate all the victims of violence. The central concept of a day of commemoration came from O'Callaghan. Trimble must have relished the idea of a former IRA killer helping to shape British and Irish policy favourable to unionism.

Trimble tried another track with the loyalists over decommissioning by opening up new secret negotiations between Sean O'Callaghan and the leadership of the UVF. When O'Callaghan met the second-in-command of the organization in East Belfast in late spring the UVF leader was somewhat dismayed that O'Callaghan had advised Trimble to bring the UDA on board, even to the extent of offering their political wing, the UDP, an office at

Stormont despite the fact that they had not been elected to the Assembly. Unfortunately the series of meetings failed to produce a breakthrough – the loyalist terror group insisted on holding on to its arms and refused to decommission unilaterally.

O'Callaghan has confirmed that one idea he floated was for Trimble to hold a meeting with the UVF's so-called Brigade Staff. By late 1999 this had still not taken place, but it is understood that Trimble did not reject the proposal out of hand. But O'Callaghan did impress upon the UVF commander that PUP statements blaming Trimble for blocking progress were playing into the hands of Sinn Fein and the IRA. During his talks with the UVF leader, he repeated the line that the republican leadership would have been delighted every time David Ervine and Billy Hutchinson attacked Trimble. As a result the PUP's comments on Trimble were moderated and the UVF eventually referred to decommissioning as being 'a noble goal'.

Although the UUP reserved its judgement on the Hillsborough declaration, Trimble was in favour of the initiative and genuinely believed it could have worked: 'I thought Hillsborough was a runner. There was a feeling that there was some chance of movement. The SDLP supported it and I believed I could have sold it, although there were some difficulties in my party. That's why we had to reserve our judgment. But I think it was possible – it could have been the solution in my mind. In the right context it could have worked,' he said.[34]

Trimble got his answer from republicans on Easter Saturday in a speech by veteran Belfast IRA leader Brian Keenan. Keenan told a republican rally at Iniskeen, Co. Monaghan that the IRA would not be forced into surrender masquerading as decommissioning. He described the Hillsborough declaration as the 'Easter bunny', adding that David Trimble had dug a hole for himself over decommissioning and republicans would not help him climb out of it. Given Keenan's stature inside the IRA, the snub to Trimble and the two governments was highly significant. There was no chance of the IRA or Sinn Fein accepting the initiative. Yet Trimble clung, naïvely as it turned out, to the notion that the republican movement had nowhere else to go. In an interview published in the *Sunday Times* on 4 April he stated that Sinn Fein would accept the Hillsborough declaration. Perhaps his optimism was merely an attempt to talk up the process, but it left the impression in many sceptical unionist minds that Trimble's analysis of republican intentions was far too benign. Just over a week after this interview both Sinn Fein and the PUP declared that they had rejected Hillsborough, marking the collapse of the first of three initiatives by Tony Blair and Bertie Ahern to implement the Good Friday deal.

The next two plans were to be even less favourable to the Ulster Unionists than Hillsborough, and were to put the long-standing relationship between Blair and Trimble under severe strain. Relations between the First Minister and his SDLP deputy were already deteriorating before the Hillsborough summit. On 20 April they got decidedly worse when Seamus Mallon launched an attack on those who in his mind had 'vandalized' the Good Friday Agreement. The Deputy First Minister accused Sinn Fein and the Ulster Unionists of wrecking the peace deal. His attack on the UUP was a critical development, since any partnership government would have to be founded on the Trimble–Mallon axis. Privately Trimble despaired at Mallon's sniping, and suspected that his deputy was lukewarm about the prospects of them working together in a power-sharing government.

In the middle of the new crisis Trimble broke another historic taboo when it was announced that he would meet Pope John Paul II in the Vatican, having received an invitation to do so at a reception for Nobel prize winners in Rome. Trimble would be the first unionist leader ever to meet a pope; the last time any unionist had got close to the present incumbent had been when Ian Paisley tried to shout him down during an address to the European Parliament in 1988. Paisley was forcibly removed from the chamber in order to let the Pope speak to MEPs.

Trimble tried to play down the poignancy of his handshake with the leader of the Catholic world. He even claimed that Orangemen in Portadown told him there was no problem with a papal meeting. 'Some recalled the receptions given to Ulstermen who fought in Italy during the Second World War,' he said. 'They told me the Vatican reception for the Ulster servicemen was great – and I'm sure some of them were Orangemen.'[35] Not all Portadown Orangemen, however, were pleased that their MP was shaking hands with the Pope. David Jones, the spokesman for the local Orange Order said: 'It's ironic to think that he can go and meet the Pope but he can't come near his own constinuency without an armed guard. People here no longer feel he represents them or loyalism in any way. I think people would only be too glad if he went over and stayed with the Pope.'[36] His colleague Ivor Young accused Trimble of reneging on his oath as an Orangeman to uphold the Protestant religion and oppose the errors of Rome. 'We all knew Trimble was a traitor, this latest escapade puts the final nail in his political coffin here in Upper Bann. There is no way that he will ever be elected here again,' Young said.[37]

More deranged Protestant fundamentalists saw the papal meeting as the ultimate betrayal. For them the Pope represented Rome, the Whore of Babylon, on which all the ills of the temporal world could be blamed. Trimble's handshake only confirmed their worst fears that the First Minister was an agent of MI5, the Vatican or the Devil – or even all of them at the same time.

The Independent Orange Order, which has strong ties to Ian Paisley's DUP, was scathing: 'We would remind David Trimble of the deeply offensive claims of spiritual supremacy made by, and for, the Pope. By meeting the Pope Mr Trimble has once again shown a blatant disregard for Orange and Protestant principles.'[38] Trimble could have reminded the Independent Orange Order that Pope Alexander VIII supported its hero, William of Orange, in his struggle against James II at the end of the seventeenth century. In fact the First Minister could have added that his meeting with the present Pope would take place in the very building where masses were held in celebration of King Billy's victory at the Boyne in 1690.

The historic handshake finally took place in the presence of Mikhail Gorbachev, the former South African President F.W. De Klerk, the Israeli Prime Minister Shimon Peres and Betty Williams, one of the founders of the Peace People. Trimble was pictured with the Pope and fifty-three other Nobel prize winners in the Consistory Hall, the room in the Vatican where the Cardinals of the Church gather to advise the Pope. Shortly before the meeting Trimble gave an interview to Vatican Radio updating the Holy See's international broadcasting arm on developments in Northern Ireland. He expressed his wish that the Pope and the Catholic Church would help to persuade the paramilitaries to 'commit themselves irrevocably to peaceful means'.[39]

When Trimble finally spoke to the Pope he told him that he hoped 1999 would be the year in which peace was finally secured. The Pope recalled his visit to Ireland twenty years before and repeated his view, expressed then, that murder could not be condoned or called by another name. Although he tried to describe the trip to Rome as a 'courtesy call' on the Pope, Trimble clearly saw some benefits in it. He accepted that there would be some criticism of the meeting but also realized that there was a wider political game for unionists to think about than their theological differences with the Church of Rome. His handshake was part of his general plan to secularize unionism. 'What I did here was kill a taboo, making it more difficult for Republicans to play a strategy game portraying unionists as being intransigent or sectarian,' he said.[40]

While in Rome Trimble kept his eye on another big political game being played out not far away – Kosovo. During the visit Mikhail Gorbachev tried to draft a critical statement on NATO's bombing of Yugoslavia, which would have been issued in the name of all of the Nobel laureates. Trimble, who had built up a rapport with the former Soviet President, tried to prevent him doing so. Instead, Trimble and F.W. De Klerk succeeded in producing a text which offered a broader analysis of the new Balkan war. 'I think the important thing to him [Gorbachev] was to make contacts with other Nobel laureates, and attempt through this to criticise the allies over their bombing campaign. But we managed to steer deliberations into more practical channels and that particular idea didn't succeed,' he said.[41] Bill Clinton and Tony Blair clearly had a lot to thank Trimble for in averting what would have been a major diplomatic embarrassment during the NATO air war against the Milosevic regime.

Blair, however, failed to reciprocate. In fact by early May some of Trimble's inner circle believed the Prime Minister was again working against their leader. On Friday, 14 May representatives of the UUP, SDLP and Sinn Fein were summoned to talks at 10 Downing Street hosted by Blair and Bertie Ahern. Most of those involved agreed that there had been some progress, although they disagreed over the extent of what was agreed. This caution, particularly among the Ulster Unionists, did not stop the Downing Street spin machine from moving into overdrive. The following morning the editors of most of the UK national Sunday newspapers were told by Number Ten to clear their front pages. Correspondents, including myself, were advised by their editors not to speak to any politicians until late into the day in order not to endanger the deal. Between five and six o'clock that evening Blair and Ahern would announce that there had been a historic deal between Sinn Fein and the UUP – an executive would be formed and decommissioning would commence later. Yet the reports of progress at the talks had been nothing but froth and there was no deal.

Many Ulster Unionists back in Belfast were dismayed at what they were hearing on the political grapevine. It seemed to them that Trimble had given Blair the impression he could live with a further compromise on decommissioning. Even some of his most trusted, liberal lieutenants such as Michael McGimpsey warned Trimble that they would not buy the package on offer in the Downing Street talks. Trimble believes his position was completely misinterpreted and then mismanaged by the Downing Street spin machine, to the point that his leadership was put in grave danger. He stated:

> The problem with the Downing Street thing was that it went on far too long. By teatime on Friday we thought something was emerging which might have been, if the details had been worked, a runner. But then as the evening went on, instead of the detail of the deal coming down in the right place, it was coming down in the wrong place. I then had to tell Blair that I could not endorse this. At Hillsborough the detail of the deal had been sorted, which enabled me to go to my Assembly party and sell it to them. The Hillsborough detail proved to the Assembly team that there would be no Sinn Fein ministers until there was some decommissioning taking place. Late afternoon at Downing Street I was proceeding in the belief that, if we got a declaration, underneath this would be the fine detail which I could sell to the party again – namely that there would be a start to decommissioning. When the detail did not come through, I warned Blair shortly before seven o'clock on Friday night that I would not support the deal as it stood. I told him that the most I could do was to go away and consider it.[42]

The plot thickened further around ten o'clock, with sharp disagreements between the UUP and the SDLP over the nature of the deal. Trimble told the SDLP he was prepared to look at the way the deal would be sequenced – an executive might be established and then decommissioning begun shortly afterwards, which was a clear shift in UUP policy. But Trimble was not simply interested in a form of words from Sinn Fein; he wanted something more concrete than a promise to do their best to persuade the IRA to disarm. 'I made it very clear that we would have to see the issue being done, so we could say to our party that we are holding the line on decommissioning,'[43] he said. He believed he had offered some ground on the UUP line of 'no guns, no government', but claimed that the nationalists failed to reciprocate. Sinn Fein had rejected Hillsborough; now it was the turn of the Ulster Unionists to dump the Downing Street initiative.

Blair, walking tall in the world over his determined approach to the Kosovo crisis, had been made to look rather foolish by the collapse of his much-vaunted Downing Street deal. He could bomb a major eastern European state like Serbia into submission, but he could not bang heads together to reach agreement in Northern Ireland. Exasperated by the lack of progress in Ulster, Blair surprised many veteran commentators in the Province by imposing the date of 30 June as the absolute and final deadline for agreement between the parties. The trouble for Blair was that 'absolute' and 'final' have a much more elastic meaning in the lexicon of Ulster's tortuous political struggle. By setting a deadline Blair had pushed Trimble into a corner. His Assembly team was concerned that the Prime Minister was preparing to renege on his own promises over 'decommissioning before government' in the 1998 Referendum. In Blair's new plan, it seemed that the only condition for an executive to be established was that General de Chastelain should be able to report that some 'progress' had been made over decommissioning. For many UUP Assembly members this was not enough: 'All the IRA had to do was talk to General de Chastelain's commission and the General could be forced to say that some progress had been made. There was no way we were going to let David sign up to a fudge like that,' said one UUP Assembly member from the liberal wing of the party.

Even outside Ulster Unionist circles there was a widespread belief that Blair had lost control of the spin doctors at Number Ten. Eight days after the Downing Street debacle the *Observer*'s editorial noted:

In the midst of the first European war since 1945 Tony Blair must be commended for continuing to shore up the Northern Ireland peace process. On other vital national issues from the economy to welfare reform Blair has handed over command to his Cabinet colleagues while he conducts the struggle against Serbian aggression in Kosovo. Only Northern Ireland has diverted his attention away from the Balkans. But in his quest to bed down the Good Friday Agreement and finally devolve powers to the Province, did he unwittingly put First Minister David Trimble at risk from his own hardliners?[44]

Mindful of the imminent European Cup final, the paper's leader borrowed a soccer analogy: 'Trimble's absence from the pro-Agreement team would be as big a blow to Blair as the loss of Roy Keane will be for Alex Ferguson in Barcelona this Wednesday.' It was changed times when the voice of the liberal British left on Sunday could speak up in defence of a unionist leader to the detriment of a popular Labour Prime Minister.

The *Observer*'s newly found concern for Trimble was in contrast to the attitude of traditional Ulster Unionist friends in the British press. Less than a week earlier the *Daily Telegraph* had taken a swipe at Trimble. In a leader on 17 May the paper warned: 'If David Trimble accepts Sinn Fein into the Northern Ireland executive before a significant amount of IRA weaponry has been surrendered, he will rightly forfeit any claim to be the leader of Unionism.' This was music to the ears of sceptics in Union First, the DUP and UKUP. Many in Trimble's party were worried by what they saw as their leader's willingness to bend on the 'no guns, no government' line, fearing that he was prepared to nominate an executive before IRA disarmament began. David Brewster broke cover on 5 June to accuse Trimble of changing party policy. His leader hit back by advising Brewster that his time would be better spent supporting his party than acting in a way that could only damage the European election campaign.

Blair's apparent softening line on decommissioning and the 'friendly fire' raining down on him from his old allies were not the only problems dogging Trimble in May. Ian Paisley was threatening to turn the forthcoming European elections into a second Referendum on the Good Friday Agreement. Worse still, the Ulster Unionist candidate (the sitting MEP, Jim Nicholson) was at the centre of a sex scandal. Trimble had known for some time about Nicholson's affair with the wife of an Armagh Borough Council official. Someone in the No unionist camp had even got hold of some tapes from a private detective who had been working for the woman's husband. These taped conversations between Nicholson (a married man with a grown-up family) and his lover, which were of a highly salacious nature, were then played down the telephone to senior Ulster Unionists, including Trimble.

In his belated confession to the party at its AGM in March Nicholson did not improve his chances of keeping the nomination. The MEP did not use the word 'sorry' in relation to the affair nor did he refer to it as a mistake, according to party delegates. Some in the party now wanted Nicholson's head, arguing that in a conservative place like Northern Ireland, where old-fashioned family values were the norm, it would be impossible to get a self-confessed adulterer elected on the UUP ticket. Among those calling for Nicholson's deselection was John Taylor, who predicted that the UUP would lose the third European seat, possibly to Sinn Fein, unless they picked another candidate. Taylor was secretly canvassing inside the UUP the idea of a dream-ticket duo – Jeffrey Donaldson and Arlene Foster as an alternative to Jim Nicholson.

By early May it appeared that the momentum to ditch Nicholson seemed unstoppable. There was, however, one force standing in the way of deselecting the sitting MEP – David Trimble. The party leader loyally defended Nicholson in spite of the opposition building up over his candidacy. Put simply, Trimble felt that Nicholson's extra-marital affair was none of anyone's business except his wife and his family. He actually felt repelled by the sight of other party members moralizing about Nicholson's character. In Trimble's mind, his MEP had performed a good service for the Province at Strasbourg and Brussels, particularly for Ulster's farming community. Nicholson's attendance record at the European Parliament, was after all, better than that of the two other MEPs, Ian Paisley and John Hume. Moreover, Nicholson had remained loyal to his leader when others were deserting him just over a year before in the run-up to the Good Friday Agreement. Trimble made it clear to his party executive that he would not throw him to the wolves. 'David doesn't judge anyone over their sexual morality. He is happy to be surrounded by all types, including gay people. He felt he owed Jim Nicholson one and he would not desert him,' one Trimble aide remarked.[45]

The task of getting Nicholson re-elected was not made easier by an eve-of-poll leader in the *Daily Telegraph*. It urged unionists to give their first-preferences to Bob McCartney, who privately predicted he was in with a real chance of taking the third seat instead of Nicholson or Sinn Fein. Once again Trimble's old friends at the *Telegraph* had stabbed him in the back.

Trimble's instincts told him that Nicholson would hold on to the seat, because even religious unionists would vote for the beleaguered MEP rather than allow Sinn Fein to snatch the seat. His instincts proved to be correct. On 14 June Ian Paisley topped the poll with 192,762 first-preference votes while John Hume (whom the SDLP had claimed would come first) came in second with 190,731. Nicholson came third with 119,507 first-preferences, just ahead of Sinn Fein's Mitchell McLaughlin. Nicholson was finally elected on the third count, thanks to transfers from their great rival Ian Paisley and the second-preferences of Robert McCartney, who was eliminated after receiving just 20,283 first-preferences. Nicholson's narrow win had thwarted a coup that Trimble's opponents had been planning in the light of a possible defeat on 14 June. The UUP leader had lived to fight another day. The results were, however, still alarming given the sharp slide in Ulster Unionist electoral support dating back from the first ceasefires.

The splits and personal rivalries within the UUP were exposed very publicly again on the day of the count. John Taylor published a letter that he had written to Trimble, in which he warned him that he would resign as a party negotiator if the decommissioning question was dodged. In response, Ken Maginnis accused Taylor of actively working against Jim Nicholson during the election campaign. Maginnis went on to claim that Taylor 'will continue to position himself to take advantage of the many difficulties that David Trimble finds himself in, which I find deplorable'.[46]

Trimble's troubles were exacerbated by an upsurge in violence in late May and early June. On 17 June the IRA informer Martin McGartland was shot and seriously wounded in a gun attack in Whitley Bay in north-east England. Like Eamon Collins (who had been found beaten to death near his home in South Armagh in January), McGartland had written an insider's account of the IRA. Following Collins's murder McGartland claimed he was on an IRA hit list. At first, wildly inaccurate reports emanating from RTE in Dublin asserted that McGartland had been shot by a local drugs gang with whom he had fallen out. However, the truth was that the attempted murder was the work of the IRA's Belfast Brigade, and McGartland was a target because a number of Belfast republicans nursed long-standing grudges against him.

Ignoring her security advisers, Mo Mowlam refused to accept that the McGartland shooting constituted a breach of the IRA ceasefire. Four days later, in an article in the *Times*, Trimble accused the Secretary of State of adopting a 'Nelsonian' attitude by turning a blind eye to ongoing terrorist violence. There was speculation in other papers, much of it fuelled directly by Glengall Street, that Trimble believed Tony Blair would have to continue to intervene personally in Northern Ireland 'until he got himself a proper Secretary of State'. In the same article Trimble issued a very public warning to Blair not to appease republicans in light of the 30 June deadline and the Prime Minister's threat that this would be Ulster's final chance to do a deal:

> Most British people still regard Tony Blair as having the potential to be one of the greatest Prime Ministers. He is now fresh from his success in an honourable war. One fought for humanitarian reasons, not a war fought for oil or power or aggrandisement. He is riding high. But he is in danger of being brought low, of finding his integrity questioned and his honour besmirched. People in Northern Ireland, who last year believed him, are now beginning to lose faith.[47]

He then drew an analogy with the Balkans, where Blair insisted that the Kosovo Liberation Army decommission its weapons once the Serbs withdrew. Trimble contrasted Blair's determined response to the KLA to his apparent weakening on the question of IRA disarmament: 'It would be very sad for us all if a Prime Minister who had garnered so much credit for his country by opposing terrorism in the Balkans should find himself, through understandable impatience, giving too much comfort to those who have not yet crossed the bridge from terrorism to democracy in Northern Ireland.'[48]

Critics of the UUP leader's strategy of flattering and wooing Blair now believed their scepticism had been justified all along. The *Daily Telegraph* – the only national paper opposed to the Good Friday Agreement – took a swipe at Trimble for placing too much faith in the Prime Minister. One of their chief feature writers, Paul Goodman, spotted widening cracks in the Blair–Trimble alliance. He argued that Blair had broken his promises the previous May when he said that prisoners would be kept in jail unless violence ended for good. The murder of Eamon Collins along with that of two drug dealers, the attempted killing of Martin McGartland, the UVF murder of loyalist dissident Frankie Curry and the continuance of punishment beatings and shootings did not indicate that violence was being forsaken for ever. And yet 250 IRA, UDA and UVF prisoners had already walked to early freedom from the gates of the Maze. In Goodman's eyes, Trimble had been had. 'I wonder whether Mr Trimble has fallen victim to "Stockholm syndrome", by which those who are kidnapped fall in love with their kidnappers,' he wrote.[49] In his view, Trimble was trapped inside his personal relationship with Blair, putting far too much blind trust in his friend.

Goodman's warning was realized on the very day of his portent to Trimble. Blair too used the *Times* to set out his plans to break the deadlock over decommissioning and reach his 30 June deadline. In his article he admitted that decommissioning was not a prior condition set down in the Good Friday deal. He then laid out three steps that the parties could take to reach devolution: '(a) There is a clear guarantee of decommissioning by Sinn Fein; (b) It is done in accordance with a timetable laid down by the Commission on Decommissioning, ending in completion in May 2000; (c) There is a cast-iron, fail-safe device that if it didn't happen according to the timetable, that executive wouldn't continue.'[50]

The Ulster Unionists immediately rejected the proposals: Blair was asking them to jump into an executive that included Sinn Fein before any guns were handed over or weapons were rendered unusable. Trimble was known to be exasperated by Blair's attitude. He believed there was no evidence that decommissioning would happen after they had set up the executive. The sceptics such as Jeffrey Donaldson, David Brewster and the Union First cabal were having a field day. As one of them put it: 'Phoney Tony was making a fool out of Trimble. Here was our leader telling us he had Blair's ear, and then suddenly Tony backs down and gives in to Dublin, the SDLP and Sinn Fein.'[51]

And there was worse to come for Trimble. After eighteen hours of intense discussion the talks adjourned around 3.40 a.m. without agreement on a formula for decommissioning and devolution. Blair's spin machine then took off again. Shifting the focus away from the failure to hit his 30 June 'absolute' and 'final' deadline, the Downing Street press office fed the world's press, camped outside

Castle Buildings, the line that they had encountered a 'seismic shift' in the attitude of Sinn Fein towards decommissioning. A number of news organizations got completely carried away by this. *Channel 4 News* trumpeted the so-called 'seismic shift' as one of the most historic developments in Ireland since partition: republicans, it appeared, were at last accepting the principle of disarming the IRA. Yet on the same programme that evening Sinn Fein's Vice-President, Pat Doherty, flatly denied that there had been any radical shift in republican policy towards decommissioning. The First Minister, too, was sceptical. Trimble's central problem during four separate meetings with Sinn Fein had been that any formula Gerry Adams's team put forward was always written in 'aspirational language'. There were no solid commitments on paper that decommissioning would happen. 'The Shinners kept saying to me, "Of course we might fail." Once I heard that, I knew they were not serious – there had been no seismic shift,' he recalled.[52]

A day later the British and Irish governments, tired of the indecision among the parties, published their own set of proposals to move things forwards. On the same day General de Chastelain's commission published its report, which noted that no party, including Sinn Fein, had suggested that decommissioning should not happen by May 2000. The report, however, gave no indication of any new movement towards the actual decommissioning of weapons. Blair and Ahern's plan, entitled *The Way Forward*, suggested the creation of an executive by 15 July, with power being devolved to the Province three days later. General de Chastelain's decommissioning body would then specify when disarmament would start. If the commitments under this plan were not met, the operation of all institutions set up by the Agreement would be suspended. Blair in particular was asking Trimble once more to modify his policy of 'no guns, no government'.

But the Prime Minister was not alone in wanting Trimble to shift. A number of Trimble's key advisers outside the UUP, such as Paul Bew and Eoghan Harris, came up with a plan which would make it easier for him to embrace *The Way Forward*. Their strategy was for Trimble to write a postdated letter of resignation as First Minister and put it in the hands of UUP trustees, perhaps a senior Ulster Unionist figure such as Josias Cunningham. Trimble would then form the executive with Sinn Fein before the guns were handed over. If within a matter of weeks there was no sign of any decommissioning, then the party trustees could activate Trimble's resignation letter and force him to bring down the executive. Bew and Harris wanted Trimble to 'put it up to Sinn Fein', to test their sincerity.

However, given the recent upswing in violence and the fact that the talks were talking place at the height of the loyalist marching season the UUP was in no mood to dilute its stance any further. According to close aides, Trimble was interested in going with the Bew–Harris plan but knew that if he did so he risked splitting the party. In the interest of UUP unity, this time he rejected the initiative. There was only one course now open to him – if Mo Mowlam triggered the mechanism for the executive's establishment he would veto its creation.

There was one chink of light in an otherwise gloomy political landscape in early July; surprisingly, it shone from the direction of Drumcree. The Orange Order, having perhaps learned its lesson from 1998's PR disaster following the Quinn children's murder, decided to wind down its protest in Portadown. Troublemakers were urged to stay away from the Drumcree hill, and Orangemen in other parts of Northern Ireland were advised to attend their own demonstrations over the Twelfth fortnight rather than congregate in Portadown. Trimble played a key part in building relations between Blair and the Portadown Orangemen. While most Orangemen on the hill probably still regarded the local MP as a traitor to the loyalist cause, some of his old friends were coming back to him. Harold Gracey had met Trimble a number of times prior to the Drumcree march. The new Orange strategy was not to make a full frontal attack on the impenetrable fortifications that the British Army had erected around Drumcree to prevent the Orangemen reaching the Garvaghy Road. Portadown may have resembled an armed camp, but the security was an effective deterrent against a mass Orange assault. Instead, the Order would try to woo Blair, just as Trimble had, and win him over. It remains to be seen if they will succeed, although something of a rapport has been established between Gracey and Blair in Downing Street. Whether or not Blair will treat Gracey the way he has Trimble, with promises and flattery in lieu of real concessions, is an open question.

On the wider political front, it is interesting that Trimble continues to be careful about laying the blame directly on Downing Street, especially given the 'seismic shift' in the Prime Minister's attitude to decommissioning – that is, a shift towards the nationalist view of the issue. Trimble says:

> A serious mistake was made with the target date. I am not sure who was responsible for that because it meant that he ran out of time. The entire concept was flawed because it was based on assumptions that the intention of the republican movement was benign. There was no evidence of that. People were misled, perhaps. Was it the fault of Adams and McGuinness, who might have been giving Blair the wrong impression? My own feeling about Blair during that last week was that he was quite concerned the way things were developing.[53]

Trimble denies that his relationship with the Prime Minister was seriously damaged by the debacle: 'I don't think so, because I met him afterwards and it was perfectly amicable. Things had ended up in a way that neither of us wanted, but we didn't fall out.'[54] He still even has a kind word or two to say about Alastair Campbell, who first transmitted that infamous signal of a 'seismic shift' to the world's media. Trimble says that his relationship with Campbell is still a good one, despite the problems the Downing Street spin machine caused him in the last week of June.

When the day finally dawned for the executive's birth Trimble decided he would be absent without leave. As the rest of the parties entered the chamber of the old Stormont Parliament where Trimble had sat alongside Bill Craig in the heady days of Vanguard a quarter of a century before, the UUP opted to boycott the Assembly. For the first time in nearly three years Trimble entered Glengall Street with a united party. When he stepped outside to talk to the press he had his entire Assembly party, including some notable rebels like Peter Weir, around him. Jeffrey Donaldson, the Agreement's chief sceptic, was at his leader's back. Trimble's excuse for failing to turn up for the vote to create the executive was that the UUP's presence would only provoke the DUP and other anti-Agreement unionists into a circus of recriminations and blame. So the Ulster Unionists would boycott the Assembly. Abstentionism had once been the favoured tactic of republicans in Northern Ireland; now it had become a device for the UUP. By lunchtime Trimble's position as First Minister was looking shaky and he was being blamed for a crisis in the peace process.

In the Assembly, meanwhile, there was the farcical spectacle of the SDLP and Sinn Fein nominating their ministers for the various departments that would run Northern Ireland. Their place in the sun lasted around half an hour – the absence of the Ulster Unionists meant that there could not be cross-community support for the new executive. Northern Ireland's first power-sharing government in twenty-five years fell in less than an hour. The collapse was personified in the sad, weary figure of Seamus Mallon, the Deputy First Minister, who announced his resignation and blamed the Ulster Unionists. Speaking 'more in sorrow than in anger', Mallon said: 'They used this crisis to bleed more concessions out of two sovereign governments to try and bleed this process dry.'[55]

Trimble continued to put a brave face on things, insisting that it did not spell the end of the Good Friday Agreement: 'Even if we have to park it for a while, things can still move forward. What we want is to leave the message that things are still possible – they can still succeed.'[56] He knew he would be blamed for the failures, even having to defend himself against accusations on Ulster Television that he no longer deserved to hold on to the Nobel peace prize. The fundamental fault in the Trimble project in the early summer of 1999 was his over-reliance on Tony Blair. The Prime Minister had undoubtedly set down an impossible deadline at the worst possible time of year, the middle of the loyalist marching season. But Blair's insistence on the 30 June cut-off date, his concessions to nationalists over decommissioning in *The Way Forward* and the pressure on the parties to try to form the executive on 15 July damaged Trimble's credibility on two levels. Inside his party he was now seen as having put far too much faith in a Prime Minister whom many now believed was more afraid of IRA bombs in London than of the wrath of Trimble accusing him of treachery. In the eyes of a growing band of Ulster Unionists, the Prime Minister had conned David Trimble with his letter of reassurance on Good Friday. Those Blair pledges were not worth the paper or the giant bill-boards on which they were written. When the crunch came, Blair chose to appease Gerry Adams rather than the leader of Ulster Unionism. Conversely, in the wider community the British government had created the impression of reaching a breakthrough on decommissioning – a breakthrough which many saw as having been spurned by David Trimble.

As he prepared to go on holiday to Switzerland and Italy at the end of July, Trimble must have wondered how he could break out of the pincer movement attacking his leadership of party and country. He was seen by an increasing number of UUP members as Blair's dupe; he was also painted as the peace-wrecker by his enemies in the outside world, particularly in the United States where a group of US Congressmen sympathetic to the Irish republican cause had launched a campaign to have his Nobel prize taken from him.

But a few weeks later, while he drank red wine, mused over a few weighty historical tomes and listened to opera CDs under the same Italian sun that Tony Blair was enjoying, Trimble must have been relieved that he had not agreed to the Bew–Harris plan to set up the Northern Ireland executive at that time. Listening to the BBC world service, he heard the news that a taxi driver called Charles Bennett had been shot dead in West Belfast and that the IRA was being blamed. There were also revelations about how the FBI had foiled a sophisticated gun-running plot in Florida involving a number of Irish people. It later transpired that it was an IRA operation and that up to forty hand-guns and machine-pistols had been smuggled into Northern Ireland where they were destined for the Provos' Belfast Brigade. The events of late summer 1999 convinced him he had been right to boycott the Assembly, for he would surely have been deposed as UUP leader even if he had survived the storm in the party caused by joining a government with Sinn Fein. Had that Northern Ireland executive been in existence at the time of the Florida arms plot and the Bennett murder, Trimble would have been sitting in a government whose ministers included men from a party with a military wing that smuggled illegal guns into its own jurisdiction. Moreover, the new Northern Ireland government would have been the only one in the free democratic world, with the exception of the United States, with a branch of the state operating a *de facto* policy of capital punishment. Trimble risked being ridiculed as the man who said no to a power-sharing executive, but he had survived to fight another day. He was still First Minister of all Northern Ireland, only just, but at least he was no longer the lost leader of Ulster Unionism, as Brian Faulkner had been twenty-five years before.

A Last Leap of Faith

At the Killyhevlin Hotel in Enniskillen David Trimble sat alone, laughing to himself in the room set aside for journalists covering his party's last annual conference of the century on Saturday, 9 October. He watched on the video monitor as his adviser from the Republic, Eoghan Harris, assailed party members for their insistence that the IRA give up guns before Sinn Fein entered a power-sharing government. Trimble was clearly enjoying the spectacle of Harris banging the rostrum and screeching at the delegates over their moralistic stance of 'no guns, no government'.

There were gasps of shock from the floor, heads shook and eyes popped as Harris thundered away. 'He's going to have a heart attack,' shouted Ken Maginnis[1] at one stage as Harris ranted and raged at the delegates during a debate on the media and unionism. Harris served up some hard truths for the delegates to swallow: 'You are in the business of making peace, of making a historic accommodation with republicanism and thus securing the union.' As someone who had opposed the Provos for thirty years while a member of Official Sinn Fein and the Workers' Party, he had some words of advice for the UUP. 'Look, Sinn Fein fought for thirty years. It's like a kid wanting a bike for Christmas. The bike they wanted was a united Ireland. They didn't get the bike. Please give them the stickers.'[2]

While Harris's remarks caused outrage amongst some delegates, Trimble, tucked away outside the conference room, just kept laughing. Perhaps, as a disciple of Karl Popper, he was simply delighting in this unprecedented theatre of ideas being acted out at his own party's conference. Or maybe he was just encouraging debate to enliven a party conference which is normally dull and predictable. The truth, however, was that Trimble was using Harris to limber his party up for a leap of faith, in order to shift the UUP's policy away from its absolutist 'no guns, no government' stance.

The location of the conference was certainly a poignant one for a party pondering on whether to take such a giant step. The Killyhevlin Hotel lies only a few miles from the Irish Republic, and this part of the border has seen scores of attacks on Protestant farmers driven from their homes in the IRA's twenty-five-year terror campaign. A short distance down the road is the war memorial where on Remembrance Sunday 1987 an IRA bomb killed eleven local Protestants honouring the dead of two world wars. In 1996 the hotel itself was the target of a Continuity IRA bomb attack which caused extensive damage and was seen as a sectarian attack on a Protestant-owned business in Fermanagh. Trimble, in his bid to persuade his party to take the leap of faith, had to battle with the force of bitter Protestant memory that coloured so much of life for unionists in places like Enniskillen.

His own speech contained the first clear hint that the UUP leader was making a tactical retreat from 'no guns, no government'. Trimble seemed to suggest that there was a possibility of a government with Sinn Fein before IRA guns, as long as those guns came shortly afterwards. 'To me "jump together" or "choreography" or "sequencing" all refer to the same thing – making sure that devolution is accompanied by decommissioning,' he told the five hundred delegates, quite a few of whom were deeply sceptical about any deal with Sinn Fein. The codeword was obviously 'accompanied', suggesting a time lapse between the establishment of an executive and the start of actual decommissioning. Like Harris, Trimble had some uncomfortable truths for his delegates to swallow. He warned them that there was no going back to the old days of unionist majority rule. Nor could they ignore the growing Sinn Fein vote. He reminded them that Ulster Unionists were already sitting down in power-sharing arrangements with nationalists and republicans in local government. He then challenged his critics to provide any alternative to his strategy – on the day, at least, there was no dissent from the floor.

It was an audacious and hard-hitting message to his party faithful. The speech also reflected his growing impatience with those in the UUP who refused to bend. In Trimble's view the leap of faith is both a political and personal version of Pascal's wager. For the seventeenth-century French philosopher, belief in God is a gamble: if you believe and there is an afterlife in heaven, then it was worth the trouble after all; if you believe and there is nothing, you have not lost anything by having faith. Similarly if Trimble were to gamble that the Provos' war is over and they will decommission and this turns out to be true, then the risk was worth it; conversely, if he were to test their sincerity and it turns out they were never serious about disarming, then at the very least he will not be blamed for the process collapsing. Moreover, he would still have his place in history as someone who had tried to make peace. There was, in his own often repeated words, 'after all a life after politics'. In short, the wager would still be worth taking.

In the bar of the Killyhevlin after the main speeches Trimble appeared in high spirits. It had clearly been a good conference for him and his loyalists. The leader had thrown down a challenge to his critics, whose voices were notably muted during the debates. His outside ally Eoghan Harris had disturbed the party's normally peaceful annual gathering. Judging at least by the numbers waiting to shake Harris's hand or buy him a drink, the columnist and film-maker had made at least some of the UUP faithful think the unthinkable. Trimble and his party chairman Denis Rogan, meanwhile, had more good news to disseminate among the delegates – Mo was to go.

For over a week Trimble had been aware that Blair was about to move Mo Mowlam out of Stormont and back to London as his cabinet enforcer. Mowlam had dug in her heels when rumours first surfaced that she was moving during the mini-reshuffle in July. Now she was definitely on her way out and Peter Mandelson, the one New Labour politician whom Trimble and his allies had wanted as the new Northern Ireland Secretary, was taking over the reins. If Trimble was considering taking the leap of faith, as Harris and others were urging him to do, he needed someone of Mandelson's calibre and skills to sell a new deal on decommissioning to a mistrustful unionist population.[3]

Trimble's confidence at the UUP conference was in sharp contrast to his mood only a month earlier when all had seemed lost for the pro-Agreement unionist camp. Chris Patten's report on the RUC's future, launched on 9 September in Belfast, had delivered a devastating blow to Trimble's leadership. Prior to the publication of Patten, Trimble had rashly predicted that a lot of the speculation regarding the recommendations of the report, such as name changes and the ditching of the badge, was groundless. Yet when the report was released the worst unionist fears were realized. Trimble's deputy, John Taylor, had always taken a less optimistic view of the Patten Report. As far back as August he had predicted that Patten would have dire consequences for the Agreement: 'The proposal to change the name of the service is an insult to present RUC members and the vast majority of people in Northern Ireland. These proposals are dynamite and, when they are released three days after the start of the Mitchell review, could be the final blow to the Belfast Agreement,' he said.[4]

By then Taylor had decided to take no more part in the talks with Sinn Fein at Stormont. The revelations about IRA gun-running in Florida and the murder of Charles Bennett had provoked him into withdrawing his support: the man on whom Trimble had relied so heavily in the run-up to the Good Friday Agreement in Easter week 1998 had deserted him. According to one of Trimble's inner circle, Taylor's support had been waning for several months. As far back as March Taylor had expressed disquiet over the Republic's attempt to renegotiate elements of the North–South strand in the Agreement. He is understood to have told one of Trimble's advisers that he was deeply worried that Dublin would be able to extend the remit of the cross-border bodies once the unionists implemented the Agreement in full. He suspected that the Irish government would continually ask for more control once the UUP established the executive in Belfast. Given these fears, in combination with Taylor's public campaign to stop Jim Nicholson being renominated as the party candidate for Europe, it is hardly surprising that Trimble's mercurial deputy jumped ship.

Taylor's defection and the outrage caused by the Patten Report within the unionist community left Trimble depressed and uncertain about his political future. The headline-grabbing elements of the report, such as the changing of the RUC's name to the Northern Ireland Police Service, the dumping of the harp and crown cap badge, and the establishment of policing boards which would include Sinn Fein representatives, convinced sceptical unionists that the Agreement was producing nothing for their community. Indeed, it seemed to them that all the benefits of the Agreement appeared to be flowing the nationalists' way. Trimble's personal anger at Patten was visible at a British-Irish Association meeting in Oxford the weekend following the report. One of the delegates said Trimble 'could barely conceal his rage' over what the former Tory chairman, who also attended the conference, had recommended.[5]

Trimble may have denounced the Patten Report but his critics, ranging from Ian Paisley's DUP to his own party colleagues, could argue with some justification that these changes, no matter how unacceptable to unionists, were the logical outcome of his having signed the Good Friday Agreement in the first place. In the midst of this despair, however, Trimble gained some fresh encouragement and advice from Eoghan Harris. Since July Harris had been urging Trimble to put the Provos to the test, set up the executive and wait for them to decommission. If they did not, he would then be justified in pulling down the whole political edifice known as the Good Friday Agreement. Now Harris had some more uncomfortable counsel for the UUP leader.

Two days after Patten was published Harris sent Trimble two detailed private letters outlining what he should do next. In the first he urged the UUP leader not to get hung up over the report: 'As it turns out I believe that Patten was not as bad as predicted, that the police are broadly willing to work the new deal, and that efforts to politicise the issue are profoundly damaging to the position of the police, confirming Catholic suspicions that Unionists see the police as ideologically theirs.' Then Harris turned to the main issue: whether the IRA campaign was over and what was to be done about decommissioning:

> For five days I read and rang everybody who really knows and asked them straight out what they believed in their heart of hearts. At the end of that process I am perfectly satisfied (a) that the war is over (b) that Sinn Fein, in increments, will come into the process and in five years or so will publicly make it clear, what they now privately accept, that they accept the constitutional position of Northern Ireland is permanent for practical purposes.

Harris also warned Trimble that his party, and unionism in general, were again in danger of losing the PR battle to republicans:

Right now the Unionist image is mud in America, Britain and the Republic. And that perception is not wholly wrong. . . . A few weeks ago there was a good objective case for backing Blair and seating Sinn Fein and then seeing whether they delivered on decommissioning. You and the UUP could not do that because of the internal situation, and the UUP fear of Paisley turning its flank. But that still does not make it the right political decision for the people of Northern Ireland.

On page three of the letter Harris advised Trimble that if he decided to take a leap of faith he would find himself in a win-win situation:

Tell my party that I believe the war is over and that I want to work the Belfast Agreement and let the British Government deal with Sinn Fein/IRA if they fail to deliver. This is a win-win situation because while (a) I might be drawn out for a short time the logic of events would soon force moderate unionism to take me back. (b) I might win in which case I look like a man. (c) Win or lose in the party I win with the people, and with the history books.

The critical point of Harris's first letter came on page four, when he urged Trimble to put it to his party:

The recognition of necessity says you should call a meeting of the widest possible party membership, or a special conference, and put it to them that you want to take a calculated risk for peace. That would put it up to them, to Blair and to the whole world – and they would in turn have to pressurize the Provos. My gut instinct, talking to a good cop the other day, is that this is what decent unionists, deep down, want you to do. To go for it. To try and make it work.

There was also a note on Trimble's personal life and his place in history if, having accepted Harris's advice, he failed to deliver his party: 'Suppose the worst comes to the worst and you lose – what have you really lost? A post that had no power to deliver what you wanted to do. You still have a wife, a family, a lectureship and the respect of the whole world. Maybe you would be out in the cold for a few months. But mark my words, they would have to beat a path to your door within weeks.'

In the second letter sent to Trimble that day, more passionate than the first, Harris urged him not to lose his head over the RUC reforms proposed in Patten. In Harris's eyes there was nothing wrong with a new police force 'called the Northern Ireland anything . . .'; in effect it was still a British police force which Sinn Fein, like everyone else, would have to accept. Then he turned on Trimble for his outright rejection of the Patten Report: 'But for the life of me, having spoken to four tough serving policemen who are sanguine about the Report, I cannot see why it should bother politicians – that is of course unless Unionists see the RUC as politzeisoldaten, political soldiers. If so we shall never have peace.'[6]

It is difficult to assess how much this savage analysis impacted on Trimble's thoughts in the weeks after the publication of the Patten Report and Taylor's desertion from the pro-Agreement camp. But the fact is that within a fortnight he had convened a secret meeting of his twenty-seven loyal Assembly members, along with Harris, the Belfast-born writer Malachi O'Doherty and Professor Paul Bew. It is clear that the closed session on 26 September in the Trust House Forte Hotel near Glasgow airport, during which Harris repeated the need for flexibility on 'no guns, no government', reflected Trimble's strategy to widen the debate on decommissioning, perhaps even to force his Assembly team to think the unthinkable. If Trimble was preparing himself and his party to switch tactics on decommissioning, Harris's intervention certainly helped. Moreover, Harris provided Trimble with some intellectual steel at a time when it appeared that his nerve was about to be broken.

While O'Doherty and Bew presented the Assembly team with an objective analysis of the current position of republicanism and the balance of forces facing unionism, Harris launched into an outright attack on 'no guns, no government'. He told the gathering, which comprised both sceptics and Trimble loyalists, that the Provos were now serious about peace: 'Do you think that having hung out in the White House and dined out in the best restaurants they [the Provos] are going back to safe houses and fry-ups?' The final segment of his speech was presented under the old Leninist sub-title 'What is to be done?'. For the former Marxist strategist who had once helped guide the Official IRA away from violent republicanism there was only one road open to Trimble and his party – to set up a government before PIRA decommissioning. 'Now boys, take a deep breath,' he told them. 'To win this war you have to do three things. (a) Purge the party. (b) Speak to Sinn Fein dead cool, as if you knew the war was over. (c) Sell the Agreement to your own side with or without decommissioning.'

Harris's heresy was not appreciated by every Assembly member at the Glasgow gathering; Pauline Armitage, for instance, who represents the UUP in East Londonderry, was unimpressed. It is a measure of the problems faced by Trimble in modernizing Ulster Unionism that Armitage still regards Harris and O'Doherty, writers with Catholic antecedents who are intellectual foes of the IRA, with deep suspicion precisely because of their backgrounds. Others in the Assembly team who were always sceptical about the Agreement, such as Roy Beggs Junior, were, however, being gradually won over. Harris recalls chatting with Beggs after the speeches. 'Young Beggs said to me, "Eoghan, I can see your point. I'm getting there, but not just yet." When I heard that, I knew I must be doing something right.'[7]

Ever since he entered negotiations with Sinn Fein and subsequently signed the Good Friday deal Trimble has faced an internal battle for the soul of unionism. At the Killyhevlin conference, those who had opposed the Agreement from its outset wore badges smugly proclaiming: 'Don't blame me I voted No'. Many of the speakers who denounced the peace accord did so from a moralistic standpoint – sitting down with 'unreconstructed terrorists' was tantamount to a mortal sin. Even within the more secular UUP there is a strong tendency towards Evangelical Christianity, which sees the world in two-dimensional terms: good versus evil, democrat versus terrorist. Strategic politics is like a game of three-dimensional chess, whereas many in the UUP would prefer to play moral draughts. Trimble's trouble is that he has to contend with his moral-draughts players while trying to guess the next move of his more astute republican opponents in the three-dimensional chess match. Unlike the Evangelicals and the moralists, he has been prepared to put aside his personal disdain for those who had once directed the IRA's terror campaign (a campaign in which his close friend and academic colleague Edgar Graham had died practically in front of him sixteen years earlier) and test their sincerity.

The forces of Protestant memory and morality were pressing down on Trimble from the resumption of talks with Sinn Fein on 6 September under the chairmanship of George Mitchell. Trimble had backed a legal bid by a victim of IRA violence to challenge Mo

Mowlam's ruling in the summer that the Bennett murder and the Florida arms plot were not breaches of the IRA's ceasefire. Michelle Williamson, who had lost her mother and father in the Shankill bomb in October 1993, launched a High Court challenge to seek to overturn Mowlam's decision. However, on the first day of the court case Williamson appeared to rebuke Trimble for supporting her case while sitting down with Sinn Fein in the Mitchell Review of the Good Friday Agreement: 'If he wants to support me that's fine. He can't bring politics into this. . . . I will not be used. I am fed up having to explain Mr Trimble's actions to Tom, Dick and Harry,' she told reporters outside the court. Accompanying her to the case was the arch-sceptic of the Good Friday Agreement, Jeffrey Donaldson.[8]

Despite such pressures, Trimble was determined to remain inside the Review. Mitchell had decided to take a completely different track to the 'absolute final deadlines' and 'seismic shift' spinning of early summer. There would be no media hothouse in Castle Buildings with parties standing on the steps briefing against each other or premiers applying public pressure on the participants to reach a deal. Instead Mitchell imposed a quiet, patient and diplomatic tone on the talks. If necessary, said the former head of the US Senate, the pro-Agreement parties would even meet outside Northern Ireland. One of his central aims in this new departure was to get the Ulster Unionists and Sinn Fein to speak to each other directly – even to sit down and have a meal together. Mitchell was particularly concerned with getting Trimble and his chief negotiator Reg Empey around a table alone with Gerry Adams and Martin McGuinness.

To enable the leaderships of the UUP and Sinn Fein to get closer, on 18 October Mitchell shifted the venue to the US ambassador's residence in London; he later called the London meetings 'an important juncture in the talks'.[9] By then there was a new rapport developing between Trimble, Empey, Adams and McGuinness. One of Trimble's aides who stayed at his side throughout the ten weeks of talks in London and Belfast recalled one of the first sit-down meals shared by the UUP and Sinn Fein in the ambassador's residence: 'There was Trimble and Empey facing Adams, McGuinness and Gerry Kelly. Mitchell was also there around the table for an evening meal. Just before the starters were brought out Gerry Kelly leaned across the table towards us and said, "Whatever you do, don't talk about fishing to Martin McGuinness or we'll be here all night." That seemed to break the ice.'[10] McGuinness, a keen fly fisherman, is notorious in republican circles for spending hours proselytizing about the merits of the sport.

Despite the new dinner-table bonhomie between the UUP and Sinn Fein there seemed little chance, at least in public, of a breakthrough round the conference table. Gerry Adams broke off from the talks on 21 October for a thirty-hour speaking engagement in New York. During a Sinn Fein fund-raising dinner in Manhattan he said there was only a 'slim possibility' of success at the talks.[11] His gloom echoed the view of the Dublin government, including the Irish Foreign Minister David Andrews who also warned that weekend that the Mitchell Review could fail.[12]

Yet behind closed doors, particularly in the offices of David Trimble's Assembly team in Stormont, there was a critical shift in position. On the same day that Adams offered his pessimistic analysis of the review, Trimble finally put the Harris option to the Assembly party. No decision was taken, nor did Trimble insist that they vote on the plan. However, on the basis of evidence that the UUP leader was now inching away from an absolutist 'no guns, no government' policy, George Mitchell agreed that the Review should be extended into November.

It is now obvious in hindsight that Harris's advice to Trimble, his Assembly team and then to his party conference was a major factor in enabling the UUP leader to tilt Ulster Unionism delicately away from 'no guns, no government'. By the beginning of November some of Trimble's closest allies were admitting that the policy had indeed run its course and that it was time to try a new route to devolution and decommissioning. Trimble was certainly prepared to take the leap of faith if the IRA and Sinn Fein could be persuaded eventually to decommission their weapons after the executive was formed.

Harris's assertion that the Provo war was probably over was bolstered by the events of the last week of the Mitchell Review. Sinn Fein and the Ulster Unionists began a series of carefully worked out moves aimed at establishing trust between the parties. Republicans started the choreography by speaking positively about decommissioning for the first time in the peace process. In a statement released on 17 November Gerry Adams said: 'All four parties to the agreement have an obligation to bring decommissioning about. Sinn Fein is committed to discharging our responsibilities in this regard.' On the same day Trimble spoke to reporters on the steps of Castle Buildings and acknowledged the republicans' right to pursue a united Ireland through peaceful means. Each of the parties acknowledged each other's internal difficulties with dissidents. Twenty-four hours later the IRA delivered a terse message which confirmed, again for the first time, that they would appoint a representative to speak with General de Chastelaine's decommissioning body – at least once the executive had been established. To republican sceptics like Anthony McIntyre, the former IRA prisoner, the Provos had crossed a historic Rubicon. They had accepted, in principle at least, that decommissioning was, if not a precondition, an obligation under the Agreement. Just a few years before republicans had laughed off any suggestion that some of their weapons would ever have to be surrendered.

To McIntyre and other republican observers, Trimble had achieved something which Tony Blair, Bertie Ahern and even Bill Clinton had been unable to deliver – the IRA jumping on the decommissioning train whose journey had only one terminus, actual disarmament. In McIntyre's mind, even if Trimble had to shift tactics to move from prior decommissioning, his goal remained the same and the combined IRA–Sinn Fein statements brought that goal ever closer.[13]

The endgame of the Northern Ireland peace process has been like a pendulum of pressure swinging from one side to the other. The pendulum was clearly swinging towards Trimble and his Ulster Unionists in mid-November. On Friday, 18 November Trimble used a press conference in Glengall Street to announce a special meeting of the Ulster Unionist Council – the party's 860-strong ruling council – in order to overturn 'no guns, no government' for 27 November. The divisions within the UUP over the new Mitchell deal (guns before government within a time frame of around eight weeks) were encapsulated in an unprecedented stand-up row in front of the media at the press conference. In the middle of Trimble's speech David Brewster, one of the party's honorary secretaries from East Londonderry who opposed the Good Friday Agreement, interrupted him. The spat was sparked by a mistake in the statement that Trimble's press officers had handed out to the media. Endorsing the Mitchell deal, Trimble had said: 'We believe that the statements by Sinn Fein and the IRA represent for the first time a real step forward.' The trouble was with the 'We'. Brewster protested furiously that a party officers' meeting earlier that morning had not endorsed that view – the position was Trimble's personally. 'It's time for a bit of honesty in this party,' shouted Brewster. Ken Maginnis, standing in the wings, smouldered with rage at Brewster.

As a result Trimble was forced to issue a second statement replacing the 'We' with 'I'. He had not checked his release with his spin doctors, including Ray Haydn, who had been hired once again to help him sell the deal to his party. It had been an embarrassing start to the fourth Trimble PR campaign and illuminated, for the entire world to see, the deep divisions inside the UUP. (Haydn summed up the difficulties in selling the deal: 'This is the Agreement, the Referendum, the Assembly and Euro elections all rolled into one. The next seven days will be hell.'[14])

Trimble's opponents, principally Jeffrey Donaldson, David Brewster and Arlene Foster, even held a rival press conference just minutes after he left the room for interviews. Their ability effectively to hijack Trimble's press launch illustrated the danger of indulging critics too much. He has resisted at least one of Harris's many pieces of advice, namely to suppress his dissenters and root out his internal enemies; Trimble has preferred to defend their right to speak out and undermine him, much to the frustration of his inner circle which wanted a wide-ranging purge of the party.

Donaldson, Brewster and Foster reflected a widely held view inside the party that Trimble had buckled under pressure – that he did not have the courage to say No. Moreover, in their eyes he had broken the promises made in all the UUP's recent manifestos that the Ulster Unionists would not sit down with Sinn Fein in government until guns were handed over. Trimble, on the other hand, having listened to the advice of former republicans like Harris and O'Callaghan, desperately wanted to put Sinn Fein and the IRA to the test. Even if the IRA reneged on its obligation to disarm, he argued, unionists would still be in a strong position to bring down the executive and lay the blame for the Agreement's failure at the republican movement's door. Once the UUP bought the Mitchell deal, he contended, the pendulum would swing back in Sinn Fein's direction and the pressure would be on the republicans to deliver up arms. Gerry Adams would have a more worrying time over Christmas and the Millennium than David Trimble would. In essence, the debate between Trimble, Empey and Maginnis on one side and Donaldson, Brewster and Foster on the other was part of the struggle for the soul of unionism – the tension between the rational and emotional, the conflicting demands of the moral and the strategic imperatives.

One Ulster Unionist politician notably absent from the frantic activity of the second week in November was John Taylor. The deputy leader was the man whose nod of approval on Good Friday 1998 enabled Trimble to sign the historic peace deal. Without Taylor's support on the day, it is difficult to see how Trimble could have been able to carry his party. The Agreement would have foundered. Taylor's newly found scepticism over the Agreement had been a major concern for Trimble: if he spoke out against the Mitchell deal in the next seven days, the vote might go against the party leader.

Taylor spent the week in Iran on the first British parliamentary visit to the Islamic Republic since the 1979 revolution. The British embassy in Tehran is situated in a boulevard called Bobby Sands Street, renamed by the ayatollahs in honour of the IRA hunger striker. As he passed down it, did Taylor wonder whether Harris and O'Callaghan had been right, that the war that Sands fought was truly over? Taylor's stance on the big day would help make or break the Mitchell deal. Once again Trimble was at the mercy of the man whom he had defeated in the 1995 leadership contest; indeed, the venue initially chosen for the Ulster Unionist Council vote was the Ulster Hall, the site of Trimble's victory four years earlier. However, as if to reflect new times, the venue was switched to Belfast's modernist Waterfront Hall.

Taylor's desertion was not the only problem Trimble faced in the final showdown with his party. The Assembly team's deputy whip, Derek Hussey, resigned on the day of the fraught press conference. Hussey had previously supported Trimble, but now found it impossible to take the step his leader required of him. The following day there was further confusion over a Sinn Fein statement made in the United States which seemed to suggest that the IRA would never decommission, that republicans were in fact stringing Trimble along. Unionist opponents, particularly Robert McCartney, seized upon the words of Pat Doherty, Sinn Fein's Vice-

President, as clear evidence that Trimble was being conned. In response, Trimble issued a warning on Radio 4's *Today* programme: 'Were Sinn Fein to continue to give the impression that they are going to double-cross me, I would cancel next Saturday's meeting.' In a bid to save the process from crashing before it got off the ground, Sinn Fein faxed a detailed statement committing Doherty and the rest of the republican leadership to the deal that George Mitchell had worked out during the ten-week Review. But regardless of Sinn Fein's damage limitation exercise, Trimble had sustained a third major blow in his bid to shift party policy. To McCartney et al. Trimble was no longer Tony Blair's dupe but Gerry Adams's dupe.

Despite this, Trimble's mood in those last seven critical days was determined and resilient. He knew there was no other way to reach the twin prizes of decommissioning and devolution. He also realized that if unionists rejected the deal the alternative would be far more detrimental to the union in the long run. The British and Irish governments would implement those aspects of the Agreement that the unionists did not like, such as prisoner releases, police reforms and so on, and the two governments would run Northern Ireland together in a form of joint authority. If his party could take the final leap of faith unionists could find themselves masters of their own destiny for the first time in three decades. But without that leap unionism would remain politically impotent, friendless and powerless in the world.

The new Northern Ireland Secretary, Peter Mandelson, had wanted to launch a Province-wide campaign deploying the forces of business, the trade union movement, the Churches and the voluntary sector to put pressure on the Ulster Unionist Council to back Trimble. On 20 November, one week before the crucial vote, Mandelson spoke in support of Trimble's position at the Women's Coalition's annual conference. Trimble's advisers were horrified, and informed the Secretary of State that using the cross-community Women's Coalition as a platform to persuade sceptical Ulster Unionists to back the Mitchell deal had been a mistake. Most UUP members, even those strongly in favour of a leap of faith, mistrusted the Coalition and regarded it as a hotchpotch of left-wing do-gooders and woolly thinkers. In sharp contrast, the average Ulster Unionist was hard-headed and found the touchy-feely politics of the Women's Coalition repellent. Trimble's inner circle, including Eoghan Harris, sent Mandelson several memos urging him to play a behind-the-scenes role rather than go for an up-front flags-and-balloons rerun of the Yes campaign. Mandelson, it seems, heeded their advice, even to the extent of adapting what he wore. Harris advised Mandelson to dress more sombrely and wear darker ties in the days running up to the vote, in a bid to chime sartorially with the conservative dress of the average UUC member.

In the last five days up to the UUC meeting the Secretary of State concentrated his efforts on two key fronts: the RUC and John Taylor. On Tuesday, 23 November the British government announced that the George Medal for bravery was to be awarded collectively to the RUC, despite Chris Patten's proposals that the police force be renamed and its crown and harp cap badge be replaced. Although some in the unionist community, especially the DUP, regarded the award as a bribe, the majority viewed the medal as a great honour for thirty years' service in the fight against terrorism. It would be wrong to conclude that the award would help tilt the Ulster Unionists towards abandoning 'no guns, no government', but it did create the impression that there was a new Secretary of State who appreciated the fears and concerns of the unionist community.

More importantly, Mandelson worked hard behind the scenes to persuade John Taylor to stand behind Trimble, presenting the UUP deputy leader with a three-page note assuring him that, in the event of the IRA refusing to decommission, the entire edifice of the Good Friday Agreement would collapse. Trimble himself remained confident of victory, despite reports on 25 November in the *Daily Telegraph* that UUC delegates were split fifty-fifty over the policy change. Twenty-four hours before the vote he received another boost in the form of a card from Nora Bradford, the widow of the late South Belfast MP murdered by the IRA. Mrs Bradford expressed her support for Trimble's efforts and said she was 'right behind him'. He even received her permission to mention her card during the debate the next day.

Trimble also obtained more advice from Harris on how to structure his keynote speech to the 860 delegates. Although he did not offer to write the speech this time, Harris advised Trimble to break it into three Aristotelian segments.

I told him the best advice for writing any speech comes from Aristotle's *The Rhetoric*, in which he breaks down an argument into three parts – character, argument and emotion. I told Trimble he should start his speech with a reference to his character, his background, his history including the opposition to Sunningdale and his Vanguard days. Then he should move on to the fine detail of the argument, the detailed reasons why they must back the deal. And then finally to switch to emotion. I believe in hindsight he took this advice on board – I even provided him with a rough guide for the times he should apply to each of the three parts of his speech.[15]

Trimble, however, could not rely on Aristotelian rhetoric alone to win the argument at the Waterfront Hall. From early on the morning of the 27th it was clear that Taylor would be won over if Trimble gave him and the party personal guarantees. The UUP were returning to the Bew–Harris plan of July, the post-dated cheque of resignation. Trimble agreed that he and the three UUP ministers in a future executive would resign in February 2000 if his leap of faith turned out to be misplaced. In addition to Mandelson's personal assurances, the Trimble post-dated cheque of resignation persuaded Taylor to come on board once again.

Ironically, Taylor wanted to speak during the three-hour debate, which began shortly after ten o'clock, but failed to do so. There were already twenty-seven UUC members on the list to speak, and the last-minute nature of Taylor's conversion prevented him from getting on to the podium. The most heated and fractious moment of the debate came during Trimble's own speech, when he referred to his murdered colleague Edgar Graham. He admitted that had the IRA not killed him it would have been Graham rather than him standing on the platform today as UUP leader. At the mention of Graham's name John Hunter, Trimble's former ally turned bitter foe, shouted out from the floor: 'And you let him down.' Trimble was physically taken aback by the interruption and responded firmly: 'I did not let him down.' It was at this moment that he mentioned his other murdered colleague, Roy Bradford, and the support he had received from his widow Nora. This was the 'emotional' segment of the speech, during which Harris had told him to tug at the delegates' heartstrings. According to Ray Haydn, it appeared to have worked.

Yet it would be a mistake to underestimate Trimble's own personal standing in the party as a key factor in winning the vote. Many delegates, including those from where Jeffrey Donaldson grew up, Kilkeel in Co. Down, acknowledged that Trimble won the admiration even of those who were sceptical about the entire peace process. He may lack the populist touch – he may find it difficult mingling with crowds, kissing babies and slapping backs – but Trimble had one advantage over his doomed predecessor Brian Faulkner. The former Northern Ireland Prime Minister was seen as a patrician member of the Big House class of unionism, which made him an easy target for ordinary unionists. Trimble, on the other hand, comes from a more humble background; he is a self-made man with none of the trappings of isolated grandeur that characterized Faulkner or Terence O'Neill. Moreover, Trimble's work-rate and energy daunt even his opponents. To many of the foot soldiers of Ulster Unionism represented on the UUC in the Waterfront Hall, Trimble has been a tireless leader whom even the most sceptical find hard to attack openly.

In January 1974 Brian Faulkner had failed to sell the Sunningdale power-sharing deal to his party. The Ulster Unionist Council rejected the arrangement by 427 votes to 374. The man who proposed its rejection was John Taylor. Faulkner subsequently lost the leadership of his party and the UUP split. Twenty-five years later Trimble knew he could be facing the same fate as Faulkner as the vote was about to be announced shortly before two o'clock. The result, however, illustrated how much had changed in Northern Ireland in a quarter of a century. The UUC had backed the policy shift by 480 votes to 329. Almost 60 per cent of the party were in favour of the compromise over 'no guns, no government' – Trimble had triumphed again. There was no repetition of the acrimony at the time of the Faulkner split; there were no walkouts, no heckling and no resignations on the steps of the Waterfront Hall. Even Willie Thompson, the UUP's MP for West Tyrone, later reconsidered his threat to resign from the party a few days after the vote. And following his victory, Trimble threw down a challenge to the leadership of the republican movement: 'We've done our bit. Mr Adams, it's over to you. We've jumped, you follow.'[16]

Over the following seven days the vote at the Waterfront Hall triggered a chain reaction of remarkable events on both sides of the

Irish Sea. On Monday, 29 November the executive was finally formed, with two Sinn Fein ministers taking their seats. Undoubtedly the most controversial appointment in unionist eyes was Martin McGuinness's elevation from former IRA chief of staff to Minister for Education in Northern Ireland. Although Trimble was able to deflect some DUP criticism after Paisley's party nominated two of its most able Assembly men, Peter Robinson and Nigel Dodds, as ministers in the new cabinet, his party was deluged with complaints about McGuinness's new role. The sight of a man once dedicated to physically destroying the Northern Ireland state sitting in the Department of Education's headquarters in the unionist stronghold of North Down outraged thousands of ordinary unionists.

Perhaps in the short to medium term David Trimble's party would pay a heavy electoral price for agreeing to an arrangement which put Martin McGuinness in charge of their children's education. However, over the last five years Trimble has always looked to the longer term in his handling of the peace process. McGuinness's bum on the ministerial chair may be a temporary if highly public political victory for the Provos, but what of the long run? McGuinness and his Sinn Fein colleagues once vowed to storm the Bastille of unionism and tear it down. At the end of the twentieth century they were 'Stormonting' instead of 'storming' the very system they had once vowed to overthrow with violence. The old revolutionaries were now part of a reconstituted Stormont regime. In that sense the Provos had lost the battle of history, their revolutionary mission was now at rest in the confines of the Education Minister's office.

Trimble's perennial problem has been to convey to a unionist electorate, brought up on black and white moral certainties, how the Good Friday Agreement and its outworking could eventually trap the mainstream republican movement into constitutional politics for ever. Trimble was always aware that unionists would have to face unpalatable scenarios like that in order to achieve the wider prize of a stable and devolved Northern Ireland within the union. Martin McGuinness as Minister of Education may turn the stomachs of thousands of ordinary unionists, but for Trimble it is a price worth paying in order to attain the wider, bigger goal.

Of course, Trimble's own position was still contingent on the IRA's willingness (or lack of it) to decommission in the first half of

2000. He is clearly vulnerable to the Provos' whims, but this is not of necessity a weakness. Paradoxically, his vulnerability has won him new friends across Ireland, Britain and the United States and strengthened his position vis-à-vis the Provos. British national newspapers from the centre-left *Observer* to the right-wing *Daily Mail* showered him with praise following his victory in the Waterfront Hall. If the IRA flatly refuses to decommission, then the weight of public opinion in Britain and Ireland and their governments will come down heavily upon the republican movement. The IRA's failure to disarm might trigger a fresh leadership crisis inside the UUP and precipitate the end of Trimble's tenure as leader. But at the very least he can walk away from the process having tried beyond the call of duty to shift unionism away from the sterile politics of 'No' towards something fresh and different.

To return to the Middle Eastern analogy at the beginning of this book, Trimble has clearly, like Rabin at the Oslo talks, been prepared to give up some ground to his historical enemies in order to cling on to what matters most. Just as Rabin was prepared to cede territory to the Arabs for peace, Trimble has been willing to allow the IRA's political wing to seize control of some of the trappings of state power so as to enable that the state itself, Northern Ireland, to remain inside the United Kingdom. For such compromises Rabin paid for his life. And while a physical threat from dissident loyalists (albeit a diminished one since the RUC's drive against the Orange Volunteers in October–November 1999) still hangs over Trimble and his family, the likely price he will have to pay if the IRA fail to decommission their weapons is to lose his party. Clearly he is vulnerable but at the same time credible in the eyes of the world for having taken such an enormous gamble.

Trimble was probably talking about himself when, during his Nobel acceptance speech, he referred to the 'politicians of the possible', those leaders of liberal democracies who govern by practical politics rather than rigid ideological programmes. In contrast to the theological and political convictions of his old rival Ian Paisley, Trimble has attempted to remould unionism and prepare it for the twenty-first century. He is a politician of the possible who long ago realized that the new balance of forces in Britain and the world was largely ranged against unionism. Unionists face a British government under a popular and seemingly immovable Prime Minister more determined than ever not to allow their leaders in Ulster perpetually to veto change in Northern Ireland. The use of the Orange Card by Tory politicians in twentieth-century history may have been somewhat exaggerated. Yet the only certain thing in this new century is that there is no one at Westminster able or willing to play the Orange Card ever again.˙ Instead of railing against those forces massed against him and his people, Trimble has tried to reshape unionism to adapt to these new times.

However, it has taken more than just tactical acumen and far-reaching strategic thinking to get Ulster Unionism to where it is at the beginning of the twenty-first century. Trimble may lack the common touch; he has made a number of poor personal judgements about his would-be allies in the party; he often overlooks those who have helped most in times of need; in 1999 he placed too much faith in the word of Tony Blair; and perhaps periodically he has fallen foul of Bob McCartney's prophecy of being tempted at the top of the temple by world leaders. But no one can question his courage in constantly putting his own leadership on the line and risking complete alienation from the community in which he originated. Nor can his willingness to push unionists down a road many of them never dreamed of travelling along be put down simply to the temptations and flatteries of high office. At a personal level, he is a man who is awkward with the great occasion and global adulation. Even on the day he won the Nobel prize his first reaction was to describe the accolade as a bit 'premature'.

Trimble's journey from the movement that smashed Sunningdale in 1974 to the statesman who saved the Good Friday Agreement twenty-five years later has been a remarkable one. The real motivation for Trimble's transformation lies in the paradoxical conservatism brilliantly illuminated in Giuseppe di Lampedusa's novel *The Leopard*. Tancredi, the nephew of the central character, Don Fabrizio, urges his uncle to embrace social changes in Sicily in order to preserve their aristocratic status and gently manage their decline: 'Unless we ourselves take a hand now, they'll foist the republic on us. If you want things to stay the same things will have to change.' *The Leopard* is set in the mid-nineteenth century at the time of the Italian *Risorgimento*, but Tancredi's maxim is equally applicable to David Trimble's career as he seeks to manage change in Ireland at the start of the twenty-first century.

Epilogue: 'We've Jumped, You Follow'

The location for the final showdown of 2000 was entirely appropriate. The clash between David Trimble and his internal opponents, led by Jeffrey Donaldson, took place inside a room set aside for the conductor of the Ulster Orchestra in Belfast's Waterfront Hall. The chamber overlooked the sight of new upmarket apartments worth up to £500,000, a forest of cranes over the cityscape and several new e-commerce and dotcom businesses. These new wealth generators had sprung up since the ceasefires on top of the old industries of shipbuilding and engineering that had transformed Belfast from a minor port town into one of the powerhouses of the British Empire, laying the economic foundations of Partition in the first decade of the twentieth century. The engineering works, the rope-making factories and even the shipyard itself have either closed down or are contracting to a skeleton staff, the certainties of Protestant industrial strength fading away like those absolutist imperatives of unionist political authority – No Surrender, Not an Inch, What We Have We Hold.

As Trimble sat waiting for the delegation from the No camp to arrive he must have gazed out on the new Belfast skyline and wondered which version of unionism would triumph on Saturday, 28 October. Would it be the risk-taking, power-sharing, secular, inclusive project he had led since Good Friday 1998 or the sullen, stubborn, exclusively Protestant traditional unionism represented by Donaldson and his allies. The First Minister was flanked by the Dublin-educated Michael McGimpsey, Northern Ireland's 'Minister for Fun', who for so long carried the lonely torch for liberal, Labourite unionism inside the UUP. Alongside McGimpsey was Sir Reg Empey, the Economy Minister, who had pointed during the morning debate to the new boom Belfast was enjoying. Trimble's delegation also included James Cooper from Co. Fermanagh, another representative of the party's liberal wing from a border county where Protestants and unionists have a unique sense of encirclement and siege.

Into the conductor's room marched Donaldson accompanied by two of Trimble's fellow MPs, Willie Ross and the Reverend Martin Smyth. The fourth member of the No delegation was Jim Rodgers, a Belfast City Councillor and former opponent of Trimble and Bill Craig back in the days of Vanguard's Voluntary Coalition. They had come on Trimble's request to discuss a compromise motion at the Ulster Unionist Council's meeting. It had been called to review the UUP's participation in coalition government with nationalists including the IRA's political wing, Sinn Fein. Many delegates were frustrated by the IRA's lack of movement on decommissioning its huge arsenal. They were further tested by ongoing IRA violence and a sophisticated Provo plot to smuggle new arms from Florida into Northern Ireland. Faith in the IRA and Sinn Fein was at its lowest within all sections of the UUP. The party had taken a hammering at the polls. The question was what to do next.

Donaldson and his allies forwarded a motion, which would have set a fixed timetable on the UUP remaining in government. In essence the proposal was that if the IRA had not started to engage with General de Chastelain's Decommissioning Body by the end of November, the party would pull out of the executive at Stormont thus bringing the experiment in power-sharing and with it devolution to an end. Trimble on the other hand did not want his hands tied with timetables and deadlines, preferring progressively to impose sanctions on Sinn Fein in order to nudge republicans towards new talks with General de Chastelain.

Around noon Trimble and his camp decided to find a compromise with their internal opponents in the form of a composite motion. They suspected (correctly as it turned out) that the No camp itself was badly divided both on strategy and objectives. Donaldson was not an outright opponent of devolution. He had earlier proposed the expulsion of Sinn Fein from the executive which, in his opinion, could still run on power-sharing lines with the SDLP. Ross and Smyth however had always been lukewarm on devolution preferring to integrate Northern Ireland fully into the UK. Sharing power for them was a total anathema. The composite motion, Trimble's strategists concluded, would drive a wedge between Donaldson on one side and Ross and Smyth on the other.

But Donaldson and his allies imagined they were at last smelling blood. His fresh-faced shock troops in the Young Unionists, many of whom in their premature three-piece suits resembled Tory Boy, the teenage Conservative fanatic invented by comedian Harry Enfield, strutted about the Waterfront like peacocks. They briefed journalists that Donaldson's motion would win the day amongst the 860 delegates and that the executive would fall within weeks. Trimble, they promised, would soon be out of a job. Given the confidence of the No camp it was unlikely they were ever going to accept the compromise offered to them in the conductor's room overlooking the river Lagan. The Donaldson-led delegation withdrew from the talks to decide on their strategy. After half an hour the meeting was resumed and Trimble was informed his compromise was unacceptable. There would be a straight vote between Donaldson's set deadline and Trimble's more open-ended motion. A *de facto* leadership challenge was about to begin, the fourth since Trimble had gone into government with Sinn Fein eleven months earlier. Close aides described the embattled First Minister that lunchtime as 'very cool but thoughtful'. His sang-froid was in sharp contrast to the mood of those closest to him. Several of his supporters mixing with the journalists assembled on the second floor of the glass-fronted circular building wore grave expressions. They privately confided that they feared the worst.

Shortly before a quarter to three, Denis Rogan, the party's Chairman, led Trimble into the press centre. Lord Rogan sat down with his leader, Daphne Trimble and Sir Reg Empey. There were audible sighs of relief from some of Trimble's colleagues as Lord Rogan read out the result: the UUP leader's motion received 445 votes, while Donaldson's proposal won 374. Trimble, the Houdini of Ulster politics, had fought off another leadership shove and for the first time in eighteen months his support amongst his party's ruling body had actually increased.

He had secured his position partially because he was prepared to toughen up his stance on Sinn Fein in government. Trimble had signalled a week earlier in the *Observer* that he was prepared to use his veto as First Minister to bar Sinn Fein ministers from attending meetings of the body dealing with all-Ireland matters. He would only lift the ban if the IRA restarted talks with General de Chastelain. In the immediate aftermath of the UUC meeting Sinn

Fein expressed surprise and shock at the ban. Martin McGuinness, the Province's Education Minister, complained that his First Minister had not indicated he was about to impose the sanction during a Cabinet meeting on the Thursday before the vote. But seven days earlier Trimble had warned: 'It is not going to be a simple walk-out as we don't want things crashing down, or force the Shinners [Sinn Fein] out of the process. But we have to show we are serious while wanting the executive to survive.' His 'proportionate response' would entail withdrawing cooperation from the North/South Ministerial Council, code for barring Sinn Fein.

In the short term the strategy worked. The power-sharing executive remained intact albeit with one of his main partners (Sinn Fein) bitterly resentful at being excluded from the one element of the Good Friday Agreement dearest to their hearts – the all-Ireland North/South Ministerial Council. Trimble had postponed another crisis in the peace process at least until January 2001.

The previous eleven months had been a roller-coaster ride with the historic coalition firstly nose-diving into suspension only to be resorted four months later. In between suspension and restoration lay delicate negotiations between the parties, the two governments and the IRA, combined with another public leap of faith by Trimble in the most powerful place on earth, Washington DC. And, throughout this incredible journey, there was one overarching and very familiar theme – decommissioning.

By the end of January 2000 Trimble's words ('We've jumped, you follow') on the day he persuaded his party to enter the executive were beginning to haunt him. Three months after he had pledged to establish the government in Belfast upon an IRA initiative on arms, the Provos appeared unwilling to move. By the start of the first week of February pro-Agreement unionists were increasingly nervous as the clock ticked towards the deadline set down by Trimble on IRA decommissioning.

On Wednesday, 2 February Peter Mandelson held one of several meetings with the party's president, Josias Cunningham, the man who held Trimble's resignation letter as First Minister in cold storage. Cunningham made it very clear to the Northern Ireland Secretary that he would activate the resignation if there was no sign of the IRA shifting on the weapons question by Friday. Mandelson was left in no doubt that the government in Stormont would collapse, with the likelihood that it would be next to impossible to put it together again. Mathematics militated against any return to government now that several of Trimble's Assembly team had defected to the No unionist benches. A majority of unionist members in the chamber no longer supported the Agreement. The requirement that a majority of representatives from each community back the peace deal meant there could be no new government. The only alternative was to suspend devolution while the arms question was tackled.

When Mandelson finally transferred power from Belfast back to London around teatime on Friday, 4 February the mood of Trimble and his followers was a mixture of relief and sadness. One close colleague described his leader's attitude to suspension:

> He was glad that Mandelson had stood beside him after all the bad experiences with Mo Mowlam. There was relief because there was no chance of getting the numbers in the Assembly to reconstitute another executive. But David was sad that the experiment had only lasted three months. He genuinely believed the government had been working well.

While nationalist Ireland ganged up against Mandelson and Trimble there was one surprising new source of support from across the Atlantic. Trimble and his press aides, David Kerr and Phillip Robinson, were taken aback by the level of support he received post-suspension in the United States media. Heavyweight newspapers such as the *Washington Post*, the *New York Times* and *New York Post* sided with the First Minister, blaming the IRA's stubborn refusal to compromise on arms as the main reason for suspension. Trimble's stock was up among the chief opinion formers of the United States, ironically at a time when his standing amongst ordinary unionist voters and his supposed nationalist partners in peace had reached a new low. Just over a month after his government went into suspended animation, Trimble would use a speech to American journalists, some of whom had backed his cause in February, as a platform to pressurise republicans to compromise over decommissioning.

The British government's willingness to rescue Trimble by suspending devolution again illustrates how important the UUP leader's survival was to Tony Blair. Mandelson, for all his dabbling in the black arts of spin, was also a valuable asset in securing Trimble's and thus the unionist community's continued participation in the Agreement. He had managed to bridge the vast chasm of mistrust that had opened between the UUP and the last Secretary of State, Mo Mowlam. Privately, Trimble admitted he might not have been able to rely on Dr Mowlam in resisting pan-nationalist demands to ignore the UUP ultimatum and press on regardless of the Ulster Unionists resigning from government.

The furore over suspension also illuminated the damaging divisions and lack of coordination between so-called partners in peace. Seamus Mallon, Trimble's deputy, along with Bertie Ahern and his bullish Foreign Minister Brian Cowen, appeared willing to sacrifice the UUP leader rather than put pressure on the IRA to change their hardline stance on illegal arms. The unedifying spectacle of the Deputy First Minister haranguing his First Minister only increased the mistrust between the two men. Acrimony between Northern Ireland's two principal political leaders has justifiably earned them the nickname 'the Odd Couple'.

Having alienated most of nationalist Ireland in February, Trimble flew to Washington the following month for the annual round of Presidential handshakes and meetings on Capitol Hill in the build-up to St Patrick's Day. It was from here that he gambled again, risking the alienation of his base support back home. While being fêted by the American media during a breakfast with the National Press Club, Trimble dropped a bombshell on his party and blew a hole in the image nationalists had painted of him as the wrecker of the Agreement. Addressing some of Washington's media high-flyers, Trimble announced that what he needed was a sign from the IRA that 'the war is over, that there will never be recourse to violence again'. Then he moved to the central message of his speech.

> I have made it clear that we are prepared to be involved in a fresh sequence which will probably not involve arms up-front but will have to involve the issue being dealt with. I'm prepared to recommend to my party that we try again, but I can only do that where there is good reason to believe it will work.

To underpin his new message to the IRA, Trimble repeated his offer to jump first (again) in an interview with the *Boston Herald*. He told the American paper:

> If they [the IRA and Sinn Fein] expect us to do the same thing [forming a government again], we'll need something a bit more

concrete. That I think is simple human nature . . . the sooner it's resolved the better. The sooner we bounce back the better.

In other words, Trimble was ready to make another leap of faith in the IRA, to set up the government before the arms or arms dumps were offered up. Across the Atlantic even his closest advisers were stunned. Jeffrey Donaldson phoned David Kerr, who was on holiday in Edinburgh visiting his girlfriend, to ask what was going on. Kerr, Trimble's chief press officer, was perplexed and confessed to Donaldson that he knew nothing about his leader's Washington speech. Kerr was not alone. None of Trimble's inner circle such as Michael McGimpsey or Ken Maginnis had been briefed about his latest shift from 'no guns, no government'. The only people Trimble had confided in were some of his non-UUP advisers in North America who were crucial in persuading the First Minister to take another risk for peace.

The National Press Club speech was an audacious initiative underlining again Trimble's willingness to gamble his own position as UUP leader in the interests of the wider political process. His closest allies back in Northern Ireland were alarmed that their leader was pushing his legendary luck too. One adviser in the UUP described the mood among the Trimbleistas after St Patrick's Day:

It was a bolt from the blue, no one knew he was going to do it. And it left us having to pick up the pieces back at home. People in the party went ballistic with this solo run, even his closest supporters. He had shifted policy again without consulting anyone.

The aim of the National Press Club speech had been to make it easier for the IRA to come up with some formula to break the deadlock over arms. It created the impression that unionists had again moved first and that any IRA gesture on weapons would not be seen as the Provos dancing to Trimble's tune. Trimble has confessed that his reasoning was partly due to the fact that Gerry Adams was about to visit Bill Clinton in the Oval Office. His speech was designed to put the pressure back on Sinn Fein and the IRA.

I knew Adams was going in to see Clinton and I wanted to put the ball at the President's feet. My aim was to show unionists were willing to move and that this would prompt Bill Clinton to pressurise republicans to start movement on the arms issue.

The move was a deft piece of high-political manoeuvring, a new form of sequencing aimed at getting government back in Belfast and securing something from the IRA on decommissioning. While observers and commentators on both sides of the Atlantic appreciated the logic behind Trimble's new shift, the reactions in his party ranged from exasperation to vengeful anger.

Trimble however had calculated that he would face a serious challenge from the No camp. He has finally revealed that his National Press Club statement was an attempt to prepare his party for a second leap of faith. He was expecting trouble at the party's Annual General Meeting the following month and the best way to sell the new initiative was to drop his plan on the UUP and take a gamble:

> It was better to have the idea of a new sequence with the IRA and ourselves before the AGM. It gave people time to absorb the implications so they couldn't accuse me on the day of misleading them. There was no point issuing a change of tactics at the meeting, it was better strategy to let them know in advance.

His opponents did not have long to wait to punish their leader for what they saw as another sop to the republican movement. On 24 March 2000 Trimble finally faced the inevitable, a full-frontal leadership challenge. At its heart it was a struggle between the future of Ulster Unionism in the new century. In the right-wing corner was the Reverend Martin Smyth, a contender from old-style unionism with its emphasis on the link with the Orange Order, the Protestant faith and loyalty to the crown. In the left corner stood Trimble and his new brand of secular unionism.

Smyth, a 68-year old Presbyterian Minister and Party Chief at Westminster, had held the South Belfast seat since Robert Bradford's murder in 1982. His loyalist credentials included being the former Grand Master of the Orange Order and a party spokesman since the late 1970s when he broke with Vanguard. He and Trimble had been on opposing sides of the unionist divide since the Troubles began. Smyth left Vanguard over Trimble and Bill Craig's proposal for Voluntary Coalition with nationalists in 1975. The South Belfast MP had lost the leadership challenge in 1995 and canvassed against Trimble during the 1998 referendum on the Good Friday Agreement. His challenge however was not met with joyous enthusiasm among other anti-Agreement UUP members such as Jeffrey Donaldson. The Lagan Valley MP had opposed any leadership contest, regarding it as premature. He even failed to turn up to Smyth's final press conference on Friday 24 March at Belfast's Europa Hotel. Those attending the launch included many from the pension-age generation of unionists who harked back to an alleged golden age of one-party rule. Joining them were the Young Unionists, Ulster's equivalent to the now-defunct ideologically extreme Federation of Conservative Students. Their far-right brand of unionism unnerved a party leadership determined to foster a new liberal image of the UUP across the world.

Smyth's press conference was chaired by Peter King, the head of the Young Unionists, who admitted that Smyth was only 'right at the time' to lead the UUP, a tacit admission that the right would have preferred a more robust challenger such as Donaldson.

Trimble's own campaign kicked off half an hour later in the UUP's Glengall Street headquarters, just yards from the Europa. It was a much slicker, carefully choreographed affair, which began with eighteen of the party's twenty-eight Assembly members filing into the conference room and bursting into applause when Trimble entered the room. His mercurial deputy John Taylor, who had been extremely sceptical about re-entering government with Sinn Fein, accompanied him. Asked the evening before if Smyth was a serious challenger or simply a stalking-horse for the right, Taylor replied in characteristic fashion: 'Stalking-horse, oh no. Martin's a carthorse.' With Taylor at his side, Trimble brimmed with confidence. He predicted that he would not only win but also decisively end the damaging strain of scepticism that had blighted his leadership over the previous two years. Michael McGimpsey summed up the mood in the Trimbleite camp: 'It was time to put up or shut up.'

Comparisons with other British political leaders though were not favourable for Trimble. In June 1995 John Major issued a similar 'put up or shut up' challenge to his Euro-sceptics, or 'bastards' as he colourfully described them on an ITN tape. That challenge was taken up enthusiastically by John Redwood. And even though Major triumphed by 218 votes to 89, the Euro-sceptic lobby refused to shut up. Major limped on until electoral oblivion on 1 May 1997, a mortally wounded leader continually ambushed by his right-wing opponents. The Agreement-sceptics of Ulster Unionism would pursue Trimble regardless of the leadership result and snipe at his handling of the peace process. Like Major, Trimble had spent too much time indulging his internal critics rather than routing them.

The meeting to decide Trimble's destiny was held at the King's Hall, normally a venue for rock concerts and the annual Royal Agricultural Show when farmers, particularly those from rural Protestant redoubts, bring their livestock and produce to town. The last few gatherings of the agricultural community had been overshadowed by the terminal crisis impacting on farming. On a bone-chilling Saturday morning in late March there was a similar sense of despondency among UUP delegates, who were fed up with the faction-fighting and policy shifts of the previous two years.

John Taylor in his description of Martin Smyth as a 'cart-horse' failed to take into account the candidate's ability to tap into widespread fears in the party. The Trimble camp seriously under-estimated the opposition to the leader's Washington initiative. An hour before the votes were cast his allies were predicting that Smyth would get around 40 per cent of the vote. In fact the result was another very close-run thing. Trimble was said to be 'shaking and white with fear' as the votes tallied up and it became clear Smyth was doing much better than anyone had expected. Anti-Agreement unionists were jubilant when the final result was announced: 457 delegates (or 56.7 per cent of the UUC) backed Trimble while a surprising 348 members (43.22 per cent) had opted for a change in leadership and voted for Smyth.

A few hours later Trimble received a second stunning blow from the anti-Agreement camp. Shortly after four o'clock a motion was passed calling on the UUP to link re-entry into talks with no change in the RUC's name. The proposal had been moved by David Burnside, Trimble's Vanguard *alterkampfen*. Trimble, along with non-party figures like former RUC Chief Constable Ronnie Flana-gan, had opposed the motion, which he believed would tie his hands in future negotiations.

The double-whammy at the King's Hall demonstrated that Trimble might have been a hero abroad but to many was another Lundy-like hate figure at home. Like a previous Nobel laureate, Mikhail Gorbachev, Trimble was fêted in world capitals as an international statesman. But as with Gorbachev prior to the collapse of the Soviet Union, Trimble was mistrusted and in many cases loathed by many of his former supporters at home. Yet despite this blow to his authority in his domestic constituency he appeared upbeat at the press conference that followed an acrimonious and draining day. When he was asked how long the world could wait for him to call it a day, Trimble bit back: 'Don't hold your breath waiting.'

The shock of the narrow margin of victory was not lost on his closest aides and advisers. They had actually expected his stock within the party to rise following his victory of sorts the previous month when the British government suspended the executive. Peter Mandelson had underwritten Trimble's 31 January deadline. New Labour had finally stood by the Ulster Unionists on a critical issue, in sharp contrast to the Tories' duplicity in the Molyneaux era. Moreover, Martin Smyth was a figure associated with the heavy defeats and isolation of that period. But Smyth had done spectacularly better than even his own circle had privately predicted. The King's Hall vote was, to borrow Trimble's own jibe at his opponents from the traditional wing of the party, 'the revenge of the Woodentops'.

Despite the setback Trimble clung on given the growing anticipation throughout April that the IRA was preparing to make an historic gesture on arms. Trimble, embattled within his own party and rapidly losing the trust of his electorate outside, was to be provided with another get-out-of-jail card from, of all people, the Provos. Once again his legendary luck did not let him down.

By the beginning of April it became apparent that a deal was in the making. Tony Blair kept Trimble aware of the negotiations involving the British and Irish governments and the IRA. But the UUP were outside this tri-partite loop working towards a new initiative on guns; the only control the Ulster Unionists could exercise over the process was a veto on the final shape of the plan. Friday, 5 May was set aside for a range of all-party talks co-hosted by Blair and his Irish counterpart Bertie Ahern. The timing was significant. Hints of a breakthrough that could lead to the restoration of the Stormont government were made on the eve of the talks, the day Londoners voted for a new mayor. As it became clear that Ken Livingstone would be elected instead of New Labour's Frank Dobson, the Downing Street spin machine attempted to shift the national political focus from London to Belfast. The parties converged on Mandelson's residence, Hillsborough Castle, on Friday morning. David Kerr recalls that Sinn Fein turned up with a high-powered delegation including the convicted IRA gunrunner and the man alleged to control arms bunkers in the Republic, Martin Ferris. 'The Provos resembled a football team that had turned up for a rigged game,' says Kerr. 'I remember David Trimble turning to me and saying, "Something's up because Ferris is in town." You got the feeling the deal had already been done.'

Kerr was extremely nervous that Blair and Ahern would attempt to bounce Trimble into something he could not sell to the UUP or the unionist community. His mind flashed back to the last talks at the same venue the year before when Alastair Campbell, Blair's Press Secretary, briefed the media about an alleged 'seismic shift' in the IRA's attitude over decommissioning. At Hillsborough '99 Kerr had strongly advised Trimble not to buy into the package as it gave no guarantees that the IRA would do anything about their arsenal. It was characteristic of Trimble that the UUP leader ignored his own press secretary's counsel and appeared to give the nod to Blair's plan for arms being put beyond use coupled with a day of national reconciliation. Kerr thought the idea of allowing illegal armed groups to participate in a symbolic day of remembrance during which some arms bunkers were sealed would provoke unprecedented moral outrage in the unionist community. The idea that illegal armies were equated with the army and police was unpalatable even to the strongest pro-Agreement unionist, Kerr concluded.

Trimble's determination to forge ahead illuminated what many of his closest friends see as one of his fundamental flaws. He has a tendency to be flattered and influenced by outsiders, whether admirers in the United States or external strategists such as Sean O'Callaghan, who came up with the concept of bunkers being sealed in tandem with the day of national reconciliation. Kerr represented the local unionist voice more fearful of backlashes in Waringstown and Lisnaskea than adulation in Washington and London.

Nonetheless, the shape of the May 2000 IRA proposal, minus the day of reconciliation, appeared remarkably similar to the 'sealed bunkers' deal at Hillsborough thirteen months earlier. During the morning of 5 May Blair held a private meeting with Trimble's ever-sceptical deputy John Taylor. Blair asked Taylor what was important to the UUP in the current climate beyond the decommissioning question. Taylor replied that there were two matters of concern. Firstly, that Sinn Fein ministers should not be allowed to pull down the Union flag from departmental buildings. Secondly, that the Crown and Harp badge of the RUC be retained in some form when the new Police Service was established. It later emerged that Blair could deliver on the first matter. Peter Mandelson used his reserve powers as Northern Ireland Secretary to impose the flying of the Union flag on specified days on all departmental buildings, including those ministries headed by Sinn Fein. The latter issue would have to be deferred while Parliament debated the Patten Report and implemented the envisaged reforms.

Around noon that Friday several impromptu meetings were taking place in Hillsborough Castle's rose garden, where Mandelson often walked his pet Labrador Bobby. David Kerr spotted Blair huddled around John Hume and Seamus Mallon, while in another corner Bertie Ahern stood talking with his officials from the Department of Foreign Affairs. One notable absentee from these discussions was Brian Cowen, the Irish Foreign Minister. Cowen had set off a damaging row with the UUP when a leak from a Senior British diplomat described Cowen's aim to hollow out the British presence in Northern Ireland. But on the day of the critical negotiations aimed at restoring power-sharing government, Cowen was relegated to the sidelines. Trimble and his colleagues were amused to spot the Foreign Minister – or 'Biffo', as he is known colloquially in Dublin and even his own constituency – sitting alone on a bench in the rose garden, reading the newspaper. As one Trimble aide put it: 'Biffo had become Mo.'

Shortly after lunch David Kerr and Phillip Robinson were sitting in the room set aside for the UUP inside Hillsborough Castle. Ken Maginnis passed the time musing over the *Daily Express* crossword. Suddenly Kerr and Robinson were startled to find Blair and his entourage entering the room. The two UUP press officers got up to leave but Maginnis told them to stay – they were also entitled to hear what was coming. Blair's first words to Trimble and the UUP delegation were: 'I don't want to see this repeated by Frank Miller in the *Irish Times*.' The Prime Minister then outlined exactly what was to happen. The deal would see the executive up and running on 22 May if the IRA gave a commitment to put their guns completely and verifiably beyond use. In effect this meant the IRA sealing bunkers and opening their dumps up to inspection by international observers. The plan also included the rapid implementation of the Patten Report. Peter Mandelson said later that the opening of arms dumps was the clearest signal that the IRA's war was over. The following morning the IRA made clear their plans. With the onus now back on Trimble, he had to sell another deal to his increasingly sceptical party.

Another Ulster Unionist Council meeting was convened for Saturday, 20 May at the Waterfront Hall to decide if the UUP would go back into government with Sinn Fein and the SDLP. In the days building up to the meeting the phone calls between David Trimble's office and a corner of the Pacific Far East became more and more frantic. Trimble and his campaign team at Stormont's parliament buildings kept in constant contact with John Taylor. Ever since the IRA announcement on 6 May, Trimble had known Taylor would once again be crucial in convincing the party to return to the power-sharing coalition.

To Trimble's frustration, his deputy had initially welcomed the IRA statement and then appeared to backtrack, demanding further concessions from the British government on flags and policing. The problem was exacerbated by the fact that Taylor had gone AWOL, taking himself off on an Industrial Development Board sponsored trip to Japan and Taiwan just when his leader needed him at his side. While Taylor breezed through Far Eastern factories Trimble toured rural towns and villages of Protestant Ulster, drumming up support for his analysis that the IRA was effectively over. One of Trimble's team who had travelled with him in the northwest of the Province on the Thursday before the UUC meeting noticed that his leader was 'physically shaking in the car'. Whether this was due to nerves, sheer exhaustion, or a mixture of both, he declined to say.

The trans-continental telephone chats however seemed to pay off. The UUP leader's unpredictable ally drafted an article in a hotel bedroom in Taipei on the eve of the vote. Trimble's campaign – in the face of a very determined and well-organised opposition that had hired PR agent David Lyle to advise them – was shored by another source, Sean O'Callaghan. The former IRA killer agreed to speak at a number of UUP meetings in the Greater Belfast area outlining why he thought the Provos' 6 May statement meant the war was over. O'Callaghan recalls:

I told them that I came from a republican family and had been in the IRA and yet with every fibre of my being I believed the IRA's 6 May statement meant that the war was over for good. I told them at every opportunity that they should back Trimble and get into government with Sinn Fein.

Although in the end the result was narrow – 53.2 per cent in favour of restoring the government, 46.8 per cent against – Trimble's opponents appeared badly shaken by their defeat. The UUP's anti-Agreement faction had fought a sophisticated and precise campaign over the previous fortnight to persuade swinging voters to back out of re-entering coalition. Many in the No camp firmly believed that this was their best chance finally to overthrow Trimble. They had failed and now the historic power-sharing coalition between unionists, nationalists and republicans was back in business. Trimble had once again taken the IRA on trust but warned that his party could still walk out of the executive if the Provos failed to keep to their promises.

A jaded-looking Trimble, facing chants of 'traitor, traitor' from a band of extreme loyalists outside the building, admitted that he had stretched his party to breaking point. He warned:

> There is a limit to how far we can stretch ourselves without an adequate response being made by the IRA ... It's patently obvious those promises must be delivered and let there be absolutely no doubt that I and my colleagues will hold the republicans to the promises they have made. If there is foot-dragging or delay there will be difficulties.

Flanked by Daphne and Party President Josias Cunningham, the man who had held the post-date cheque, the letter of resignation as First Minister, Trimble then remarked that Sinn Fein needed to be 'housetrained' before they became fully fledged democrats. The comments sparked an angry reaction within nationalist Ireland: people were indignant that Trimble was comparing republicans to dogs. Apart from ignoring the fact that the UUP leader was speaking metaphorically, it seemed a bit rich of nationalists to be so vocally outraged over the unfortunate use of a phrase by Trimble while staying silent over IRA punishment beatings, arms importations and murder – all clear breaches of the Agreement and the Mitchell principles on non-violence.

Between restoration and his party's conference on 6 October the peace process was punctuated with a series of minor crises. There were violent clashes at Drumcree, which spread to loyalist parts of Greater Belfast and East Antrim but never matched the tempo of previous protests that had threatened to destabilise the Province.

More alarming for unionism was the eruption at the end of August of a loyalist feud on the Chancel Road between one faction of the UDA and the UVF. The fact that some of the men in the thick of the battle were prisoners recently released from jail under the Agreement's early-release scheme only increased the average unionist voter's fears that Northern Ireland was becoming a Mafia state. With seven dead and hundreds expelled from their homes, the anti-Agreement wing of unionism could argue (with some justification) that the Agreement freed paramilitaries who then brought inter-Protestant violence back on to loyalist streets. Trimble made a number of attempts to bring the two sides together. A fortnight after the shooting war on the Shankill began, Trimble dispatched Sean O'Callaghan to Belfast. The IRA's most famous 'Pentiti' helped organise a meeting at the home of an Ulster Unionist councillor in Belfast attended by representatives of both the UVF and UDA. O'Callaghan had been in contact with several key players in the loyalist movements since Trimble first made overtures about a token gesture on arms. But despite his familiarity with the men gathered at the hastily convened peace talks, the two sides failed to hammer out a lasting truce.

Against a backdrop of internecine loyalist violence, squabbling between the coalition partners over the implementation of the Patten Report and the absence of another IRA move on arms, Trimble's party had to fight a Westminster by-election. Even before the parties descended on the electorate of South Antrim, a rural constituency on the edge of Belfast, Trimble suffered a major setback. His preferred candidate to replace the late Clifford Forsythe was David Campbell, his chief-of-staff at the Assembly, who was intensely loyal to his leader but remained on good terms with anti-Agreement elements of the UUP, including the Orange Order.

The South Antrim Unionist Association however rejected Campbell and instead plumped for Trimble's old Vanguard comrade, David Burnside, who had by now shifted to the No camp of the party. Although he and Burnside remained on good terms, close Trimble allies later reflected that Burnside's failure to take what had been a safe UUP seat was a blessing in disguise. Burnside had become a thorn in Trimble's side having moved to the right of his leader, most significantly in putting forward the motion to tie UUP participation in power-sharing government to the retention of the RUC's name. Several of Trimble's inner circle have confessed they breathed a sigh of relief that Burnside did not get elected. They suspected that his presence at Westminster would have been more destabilising for the pro-Agreement faction and, moreover, Burnside would have eventually used his position to launch a serious leadership challenge.

On one level the election of Ian Paisley's candidate, the Reverend William McCrea, in this strongly Ulster Unionist constituency resembled a political revolution. The DUP had overturned a massive UUP majority in what McCrea and Paisley turned into a referendum on the Agreement. The unionist electorate appeared to have rejected the Good Friday deal and David Trimble. However, the pitiful turnout – 43 per cent – suggested that many unionist voters, especially those in middle-class redoubts, had no enthusiasm for an anti-Agreement candidate like David Burnside. On the canvass Trimble received a more enthusiastic welcome in places like Ballyclare, Templepatrick and Glengormley (satellite towns of Belfast) than Burnside. For the first time in his career Trimble seemed to enjoy pounding the pavements on the political hustings. One of his press officers remarked during a trip to a country fair at Burnside village that Trimble 'had become a man of the people, who the people could warm to'. Burnside sought to rely on the adulation of *Daily Telegraph* leader writers, London *Times* columnists and even Tory ultras like Lord Tebbit. Yet despite the best efforts of London's laptop loyalists, most unionists stayed away from the polling booth. On a low turn-out the DUP was able to get its traditional vote out in strongholds like the loyalist estates of Antrim town to snatch the seat by 1200 votes.

The real lesson perhaps for the loss of South Antrim is David Trimble's inability to get a grip of his party that at local level was able to defy UUP HQ in Glengall Street and choose its own candidate. The UUP remained an archaic political institution with a degree of rebellious autonomy that would no longer be tolerated by either Labour or Conservatives on the other side of the Irish Sea. A Province-wide opinion poll conducted after South Antrim for Ulster Marketing Surveys indicated that Trimble had more support in the country than the bald result of the by-election suggested. A quarter of all voters said they would cast their votes for the UUP, a figure higher than the level of support the party received in the Assembly elections. In contrast the DUP's overall level of support had fallen from 17 per cent in 1998 to 12 per cent. In addition a majority of UUP voters, 52 per cent, (almost directly correlating with Trimble's core vote at UUC meetings throughout the year) said they still backed the Agreement. The poll was the best indicator that if Trimble and his team tried hard enough they could still drum up enthusiasm for the peace deal and his handling of the process. It was also apparent that when he and the party moved, or were perceived to have moved towards the right, many pro-Agreement unionists simply turned off and stayed at home.

One of Trimble's chief flaws as leader of Northern Ireland's largest party is that he has indulged his critics and internal enemies. The first sign that his patience with them was being severely tested took place on 6 October when the UUP held its annual conference. In a blistering attack, which presaged his victory at the UUC meeting in the Waterfront Hall twenty days later, Trimble finally launched into his opponents. 'Stop undermining the leadership of this party,' he warned them.

His triumph over Donaldson and co. on 26 October came of course at a price. His bar on Sinn Fein ministers attending the North/South Ministerial Council meetings has been challenged in the courts. Republicans warn that his move has made it less unlikely that the IRA will re-open talks with de Chastelain's decommissioning body. However, at the end of 2000, with outgoing President Bill Clinton on his way back for a final farewell to Northern Ireland (the one real success of his foreign policy), the British and Irish governments are piecing together a series of moves aimed at delivering new discussions between the Provisionals and the General, lifting the Trimble ban on Sinn Fein, and expanding the role of the two international observers, Matti Ahtasari and Cyril Ramaphosa, tasked with inspecting IRA arms dumps.

On the question of IRA weapons, Trimble remains pragmatic about their disposal. If bunkers are sealed and globally acclaimed figures like the retired Finnish general and the former African National Congress guerrilla confirm that arms have been put beyond use, this in Trimble's eyes is 'decommissioning by other means'. While the UUP leader will have quite likely faced another challenge to his authority at the UUC meeting in January 2001, the real deadline for David Trimble is May 2001, if and when Tony Blair calls a general election. If the UUP vote declines further, loses MPs and perhaps even is supplanted by Paisley's DUP as the principal voice of unionism, then Trimble's tenure as leader will be over. This bleak scenario is complicated further by the prospect of local government elections, which the DUP will also turn into a fresh referendum of unionist support for the Agreement and the

Trimble project. The one problem for the DUP is the possibility of the British government holding the local government elections on the same day as the national contest. This would inevitably push up the overall turnout, favouring as always the UUP rather than the Democratic Unionists.

Since the Good Friday Agreement was signed, a key Sinn Fein tactic has been to portray the settlement as merely a 'stepping-stone' towards a united Ireland. The Provisionals' spokesmen have set off a series of green flares aimed at preventing the republican base from zeroing in on the partitionist core of the historic compromise. But in the last quarter of 2000 the green mists that have shrouded the political battlefield, luring rank-and-file republicans into believing they were crossing no-man's-land to place the Irish tricolour triumphantly over the unionist trenches, are finally clearing. The veto was intact as a result of Trimble's ban, it proved that unionists still exercised a degree of control over the political institutions, including the most important one to Sinn Fein cross-border bodies. Combined with Peter Mandelson's decision to impose the flying of the Union flag over ministries controlled by Martin McGuinness and his colleague Bairbre de Brun, the ban marked a significant victory for Ulster Unionism after years of apparent retreat and regression. The two controversies underpin the suspicions of republican sceptics that British sovereignty over the North of Ireland has not been surrendered or that the veto still exists. Bizarrely, Trimble and his allies have played down these achievements rather than trumpet them to the unionist electorate.

One of the recurring patterns of unionist history in the twentieth century has been the squandering of power and influence in the UK and the world at large for the sake of narrow short-term triumphalism and sectarian domination. The Unionist Party, having secured a state apart from Michael Collins's Free State in 1921, helped create through discrimination and repression a recalcitrant and ultimately rebellious minority within its borders. Unionism lost Stormont and its hegemony over the Province in 1972 partly because it resisted the moderate reformist demands of the Northern Ireland Civil Rights Movement. Having scored a victory of sorts in the 1974 Ulster Workers' Strike, mainstream unionist parties then failed to be magnanimous and reach out for a new power-sharing deal with nationalists. Overestimating their influence with Margaret Thatcher and the Conservative Party, the UUP indulged in fantasies such as integration, believing for some time in the then Prime Minister's fictional comment that Ulster was as British as her Finchley constituency. At the beginning of the new century unionism is once again in danger of repeating past mistakes. The leader of the main unionist party has managed to give the Protestant/loyalist population some control over their destiny for the first time since direct rule was imposed. In addition, Trimble has opened up the possibility of reshaping unionism to make it more attractive to the ever-confident Catholic middle-class, the very people who will be needed in the future to save the union from eclipse by the growing nationalist electorate in Northern Ireland.

During a discussion of the first edition of this book at BBC's Millbank Studio last April, one of the contributors to the programme sitting alongside the author expressed dismay at the possibility of Trimble being ditched by his own people. The British politician who was perplexed that Trimble could be out of a job within a year was none other than the Shadow Home Secretary and darling of the Tory Party's right wing, Anne Widdicombe. 'They [the No unionist camp] will live to regret this if they lose David Trimble,' Ms Widdicombe said repeatedly. 'They will live to regret it.'

If Anne Widdicombe, the champion of an Arcadian Britain of home-spun morality, family values and outmoded nationalism, regards unionism minus Trimble as a dreary prospect, what hope then for traditional unionism in persuading Tony Blair, Gordon Brown or Peter Mandelson to turn back the tide of change in Northern Ireland?

Following the signing of the Good Friday Agreement Trimble confided to his closest associates that he believed he could be the first unionist leader to see off Ian Paisley. Judged solely on recent elections Trimble's prophecy may not be fulfilled. Paisley, the colossus of Ulster politics, the personification of traditional unionism, will undoubtedly lead his party in the immediate aftermath of the coming general election. The future of Trimble, the advocate of new unionism, rests on much less stable foundations. Severe losses at the polls will precipitate the most serious challenge to his leadership. Whatever the outcome of the next electoral test for the Agreement and new unionism, one thing is certain: if Paisley defeats another reforming, compromising, modernising unionist rival it will mean further regression and loss of influence for the unionist community. In seeing off Trimble, the robust defenders of old-style unionism will have mortally wounded the union itself.

Notes

CHAPTER 1: A STATE OF SIEGE, A SENSE OF SERVICE

1. A.T.Q. Stewart, *The Narrow Ground*
2. Foreword by David Trimble in C.D. Milligan, *The Walls of Derry: Their Building, Defending and Preserving*
3. Interview with David Trimble, 21 December 1998
4. Interview with David Trimble, 21 December 1998
5. Interview with David Trimble, 21 December 1998
6. Interview with David Trimble, 21 December 1998
7. Interview with David Trimble, 21 December 1998
8. Interview with David Trimble, 21 December 1998
9. Statement of witness to RUC, 16 February 1999
10. Statement of witness to RUC, 16 February 1999
11. Interview with David Trimble, 21 December 1998
12. Interview with Leslie Cree, 4 January 1999
13. Interview with Leslie Cree, 4 January 1999
14. Interview with Leslie Cree, 4 January 1999
15. Interview with Leslie Cree, 4 January 1999
16. Interview with Alan McKillen, 18 January 1999
17. Interview with Alan McKillen, 18 January 1999
18. Interview with David Trimble, 21 December 1998
19. Interview with Herbie Wallace, 15 April 1999
20. Interview with Herbie Wallace, 15 April 1999
21. Interview with Herbie Wallace, 15 April 1999
22. Interview with David Burnside, 7 December 1998
23. Interview with Herbie Wallace, 15 April 1999
24. *North Down Spectator*, 5 July 1968
25. Interview with Tina/William McCombe, 5 May 1999
26. Interview with Tina/William McCombe, 5 May 1999
27. Interview with David Trimble, 21 December 1998
28. Interview with David Trimble, 21 December 1998
29. Interview with John Hunter, 11 January 1999
30. Interview with John Hunter, 11 January 1999
31. Interview with David Trimble, 21 December 1998
32. Private interview, 5 January 1999
33. Private interview, 5 January 1999
34. Private interview, 5 January 1999

CHAPTER 2: VANGUARD DAYS

1. Interview with Anthony Alcock, 10 November 1998
2. Interview with Reg Empey, 8 December 1998
3. Interview with David Burnside, 18 December 1998
4. Interview with David Burnside, 18 December 1998
5. Private interview, 25 November 1998
6. Interview with Andy Tyrie, 12 January 1999
7. Interview with Sam McClure, 11 January 1999
8. Interview with Sam McClure, 11 January 1999
9. Interview with Sam McClure, 11 January 1999
10. Interview with David Trimble, 28 January 1999
11. Interview with Jim Wilson, 3 November 1998
12. Interview with Glen Barr, 10 December 1998
13. Don Anderson, *14 May Days*
14. Interview with David Trimble, 28 January 1999
15. Interview with Fred Crowe, 10 December 1998
16. Interview with Fred Crowe, 10 December 1998
17. Interview with Reg Empey, 8 December 1998
18. Interview with Tom Hadden, 14 April 1999
19. *Sunday News*, 20 January 1974
20. *Sunday News*, 20 January 1974
21. Interview with John Laird, 17 February 1999
22. Interview with David Trimble, 28 January 1999
23. Don Anderson, *14 May Days*
24. Interview with Sam McClure, 11 January 1999
25. *Belfast Telegraph*, 14 April 1999
26. *Belfast Telegraph*, 14 April 1999
27. *Belfast Telegraph* 11 April 1975
28. *Belfast Telegraph*, 17 April 1975
29. *Belfast Telegraph*, 27 April 1975
30. *Belfast Telegraph*, 27 June 1975
31. Private interview, 25 November 1998
32. *Belfast Telegraph*, 13 October 1975
33. *Hansard*, 4 March 1976
34. *Hansard*, 4 March 1976
35. Interview with David Trimble, 2 February 1999
36. Interview with Gerry Fitt, 10 May 1999
37. Interview with Glen Barr, 10 December 1998
38. *Belfast Telegraph*, 17 November 1976
39. Author present, 11 January 1999

CHAPTER 3: FROM OUT OF THE WILDERNESS

1. Interview with Herbie Wallace, 15 April 1999
2. Interview with David Trimble, 3 June 1999
3. Interview with Brian Garrett, 11 December 1998
4. Interview with Herbie Wallace, 15 April 1999
5. Interview with Michael McGimpsey, 2 December 1998
6. Interview with Harry West, 1 December 1998
7. Interview with Jim Wilson, 28 January 1999
8. Interview with John Taylor, 7 May 1999
9. Private interview, 27 January 1999
10. Interview with Tom Hadden, 14 April 1999

11. Interview with Tom Hadden, 14 April 1999
12. Interview with Herbie Wallace, 15 April 1999
13. *Belfast Telegraph*, 18 October 1980
14. Interview with Herbie Wallace, 15 April 1999
15. Private interview
16. Interview with Brian Garrett, 11 December 1998
17. Interview with Herbie Wallace, 15 April 1999
18. Private interview
19. Private interview
20. Interview with Herbie Wallace, 15 April 1999
21. Interview with Paul Bew, 2 March 1999
22. *Belfast Telegraph*, 18 October 1980
23. Interview with Davy McNarry, 11 February 1999
24. Interview with David Trimble, 2 June 1999
25. Private interview
26. Interview with Gordon Lucy, 6 January 1999
27. David Trimble, *The Easter Rebellion of 1916*
28. Eamon Phoenix, *Northern Nationalism*
29. Interview with David Trimble, 11 January 1999
30. Interview with David Trimble, 11 January 1999
31. *Ulster Newsletter*, 3 October 1985
32. *Belfast Telegraph*, 13 December 1985
33. Private interview with second-in-command of Ulster Volunteer Force
34. Private interview with second-in-command of Ulster Volunteer Force
35. *Ulster Newsletter*, 6 November 1986
36. *Ulster Newsletter*, 6 November 1986
37. *Ulster Newsletter*, 6 November 1986
38. *Ulster Newsletter*, 6 November 1986
39. *Ulster Newsletter*, 6 November 1986
40. Interview with Andy Tyrie, 30 November 1998
41. Interview with Andy Tyrie, 30 November 1998
42. *Ulster Newsletter*, 17 August 1989
43. *Ulster Newsletter*, 17 August 1989
44. *Ulster Newsletter*, 17 August 1989
44. Private interview, 24 January 1999
45. Interview with Ruth Dudley Edwards, 18 November 1998
46. Interview with John Taylor, 7 May 1999
47. Interview with John Taylor, 7 May 1999
48. Interview with David Trimble, 2 June 1999

CHAPTER 4: THE ROAD TO WESTMINSTER

1. Private interview, 27 April 1999
2. Interview with Fred Crowe, 10 December 1998
3. Interview with Simon Lee, 16 February 1999
4. Private interview, 26 January 1999
5. *Belfast Telegraph*, 20 May 1999
6. *Belfast Telegraph*, 18 November 1989
7. *Belfast Telegraph*, 20 May 1990
8. *Times*, 19 May 1990
9. *Irish Times*, 22 May 1990
10. *Ulster Review*, summer 1990
11. *Hansard*, 23 May 1990
12. Private interview, 26 January 1999

13. Interview with Barry White, 20 April 1999
14. Interview with Barry White, 20 April 1999
15. Interview with David Brewster, 17 February 1999
16. *Sunday Life*, 28 October 1990
17. *Belfast Telegraph*, 21 October 1989
18. *Belfast Telegraph*, 12 October 1990
19. *Belfast Telegraph*, 27 December 1990
20. Interview with Michael McGimpsey, 2 December 1998
21. Interview with Ken Maginnis, 5 May 1999
22. Interview with Michael McGimpsey, 2 December 1998
23. *The Independent*, 20 February 1992
24. Interview with the Reverend David Knox, 22 April 1999
25. Interview with the Reverend David Knox, 22 April 1999
26. Interview with the Reverend David Knox, 22 April 1999
27. Interview with the Reverend David Knox, 22 April 1999
28. *Belfast Telegraph*, 3 July 1992
29. Interview with Chris Hudson, 14 April 1999
30. *The World at One*, 26 May 1993
31. *Belfast Telegraph*, 4 May 1993
32. *Belfast Telegraph*, 30 March 1993
33. *Belfast Telegraph*, 30 March 1993
34. *Belfast Telegraph*, 30 October 1993
35. *Belfast Telegraph*, 20 November 1993
36. Letter from the Reverend Ian Paisley to John Major, 15 December 1993
37. Dail Eireann, 15 December 1993
38. *Belfast Telegraph*, 22 January 1994
39. Interview with David Trimble, 5 May 1999
40. *Hansard*, 29 May 1994
41. *Belfast Telegraph*, 26 May 1994
42. Jim Cusack and Henry McDonald, *UVF*
43. *Belfast Telegraph*, 3 August 1994
44. Paul Bew and Gordon Gillespie, *The Northern Ireland Peace Process 1993–96: A Chronology*
45. *Belfast Telegraph*, 15 September 1994
46. Private interview, 5 March 1999
47. *Belfast Telegraph*, 1 October 1994
48. *Belfast Telegraph*, 9 September 1994
49. *Belfast Telegraph*, 9 September 1994

CHAPTER 5: A MAN FOR ALL FACTIONS

1. Interview with Jim Reynolds, 15 February 1999
2. Interview with Jim Reynolds, 15 February 1999
3. Interview with Jim Reynolds, 15 February 1999
4. Interview with Gordon Lucy, 6 January 1999
5. *Belfast Telegraph*, 22 September 1995
6. Paul Bew and Gordon Gillespie, *The Northern Ireland Peace Process 1993–96: A Chronology*
7. Interview with David Trimble, 6 April 1999
8. Interview with John Taylor, 7 May 1999
9. *Belfast Telegraph*, 28 July 1995
10. Interview with David Trimble, May 1999
11. Interview with Gordon Lucy, 6 January 1999
12. Interview with Stephen King, 17 February 1999

13. Interview with Gordon Lucy, 6 January 1999
14. Interview with Stephen King, 17 February 1999
15. Private interview, 18 February 1999
16. Interview with Stephen King, 17 February 1999
17. Interview with Jack Allen, 28 April 1999
18. Interview with Chris McGimpsey, 16 November 1998
19. Interview with Ken Maginnis, 5 May 1999
20. *Sunday Business Post*, 10 September 1995
21. *Irish News*, 14 September 1995
22. *People*, 17 August 1995
23. Private interview
24. Private interview
25. Anthony Seldon, *Major: A Political Life*
26. Interview with Chris McGimpsey, 16 November 1998
27. Private interview, 9 November 1998
28. Interview with David Trimble by Jim Dougal, *Inside Politics*, BBC Radio Ulster, 8 September 1995
29. Interview with Robert McCartney, 18 February 1999
30. Interview with Viscount Cranborne, 10 January 1999
31. *Hansard*, 24 January 1996
32. *Hansard*, 24 January 1996
33. *Belfast Telegraph*, 13 February 1996
34. Private interview, August 1996
35. Interviews with David Trimble and BBC *Panorama* documentary, summer 1996
36. *Belfast Telegraph*, 16 July 1996
37. Anthony Seldon, *Major: A Political Life*
38. Interview with Chris McGimpsey, 16 November 1998
39. Interview with Gary Kent, 10 May 1999
40. Interview with Chris McGimpsey, 16 November 1998
41. Interview with Ken Maginnis, 5 May 1999
42. Interview with Jim Reynolds, 15 February 1999

CHAPTER 6: TOWARDS A LONG GOOD FRIDAY

1. Interview with David Trimble, 7 May 1999
2. Interview with Sean O'Callaghan, 10 May 1999
3. Interview with Sean O'Callaghan, 10 May 1999
4. *Daily Telegraph*, 14 July 1997
5. Interview with Sean O'Callaghan, 10 May 1999
6. *Belfast Telegraph*, 21 July 1997
7. Interview with Sean O'Callaghan, 10 May 1999
8. Interview with David Brewster, 17 February 1999
9. *Sunday Times*, 7 September 1997
10. Interview with Sean O'Callaghan, 10 May 1999
11. *Irish Times*, 27 October 1997
12. *Irish Times*, 27 October 1997
13. *Irish Times*, 27 October 1997
14. *Belfast Telegraph*, 30 October 1997
15. *Belfast Telegraph*, 12 November 1997
16. Interview with Robert McCartney, 18 February 1999
17. Interview with Sean O'Callaghan, 10 May 1999
18. Interview with Eoghan Harris, 3 February 1999
19. *Belfast Telegraph*, 8 October 1997
20. *Belfast Telegraph*, 1 December 1997

21. Private interview
22. Interview with Ken Maginnis, 5 May 1999
23. Interview with Eoghan Harris, 3 February 1999
24. Interview with John Laird, 10 November 1998
25. *Sunday Tribune*, 18 January 1998
26. *Ulster Newsletter*, 17 January 1998
27. George Mitchell, *Making Peace*
28. *Belfast Telegraph*, 6 March 1998
29. *Belfast Telegraph*, 18 March 1998
30. Interview with David Brewster, 17 February 1999
31. BBC Northern Ireland documentary *The Hand of History*
32. Interview with John Taylor, 7 May 1999
33. George Mitchell, *Making Peace*
34. Interview with David Brewster, 17 February 1999
35. Interview with Brian Garrett, 11 December 1998
36. Interview with John Taylor, 7 May 1999
37. Interview with Stephen King, 17 February 1999
38. Private interview
39. Interview with David Kerr, 28 February 1999
40. Interview with John Taylor, 7 May 1999
41. Interview with Ken Maginnis, 5 May 1999
42. Private interview
43. Interview with David Kerr, 28 February 1999
44. Interview with John Taylor, 7 May 1999
45. Interview with David Kerr, 28 February 1999
46. Interview with David McNarry, 11 December 1999
47. Interview with David McNarry, 11 December 1999
48. *Irish Independent*, 11 April 1998
49. Interview with David Trimble, 7 May 1999
50. Interview with David Trimble, 7 May 1999
51. Interview with Brian Garrett, 11 December 1998
52. Interview with David Trimble, 7 May 1999
53. Sir David Fell, *Strand Two: The North–South Ministerial Council, A Unionist/British Perspective*
54. Sir David Fell, *Strand Two: The North–South Ministerial Council, A Unionist/British Perspective*
55. *Sunday Life*, 18 April 1998

CHAPTER 7: A LONGER HOT SUMMER

1. *Sunday Life*, 19 April 1998
2. Private interview
3. Interview with Ray Haydn, 3 February 1999
4. Interview with Ray Haydn, 3 February 1999
5. *Belfast Telegraph*, 7 May 1998
6. *Ulster Newsletter*, 9 May 1998
7. *Belfast Telegraph*, 11 May 1998
8. Interview with Ken Maginnis, 5 May 1999
9. Interview with Eoghan Harris, 5 May 1999
10. Private interview
11. Interview with David Kerr, 8 May 1999
12. Interview with Ray Haydn, 3 February 1999
13. Interview with Sean O'Callaghan, 20 April 1999
14. *Belfast Telegraph*, 19 May 1998

15. Interview with David Kerr, 21 July 1999
16. Interview with Ray Haydn, 3 February 1999
17. Interview with Chris McGimpsey, 17 December 1998
18. Interview with Ray Haydn, 3 February 1999
19. *Belfast Telegraph*, 21 May 1998
20. *Belfast Telegraph*, 21 May 1998
21. Private interview, 5 December 1998
22. *Sunday Times*, 7 June 1998
23. *The Independent*, 22 May 1998
24. Private interview
25. Interview with Eoghan Harris, 2 February 1999
26. *Belfast Telegraph*, 8 June 1998
27. Private interview, 3 March 1999
28. *Prime Time*, RTE, 11 June 1998
29. *Sunday Life*, 14 June 1998
30. *Belfast Telegraph*, 18 June 1998
31. *Belfast Telegraph*, 23 June 1998
32. Interview with Stephen King, 17 February 1999
33. Interview with Ray Haydn, 5 March 1999
34. *Sunday Life*, 5 July 1998
35. Private interview
36. *Sunday Life*, 5 July 1998
37. *Belfast Telegraph*, 1 July 1998
38. *Irish Times*, 2 July 1998
39. *Belfast Telegraph*, 1 July 1998
40. Interview with John Taylor, 7 May 1999
41. Interview with John Taylor, 7 May 1999
42. *Belfast Telegraph*, 1 July 1998
43. Private interview

CHAPTER 8: NOBEL, NO GUNS, NO GOVERNMENT

1. Interview with Ray Haydn, 2 March 1999
2. Interview with David Trimble, 7 May 1999
3. Interview with Ray Haydn, 2 March 1999
4. *Belfast Telegraph*, 19 August 1998
5. *Observer*, 6 August 1998
6. *Irish Times*, 20 August 1998
7. *New Statesman*, 29 August 1998
8. *Irish Times*, 2 September 1998
9. *Observer*, 6 August 1998
10. Interview with David Trimble, 20 August 1999
11. Interview with David Trimble, 20 August 1999
12. *Belfast Telegraph*, 14 August 1998
13. *Belfast Telegraph Extra*, 10 October 1998
14. Interview with David Trimble, 7 May 1999
15. *Irish Independent*, 3 October 1998
16. *Belfast Telegraph*, 15 October 1998
17. Private interview
18. *Belfast Telegraph*, 16 October 1998
19. *Observer*, 6 September 1998
20. Private interview
21. Interview with John Taylor 30 November 1998
22. Interview with Dr Arthur Aughey, 9 February 1999

23. Interview with David Trimble, 7 May 1999
24. Interview with David Kerr, 20 August 1999
25. Interview with David Trimble, 7 May 1999
26. *Belfast Telegraph*, 8 December 1998
27. Private interview
28. *Sunday Times*, 14 February 1999
29. Interview with David Trimble, 7 May 1999
30. *Belfast Telegraph*, 17 February 1999
31. *Sunday Life*, 21 February 1999
32. *Sunday Life*, 18 April 1999
33. Interview with Sean O'Callaghan,
34. Interview with David Trimble, 7 May 1999
35. *Sunday Life*, 18 April 1999
36. *Star*, 21 April 1999
37. *Irish Independent*, 23 April 1999
38. *Belfast Telegraph*, 21 April 1999
39. Vatican Radio, 22 April 1999
40. *Sunday Life*, 25 April 1999
41. *Sunday Life*, 25 April 1999
42. Interview with David Trimble, 7 May 1999
43. Interview with David Trimble, 7 May 1999
44. *Observer*, 23 May 1999
45. Private interview
46. Interview with Ken Maginnis, 14 June 1999
47. *Times*, 22 June 1999
48. *Times*, 22 June 1999
49. *Times*, 22 June 1999
50. *Times*, 25 June 1999
51. Private interview
52. Interview with David Trimble, 7 May 1999
53. Interview with David Trimble, 7 May 1999
54. Interview with David Trimble, 7 May 1999
55. *Hansard*, Northern Ireland Assembly, 15 July 1999
56. *Belfast Telegraph*, 16 July 1999

CHAPTER 9: A LAST LEAP OF FAITH

1. *Irish Times*, 11 October 1999
2. Speech by Eoghan Harris, 9 October 1999
3. Sean O'Callaghan told me six months prior to the October 1999 conference that Mandelson was the firm favourite to replace Mowlam when Blair got around to changing the cabinet
4. *Daily Telegraph*, 26 August 1999
5. Interview with Eoghan Harris, 16 September 1999
6. Interview with Eoghan Harris, 16 September 1999
7. Interview with Eoghan Harris, 11 November 1999
8. *Irish News*, 23 September 1999
9. BBC Radio Ulster, 18 November 1999
10. Private interview, 28 October 1999
11. *Irish News*, 21 October 1999
12. *Irish News*, 23 October 1999
13. Interview with Anthony McIntyre, 18 November 1999
14. Interview with Ray Haydn, 18 November 1999
15. Interview with Eoghan Harris, 29 November 1999
16. *Observer*, 28 November 1999

Bibliography

ANDERSON, Don, *14 May Days: The Inside Story of the Loyalist Strike of 1974*, Gill and Macmillan, 1994

BEW, Paul and Gordon Gillespie, *The Northern Ireland Peace Process 1993–96: A Chronology*, Serif, 1996

BEW, Paul, Henry Patterson and Paul Teague, *Between War and Peace: The Political Future of Northern Ireland*, Lawrence and Wishart, 1997

BRUCE, Steve, *The Edge of the Union: Ulster Loyalist Political Vision*, Oxford University Press, 1994

BRUCE, Steve, *The Red Hand*, Oxford University Press, 1992

CUSACK, Jim and Henry McDonald, *UVF*, Poolbeg, 1997

FELL, Sir David, *Strand Two: The North–South Ministerial Council, A Unionist/British Perspective*, Jigsaw Group, June 1998

FLACKES, W.D. and Sydney Elliot, *Northern Ireland: A Political Directory 1968–93*, Blackstaff, 1993

MITCHELL, George, *Making Peace*, Heinemann, 1999

O'BRIEN, Conor Cruise, *Memoir: My Life and Themes*, Profile Books, 1998

PARKINSON, Alan F., *Ulster Loyalism and the British Media*, Four Courts Press, 1998

PHOENIX, Eamon, *Northern Nationalism: Nationalist Politics, Partition and the Catholic Minority in Northern Ireland 1890–1940*, Ulster Historical Foundation, 1994

SELDON, Anthony, *Major: A Political Life*, Phoenix, 1997

STEWART, A.T.Q., *Edward Carson*, Gill and Macmillan, 1981

STEWART, A.T.Q., *The Narrow Ground*, Blackstaff, 1997

TRIMBLE, David, *The Easter Rebellion of 1916*, Ulster Society, 1992

TRIMBLE, David, *The Foundation of Northern Ireland*, Ulster Society, 1991

Index

Adams, Davy 189
Adams, Gerry 67, 125, 131, 133, 140, 151, 165, 167–8, 181, 184, 216, 251, 254, 264–7, 287, 315–16, 319, 333
Ahern, Bertie 184–5, 196, 200, 203–4, 206, 210, 261–2, 285–6, 290, 292, 294, 302, 332, 337, 338, 339
Ahtasari, Matti, 344
Alcock, Prof. Anthony 35
Alderdice, Dr John 207
Allen, Jack 107, 109, 156–7, 240
Alliance Party 120, 169, 207
Amnesty International 285
Ancram, Michael 147
Anderson, Don 42, 47, 53
Andrews, David 192, 196, 316
Anglo–Irish Agreement (1985) 91–6, 104, 111–12, 119, 129, 196
Annesley, Sir Hugh 148–9, 173
Armagh Four Committee 118–19
Armitage, Pauline 250, 255, 268, 314
Armstrong, Billy 268
Armstrong, Colin 263
Ash (pop group) 232–5
Atkins, Sir Humphrey 76, 82
Attwood, Tim 232, 233, 235
Aughey, Dr Arthur 99, 278

B Specials 20–2, 29, 31, 90
Baird, Ernest 50, 60–2, 65, 125
Barr, Glen 41, 50, 52, 54, 55, 61, 63, 65, 231–2, 247
Beggs, Roy 192, 226, 242, 267
Beggs, Roy Jr 250, 268, 286, 314
Begley, Thomas 151
Benson, Tom 268
Bernie, Esmond 268
Between War and Peace (Bew) 197
Bew, Paul 81–2, 103, 197, 254, 289, 302–3, 313
Bingham, Revd William 182, 190, 230, 256, 257
Black, Phillip 245–6
Blair, Tony 62, 170, 177, 179, 183, 191, 197, 200, 241, 260, 262, 269, 272, 277, 297, 326
  and decommissioning 165–6, 246–7, 300–4
  Downing Street initiative 294–6
  DT's relations with 132–3, 176, 178, 246, 300–1, 304, 305–6, 331, 337
  Hillsborough initiative 290–2
  and Hillsborough negotiations (2000) 337–9
  and Referendum campaign 229, 231–2, 236

and Stormont talks 185, 186, 192, 202–3, 207–11, 214
Boal, Desmond 47–8, 283
Bono 231–5
Boyle, Kevin 46
Bradford, Hazel 159
Bradford, Nora 321, 322
Bradford, Revd Robert 49, 50, 52, 70–1, 77, 334
Brady, Archbishop Sean 195
Brewster, David 117, 160, 185, 186, 188, 201, 204, 206, 267, 297, 301, 317–19
Brooke, Peter 112, 115, 119–20
Bruton, John 143, 153, 162–3, 168, 173, 184
Burnside, David 24, 36, 37, 38, 110, 128, 177, 189, 336, 342–3
Byrne, Joe 270

Cahill, Joe 22
Cahoon family 9, 10–12, 27, 42
Callaghan, James 29, 106, 133
Campaign for Equal Citizenship 99, 100, 110, 147, 230
Campbell, Alastair 304, 338
Campbell, David 207, 258, 342
Campbell, Patricia 223
Campbell, Sheena 112
Carson, Sir Edward 9, 184, 76, 86, 89, 90, 263, 275
Cheevers, Tommy 231, 247
Chichester Clark, James 29, 30
Clinton, Bill 163, 167, 168, 187, 199–200, 211, 264–5, 332, 333–4, 344
Collins, Eamon 299, 301
Collins, Michael 89–90, 101, 266
Combined Loyalist Military Command 120, 121, 144
Committee, The (Channel 4 TV) 96
Committee, The (McPhelimy) 244–5
Common Sense (UDA document) 98–9
Continuity IRA 187, 193, 308
Cooper, James 328
Coulter, Jean 75, 288
Coulter, Robert 268
Council of Ireland 46–7, 57, 58, 188, 192, 199, 213
Council of the British Isles 49, 101, 121, 213
Cowen, Brian 332, 339
Craig, Bill 34–5, 37–40, 42, 44, 46, 49, 57, 59–61, 63–7, 71, 82, 83, 90–1, 185, 287–8, 334
Craig, Sir James 89–90, 100–1, 125, 163, 263, 266
Cranborne, Lord 110, 163–5, 180, 182, 189, 230–1, 289

Crane, Robert 107
Cree, Leslie 18–19, 21, 36, 51
Crowe, Fred 44–5, 82, 91, 93, 107–8
Crozier, Ian 188
Cunningham, Josias 152, 302, 330, 341

Daly, Cardinal Cathal 127
de Brun, Bairbre 266, 345
de Chastelain, Gen. John 246, 275, 296, 317, 328, 344
Democratic Left Party 158, 184
Democratic Unionist Party 43, 49, 59, 66, 77, 92, 110, 120, 128, 130–1, 138, 168–9, 186, 215, 221, 241, 251, 273, 297, 311, 321, 324, 343, 344–5
De Rossa, Proinsias 157–8, 184, 191, 194, 267
de Valera, Eamon 14, 89, 90, 184
Devlin, Bernadette 23
Devlin, Paddy 39, 59, 66
Dobson, Frank 337
Doherty, Pat 302, 319–20
Donaldson, Jeffrey 121, 138, 168, 180, 186, 205–10, 219–20, 223–4, 226–7, 229, 241–3, 250, 251, 263, 267, 268, 298, 301, 304, 315, 318–19, 323, 327, 328–9, 333, 335, 344
Downing Street Declaration 130–1
Drumcree 1–4, 6, 22, 148–52, 154, 157, 158, 166, 169–74, 182, 183, 231, 247, 255–7, 303
Dudley Edwards, Ruth 103, 116, 159, 161, 171, 180, 289
Durkan, Mark 174

Eames, Archbishop Robin 130
Easter Rebellion of 1916 87–9
Empey, Sir Reg 35–6, 38, 40, 45, 60, 112, 121, 201, 210, 223, 240, 250–1, 315, 319, 327–8, 329
Ervine, David 134, 186, 204, 249, 291

Faul, Father Denis 285
Faulkner, Brian 22, 30–1, 43–4, 46–7, 49, 54–5, 61, 65, 66, 100, 192, 213, 253, 323
Fell, Sir David 215–17
Ferris, Martin 338
Fianna Fail 75, 159, 184, 286
Finlay, Fergus 126
Fitt, Gerry 46, 49, 56, 64–6, 213
Fitzgerald, Garret 84–5, 92
Flanagan, Chief Constable Ronnie 336
Forsythe, Clifford 192, 226, 267, 342
Fortnight 74–8
Foster, Arlene 207, 223, 243, 298, 318–19
Foundation of Northern Ireland 89–90
Frameworks 143–7, 196–7, 204, 215–16
Friends of the Union 110, 189–90
Fulton, Mark 287

Gardiner, Sam 109, 113
Garland, Roy 204
Garrett, Brian 70, 78, 80, 205, 214
Gilman, Bill 173
Good Friday Agreement 185–220, 244, 247, 268, 271, 276–7, 285, 288, 301, 305, 311, 324, 330, 342, 345, 346
    Referendum 198–9, 206, 219–41, 296, 335
Goodman, Paul 300–1
Gorbachev, Mikhail 272, 293, 294, 336
Gordon, Richard 175
Gore, Al 138
Gorman, Ed 113–14
Gorman, Sir John 265
Goulding, Cathal 22, 30
Gow, Ian 110

Gracey, Harold 2, 113, 149–50, 303
Graham, Edgar 68–71, 83, 252, 322
Graham, Constable John 179–80
Graham, Pearl 217
Green, George 36–7, 44, 61, 63
Grimason, Stephen 254

Hadden, Prof. Tom 46, 74–5, 78
Haggan, Gary 110
Hargreaves, Ian 175
Harris, Eoghan 191, 194, 226, 242, 268, 277, 302–3, 307–9, 311–14, 316, 318, 321–2
Haughey, Charles 76–7, 111–12, 125
Haughey, Denis 176
Haydn, Ray 222–3, 228–9, 233–4, 237–9, 240, 242, 249, 254, 258–60, 272–3, 318, 322
Hayes, Gerry 115
Hayes, Maurice 269
Heath, Edward 30–1, 34, 42, 49
Hegarty, Dr Seamus 262
Hermon, Sir Jack 69, 231, 237–8
Herron, Tommy 41
Hoey, Kate 189, 230, 231, 238
Holmes, Sir John 197
Hudson, Chris 126, 129, 228
Hume, John 55–6, 66, 72, 77, 98, 125–8, 132, 140, 164, 178, 199, 232–3, 235–6, 252, 271, 277, 280, 281, 298–9, 339
Hunter, John 28, 87, 154, 160, 188, 201, 204, 206, 209, 243, 251, 322
Hussey, Derek 268, 319
Hutchinson, Billy 249, 276, 284, 291

Independent Orange Order 293
INLA 85, 193
International Decommissioning Commission 264, 266, 275, 287, 290, 302, 317, 328, 344
IRA 13–15, 21–2, 87, 89
    Official 30–1, 45, 82, 136–7, 158, 220
    Provisional 30–1, 43, 45, 59, 112, 131–3, 158, 168, 199, 287, 306, 317, 324–5, 328, 330, 333, 337–8, 340, 341, 345
    ceasefire 57, 119, 129, 134–41, 142, 144, 147, 148, 152, 163, 166, 167, 177, 179, 181–2, 183, 185, 284, 300, 315
    violence 33, 68–71, 75, 80, 117–18, 121–2, 127, 129, 134, 163, 165–7, 174, 179–80, 187, 193, 264, 299, 306, 308
Irish Labour Party 125–6

Jack, Captain W.H. 8, 9, 42
John Paul II, Pope 292–3
Johnston, Constable David 179–80
Jones, Colette 110, 111, 112, 115
Jones, David 292
Jordan, Raymond 57, 59

Keenan, Brian 291
Kelly, Gerry 158–9, 220, 265, 315
Kennan, George 277, 278, 279
Kennedy, Edward 199
Kennedy, Laurence 110
Kent, Gary 174–5, 176, 177, 289
Kerr, David 208–10, 223, 227, 232–3, 254, 258, 260, 270, 281, 331, 333, 337–8, 339
Kilfedder, Jim 147
King, Peter 267, 335
King, Steven 154, 155, 156, 201, 205–6, 211, 219, 226, 249
King, Tom 92, 93, 94
Knox, Revd David 122–4

Laird, John 49, 60, 86, 195, 247
Larkin, Aidan 58
Lee, Simon 108, 114
Lemass, Sean 21
Lennon, Father Brian 158
Livingstone, Ken 337
Lloyd, John 99, 191, 289
Logue, Hugh 47, 188
Loyalist Volunteer Force 197, 208, 221, 228, 274–5, 287
Lucy, Gordon 86, 144–5, 154–5
Lundy, Governor 11
Lyle, David 340

McAleese, Mary 79, 262
McAliskey, Bernadette 107, 141
McCann, Eamon 232, 233
McCartney, Robert 99, 138, 147–8, 162, 169, 172,
    183, 186, 189, 225, 227, 228, 231, 238, 241,
    250, 282, 298–9, 319, 326
McCausland, Nelson 87, 145, 160, 187, 188, 200
McClinton, Kenny 274–5
McClure, Sam 39–40, 55, 57, 67, 95–6, 128, 238
McCombe, Tina (William) 25, 31
McCrea, Revd William 134, 169, 343
McCusker, Harold 69, 92, 106–7, 108, 113, 118
McCusker, Jennifer 107, 109
McGartland, Martin 299–300, 301
McGimpsey, Chris 120–1, 126, 157, 159, 174–7, 234,
    249, 250
McGimpsey, Michael 71, 104, 120–1, 126, 234, 250–
    1, 295, 327, 333, 335
McGuinness, Martin 4, 134, 138, 140, 146, 174, 181,
    187, 220, 251, 264–7, 287, 315–16, 324, 330,
    345
McGurran, Malachy 45
McIntyre, Anthony 254, 317
MacIntyre, Donald 239–40
McKelvey, Archie 124
McKenna, Brendan 149, 172, 190
McKillen, Alan 19
McLaughlin, Mitchell 166, 230, 286, 299
McMichael, John 95–6, 98–9, 128, 244
McNamara, Kevin 132–3
McNarry, David 82, 211
McPhelimy, Sean 244
Maginnis, Alban 56–7, 58
Maginnis, Ken 97, 121, 126, 151–4, 156–7, 162, 166,
    178, 186, 194, 201, 205, 209, 210, 221, 226,
    229, 239–43, 250, 258–60, 299, 307, 318, 319,
    333, 339
Major, John 28, 122, 127–31, 136, 140, 142, 143,
    147, 161, 163–8, 173, 177–8, 246, 335
Mallon, Seamus 94, 146, 198, 213, 252, 256–7, 262,
    270–1, 277, 283, 286, 292, 305, 332, 339
Mandelson, Peter 242, 289, 309, 320–1, 330–1, 337,
    339, 345
Marr, Andrew 176
Mason, Roy 66
Maxwell, Sir John 88
Mayhew, Sir Patrick 128, 171
Mitchell, George 164–6, 169, 193, 197, 202–4, 210,
    251, 314–18, 320
Molloy, Francie 265
Moloney, Ed 195–6
Molyneaux, James 13, 73–7, 84–5, 91, 93, 98, 102,
    105, 115, 119–21, 125–6, 130–4, 136, 138, 142–
    8, 152, 164, 199, 220, 228, 234
Mowlam, Mo 185, 191–2, 197, 201, 203, 225, 227,
    236–7, 246, 274, 300, 303, 309, 315, 330, 332

Nationalist Party 26
Nelson, Drew 87, 160, 186, 251

Neshitt, Dermot 68, 201
New Dialogue 174, 289
New Ireland Forum 79, 84–5
Nicholson, Jim 94, 103–4, 117, 152, 297–9, 310
Nobel Peace Prize 1, 2–3, 271–3, 277–81, 305, 306
North-South Ministerial Council 212, 215–16, 270,
    277
Northern Ireland Office 94, 95, 97, 120, 185, 259,
    272, 274
Northern Ireland Unionist Party 283

O'Brien, Conor Cruise 228, 282–3
O'Callaghan, Sean 69, 180–4, 186–7, 189–90, 205,
    229–31, 256, 274–6, 289–91, 338, 340, 342
O'Doherty, Malachi 199, 313, 314
O'Dowd, Niall 196–7
Official Unionists 43, 44, 66
O'Halloran, Marie 114
O'Neill, Terence 21–2, 24, 26, 29, 34, 253, 323
Orange Volunteers 38, 218, 273, 287, 325
Oz, Amos 3, 4, 278

Paisley, Ian 21, 35, 50, 60–1, 63–5, 76–7, 96, 111,
    115, 118, 125, 129–31, 136, 162, 168, 172, 186,
    190, 196, 239, 263, 268, 290, 325, 343, 344,
    346
    and Assembly 250, 251, 286
    at Drumcree 149–51, 157, 257
    as MEP 72, 292, 298, 299
    and Referendum 220, 223, 227, 230, 237, 239,
        241, 297
Paisley, Ian Jr 120, 248
Paisley, Sylvia 69
Parades Commission 231–2, 247
Passmore, Thomas 60, 75
Patten Report 237, 309–11, 313, 321, 339, 342
Patterson, Henry 82, 187
Pollak, Andy 78
Powell, Enoch 64, 73, 98, 102
Powell, Jonathan 208, 229, 230, 275, 290
Progressive Unionist Party 134, 167, 186, 190, 204,
    240, 249, 276, 284, 291, 292

Quinn children 257, 303

Rabin, Yitzak 5, 6, 325
Ramaphosa, Cyril, 344
Real IRA 187, 261, 262
Red Hand Commando 38, 39, 43, 61
Red Hand Defenders 4, 273, 287
Redmond, John 89, 263
Redwood, John 335
Rees, Merlyn 50, 54, 55, 57, 63
Reynolds, Albert 125, 129–30, 132, 140
Reynolds, Lee 142–3, 144–6, 154, 178
Ringland, Trevor 237, 242
Robinson, Peter 66, 111, 190, 268, 272, 324
Robinson, Phillip 331, 339
Rodgers, Jim 145, 328
Rogan, Denis 240, 251, 262, 309, 329
Ross, William 154, 156, 160, 192–3, 219, 226, 236,
    242, 267, 328–9
RUC 13, 29, 51, 66, 93, 94, 151, 169–71, 173, 174,
    237, 321, 336, 339, 342
    see also Patten Report
Ryder, Chris 75

Sands, Jim 245
Saulters, Robert 183
SDLP 53, 55–9, 60, 62, 64, 66, 83, 89, 92, 94, 115,
    120, 137, 165, 172, 188, 249, 271, 291, 295,
    328

in Assembly 43, 46–7, 252, 276–7, 282, 284, 305
and decommissioning 264, 270, 279
and Referendum campaign 232–3
at Stormont talks 186, 200, 213
Seawright, George 92
Simpson, John 62
Sinn Fein 22, 83, 89, 127, 129, 131, 134, 136, 137,
139, 140, 144, 147, 166, 167, 172–4, 177, 179–
81, 263, 265, 290, 292
at all-party talks 162–4, 183, 185–6, 192–3, 195–
7, 200–1, 337–8
Ard Feis 220, 224–5
in Assembly 212, 251, 252, 267, 305, 324
and decommissioning 264, 266, 286–7, 291, 302,
316–17, 319, 328, 329–34
election results 79, 92, 169, 184
and Good Friday Agreement 207, 212, 220, 241,
345
and Mitchell Review 314–16
and Referendum 220, 225, 232–3
Smith, Harry 52–3
Smith, John 129, 132–3, 165
Smyth, Revd Martin 73, 115, 137, 154, 156, 160,
192, 226, 242, 265, 328–9, 334–5, 336, 337
Spring, Dick 125, 127, 129, 131
Stewart, A.T.Q. 10, 11
Stone, Michael 227, 229
Sunningdale Agreement 46, 47, 49, 57, 61, 188, 198,
213, 323

Taylor, John 50, 63, 72–3, 82, 97, 103–4, 115, 136,
138, 151, 153–7, 162, 186, 193, 198, 201–3,
205, 207–11, 221, 226, 253, 254, 267, 276, 284,
298–9, 310, 319, 321–3, 335, 336, 338, 340
Thatcher, Margaret 66, 71, 73–4, 76–7, 84–5, 90–4,
119, 143, 345–6
Third Force 77, 101
Thompson, Willie 50, 160, 188, 192, 219, 226, 242,
261, 323
Trimble, Daphne 79–80, 113, 123–4, 153, 194, 223,
242, 259, 272, 281, 329, 341
Trimble, David:
academic career 25–7, 56–8, 66, 74, 78–9, 108,
122
adolescence 18–19
appearance 18, 28, 43, 50
awards 1, 2–3, 271–2, 277
birth and childhood 13, 14–15
education 15–17, 20, 22–4
employment 20, 21
family life 113, 122–4, 171, 194–5, 273, 281
friendships 18–19, 45, 103, 122
image of 191, 222–3
interests 19, 81, 116, 126, 253
as journalist 74–8
labelled as traitor 4, 6, 11, 38, 215, 263, 273–4,
293, 303
marriages 25, 45–6, 80
and paramilitaries 38–42, 61–2, 94–8, 127–8, 238,
244–5, 287
personality 20, 25, 28, 42, 50, 80, 82, 123–4, 194–
5, 205, 214, 226, 228, 235, 246, 253–4, 326,
344
political career 2, 5–6, 23–4, 36–7, 43–4, 49, 52–5,
57–62, 71, 85, 87, 93, 103–9, 113, 115–17,
119, 122, 141–2, 152–3, 157
threat to 6, 7, 273, 325
Trimble, Heather 24, 25, 45, 80
Trimble family 12–13, 15, 17, 25, 80
Trouble with Guns (O'Doherty) 199
Tyrie, Andy 38, 40, 50, 54, 65, 96, 98–9, 128, 238,
244

U2 232–5
UK Unionist Party 242, 243, 251, 282–3, 297
Ulster Clubs 95–8, 100, 103, 128, 171, 221, 245
Ulster Defence Association 33, 38, 40, 41, 61, 62, 65–
6, 96, 98–100, 102, 127–9, 137, 167, 227, 238,
275, 276, 290, 342
Ulster Defence Regiment 45, 59, 93, 118–20
Ulster Democratic Party 142, 167, 186, 190, 204,
227, 240, 290
Ulster Loyalist Coordinating Committee 62
Ulster Resistance 96, 101, 239
Ulster Society 85–7, 90, 95, 144, 154, 157, 168
Ulster Unfettered 62, 99, 101, 121
Ulster Unionist Party 120–1, 125–6, 128, 186–8, 201,
204–10, 218–21, 223, 226–7, 241–3, 251, 252,
268, 328, 343
annual conferences 8, 82, 104, 188, 307–9, 314,
344
Council 83, 144, 154, 200, 211, 218–20, 240, 267,
284, 288–9, 317, 319, 320, 323, 328
Devolution Group 69
Graduate Association 186
Labour Group 175
leadership contests 153–7, 329, 334, 335–7, 344,
346
MPs 92, 94, 97, 106, 116, 122, 128, 165, 177–8,
192–3, 219–20, 223, 226, 242, 327
Young Unionists 35–6, 69, 78–9, 114–15, 117,
139, 142, 144, 154, 156, 187, 219, 223, 234,
329, 335
Ulster Volunteer Force 9, 29, 38, 40, 52, 61, 66, 88,
96, 112, 118, 127, 129, 137, 167, 170, 227, 238,
245, 275–6, 290–1, 342
Ulster Workers' Council 49–55
Union First 267–8, 297, 301
Unionist Party of Northern Ireland 61, 66
United Loyalist Council 41, 42
United Ulster Unionist Council 49–50, 52, 54, 58, 60–
5
United Unionist Action Council 65
United Unionists 220–1, 228, 267

Vanguard 34–47, 49, 57, 59–67, 72, 77, 78, 95, 127,
139, 246, 334
Service Corps 39–42, 95, 244
Voluntary Coalition 60–1, 63, 64, 66, 72, 102,
125, 161, 185, 213, 328, 334

Walker, Cecil 159–60, 221
Wallace, Herbie 23, 24, 46, 68, 71, 78, 79, 80, 81
Watson, Denis 182, 243, 267
Way Forward, The 302, 305
Weir, Peter 114–15, 201, 206–7, 243, 250–1, 267,
284, 304
West, Harry 49, 50, 61, 65, 66, 72–3, 75, 242–3
What Choice for Ulster? 100
Wheeler, Tim 234–5
White, Barry Jr 116, 289
Whitelaw, William 33, 43, 46
Widdicombe, Anne 346
Williams, Betty 272, 293
Williamson, Michelle 315
Wilson, Harold 29, 50, 53–5, 57
Wilson, Jim 41, 72, 104, 161, 218, 223, 240, 250–1
Wilson, Padraig 225
Women's Coalition 320
Workers' Party 82, 106, 112, 191, 233
Wright, Billy 139, 170–2, 174, 193, 287
Wright View, The 273

Young, Ivor 2, 3, 293

A NOTE ON THE AUTHOR

Henry McDonald has been BBC Northern Ireland's Security correspondent and Northern Ireland Correspondant for the *Sunday Times*. He is now Ireland Correspondent for the *Observer*. He is a contributor to the *Spectator* and a frequent broadcaster. He is the author of *Irishbatt – the Story of Ireland's Blue Berets in Lebanon*, and the co-author of *INLA – Deadly Divisions* and of *UVF*.